The Constitution of Society

The Constitution of Society

Outline of the Theory of Structuration

Anthony Giddens

University of California Press
Berkeley and Los Angeles

First published in the
United States by the University of California Press, 1984

Library of Congress Catalog Number 84-040290

ISBN 0-520-05292-7

Typeset by Pioneer, East Sussex
Printed and bound in Great Britain by
Bell and Bain Limited, Glasgow

Contents

Preface

For some while, and in a number of previous publications, I have been seeking to establish an approach to social science which departs in a substantial fashion from existing traditions of social thought. This volume provides a summation of those previous writings, setting them out in what I hope is a developed and coherent manner. The vague term 'approach' to social science actually conveys very well what I take to be the methodological implications of structuration theory. In social science, for reasons expanded upon in considerable detail in what follows, conceptual schemes that order and inform processes of inquiry into social life are in large part what 'theory' is and what it is for. I do not mean by this, of course, that it is not the aim of social theory to illuminate, interpret and explain substantive features of human conduct. I mean that the task of establishing and validating generalizations — I shall not say 'laws' — is only one among various other priorities or aims of social theory. The task of constructing sets of stably established generalizations, which is (perhaps) the lynchpin of the endeavours of the natural sciences, is not an ambition of much relevance to social science. Or so I propose.

Many people have been good enough to look through and comment upon earlier drafts of the book or have otherwise contributed very directly to its final form. I would like to thank the following persons in particular: Mrs D. M. Barry, John Forrester, Diego Gambetta, Helen Gibson, Derek Gregory, David Held, Sam Hollick, Geoffrey Ingham, Robert K. Merton, Mark Poster, W. G. Runciman, Quentin Skinner, John B. Thompson and Jonathan Zeitlin.

A.G.
January 1984

B

Abbreviations

CCHM   *A Contemporary Critique of Historical Materialism,* vol.1
         (London: Macmillan/Berkeley: University of California
         Press, 1981)

CPST   *Central Problems in Social Theory* (London: Macmillan/
         Berkeley: University of California Press, 1979)

CSAS   *The Class Structure of the Advanced Societies,* rev. edn
         (London: Hutchinson/New York: Harper & Row, 1981)

NRSM   *New Rules of Sociological Method* (London:
         Hutchinson/New York: Basic Books, 1976)

PCST   *Profiles and Critiques in Social Theory* (London:
         Macmillan/Berkeley: University of California
         Press, 1982)

SSPT   *Studies in Social and Political Theory* (London:
         Hutchinson/New York: Basic Books, 1977)

All by Anthony Giddens.

Introduction

The backdrop to this book is to be found in a series of significant developments which have taken place in the social sciences over the past decade and a half. These have been concentrated in substantial part in social theory, and bear especially upon that most maligned and most provocative of the social sciences, sociology. Sociology is by its very nature controversial. However, for a considerable period after the Second World War, particularly in the English-speaking world, there was a broad consensus about its nature and tasks and about those of the social sciences as a whole. There was, it could be said, a middle ground shared by otherwise competing perspectives, a terrain on which intellectual battles could be fought out. During that period sociology was an academic growth area, a subject with a burgeoning reputation, even if it remained distinctly unpopular in many circles. It was dominated internationally by American sociology, and in social theory the influence of Talcott Parsons was marked.[1] The prestige enjoyed by Parsons's ideas can be exaggerated retrospectively — many found his taste for abstraction and obscurity unattractive, and he had his fair share of critics and detractors. However, *The Structure of Social Action,* first published in the late 1930s but widely known only in the post-war period, was in more than one way a key work in the formation of modern sociology. In it Parsons established a systematic pedigree for social theory, based upon an interpretation of European thought in the nineteenth and early twentieth centuries. The work of Durkheim, Max Weber and Pareto loomed large, but Marx played a very slight role indeed. The writings of the 1890—1920 generation had supposedly gone beyond Marx in all important respects, sifting out what was valuable and discarding the dross.

The book also set up an approach to social theory of a very definite type, combining a sophisticated version of functionalism and a naturalistic conception of sociology. Parsons's subsequent writings elaborated these views in considerable detail, emphasizing that although human action has very special and distinctive attributes, social science by and large shares the same logical framework as natural science. Himself writing and working in an American context, Parsons's attempt to pinpoint the origins of his thought in European social theory actually served to reinforce the dominant position of American sociology. For Durkheim, Weber and Pareto were regarded as forerunners of the development of the 'action frame of reference', to be given its full expression by Parsons and his colleagues. Sociology may have its main theoretical origins in Europe, but the further elaboration of the subject was a task that had been largely transferred across the Atlantic. Curiously, this result was achieved at the expense of a concomitant recognition of the importance of indigenous American contributions to social theory; G. H. Mead received short shrift in *The Structure of Social Action,* as Parsons came later to acknowledge. To this day, however, there are textbooks on social theory, or 'sociological theory', emanating from the United States, which begin with the classic European thinkers but then convey the impression that social theory in Europe subsequently came to a stop — any further progress is taken to be a purely American affair.

But even within the confines of the debates deriving directly from Parsons's writings, some of the leading contributors were European. Marxism has long been a much more important influence in European than in American intellectual culture, and some of Parsons's most perceptive critics drew inspiration from Marx as well as from readings of Weber rather different from those which Parsons had made. Dahrendorf, Lockwood, Rex and others of a similar standpoint took the theoretical content of Parsons's work much more seriously than did his American radical critics (C. Wright Mills and, later, Gouldner). The former group regarded Parsons's contributions as of major importance but as one-sided in neglecting phenomena they saw as primary in Marx — class division, conflict and power. They were not themselves Marxists, but they envisaged something of a fusion between Parsonian and Marxist concepts. While there were many important innovations within Marxism during this period — such as the revival of interest in the 'young Marx', attempts to merge Marxism and phenomenology, and subsequently Marxism and structuralism — these were not well known to those who called themselves 'sociologists', even in Europe. Those who regarded themselves as both sociologists and Marxists tended to share the basic assumptions of functionalism and naturalism, which is one reason why much common ground for debate was found.

The fissures in this common ground opened up remarkably suddenly in the late 1960s and early 1970s, and they went very deep. There is no doubt that their origins were as much political as intellectual. But whatever their provenance, they had the effect of largely dissolving whatever consensus had existed before about how social theory should be approached. In its place there appeared a baffling variety of competing theoretical perspectives, none able fully to recapture the pre-eminence formerly enjoyed by the 'orthodox consensus'. It became apparent to those working in sociology that all along there had in fact been less of a consensus about the nature of social theory than many had imagined. Some traditions of thought, such as symbolic interactionism, had all the while been accorded considerable support without storming the citadel of the orthodox consensus. Other schools of thought that had developed in large part separately from the main body of the social sciences were taken seriously for the first time, including phenomenology and the critical theory of the Frankfurt philosophers. Some traditions which had seemed moribund were given a new impetus. Although Weber had been influenced by the hermeneutic tradition and had incorporated its main concept of *verstehen* into his work, most of those connected with sociology would certainly not have regarded 'hermeneutics' as part of their lexicon. But, partly in conjunction with phenomenology, interpretative traditions in social thought again came to the fore. Finally, other styles of thought, such as ordinary language philosophy, were adopted into social theory in various ways.

With these developments the centre of gravity in respect of innovative contributions to social theory moved back towards Europe.[1]* It became obvious that a great deal of the more

---

*References may be found on pp. xxxvi—xxxvii.

interesting theoretical work was going on there — and for the most part in languages other than English. European social theory was, and is, not only alive but kicking very vigorously. But what is the outcome of these stirrings? For the loss of the centre ground formerly occupied by the orthodox consensus has seemingly left social theory in a hopeless disarray. Notwithstanding the babble of rival theoretical voices, it is possible to discern certain common themes in this apparent confusion. One is that most of the schools of thought in question — with notable exceptions, such as structuralism and 'post-structuralism' — emphasize the active, reflexive character of human conduct. That is to say, they are unified in their rejection of the tendency of the orthodox consensus to see human behaviour as the result of forces that actors neither control nor comprehend. In addition (and this does include both structuralism and 'post-structuralism'), they accord a fundamental role to language, and to cognitive faculties in the explication of social life. Language use is embedded in the concrete activities of day-to-day life and is in some sense partly constitutive of those activities. Finally, the declining importance of empiricist philosophies of natural science is recognized to have profound implications for the social sciences also. It is not just the case that social and natural science are further apart than advocates of the orthodox consensus believed. We now see that a philosophy of natural science must take account of just those phenomena in which the new schools of social theory are interested — in particular, language and the interpretation of meaning.

It is with these three core sets of issues, and their mutual connections, that the theory of structuration, as I represent it in this book, is concerned. 'Structuration' is an unlovely term at best, although it is less inelegant in the Gallic context from which it came. I have not been able to think of a more engaging word for the views I want to convey. In elaborating the concepts of structuration theory, I do not intend to put forward a potentially new orthodoxy to replace the old one. But structuration theory is sensitive to the shortcomings of the orthodox consensus and to the significance of the convergent developments noted above.

In case there is any doubt about terminology here, let me emphasize that I use the term 'social theory' to encompass issues that I hold to be the concern of all the social sciences. These issues are to do with the nature of human action and the acting self; with how interaction should be conceptualized and its relation to institutions; and with grasping the practical connotations of social analysis. I understand 'sociology', by contrast, to be not a generic discipline to do with the study of human societies as a whole, but that branch of social science which focuses particularly upon the 'advanced' or modern societies. Such a disciplinary characterization implies an intellectual division of labour, nothing more. While there are theorems and concepts which belong distinctively to the industrialized world, there is no way in which something called 'sociological theory' can be clearly distinguished from the more general concepts and concerns of social theory. 'Sociological theory', in other words, can if one likes be regarded as a branch of social theory more generally, but it cannot sustain a wholly separate identity. This book is written with a definite sociological bias, in the sense that I tend to concentrate upon material particularly relevant to modern societies. But as an introduction to structuration theory it is also intended in substantial degree as a formulation of the tasks of social theory in general and is 'theory' in the same sense. That is to say, the focus is upon the understanding of human agency and of social institutions.

'Social theory' is not a term which has any precision, but it is a very useful one for all that. As I represent it, 'social theory' involves the analysis of issues which spill over into philosophy, but it is not primarily a philosophical endeavour. The social sciences are lost if they are not directly related to philosophical problems by those who practise them. To demand that social scientists be alive to philosophical issues is not the same as driving social science into the arms of those who might claim that it is inherently speculative rather than empirical. Social theory has the task of providing conceptions of the nature of human social activity and of the human agent which can be placed in the service of empirical work. The main concern of social theory is the same as that of the social sciences in general: the illumination of concrete processes of social life. To hold that philosophical debates can contribute to this concern is not to suppose that such debates need to be resolved conclusively before worthwhile social research can be initiated. On the contrary, the prosecution of social research can in principle cast light on philosophical controversies just as much as the reverse. In particular, I think it wrong to slant social theory too unequivocally towards abstract and highly generalized questions of epistemology, as if any significant developments in social science had to await a clear-cut solution to these.

A few remarks are necessary about the 'theory' in social theory. There are certain senses often attributed to 'theory' in the social sciences from which I want to maintain some considerable distance. One conception used to be popular among some of those associated with the orthodox consensus, although it is no longer widely held today. This is the view — influenced by certain versions of the logical empiricist philosophy of natural science — that the only form of 'theory' worthy of the name is that expressible as a set of deductively related laws or generalizations. This sort of notion has turned out to be of quite limited application even within the natural sciences. If it can be sustained at all, it is only in respect of certain areas of natural science. Anyone who would seek to apply it to social science must recognize that (as yet) there is no theory at all; its construction is an aspiration deferred to a remote future, a goal to be striven for rather than an actual part of the current pursuits of the social sciences.

Although this view does have some adherents even now, it is far removed from anything to which I would hold that social theory could or should aspire — for reasons which will emerge clearly enough in the body of the book which follows. But there is a weaker version of it which still commands a very large following and which invites rather longer discussion even in this prefatory context. This is the idea that the 'theory' in social theory must consist essentially of generalizations if it is to have explanatory content. According to such a standpoint, much of what passes for 'social theory' consists of conceptual schemes rather than (as should be the case) 'explanatory propositions' of a generalizing type.

Two problems have to be separated here. One concerns the nature of explanation in the social sciences. I shall take it for granted that explanation is contextual, the clearing up of queries. Now it *might* be held that the only queries worth their salt in social science are those of a very generalized kind, which can therefore be answered only by reference to abstract generalizations. But such a view has little to commend it, since it does not help to clarify the explanatory import of much of what social scientists (or natural scientists either, for that matter) do. Most 'why?' questions do not need a generalization to answer them, nor do the answers logically imply that there must be some generalizations lurking around which could be invoked to back up the answers. Such observations have become fairly commonplace in the philosophical literature, and I shall not try to extend them further. Much more contentious is a second claim I defend, and elaborate in the book, that the uncovering of generalizations is not the be-all and end-all of social theory. If the proponents of 'theory as explanatory generalization' have too narrowly confined the nature of 'explanation', they have compounded the error by failing to inquire closely enough into what generalization is, and should be, in social science.

Generalizations tend towards two poles, with a range and variety of possible shadings between them. Some hold because actors themselves know them — in some guise — and apply them in the enactment of what they do. The social scientific observer does not in fact have to 'discover' these generalizations, although that observer may give a new discursive form to them. Other generalizations refer to circumstances, or aspects of circumstances, of which agents are ignorant and which effectively 'act' on them, independent of whatever the agents may believe they are up to. Those I shall call 'structural sociologists' tend to be interested only in generalization in this second sense — indeed, this is what is meant when it is claimed that the 'theory' in social theory should comprise explanatory generalizations. But the first is just as fundamental to social science as the second, and each form of generalization is unstable in respect of the other. The circumstances in which generalizations about what 'happens' to agents hold are mutable in respect of what those agents can learn knowledgeably to 'make happen'. From this derives the (logically open) transformative impact which the social sciences can have upon their 'subject matter'. But from it also comes the fact that the discovery of 'laws' — i.e., generalizations of type 2 — is only one concern among others that are equally important to the theoretical content of social science. Chief among these other concerns is the provision of conceptual means for analysing what actors know about why they act as they do, particularly either where they are not aware (discursively) that they know it, or where actors in other contexts lack such awareness. These tasks are primarily hermeneutic in character, but they are an inherent and necessary part of social theory. The 'theory' involved in 'social theory' does not consist only, or even primarily, of the formulation of generalizations (of type 2). Neither are the concepts developed under the rubric 'social theory' made up only of those which can be fed into such generalizations. Quite to the contrary, these concepts must be related to others referring to the knowledgeability of agents, to which they are inevitably tied.

Most of the controversies stimulated by the so-called 'linguistic turn' in social theory, and by the emergence of post-empiricist philosophies of science, have been strongly epistemological in character. They have been concerned, in other words, with questions of relativism, problems of verification and falsification and so on. Significant as these may be, concentration upon epistemological issues draws attention away from the more 'ontological' concerns of social theory, and it is these upon which structuration theory primarily concentrates. Rather than becoming preoccupied with epistemological disputes and with the question of whether or not anything like 'epistemology' in its time-honoured sense can be formulated at all, those working in social theory, I suggest, should be concerned first and foremost with reworking conceptions of human being and human doing, social reproduction and social transformation. Of prime importance in this respect is a dualism that is deeply entrenched in social theory, a division between objectivism and subjectivism. Objectivism was a third -ism characterizing the orthodox consensus, together with naturalism and functionalism. In spite of Parsons's terminology of 'the action frame of reference', there is no doubt that in his theoretical scheme the object (society) predominates over the subject (the knowledgeable human agent). Others whose views could be associated with that consensus were very much less sophisticated in this respect than was Parsons. By attacking objectivism — and structural sociology — those influenced by hermeneutics or by phenomenology were able to lay bare major shortcomings of those views. But they in turn veered sharply towards subjectivism. The conceptual divide between subject and social object yawned as widely as ever.

Structuration theory is based on the premise that this dualism has to be reconceptualized as a duality — the duality of structure. Although recognizing the significance of the 'linguistic turn', it is not a version of hermeneutics or interpretative sociology. While acknowledging that society is not the creation of individual subjects, it is distant from any conception of structural sociology. The attempt to formulate a coherent account of human agency and of structure demands, however, a very considerable conceptual effort. An exposition of these views is offered in the opening chapter and is further developed throughout the book. It leads on directly to other main themes, especially that of the study of time-space relations. The structural properties of social systems exist only in so far as forms of social conduct are reproduced chronically across time and space. The structuration of institutions can be understood in terms of how it comes about that social activities become 'stretched' across wide spans of time-space. Incorporating time-space in the heart of social theory means thinking again about some of the disciplinary divisions which separate sociology from history and from geography. The concept and analysis of history is particularly problematic. This book, indeed, might be accurately described as an extended reflection upon a celebrated and oft-quoted phrase to be found in Marx. Marx comments that 'Men [let us immediately say human beings] make history, but not in circumstances of their own choosing.'* Well, so they do. But what a diversity of complex problems of social analysis this apparently innocuous pronouncement turns out to disclose!

---

* The phrase is to be found in the introductory paragraphs of *The Eighteenth Brumaire of Louis Bonaparte*. It was made in a polemical vein; those who are ignorant of history, Marx says, may be condemned to repeat it, perhaps even farcically. The exact quotation in the original goes as follows: 'Die Menschen machen ihre eigene Geschichte, aber sie machen sie nicht aus freien Stücken, nicht unter selbstgewählten, sondern unter unmittelbar vorgefundenen, gegebenen und überlieferten Umständen. Die Tradition aller toten Geschlechter lastet wie ein Alp auf dem Gehirne der Lebenden. Und wenn sie eben damit beschäftigt scheinen, sich und die Dinge umzuwälzen, noch nicht Dagewesenes zu schaffen, gerade in solchen Epochen revolutionärer Krise beschwören sie ängstlich die Geister der Vergangenheit zu ihrem Dienste herauf, entlehnen ihnen Namen, Schlachtparole, Kostüm, um in dieser altehrwürdigen Verkleidung und mit dieser erburgten Sprache die neue Weltgeschichtsszene aufzuführen.' (Marx and Engels: *Werke*, Vol 8. Berlin: Dietz Verlag 1960, p. 115).

In formulating this account of structuration theory I have not been reluctant to draw upon ideas from quite divergent sources. To some this may appear an unacceptable eclecticism, but I have never been able to see the force of this type of objection. There is an undeniable comfort in working within established traditions of thought — the more so, perhaps, given the very diversity of approaches that currently confronts anyone who is outside any single tradition. The comfort of established views can, however, easily be a cover for intellectual sloth. If ideas are important and illuminating, what matters much more than their origin is to be able to sharpen them so as to demonstrate their usefulness, even if within a framework which might be quite different from that which helped to engender them. Thus, for example, I acknowledge the call for a decentring of the subject and regard this as basic to structuration theory. But I do not accept that this implies the evaporation of subjectivity into an empty universe of signs. Rather, social practices, biting into space and time, are considered to be at the root of the constitution of both subject and social object. I admit the central significance of the 'linguistic turn', introduced especially by hermeneutic phenomenology and ordinary language philosophy. At the same time, however, I hold this term to be in some part a misleading one. The most important developments as regards social theory concern not so much a turn towards language as an altered view of the intersection between saying (or signifying) and doing, offering a novel conception of *praxis*. The radical transmutation of hermeneutics and phenomenology initiated by Heidegger, together with the innovations of the later Wittgenstein, are the two main signal markers on the new path. But to pursue this path further means precisely to shake off any temptation to become a full-blown disciple of either of these thinkers.

Let me offer here a short summary of the organization of the book. Having given in the first chapter an outline of the chief concepts involved in structuration theory, in the second I begin the more substantive part of the volume with a discussion of consciousness, the unconscious and the constitution of day-to-day life. Human agents or actors — I use these terms interchangeably — have, as an inherent aspect of what they do, the capacity to understand what they do while they do it. The reflexive capacities of the human actor are characteristically involved in a continuous manner with the flow of day-to-day conduct in the contexts of social activity. But reflexivity operates only partly on a discursive level. What agents know about what they do, and why they do it — their knowledgeability *as* agents — is largely carried in practical consciousness. Practical consciousness consists of all the things which actors know tacitly about how to 'go on' in the contexts of social life without being able to give them direct discursive expression. The significance of practical consciousness is a leading theme of the book, and it has to be distinguished from both consciousness (discursive consciousness) and the unconscious. While accepting the importance of unconscious aspects of cognition and motivation, I do not think we can be content with some of the more conventionally established views of these. I adopt a modified version of ego psychology but endeavour to relate this directly to what, I suggest, is a fundamental concept of structuration theory — that of *routinization*.

The routine (whatever is done habitually) is a basic element of day-to-day social activity. I use the phrase 'day-to-day social activity' in a very literal sense, not in the more complex, and I think more ambiguous, way which has become familiar through phenomenology. The term 'day-to-day' encapsulates exactly the routinized character which social life has as it stretches across time-space. The repetitiveness of activities which are undertaken in like manner day after day is the material grounding of what I call the recursive nature of social life. (By its recursive nature I mean that the structured properties of social activity — via the duality of structure — are constantly recreated out of the very resources which constitute them.) Routinization is vital to the psychological mechanisms whereby a sense of trust or ontological security is sustained in the daily activities of social life. Carried primarily in practical consciousness, routine drives a wedge between the potentially explosive content of the unconscious and the reflexive monitoring of action which agents display. Why did Garfinkel's 'experiments with trust' stimulate such a very strong reaction of anxiety on the part of those involved, seemingly out of all proportion to the trivial nature of the circumstances of their origin? Because, I think, the apparently minor conventions of daily social life are of essential significance in curbing the sources of unconscious tension that would otherwise preoccupy most of our waking lives.

The situated character of action in time-space, the routinization of activity and the repetitive nature of day-to-day life — these are phenomena which connect discussion of the unconscious with Goffman's analyses of co-presence. In spite of their manifest brilliance, Goffman's writings are usually thought of as perhaps somewhat lightweight in respect of their theoretical content, either because he is regarded above all as a sort of sociological *raconteur* — the equivalent of a sociological gossip whose observations entertain and titillate but are none the less superficial and essentially picayune — or because what he portrays is specific to social life in modern, middle-class society, a cynical society of amoral role players. There is something in each of these views, and to a certain degree Goffman is vulnerable to them because he refrains from drawing out, in a fully systematic way, the implications of his standpoint. Where he does do so he tends to link the rituals of day-to-day social life to ethological accounts of the behaviour of the higher animals and to explicate them in those terms. This may indeed be instructive, but it is not the most useful way of relating his work to problems of social theory because it does not plug the right gaps in what he has to say. One such gap is the absence of an account of motivation, the main reason why his writings are open to the second interpretation mentioned above. I try to show how an analysis of motivation, as developed in relation to routinization and the unconscious, can bring out the systematic character of Goffman's work more fully. Goffman's emphasis on trust and tact strikingly echoes themes found in ego psychology and generates an analytically powerful understanding of the reflexive monitoring of the flux of encounters involved in daily life.

Fundamental to social life is the positioning of the body in social encounters. 'Positioning' here is a rich term. The body is positioned in the immediate circumstances of co-presence in relation to others: Goffman provides an extraordinarily subtle but telling set of observations about face work, about gesture and reflexive control of bodily movement as inherent in the continuity of social life. Positioning is, however, also to be understood in relation to the seriality of encounters across time-space. Every individual is at once positioned in the flow of day-to-day life; in the life-span which is the duration of his or her existence; and in the duration of 'institutional time', the 'supra-individual' structuration of social institutions. Finally, each person is positioned, in a 'multiple' way, within social relations conferred by specific social identities; this is the main sphere of application of the concept of social role. The modalities of co-presence, mediated directly by the sensory properties of the body, are clearly different from social ties and forms of social interaction established with others absent in time or in space.

It is not only individuals who are 'positioned' relative to one another; the contexts of social interaction are also. In examining these connections, to do with the contextuality of social interaction, the techniques and approach of time-geography, as developed by Hägerstrand, are highly illuminating. Time-geography also has as its principal concern the location of individuals in time-space but gives particular attention to constraints over activity deriving from physical properties of the body and of environments in which agents move. Reference to these is but one of the respects in which sociology can profit from the writings of geographers. Another is the interpretation of urbanism, which, I argue, has a basic part to play in social theory; and, of course, a general sensitivity to space and place is of even greater importance.

Goffman gives some considerable attention to the regionalization of encounters, and I take the notion of regionalization to be a very significant one for social theory. It has always been a main concern of the writings of geographers, but I want to regard it as less of a purely spatial concept than they ordinarily do. The situated nature of social interaction can usefully be examined in relation to the different locales through which the daily activities of individuals are co-ordinated. Locales are not just places but *settings* of interaction; as Garfinkel has demonstrated particularly persuasively, settings are used chronically — and largely in a tacit way — by social actors to sustain meaning in communicative acts. But settings are also regionalized in ways that heavily influence, and are influenced by, the serial character of encounters. Time-space 'fixity' also normally means social fixity; the substantially 'given' character of the physical *milieux* of day-to-day life interlaces with routine and is deeply influential in the contours of institutional reproduction. Regionalization also has strong psychological and social resonance in respect of the 'enclosure' from view of some types of activities and some types of people and the 'disclosure' of others. Here we again find a major point of connection between seemingly disparate ideas, those of Goffman and Foucault; both accord great importance to the socially and historically fluctuating lines between enclosure and disclosure, confinement and display.

I think it is a mistake to regard encounters in circumstances of co-presence as in some way the basis upon which larger, or 'macrostructural', social properties are built. So-called 'micro-sociological' study does not deal with a reality that is somehow more substantial than that with which 'macrosociological' analysis is concerned. But neither, on the contrary, is interaction in situations of co-presence simply ephemeral, as contrasted to the solidity of large-scale or long-established institutions. Each view has its proponents, but I see this division of opinion as an empty one and as a slightly more concrete version of the dualism in social theory already mentioned. The opposition between 'micro' and 'macro' is best reconceptualized as concerning how interaction in contexts of co-presence is structurally implicated in systems of broad time-space distanciation — in other words, how such systems span large sectors of time-space. And this in turn is best investigated as a problem of the connection of social with system integration, as I define these terms. But a vital rider has to be added to this. The relation of social to system integration cannot be grasped on a purely abstract level; the theory of urbanism is essential to it. For it is only with the advent of cities — and, in modern times, with the urbanism of the 'created environment' — that a significant development of system integration becomes possible.

We have to be very careful indeed with the concept of 'social system' and the associated notion of 'society'. They sound innocent terms, and they are probably indispensable if used with appropriate measures of caution. 'Society' has a useful double meaning, which I have relied upon — signifying a bounded system, and social association in general. An emphasis upon regionalization helps to remind us that the degree of 'systemness' in social systems is very variable and that 'societies' rarely have easily specifiable boundaries — until, at least, we enter the modern world of nation-states. Functionalism and naturalism tend to encourage unthinking acceptance of societies as clearly delimited entities, and social systems as internally highly integrated unities. For such perspectives, even where direct organic metaphors are rejected, tend to be closely allied to biological concepts; and these have usually been arrived at with reference to entities clearly set off from the world around them, having an evident internal unity. But 'societies' are very often not like this at all. To help take account of that, I introduce the terms 'intersocietal systems' and 'time-space edges', referring to different aspects of regionalization which cut across social systems recognizably distinct as societies. I also use these notions extensively in assessing interpretations of social change later in the book.

In formulating structuration theory I wish to escape from the dualism associated with objectivism and subjectivism. But some critics have felt that not enough weight is given to factors emphasized by the first of these, particularly in respect of the constraining aspects of the structural properties of social systems. To show that such is not the case I indicate in some detail what 'constraint' can be taken to mean in social theory and how the various senses that can be given to the term are understood in the theory of structuration. Recognition of the nature and significance of structural constraint does not mean succumbing to the attractions of structural sociology, but neither, as I try to make clear, do I accept a viewpoint close to methodological individualism. As conceptualized in structuration theory, 'structure' means something different from its usual usage in the social sciences. I also introduce a cluster of other concepts centring upon that of structure and endeavour to show why they are necessary. Most important among these is the idea of 'structural principles', which are structural features of overall societies or societal totalities; I also seek to show that it is through the notion of structural principles that the concept of contradiction can most usefully be specified as relevant to social analysis. These notions again cannot be expressed in purely abstract form, and I examine them with reference to three major types of society that can be distinguished in human history: tribal cultures, class-divided societies and modern nation-states associated with the rise of industrial capitalism.

Mention of history recalls the dictum that human beings make history. What exactly is it that they make — what does 'history' mean here? The answer cannot be expressed in as cogent a form as the original maxim. There is, of course, a difference between history as events which elapse and history as writing about those events. But this does not get us all that far. History in the first sense is temporality, events in their duration. We tend to associate temporality with a linear sequence, and thus history thought of in this way with movement in a discernible direction. But this may very well be a culture-bound fashion of thinking about time; even if it is not, we still have to avoid the equation of 'history' with social change. For this reason it is worth speaking of 'historicity' as a definite sense of living in a social world constantly exposed to change, in which Marx's maxim is part of a general cultural awareness, not a theorem peculiar to specialist social thinkers. History as the writing of history also poses its own dilemmas and puzzles. All I shall have to say about these is that they are not distinctive; they do not permit us to make clear-cut distinctions between history and social science. Hermeneutic problems involved in the accurate description of divergent forms of life, the interpretation of texts, the explication of action, institutions and social transformation — these are shared by all the social sciences, including history.

How, then, should we approach the study of social change? I try to show that the search for a theory of social change (where 'theory' means in this instance explaining social change by reference to a single set of mechanisms, such as the old evolutionary favourites of adaptation and differential selection) is a doomed one. It is flawed by the same kind of logical shortcomings that attach more generally to the supposition that the social sciences can uncover universal laws of human conduct. The sorts of understanding or knowledge that human beings have of their own 'history' is partly constitutive of what that history is and of the influences that act to change it. However, it is important to give particular critical attention to evolutionism because in one version or another it has been so influential in a variety of different areas of social science. I mean by 'evolutionism', as applied to the social sciences, the explication of social change in terms of schemas which involve the following features: an irreversible series of stages through which societies move, even if it is not held that all individual societies must pass through each of them to reach the higher ones; some conceptual linkage with biological theories of evolution; and the specification of directionality through the stages indicated, in respect of a given criterion or criteria, such as increasing complexity or expansion of the forces of production. A range of objections can be brought against these ideas, both in respect of their intrinsic demerits and in terms of secondary implications which evolutionism almost inevitably tends to bring in its train, even if they are not logically entailed by it. 'Historical materialism', I think, is a version of evolutionism according to these criteria, in at least one of the main ways in which that contentious term has been understood. If interpreted in this manner, historical materialism manifests several of the main and the secondary limitations of evolutionary theories more generally and has to be rejected for the same reasons.

Since I do not think it possible to compress 'history' into the kinds of scheme favoured by evolutionism in general, or by historical materialism more specifically, I speak of deconstructing rather than reconstructing them. By this I mean that accounts of social change have to take a substantially different form from evolutionism; there is no virtue in trying merely to remodel them somewhat. In addition to concepts already introduced, I make use of two others: those of 'episode' and 'world time' (the first due to Gellner, the second to Eberhard). All social life can be represented as a series of episodes; encounters in circumstances of co-presence certainly have an episodic form. But in this connection I am referring mainly to large-scale processes of change, in which there is some definite type of institutional reorganization, such as the formation of cities in agrarian societies or the formation of early states. Episodes may certainly be fruitfully compared with one another but not in complete abstraction from the context of their origin. The influence of 'world time' is relevant precisely to how far they are in fact comparable. 'World time' concerns the varying conjunctures in history that may affect the conditions and outcomes of seemingly similar episodes and the influence of what the agents involved *know* about such conditions and outcomes. I seek to indicate the analytical purchase of these notions by using as an illustration theories of state formation.

Structuration theory will not be of much value if it does not help to illuminate problems of empirical research, and in the concluding chapter I take up this issue, which I hold to be inseparable from the implications of structuration theory as a form of critique. I do not try to wield a methodological scalpel. That is to say, I do not believe that there is anything in either the logic or the substance of structuration theory which would somehow prohibit the use of some specific research technique, such as survey methods, questionnaires or whatever. Some considerations brought into play are relevant to the mode of application of particular techniques to research questions and to the interpretation of results, but that is a rather different matter. The points of connection of structuration theory with empirical research are to do with working out the logical implications of studying a 'subject matter' of which the researcher is already a part and with elucidating the substantive connotations of the core notions of action and structure. Some of the points I have made on the abstract level of theory apply directly on the level of research. A good deal of social theory, especially that associated with structural sociology, has treated agents as much less knowledgeable than they really are. The results of this can be very easily discerned in empirical work, in respect of a failure to gain information that allows access to the full range of agents' knowledgeability in at least two ways. What actors are able to say about the conditions of their action and that of others is foreshortened if researchers do not recognize the possible significance of a range of discursive phenomena to which, as social actors themselves, they would certainly pay close attention but which in social research are often simply discounted. These are aspects of discourse which in form are refractory to being rendered as statements of propositional belief or which, like humour or irony, derive their meaning not so much from the content of what is said as from the style, mode of expression or context of utterance. But to this we must add a second factor of greater importance: the need to acknowledge the significance of practical consciousness. Where what agents know about what they do is restricted to what they can say about it, in whatever discursive style, a very wide area of knowledgeability is simply occluded from view. The study of practical consciousness must be incorporated into research work. It would be an error to suppose that non-discursive components of consciousness are necessarily more difficult to study empirically than the discursive, even though agents themselves, by definition, cannot comment directly on them. The unconscious, on the other hand, poses altogether a different order of problem, certainly demanding techniques of interrogation distinct from those involved in descriptive social research.

Functionalism has been highly important in the social sciences, not only because of its prominence as a type of theorizing but also because of the empirical stimulus it has provided. The origins of fieldwork in anthropology are more or less coterminous with the impact of functionalism, and in sociology also functionalist thought has helped to generate a significant body of research work. I think it essential to understand the attractions of functionalism in this respect, while still holding that conceptually its influence has been largely pernicious. Functionalism has strongly emphasized the significance of unintended consequences of action, especially in so far as such consequences occur in a regular way and are therefore involved in the reproduction of institutionalized aspects of social systems. Functionalists have been quite right to promote this emphasis. But it is entirely possible to study unintended consequences without the use of functionalist concepts. Moreover, the designation of just what is unintentional in regard of the consequences of action can be adequately grasped empirically only if the intentional aspects of action are identified, and this again means operating with an interpretation of agency more sophisticated than is normally held by those inclined towards functionalist premises.

In structuration theory 'structure' is regarded as rules and resources recursively implicated in social reproduction; institutionalized features of social systems have structural properties in the sense that relationships are stabilized across time and space. 'Structure' can be conceptualized abstractly as two aspects of rules — normative elements and codes of signification. Resources are also of two kinds: authoritative resources, which derive from the co-ordination of the activity of human agents, and allocative resources, which stem from control of material products or of aspects of the material world. What is especially useful for the guidance of research is the study of, first, the routinized intersections of practices which are the 'transformation points' in structural relations and, second, the modes in which institutionalized practices connect social with system integration. As regards the first of these, to take an example, it can be demonstrated how private property, a cluster of rights of ownership, can be 'translated' into industrial authority, or modes of sustaining managerial control. As regards the second, what has to be ascertained empirically is how far the situated practices studied in a given range of contexts converge with one another in such a way that they enter directly into system reproduction. An alertness to the significance of locales as settings of interaction is important here; there is no reason why sociologists should not adopt some of the research techniques established by geographers, including the graphic techniques of time-geography, in order to study them.

If the social sciences are understood as they were during the period of dominance of the orthodox consensus, their attainments do not look impressive, and the relevance of social research to practical issues seems fairly slight. For the natural sciences, or at least the more advanced of them, have precisely specified and generally accepted laws, together with a fund of uncontroversial empirical observations which can be explicated in terms of those laws. Natural science has become coupled to technological capabilities of an awesome kind, destructive as well as constructive. In the eyes of those who would model social science directly on natural science, the former surely comes off a distant second best. Both cognitively and practically, the social sciences seem distinctly inferior to the natural sciences. But if we accept that social science should no longer be some sort of replica of natural science and is in some respects a quite divergent enterprise, a very different view of their relative achievements and influence can be defended. There are no universal laws in the social sciences, and there will not be any — not, first and foremost, because methods of empirical testing and validation are somehow inadequate but because, as I have pointed out, the causal conditions involved in generalizations about human social conduct are inherently unstable in respect of the very knowledge (or beliefs) that actors have about the circumstances of their own action. The so-called 'self-fulfilling prophecy', of which Merton and others have written, is a special case of a much more generic phenomenon in the social sciences. This is a mutual interpretative interplay between social science and those whose activities compose its subject matter — a 'double hermeneutic'. The theories and findings of the social sciences cannot be kept wholly separate from the universe of meaning and action which they are about. But, for their part, lay actors are social theorists, whose theories help to constitute the activities and institutions that are the object of study of specialized social observers or social scientists. There is no clear dividing line between informed sociological reflection carried on by lay actors and similar endeavours on the part of specialists. I do not want to deny that there *are* dividing lines, but they are inevitably fuzzy, and social scientists have no absolute monopoly either upon innovative theories or upon empirical investigations of what they study.

All this may perhaps be granted. But it still might not be accepted from these comments that we should take a different view of the accomplishments and impact of the social sciences to that indicated above. How could it seriously be suggested that social science has had as much influence, or more, upon the social world as natural science has had on the material world? I think, in fact, that this view can be maintained — although, of course, no such comparison could be precise, in view of the very differences between what is involved in each case. The point is that reflection on social processes (theories, and observations about them) continually enter into, become disentangled with and re-enter the universe of events that they describe. No such phenomenon exists in the world of inanimate nature, which is indifferent to whatever human beings might claim to know about it. Consider, for example, theories of sovereignty formulated by seventeenth-century European thinkers. These were the results of reflection upon, and study of, social trends into which they in turn were fed back. It is impossible to have a modern sovereign state that does not incorporate a discursively articulated theory of the modern sovereign state. The marked tendency towards an expansion of political 'self-monitoring' on the part of the state is characteristic of modernity in the West in general, creating the social and intellectual climate from which specialized, 'professional' discourses of social science have developed but also both express and foster. One could certainly make some sort of case for claiming that these changes, in which social science has been centrally involved, are of a very fundamental character. By the side of them the transformations of nature achieved by the natural sciences do not look so massive.

Reflecting upon such considerations a little further, we can see both why the social sciences may not appear to generate a great deal of original knowledge and also why theories and ideas produced in the past, apparently paradoxically, may retain a relevance to the present day which archaic conceptions of the natural sciences do not have. The best and most interesting ideas in the social sciences (a) participate in fostering the climate of opinion and the social processes which give rise to them, (b) are in greater or lesser degree entwined with theories-in-use which help to constitute those processes and (c) are thus unlikely to be clearly distinct from considered reflection which lay actors may bring to bear in so far as they discursively articulate, or improve upon, theories-in-use. These facts have consequences, particularly for sociology (to which they are most distinctly relevant) which affect both the prosecution of empirical research and the formulation and reception of theories. In respect of research they mean that it is much more difficult than is the case in natural science to 'hold up' acceptance of theories while searching for ways to test them out appropriately. Social life moves on; appealing or potentially practical theories, hypotheses or findings may be taken up in social life in such a way that the original grounds upon which they could be tested have altered anyway. There are many complex possible permutations of mutual 'feed-in' here, which combine also with the difficulties inherent in controlling variables, replicating observations and other methodological quandaries in which the social sciences can find themselves. Theories in natural science are original, innovative and so on to the degree to which they place in question what either lay actors or professional scientists previously believed about the objects or events to which they refer. But theories in the social sciences have to be in some part based upon ideas which (although not necessarily discursively formulated by them) are already held by the agents to whom they refer. Once reincorporated within action, their original quality may become lost; they may become all too familiar. The notion of sovereignty and associated theories of the state were stunningly new when first formulated; today they have in some degree become a part of the very social reality which they helped to establish.

But why do some social theories retain their freshness long after the conditions that helped produce them are past? Why, now that we are well familiar with the concept and the reality of state sovereignty, do seventeenth-century theories of the state retain a relevance to social or political reflection today? Surely exactly because they have contributed to constituting the social world we now live in. It is the fact that they are reflections upon a social reality which they also help to constitute and which both has a distance from, yet remains part of, our social world that engages our attention. Theories in the natural sciences which have been replaced by others which do the same job better are of no interest to the current practice of science. This cannot be the case where those theories have helped to constitute what they interpret or explicate. The 'history of ideas' may perhaps justifiably be regarded as of marginal importance to the practising natural scientist, but it is much more than tangential to the social sciences.

If they are correct, these ruminations lead on in a direct way to a consideration of social science as critique — as involved in a practical fashion with social life. We cannot be content with the 'technological' version of critique proposed by the orthodox consensus, a view deriving from a natural science model. The technological view of critique supposes that the 'internal critique' of social science — the critical assessments which those working in the social sciences make of each other's views — uncomplicatedly generates an 'external critique' of lay beliefs that can be the basis of practical social intervention. But, given the significance of the 'double hermeneutic', matters are much more complex. The formulation of critical theory is not an *option*; theories and findings in the social sciences are likely to have practical (and political) consequences regardless of whether or not the sociological observer or policy-maker decides that they can be 'applied' to a given practical issue.

This was not a particularly easy book to write and proved in some part refractory to the normal ordering of chapters. Structuration theory was formulated in substantial part through its own 'internal critique' — the critical evaluation of a variety of currently competing schools of social thought. Rather than allow some of these critical confrontations to obtrude into the main sections of the text, I have included them as appendices to those chapters to which they most immediately relate. (Notes associated with them similarly follow the notes that belong to relevant chapters.) The reader who wants to follow the main line of the argument in an unencumbered way can pass over them. They will, however, be of interest to anyone concerned either with how the views I defend differ from those of others or with the elaboration of themes treated in a condensed way in the core of each chapter. A variety of neologisms are used in the book, and I have placed a glossary of these at the end.

Reference

1 It would, of course, be a mistake to suppose that the influence of Parsons is confined to the past, to imagine that Parsons has been forgotten in the same way as he once suggested happened to Spencer very soon after his death. On the contrary, one of the most visible trends in social theory today is the prime part played by views drawn more or less directly from Parsons. One might instance the writings of Luhmann and Habermas in Germany, Bourricauld in France and Alexander and others in the United States. I do not intend to discuss any of this literature in detail, but it is probably worth spelling out a little why I do not have much sympathy with those aspects of the writings of such authors which are closely based on Parsons's ideas. All the writers in question are strongly critical of Parsons's connections with functionalism, of which Luhmann probably seeks to retain more than the others. In this respect, I am in accord with them, as this text should make clear enough. But in other ways, for reasons which are also documented at some length in this book, I consider that a radical break has to be made with Parsonian theorems. An important aspect of this concerns the filtering of the influence of Max Weber through the writings of Parsons. I have often been called a 'Weberian' by critics who regard this as some sort of irreparable fault. I do not see the term, as they do, as a slur, but neither do I accept it as accurately applied to my views. If I draw upon Weber, it is from an angle different from that of the aforementioned authors. Thus Habermas's Weber (surprisingly perhaps) tends to be a Parsonian-style Weber, concerned above all with the rationalization of values and with 'social differentiation', portrayed as generalized processes of development. Social life is not depicted here through the lenses I would prefer to borrow from Weber, as concerned with the multifarious practices and struggles of concretely located actors; with conflict and the clash of sectional interests; and with the territoriality and violence of political formations or states.
    Parsons regarded himself as an 'action theorist' and called his

version of social science the 'action frame of reference'. But, as I have sought to show at some length elsewhere (see *NRSM*, chapter 3), what I would regard as a satisfactory conception of action (and other related notions, especially those of intentions and reasons) is not to be found in Parsons's work. This is not, as some commentators have suggested, because a later emphasis upon functionalism and systems theory tended to swamp an earlier concern with 'voluntarism'. It is because the idea of voluntarism was flawed at source. In Parsons's thought voluntarism has always been linked with the resolution of the 'problem of order', conceived of by him as the co-ordination of potentially disruptive individual wills. It is resolved through the demonstration that actors internalize, as motives, the shared values upon which social cohesion depends. The call for an account of action becomes conflated with the demand to link a 'psychological' theory of motivation with a 'sociological' interpretation of the structural features of social systems. Little, if any, conceptual room is left for what I emphasize as the knowledgeability of social actors, as constitutive in part of social practices. I do not think that any standpoint which is heavily indebted to Parsons can cope satisfactorily with this issue at the very core of the concerns of social theory as I conceive of it in this book.

If those strongly indebted to Parsons today do not regard themselves as functionalists and have rejected the functionalist cast of Parsons's thought in greater or lesser degree, they still take over other ideas related to most versions of functionalism. These include: a fascination with 'value-consensus' or symbolic orders at the expense of the more mundane, practical aspects of social activity; the tendency to assume that societies are easily distinguishable unities, as biological organisms are; and a fondness for evolutionary-style theories. I consider each of these emphases to be seriously misleading and shall enter strong reservations about them. There can be no doubt about the sophistication and importance of the work of some authors currently endeavouring to develop Parsons's work in novel ways, particularly Luhmann and Habermas. But I think it as necessary to repudiate the newer versions of Parsonianism as I do the longer established varieties of non-Parsonian structural sociology.

1
Elements of the Theory of Structuration

In offering a preliminary exposition of the main concepts of structuration theory[1]* it will be useful to begin from the divisions which have separated functionalism (including systems theory) and structuralism on the one hand from hermeneutics and the various forms of 'interpretative sociology' on the other. Functionalism and structuralism have some notable similarities, in spite of the otherwise marked contrasts that exist between them. Both tend to express a naturalistic standpoint, and both are inclined towards objectivism. Functionalist thought, from Comte onwards, has looked particularly towards biology as the science providing the closest and most compatible model for social science. Biology has been taken to provide a guide to conceptualizing the structure and the functioning of social systems and to analysing processes of evolution via mechanisms of adaptation. Structuralist thought, especially in the writings of Lévi-Strauss, has been hostile to evolutionism and free from biological analogies. Here the homology between social and natural science is primarily a cognitive one in so far as each is supposed to express similar features of the overall constitution of mind. Both structuralism and functionalism strongly emphasize the pre-eminence of the social whole over its individual parts (i.e., its constituent actors, human subjects).

In hermeneutic traditions of thought, of course, the social and natural sciences are regarded as radically discrepant. Hermeneutics has been the home of that 'humanism' to which structuralists have been so strongly and persistently opposed. In hermeneutic thought, such as presented by Dilthey, the gulf between subject and social object is at its widest. Subjectivity is the preconstituted

*References may be found on pp. 37—9.

centre of the experience of culture and history and as such provides the basic foundation of the social or human sciences. Outside the realm of subjective experience, and alien to it, lies the material world, governed by impersonal relations of cause and effect. Whereas for those schools of thought which tend towards naturalism subjectivity has been regarded as something of a mystery, or almost a residual phenomenon, for hermeneutics it is the world of nature which is opaque — which, unlike human activity, can be grasped only from the outside. In interpretative sociologies, action and meaning are accorded primacy in the explication of human conduct; structural concepts are not notably prominent, and there is not much talk of constraint. For functionalism and structuralism, however, structure (in the divergent senses attributed to that concept) has primacy over action, and the constraining qualities of structure are strongly accentuated.

The differences between these perspectives on social science have often been taken to be epistemological, whereas they are in fact also ontological. What is at issue is how the concepts of action, meaning and subjectivity should be specified and how they might relate to notions of structure and constraint. If interpretative sociologies are founded, as it were, upon an imperialism of the subject, functionalism and structuralism propose an imperialism of the social object. One of my principal ambitions in the formulation of structuration theory is to put an end to each of these empire-building endeavours. The basic domain of study of the social sciences, according to the theory of structuration, is neither the experience of the individual actor, nor the existence of any form of societal totality, but social practices ordered across space and time. Human social activities, like some self-reproducing items in nature, are recursive. That is to say, they are not brought into being by social actors but continually recreated by them via the very means whereby they express themselves *as* actors. In and through their activities agents reproduce the conditions that make these activities possible. However, the sort of 'knowledgeability' displayed in nature, in the form of coded programmes, is distant from the cognitive skills displayed by human agents. It is in the conceptualizing of human knowledgeability and its involvement in action that I seek to appropriate some of the major contributions of interpretative sociologies. In structuration theory a hermeneutic starting-point is accepted in so far as it is acknowledged that the description of human activities demands a familiarity with the forms of life expressed in those activities.

It is the specifically reflexive form of the knowledgeability of human agents that is most deeply involved in the recursive ordering of social practices. Continuity of practices presumes reflexivity, but reflexivity in turn is possible only because of the continuity of practices that makes them distinctively 'the same' across space and time. 'Reflexivity' hence should be understood not merely as 'self-consciousness' but as the monitored character of the ongoing flow of social life. To be a human being is to be a purposive agent, who both has reasons for his or her activities and is able, if asked, to elaborate discursively upon those reasons (including lying about them). But terms such as 'purpose' or 'intention', 'reason', 'motive' and so on have to be treated with caution, since their usage in the philosophical literature has very often been associated with a hermeneutical voluntarism, and because they extricate human action from the contextuality of time-space. Human action occurs as a *durée,* a continuous flow of conduct, as does cognition. Purposive action is not composed of an aggregate or series of separate intentions, reasons and motives. Thus it is useful to speak of reflexivity as grounded in the continuous monitoring of action which human beings display and expect others to display. The reflexive monitoring of action depends upon rationalization, understood here as a process rather than a state and as inherently involved in the competence of agents. An ontology of time-space as constitutive of social practices is basic to the conception of structuration, which *begins* from temporality and thus, in one sense, 'history'.

This approach can draw only sparingly upon the analytical philosophy of action, as 'action' is ordinarily portrayed by most contemporary Anglo-American writers. 'Action' is not a combination of 'acts': 'acts' are constituted only by a discursive moment of attention to the *durée* of lived-through experience. Nor can 'action' be discussed in separation from the body, its mediations with the surrounding world and the coherence of an acting self. What I call a *stratification model* of the acting self involves treating the reflexive monitoring, rationalization and motivation of action as embedded sets of processes.[2] The rationalization of

D

action, referring to 'intentionality' as process, is, like the other two dimensions, a routine characteristic of human conduct, carried on in a taken-for-granted fashion. In circumstances of interaction — encounters and episodes — the reflexive monitoring of action typically, and again routinely, incorporates the monitoring of the setting of such interaction. As I shall indicate subsequently, this phenomenon is basic to the interpolation of action within the time-space relations of what I shall call co-presence. The rationalization of action, within the diversity of circumstances of interaction, is the principal basis upon which the generalized 'competence' of actors is evaluated by others. It should be clear, however, that the tendency of some philosophers to equate reasons with 'normative commitments' should be resisted: such commitments comprise only one sector of the rationalization of action. If this is not understood, we fail to understand that norms figure as 'factual' boundaries of social life, to which a variety of manipulative attitudes are possible. One aspect of such attitudes, although a relatively superficial one, is to be found in the commonplace observation that the reasons actors offer discursively for what they do may diverge from the rationalization of action as actually involved in the stream of conduct of those actors.

This circumstance has been a frequent source of worry to philosophers and observers of the social scene — for how can we be sure that people do not dissimulate concerning the reasons for their activities? But it is of relatively little interest compared with the wide 'grey areas' that exist between two strata of processes not accessible to the discursive consciousness of actors. The vast bulk of the 'stocks of knowledge', in Schutz's phrase, or what I prefer to call the *mutual knowledge* incorporated in encounters, is not directly accessible to the consciousness of actors. Most such knowledge is practical in character: it is inherent in the capability to 'go on' within the routines of social life. The line between discursive and practical consciousness is fluctuating and permeable, both in the experience of the individual agent and as regards comparisons between actors in different contexts of social activity. There is no bar between these, however, as there is between the unconscious and discursive consciousness. The unconscious includes those forms of cognition and impulsion which are either wholly repressed from consciousness or appear in consciousness only in distorted form. Unconscious motivational components of action, as psychoanalytic theory suggests, have an internal hierarchy of their own, a hierarchy which expresses the 'depth' of the life history of the individual actor. In saying this I do not imply an uncritical acceptance of the key theorems of Freud's writings. We should guard against two forms of reductionism which those writings suggest or foster. One is a reductive conception of institutions which, in seeking to show the foundation of institutions in the unconscious, fails to leave sufficient play for the operation of autonomous social forces. The second is a reductive theory of consciousness which, wanting to show how much of social life is governed by dark currents outside the scope of actors' awareness, cannot adequately grasp the level of control which agents are characteristically able to sustain reflexively over their conduct.

The Agent, Agency

The stratification model of the agent can be represented as in figure 1. The reflexive monitoring of activity is a chronic feature of everyday action and involves the conduct not just of the individual but also of others. That is to say, actors not only

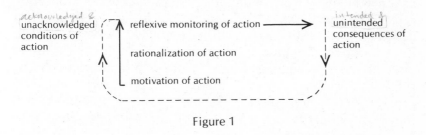

Figure 1

monitor continuously the flow of their activities and expect others to do the same for their own; they also routinely monitor aspects, social and physical, of the contexts in which they move. By the rationalization of action, I mean that actors — also routinely and for the most part without fuss — maintain a continuing 'theoretical understanding' of the grounds of their activity. As I have mentioned, having such an understanding should not be equated with the discursive giving of reasons for particular items of conduct, nor even with the capability of specifying such reasons discursively. However, it is expected by competent agents of others — and is the main criterion of competence applied in day-to-day conduct — that actors will usually be able to explain most of what they do, if asked. Questions often posed about intentions and reasons by philosophers are normally only put by lay actors either when some piece of conduct is specifically puzzling or when there is a 'lapse' or fracture in competency which might in fact be an intended one. Thus we will not ordinarily ask another person why he or she engages in an activity which is conventional for the group or culture of which that individual is a member. Neither will we ordinarily ask for an explanation if there occurs a lapse for which it seems unlikely the agent can be held responsible, such as slips in bodily management (see the discussion of 'Oops!', pp. 81—3) or slips of the tongue. If Freud is correct, however, such phenomena might have a rationale to them, although this is only rarely realized either by the perpetrators of such slips or by others who witness them (see pp. 94—104).

I distinguish the reflexive monitoring and rationalization of action from its motivation. If reasons refer to the grounds of action, motives refer to the wants which prompt it. However, motivation is not as directly bound up with the continuity of action as are its reflexive monitoring or rationalization. Motivation refers to potential for action rather than to the mode in which action is chronically carried on by the agent. Motives tend to have a direct purchase on action only in relatively unusual circumstances, situations which in some way break with the routine. For the most part motives supply overall plans or programmes — 'projects', in Schutz's term — within which a range of conduct is enacted. Much of our day-to-day conduct is not directly motivated.

While competent actors can nearly always report discursively about their intentions in, and reasons for, acting as they do, they cannot necessarily do so of their motives. Unconscious motivation is a significant feature of human conduct, although I shall later indicate some reservations about Freud's interpretation of the nature of the unconscious. The notion of practical consciousness is fundamental to structuration theory. It is that characteristic of the human agent or subject to which structuralism has been particularly blind.[3] But so have other types of objectivist thought.

Only in phenomenology and ethnomethodology, within socio-logical traditions, do we find detailed and subtle treatments of the nature of practical consciousness. Indeed, it is these schools of thought, together with ordinary language philosophy, which have been responsible for making clear the shortcomings of orthodox social scientific theories in this respect. I do not intend the distinction between discursive and practical consciousness to be a rigid and impermeable one. On the contrary, the division between the two can be altered by many aspects of the agent's socialization and learning experiences. Between discursive and practical consciousness there is no bar; there are only the differences between what can be said and what is characteristically simply done. However, there are barriers, centred principally upon repression, between discursive consciousness and the unconscious.

discursive consciousness

practical consciousness

unconscious motives/cognition

As explained elsewhere in the book, I offer these concepts in place of the traditional psychoanalytic triad of ego, super-ego and id. The Freudian distinction of ego and id cannot easily cope with the analysis of practical consciousness, which lacks a theoretical home in psychoanalytic theory as in the other types of social thought previously indicated. The concept of 'pre-conscious' is perhaps the closest notion to practical consciousness in the conceptual repertoire of psychoanalysis but, as ordinarily used, clearly means something different. In place of the 'ego', it is preferable to speak of the 'I' (as, of course, Freud did in the original German). This usage does not prevent anthropomor-phism, in which the ego is pictured as a sort of mini-agent; but it does at least help to begin to remedy it. The use of 'I' develops out of, and is thereafter associated with, the positioning of the agent in social encounters. As a term of a predicative sort, it is 'empty' of content, as compared with the richness of the actor's self-descriptions involved with 'me'. Mastery of 'I', 'me', 'you' relations, as applied reflexively in discourse, is of key importance to the emerging competence of agents learning language. Since I do not use the term 'ego', it is evidently best to dispense with 'super-ego' also — a clumsy term in any case. The term 'moral conscience' will do perfectly well as a replacement.

These concepts all refer to the agent. What of the nature of agency? This can be connected with a further issue. The *durée* of day-to-day life occurs as a flow of intentional action. However, acts have unintended consequences; and, as indicated in figure 1, unintended consequences may systematically feed back to be the unacknowledged conditions of further acts. Thus one of the regular consequences of my speaking or writing English in a correct way is to contribute to the reproduction of the English language as a whole. My speaking English correctly is intentional; the contribution I make to the reproduction of the language is not. But how should we formulate what unintended consequences are?

It has frequently been supposed that human agency can be defined only in terms of intentions. That is to say, for an item of behaviour to count as action, whoever perpetrates it must intend to do so, or else the behaviour in question is just a reactive response. The view derives some plausibility, perhaps, from the fact that there are some acts which cannot occur unless the agent intends them. Suicide is a case in point. Durkheim's conceptual efforts to the contrary, 'suicide' cannot be said to occur unless there is some kind of intent to precipitate self-destruction. A person who steps off the curb and is knocked down by an oncoming car cannot be said to be a 'suicide' if the event is accidental; it is something that happens to the individual, rather than something the individual does. However, suicide is not typical of most human acts, in respect of intentions, in so far as it can be said to have occurred only when its perpetrator intended it to occur. Most acts do not have this characteristic.

Some philosophers have argued, however, that for an event in which a human being is involved to count as an example of agency, it is necessary at least that what the person does be intentional under some description, even if the agent is mistaken about that description. An officer on a submarine pulls a lever intending to change course but instead, having pulled the wrong lever, sinks the *Bismarck*. He has done something intentionally, albeit not what he imagined, but thus the *Bismarck* has been sunk through his agency. Again, if someone intentionally spills some coffee, thinking mistakenly that it is tea, spilling the coffee is an act of that person, even though it has not been done intentionally; under another description, as 'spilling the tea', it is intentional.[4] (In most instances, 'spilling' something tends to have the implication that the act is unintentional. It is a slip intervening in a course of action in which the person is intending to do something different altogether, namely pass the cup to another person. Freud claims that nearly all such behavioural slips, like slips of the tongue, are actually unconsciously motivated. This, of course, brings them under intentional descriptions from another angle.)

But even the view that for an event to count as an instance of agency, it must be intentional only under *some* description or another is wrong. It confuses the designation of agency with the giving of act-descriptions;[5] and it mistakes the continued monitoring of an action which individuals carry out with the defining properties of that action as such. Agency refers not to the intentions people have in doing things but to their capability of doing those things in the first place (which is why agency implies power: cf. the Oxford English Dictionary definition of an agent, as 'one who exerts power or produces an effect'). Agency concerns events of which an individual is the perpetrator, in the sense that the individual could, at any phase in a given sequence of conduct, have acted differently. Whatever happened would not have happened if that individual had not intervened. Action is a continuous process, a flow, in which the reflexive monitoring which the individual maintains is fundamental to the control of the body that actors ordinarily sustain throughout their day-to-day lives. I am the author of many things I do not intend to do, and may not want to bring about, but none the less *do*. Conversely, there may be circumstances in which I intend to achieve something, and do achieve it, although not directly through my agency. Take the example of the spilled coffee. Supposing an individual, A, were a malicious spirit and played a practical joke by placing the cup on a saucer at such an angle that, when picked up, it would be very likely to spill. Individual B picks up the coffee, and it duly spills over. It would be right to say that what A did brought the incident about, or at least contributed to its coming about. But A did not spill the coffee; B did. Individual B, who did not intend to spill the coffee, spilled the coffee; individual A, who did intend that the coffee should be spilled, did not spill it.

But what is it to do something unintentionally? Is it different from bringing about consequences unintentionally? Consider the so-called 'accordion effect' of action.[6] An individual flicks a switch to illuminate a room. Although this is intentional, the fact that the turning on of the switch alerts a prowler is not. Supposing the prowler flees down the road, is caught by a policeman, and after due process spends a year in gaol on the basis of being convicted of the burglary. Are all these unintended consequences of the act of flicking the switch? Which are things the individual has 'done'? Let me mention an additional example, taken from a theory of ethnic segregation.[7] A pattern of ethnic segregation might develop, without any of those involved intending this to happen, in the following way, which can be illustrated by analogy. Imagine a chessboard which has a set of 5-pence pieces and a set of 10-pence pieces. These are distributed randomly on the board, as individuals might be in an urban area. It is presumed that, while they feel no hostility towards the other group, the members of each group do not want to live in a neighbourhood where they are ethnically in a minority. On the chessboard each piece is moved around until it is in such a position that at least 50 per cent of the adjoining pieces are of the same type. The result is a pattern of extreme segregation. The 10-cent pieces end up as a sort of ghetto in the midst of the 5-cent ones. The 'composition effect' is an outcome of an aggregate of acts — whether those of moving pieces on the board or those of agents in a housing market — each of which is intentionally carried out. But the eventual outcome is neither intended nor desired by anyone. It is, as it were, everyone's doing and no one's.

To understand what it is to do something unintentionally, we have first of all to be clear how 'intentional' should be understood. This concept I define as characterizing an act which its perpetrator knows, or believes, will have a particular quality or outcome and where such knowledge is utilized by the author of the act to achieve this quality or outcome.[8] If the characterization of agency given above is correct, we have to separate out the question of what an agent 'does' from what is 'intended' or the intentional aspects of what is done. Agency refers to doing. Switching on the light was something the agent did, and alerting the prowler was also something that agent did. It was unintended if the actor did not know the prowler was there and if for some reason, while knowing the prowler was there, the agent did not seek to use this knowledge to alert the intruder. Unintentional doings can be separated conceptually from unintended consequences of doings, although the distinction will not matter whenever the focus of concern is the relation between the intentional and unintentional. The consequences of what actors do, intentionally or unintentionally, are events which would not have happened if that actor had behaved differently, but which are not within the scope of the agent's power to have brought about (regardless of what the agent's intentions were).

I think we can say that all the things that happened to the prowler following the flicking of the switch were unintended consequences of the act, given that the individual in question did not know the prowler was there and therefore initiated the sequence unintentionally. If there are complexities in this, they are to do with how it comes about that a seemingly trivial act may trigger events far removed from it in time and space, not whether or not those consequences were intended by the perpetrator of the original act. In general it is true that the further removed the consequences of an act are in time and space from the original context of the act, the less likely those consequences are to be intentional — but this is, of course, influenced both by the scope of the knowledgeability that actors have (see pp. 90—2) and the power they are able to mobilize. We would ordinarily think of what the agent 'does' — as contrasted with the consequences ensuing from what has been done — in terms of phenomena the agent has more or less within his or her control. In most spheres of life, and in most forms of activity, the scope of control is limited to the immediate contexts of action or interaction. Thus we would say that turning on the light was something the agent did, and probably also alerting the prowler, but not causing the prowler to get caught by the policeman or to end up spending a year in gaol. Although it might be the case that these events would not have happened when and where they did without the act of flicking the switch, their occurrence depended on too many other contingent outcomes for them to be something the original actor 'did'.

Philosophers have used up a great deal of ink attempting to analyse the nature of intentional activity. But from the point of view of the social sciences, it is hard to exaggerate the importance of the unintended consequences of intentional conduct. Merton has provided perhaps the classical discussion of the issue.[9] He points out, entirely correctly, that the study of unintended consequences is fundamental to the sociological enterprise. A given item of activity may have either (a) non-significant or (b) significant consequences; and either (c) singly significant consequences or (d) multiply significant consequences. What is judged 'significant' will depend upon the nature of the study being undertaken or the theory being developed.[10] However, Merton then goes on to couple unintended consequences with functional analysis, a conceptual move which, although conventionally made in the sociological literature, I wish to reject. In particular, it is important to see that the analysis of unintended consequences does not (as Merton claims it does) make sense of seemingly irrational forms or patterns of social conduct. Merton contrasts intentional activity (manifest functions) with its unintended consequences (latent functions). One of the aims of identifying latent functions is to show that apparently irrational social activities may not be so irrational after all. This is particularly likely to be the case, according to Merton, with enduring activities or practices. These may often be dismissed as '"superstitions", "irrationalities", "mere inertia of tradition", etc'. However, in Merton's view, if we discover that they have a latent function — an unintended consequence, or set of consequences, which help to secure the continued reproduction of the practice in question — then we demonstrate that it is not so irrational at all.

Thus a ceremonial, for example, 'may fulfil the latent function of reinforcing the group identity by providing a periodic occasion on which the scattered members of a group assemble to engage in a common activity'.[11] But to suppose that such a demonstration of a functional relation provides a reason for the existence of a practice is mistaken. What is being more or less surreptitiously smuggled in here is a conception of 'society's reasons' on the basis of imputed social needs. Thus if we understand that the group 'needs' the ceremonial to enable it to survive, we see its continuation as no longer irrational. But to say that the existence of a social state A needs a social practice B to help it to survive in recognizably similar form is to pose a question that then has to be answered; it does not itself answer it. The relation between A and B is not analogous to the relation that obtains between wants or needs and intentions in the individual actor. In the individual, wants that are constitutive of the motivational impulses of the actor generate a dynamic relation between motivation and intentionality. This is not the case with social systems, except where actors behave in cognizance of what they take to be social needs.[12]

This point having been made, there can be no quarrel with Merton's emphasis upon the significance of connecting unintended consequences of action with institutionalized practices, those deeply embedded in time and space. This represents the most important of three main research contexts — separable from one another only analytically — in which the influence of unintended consequences can be analysed. One is the turning on the light/alerting the prowler/causing the prowler to flee/etc. type of example. The interest of the researcher here is in the cumulation of events deriving from an initiating circumstance without which that cumulation would not have been found. Max Weber's analysis of the effects of the Battle of Marathon on the subsequent development of Greek culture, and thence of the formation of European culture in general, is a case in point, as is his discussion of the consequences of the firing of the bullet that killed Archduke Ferdinand at Sarajevo.[13] The concern is with a singular set of events, traced through and analysed counter-factually. The researcher asks, 'What would have happened to events B, C, D, E . . . if A had not occurred?' — thereby seeking to identify the role of A in the chain or sequence.

A second type of circumstance upon which the social analyst might focus is one in which, instead of a pattern of unintended consequences initiated by a single event, there is a pattern resulting from a complex of individual activities. The discussion of ethnic segregation mentioned above is an example of this. Here a definite 'end result' is taken as the phenomenon to be explained, and that end result is shown to derive as an unintended consequence from an aggregate of courses of intentional conduct. The theme of rationality tends to surface again here, although this time there is no logical objection to be made to it. As game theorists have convincingly pointed out, the outcome of a series of rational actions, undertaken separately by individual actors, may be irrational for all of them.[14] 'Perverse effects' are only one type of unintended consequences, although it is no doubt true that situations where they occur are of particular interest.[15]

The third type of context in which unintended consequences may be traced out is that pointed to by Merton: where the interest of the analyst is in the mechanisms of reproduction of institutionalized practices. Here the unintended consequences of action form the acknowledged conditions of further action in a non-reflexive feedback cycle (causal loops). I have pointed out that it is not enough to isolate functional relations in order to explain why such feedback occurs. How, then, does it happen that cycles of unintended consequences feed back to promote social reproduction across long periods of time? In a general way, this is not difficult to analyse. Repetitive activities, located in one context of time and space, have regularized consequences, unintended by those who engage in those activities, in more or less 'distant' time-space contexts. What happens in this second series of contexts then, directly or indirectly, influences the further conditions of action in the original context. To understand what is going on no explanatory variables are needed other than those which explain why individuals are motivated to engage in regularized social practices across time and space, and what consequences ensue. The unintended consequences are regularly 'distributed' as a by-product of regularized behaviour reflexively sustained as such by its participants.

Agency and Power

What is the nature of the logical connection between action and power? Although the ramifications of the issue are complex, the basic relation involved can easily be pointed to. To be able to 'act otherwise' means being able to intervene in the world, or to refrain from such intervention, with the effect of influencing a specific process or state of affairs. This presumes that to be an agent is to be able to deploy (chronically, in the flow of daily life) a range of causal powers, including that of influencing those deployed by others. Action depends upon the capability of the individual to 'make a difference' to a pre-existing state of affairs or course of events. An agent ceases to be such if he or she loses the capability to 'make a difference', that is, to exercise some sort of power. Many interesting cases for social analysis centre upon the margins of what can count as action — where the power of the individual is confined by a range of specifiable circumstances.[16] But it is of the first importance to recognize that circumstances of social constraint in which individuals 'have no choice' are not to be equated with the dissolution of action as such. To 'have no choice' does not mean that action has been replaced by reaction (in the way in which a person blinks when a rapid movement is made near the eyes). This might appear so obvious as not to need saying. But some very prominent schools of social theory, associated mainly with objectivism and with 'structural sociology', have not acknowledged the distinction. They have supposed that constraints operate like forces in nature, as if to 'have no choice' were equivalent to being driven irresistibly and uncomprehendingly by mechanical pressures (see pp. 211—13).

Expressing these observations in another way, we can say that action logically involves power in the sense of transformative capacity. In this sense, the most all-embracing meaning of 'power', power is logically prior to subjectivity, to the constitution of the reflexive monitoring of conduct. It is worth emphasizing this because conceptions of power in the social sciences tend faithfully to reflect the dualism of subject and object referred to previously. Thus 'power' is very often defined in terms of intent or the will, as the capacity to achieve desired and intended outcomes. Other writers by contrast, including both Parsons and Foucault, see power as above all a property of society or the social community.

The point is not to eliminate one of these types of conception at the expense of the other, but to express their relation as a feature of the duality of structure. In my opinion, Bachrach and Baratz are right when, in their well-known discussion of the matter, they say that there are two 'faces' of power (not three, as Lukes declares).[17] They represent these as the capability of actors to enact decisions which they favour on the one hand and the 'mobilization of bias' that is built into institutions on the other. This is not wholly satisfactory because it preserves a zero-sum conception of power. Rather than using their terminology we can express the duality of structure in power relations in the following way. Resources (focused via signification and legitimation) are structured properties of social systems, drawn upon and reproduced by knowledgeable agents in the course of interaction. Power is not intrinsically connected to the achievement of sectional interests. In this conception the use of power characterizes not specific types of conduct but all action, and power is not itself a resource. Resources are media through which power is exercised, as a routine element of the instantiation of conduct in social reproduction. We should not conceive of the structures of domination built into social institutions as in some way grinding out 'docile bodies' who behave like the automata suggested by objectivist social science. Power within social systems which enjoy some continuity over time and space presumes regularized relations of autonomy and dependence between actors or collectivities in contexts of social interaction. But all forms of dependence offer some resources whereby those who are subordinate can influence the activities of their superiors. This is what I call the *dialectic of control* in social systems.

Structure, Structuration

Let me now move to the core of structuration theory: the concepts of 'structure', 'system' and 'duality of structure'. The notion of structure (or 'social structure'), of course, is very prominent in the writings of most functionalist authors and has lent its name to the traditions of 'structuralism'. But in neither instance is this conceptualized in a fashion best suited to the demands of social theory. Functionalist authors and their critics have given much more attention to the idea of 'function' than to that of 'structure', and consequently the latter has tended to be used as a received notion. But there can be no doubt about how 'structure' is usually understood by functionalists and, indeed, by the vast majority of social analysts — as some kind of 'patterning' of social relations or social phenomena. This is often naively conceived of in terms of visual imagery, akin to the skeleton or morphology of an organism or to the girders of a building. Such conceptions are closely connected to the dualism of subject and social object: 'structure' here appears as 'external' to human action, as a source of constraint on the free initiative of the independently constituted subject. As conceptualized in structuralist and post-structuralist thought, on the other hand, the notion of structure is more interesting. Here it is characteristically thought of not as a patterning of presences but as an intersection of presence and absence; underlying codes have to be inferred from surface manifestations.

structure in the social systems that constrain behaviour
structure in the thought systems that print behaviour

These two ideas of structure might seem at first sight to have nothing to do with one another, but in fact each relates to important aspects of the structuring of social relations, aspects which, in the theory of structuration, are grasped by recognizing a differentiation between the concepts of 'structure' and 'system'. In analysing social relations we have to acknowledge both a syntagmatic dimension, the patterning of social relations in time-space involving the reproduction of situated practices, and a paradigmatic dimension, involving a virtual order of 'modes of structuring' recursively implicated in such reproduction. In structuralist traditions there is usually ambiguity over whether structures refer to a matrix of admissible transformations within a set or to rules of transformation governing the matrix. I treat structure, in its most elemental meaning at least, as referring to such rules (and resources). It is misleading, however, to speak of 'rules of transformation' because all rules are inherently transformational. Structure thus refers, in social analysis, to the structuring properties allowing the 'binding' of time-space in social systems, the properties which make it possible for discernibly similar social practices to exist across varying spans of time and space and which lend them 'systemic' form. To say that structure is a 'virtual order' of transformative relations means that social systems, as reproduced social practices, do not have 'structures' but rather exhibit 'structural properties' and that structure exists, as time-space presence, only in its instantiations in such practices and as memory traces orienting the conduct of knowledgeable human agents. This does not prevent us from conceiving of structural properties as hierarchically organized in terms of the time-space extension of the practices they recursively organize. The most deeply embedded structural properties, implicated in the reproduction of societal totalities, I call *structural principles*. Those practices which have the greatest time-space extension within such totalities can be referred to as *institutions*.

To speak of structure as 'rules' and resources, and of structures as isolable sets of rules and resources, runs a distinct risk of misinterpretation because of certain dominant uses of 'rules' in the philosophical literature.

(1) Rules are often thought of in connection with games, as

formalized prescriptions. The rules implicated in the reproduction of social systems are not generally like this. Even those which are codified as laws are characteristically subject to a far greater diversity of contestations than the rules of games. Although the use of the rules of games such as chess, etc. as prototypical of the rule-governed properties of social systems is frequently associated with Wittgenstein, more relevant is what Wittgenstein has to say about children's play as exemplifying the routines of social life.

(2)   Rules are frequently treated in the singular, as if they could be related to specific instances or pieces of conduct. But this is highly misleading if regarded as analogous to the operation of social life, in which practices are sustained in conjunction with more or less loosely organized sets.

(3)   Rules cannot be conceptualized apart from resources, which refer to the modes whereby transformative relations are actually incorporated into the production and reproduction of social practices. Structural properties thus express forms of *domination* and *power*.

(4)   Rules imply 'methodical procedures' of social interaction, as Garfinkel in particular has made clear. Rules typically intersect with practices in the contextuality of situated encounters: the range of 'ad hoc' considerations which he identifies are chronically involved with the instantiation of rules and are fundamental to the form of those rules. Every competent social actor, it should be added, is *ipso facto* a social theorist on the level of discursive consciousness and a 'methodological specialist' on the levels of both discursive and practical consciousness.

(5)   Rules have two aspects to them, and it is essential to distinguish these conceptually, since a number of philosophical writers (such as Winch) have tended to conflate them. Rules relate on the one hand to the constitution of *meaning*, and on the other to the *sanctioning* of modes of social conduct.

I have introduced the above usage of 'structure' to help break with the fixed or mechanical character which the term tends to have in orthodox sociological usage. The concepts of system and structuration do much of the work that 'structure' is ordinarily called upon to perform. In proposing a usage of 'structure' that might appear at first sight to be remote from conventional interpretations of the term, I do not mean to hold that looser versions be abandoned altogether. 'Society', 'culture' and a range of other forms of sociological terminology can have double usages that are embarrassing only in contexts where a difference is made in the nature of the statements employing them. Similarly, I see no particular objection to speaking of 'class structure', 'the structure of the industrialized societies' and so on, where these terms are meant to indicate in a general way relevant institutional features of a society or range of societies.

One of the main propositions of structuration theory is that the rules and resources drawn upon in the production and reproduction of social action are at the same time the means of system reproduction (the duality of structure). But how is one to interpret such a claim? In what sense is it the case that when I go about my daily affairs my activities incorporate and reproduce, say, the overall institutions of modern capitalism? What rules are being invoked here in any case? Consider the following possible instances of what rules are:

(1) 'The rule defining checkmate in chess is . . .';
(2) A formula: $a_n = |n^2 + n\text{-}1$;
(3) 'As a rule R gets up at 6.00 every day';
(4) 'It is a rule that all workers must clock in at 8.00 a.m.'

Many other examples could of course be offered, but these will serve in the present context. In usage (3) 'rule' is more or less equivalent to habit or routine. The sense of 'rule' here is fairly weak, since it does not usually presuppose some sort of underlying precept that the individual is following or any sanction which applies to back up that precept; it is simply something that the person habitually does. Habit is part of routine, and I shall strongly emphasize the importance of routine in social life. 'Rules', as I understand them, certainly impinge upon numerous aspects of routine practice, but a routine practice is not as such a rule.

Cases (1) and (4) have seemed to many to represent two types of rule, constitutive and regulative. To explain the rule governing checkmate in chess is to say something about what goes into the very making of chess as a game. The rule that workers must clock in at a certain hour, on the other hand, does not help define what

E

work is; it specifies how work is to be carried on. As Searle puts it, regulative rules can usually be paraphrased in the form 'Do X', or 'If Y, do X.' Some constitutive rules will have this character, but most will have the form 'X counts as Y', or 'X counts as Y in context C'.[18] That there is something suspect in this distinction, as referring to two types of rule, is indicated by the etymological clumsiness of the term 'regulative rule'. After all, the word 'regulative' already implies 'rule': its dictionary definition is 'control by rules'. I would say of (1) and (4) that they express two aspects of rules rather than two variant types of rule. (1) is certainly part of what chess is, but for those who play chess it has sanctioning or 'regulative' properties; it refers to aspects of play that must be observed. But (4) also has constitutive aspects. It does not perhaps enter into the definition of what 'work' is, but it does enter into that of a concept like 'industrial bureaucracy'. What (1) and (4) direct our attention to are two aspects of rules: their role in the constitution of meaning, and their close connection with sanctions.

Usage (2) might seem the least promising as a way of conceptualizing 'rule' that has any relation to 'structure'. In fact, I shall argue, it is the most germane of all of them. I do not mean to say that social life can be reduced to a set of mathematical principles, which is very far from what I have in mind. I mean that it is in the nature of formulae that we can best discover what is the most analytically effective sense of 'rule' in social theory. The formula $a_n = n^2| + n$-1 is from Wittgenstein's example of number games.[19] One person writes down a sequence of numbers; a second works out the formula supplying the numbers which follow. What is a formula of this kind, and what is it to understand one? To understand the formula is not to utter it. For someone could utter it and not understand the series; alternatively, it is possible to understand the series without being able to give verbal expression to the formula. Understanding is not a mental process accompanying the solving of the puzzle that the sequence of numbers presents — at least, it is not a mental process in the sense in which the hearing of a tune or a spoken sentence is. It is simply being able to apply the formula in the right context and way in order to continue the series.

A formula is a generalizable procedure — generalizable because it applies over a range of contexts and occasions, a procedure because it allows for the methodical continuation of an established sequence. Are linguistic rules like this? I think they are — much more than they are like the sorts of rule of which Chomsky speaks. And this seems also consonant with Wittgenstein's arguments, or a possible construal of them at any rate. Wittgenstein remarks, 'To understand a language means to be a master of a technique.'[20] This can be read to mean that language use is primarily methodological and that rules of language are methodically applied procedures implicated in the practical activities of day-to-day life. This aspect of language is very important, although not often given much prominence by most followers of Wittgenstein. Rules which are 'stated', as (1) and (4) above, are interpretations of activity as well as relating to specific sorts of activities: all codified rules take this form, since they give verbal expression to what is supposed to be done. But rules are procedures of action, aspects of *praxis*. It is by reference to this that Wittgenstein resolves what he first of all sets up as a 'paradox' of rules and rule-following. This is that no course of action can be said to be guided by a rule because every course of action can be made to accord with that rule. However, if such is the case, it is also true that every course of action can be made to conflict with it. There is a misunderstanding here, a confusing of the interpretation or verbal expression of a rule with following the rule.[21]

Let us regard the rules of social life, then, as techniques or generalizable procedures applied in the enactment/reproduction of social practices. Formulated rules — those that are given verbal expression as canons of law, bureaucratic rules, rules of games and so on — are thus codified interpretations of rules rather than rules as such. They should be taken not as exemplifying rules in general but as specific types of formulated rule, which, by virtue of their overt formulation, take on various specific qualities.[22]

So far these considerations offer only a preliminary approach to the problem. How do formulae relate to the practices in which social actors engage, and what kinds of formulae are we most interested in for general purposes of social analysis? As regards the first part of the question, we can say that awareness of social rules, expressed first and foremost in practical consciousness, is the very core of that 'knowledgeability' which specifically characterizes human agents. As social actors, all human beings are highly 'learned' in respect of knowledge which they possess, and apply, in the production and reproduction of day-to-day social encounters; the vast bulk of such knowledge is practical rather than theoretical in character. As Schutz and many others have pointed out, actors employ typified schemes (formulae) in the course of their daily activities to negotiate routinely the situations of social life. Knowledge of procedure, or mastery of the techniques of 'doing' social activity, is by definition methodological. That is to say, such knowledge does not specify all the situations which an actor might meet with, nor could it do so; rather, it provides for the generalized capacity to respond to and influence an indeterminate range of social circumstances.

Those types of rule which are of most significance for social theory are locked into the reproduction of institutionalized practices, that is, practices most deeply sedimented in time-space.[23] The main characteristics of rules relevant to general questions of social analysis can be described as follows:

intensive	tacit	informal	weakly sanctioned
:	:	:	
shallow	discursive	formalized	strongly sanctioned

By rules that are intensive in nature, I mean formulae that are constantly invoked in the course of day-to-day activities, that enter into the structuring of much of the texture of everyday life. Rules of language are of this character. But so also, for example, are the procedures utilized by actors in organizing turn-taking in conversations or in interaction. They may be contrasted with rules which, although perhaps wide in scope, have only a superficial impact upon much of the texture of social life. The contrast is an important one, if only because it is commonly taken for granted among social analysts that the more abstract rules — e.g., codified law — are the most influential in the structuring of social activity. I would propose, however, that many seemingly trivial procedures followed in daily life have a more profound influence upon the generality of social conduct. The remaining categories should be more or less self-explanatory. Most of the rules implicated in the production and reproduction of social practices are only tacitly grasped by actors: they know how to 'go on'. *The discursive formulation of a rule is already an interpretation of it,* and, as I have noted, may in and of itself alter the form of its application. Among rules that are not just discursively formulated but are formally codified, the type case is that of laws. Laws, of course, are among the most strongly sanctioned types of social rules and in modern societies have formally prescribed gradations of retribution. However, it would be a serious mistake to underestimate the strength of informally applied sanctions in respect of a variety of mundane daily practices. Whatever else Garfinkel's 'experiments with trust' might be thought to demonstrate, they do show the extraordinarily compelling force with which apparently minor features of conversational response are invested.[24]

The structuring qualities of rules can be studied in respect, first of all, of the forming, sustaining, termination and reforming of encounters. Although a dazzling variety of procedures and tactics are used by agents in the constitution and reconstitution of encounters, probably particularly significant are those involved in the sustaining of ontological security. Garfinkel's 'experiments' are certainly relevant in this respect. They indicate that the prescriptions involved in the structuring of daily interaction are much more fixed and constraining than might appear from the ease with which they are ordinarily followed. This is surely because the deviant responses or acts that Garfinkel instructed his 'experimenters' to perform disturbed the sense of ontological security of the 'subjects' by undermining the intelligibility of discourse. Breaking or ignoring rules is not, of course, the only way in which the constitutive and sanctioning properties of intensively invoked rules can be studied. But there is no doubt that Garfinkel has helped to disclose a remarkably rich field of study — performing the 'sociologist's alchemy', the 'transmutation of any patch of ordinary social activity into an illuminating publication'.[25]

I distinguish 'structure' as a generic term from 'structures' in the plural and both from the 'structural properties of social systems'.[26] 'Structure' refers not only to rules implicated in the production and reproduction of social systems but also to resources (about which I have so far not said much but will do so shortly). As ordinarily used in the social sciences, 'structure' tends to be employed with the more enduring aspects of social systems in mind, and I do not want to lose this connotation. The most important aspects of structure are rules and resources recursively involved in institutions. Institutions by definition are the more enduring features of social life. In speaking of the structural properties of social systems I mean their institutionalized features, giving 'solidity' across time and space. I use the concept of 'structures' to get at relations of transformation and mediation which are the 'circuit switches' underlying observed conditions of system reproduction.

Let me now answer the question I originally posed: in what manner can it be said that the conduct of individual actors reproduces the structural properties of larger collectivities? The question is both easier and more difficult to answer than it appears. On a logical level, the answer to it is nothing more than a truism. That is to say, while the continued existence of large collectivities or societies evidently does not depend upon the activities of any particular individual, such collectivities or societies manifestly would cease to be if all the agents involved disappeared. On a substantive level, the answer to the question depends upon issues yet to be broached — those concerning the mechanisms of integration of different types of societal totality. It is always the case that the day-to-day activity of social actors draws upon and reproduces structural features of wider social systems. But 'societies' — as I shall make clear — are not necessarily unified collectivities. 'Social reproduction' must not be equated with the consolidation of social cohesion. The location of actors and of collectivities in different sectors or regions of more encompassing social systems strongly influences the impact of even their habitual conduct upon the integration of societal totalities. Here we reach the limits of linguistic examples which might be used to illustrate the concept of the duality of structure. Considerable illumination of problems of social analysis can be derived from studying the recursive qualities of speech and language. When I produce a grammatical utterance, I draw upon the same syntactical rules as those that utterance helps to produce. But I speak the 'same' language as the other speakers in my language community; we all share the same rules and linguistic practices, give or take a range of relatively minor variations. Such is not necessarily the case with the structural properties of social systems in general. But this is not a problem to do with the concept of the duality of structure as such. It is to do with how social systems, especially 'societies', should be conceptualized.

The Duality of Structure

Structure(s)	System(s)	Structuration
Rules and resources, or sets of transformation relations, organized as properties of social systems	Reproduced relations between actors or collectivities, organized as regular social practices	Conditions governing the continuity or transmutation of structures, and therefore the reproduction of social systems

Let me summarize the argument thus far. Structure, as recursively organized sets of rules and resources, is out of time and space, save in its instantiations and co-ordination as memory traces, and is marked by an 'absence of the subject'. The social systems in which structure is recursively implicated, on the contrary, comprise the situated activities of human agents, reproduced across time and space. Analysing the structuration of social systems means studying the modes in which such systems, grounded in the knowledgeable activities of situated actors who draw upon rules and resources in the diversity of action contexts, are produced and reproduced in interaction. Crucial to the idea of structuration is the theorem of the duality of structure, which is logically implied in the arguments portrayed above. The constitution of agents and structures are not two independently given sets of phenomena, a dualism, but represent a duality. According to the notion of the duality of structure, the structural properties of social systems are both medium and outcome of the practices they recursively organize. Structure is not 'external' to individuals: as memory traces, and as instantiated in social practices, it is in a certain sense more 'internal' than exterior to their activities in a Durkheimian sense. Structure is not to be equated with constraint but is always both constraining and enabling. This, of course, does not prevent the structured properties of social systems from stretching away, in time and space, beyond the control of any individual actors. Nor does it compromise the possibility that actors' own theories of the social systems which they help to constitute and reconstitute in their activities may reify those systems. The reification of social relations, or the discursive 'naturalization' of the historically contingent circumstances and products of human action, is one of the main dimensions of ideology in social life.[27]

Even the crudest forms of reified thought, however, leave untouched the fundamental significance of the knowledgeability of human actors. For knowledgeability is founded less upon discursive than practical consciousness. The knowledge of social conventions, of oneself and of other human beings, presumed in being able to 'go on' in the diversity of contexts of social life is detailed and dazzling. All competent members of society are vastly skilled in the practical accomplishments of social activities and are expert 'sociologists'. The knowledge they possess is not incidental to the persistent patterning of social life but is integral to it. This stress is absolutely essential if the mistakes of functionalism and structuralism are to be avoided, mistakes which, suppressing or discounting agents' reasons — the rationalization of action as chronically involved in the structuration of social practices — look for the origins of their activities in phenomena of which these agents are ignorant.[28] But it is equally important to avoid tumbling into the opposing error of hermeneutic approaches and of various versions of phenomenology, which tend to regard society as the plastic creation of human subjects. Each of these is an illegitimate form of reduction, deriving from a failure adequately to conceptualize the duality of structure. According to structuration theory, the moment of the production of action is also one of reproduction in the contexts of the day-to-day enactment of social life. This is so even during the most violent upheavals or most radical forms of social change. It is not accurate to see the structural properties of social systems as 'social products' because this tends to imply that pre-constituted actors somehow come together to create them.[29] In reproducing structural properties to repeat a phrase used earlier, agents also reproduce the conditions that make such action possible. Structure has no existence independent of the knowledge that agents have about what they do in their day-to-day activity. Human agents always know what they are doing on the level of discursive consciousness under some description. However, what they do may be quite unfamiliar under other descriptions, and they may know little of the ramified consequences of the activities in which they engage.

The duality of structure is always the main grounding of

continuities in social reproduction across time-space. It in turn presupposes the reflexive monitoring of agents in, and as constituting, the *durée* of daily social activity. But human knowledgeability is always bounded. The flow of action continually produces consequences which are unintended by actors, and these unintended consequences also may form unacknowledged conditions of action in a feedback fashion. Human history is created by intentional activities but is not an intended project; it persistently eludes efforts to bring it under conscious direction. However, such attempts are continually made by human beings, who operate under the threat and the promise of the circumstance that they are the only creatures who make their 'history' in cognizance of that fact.

The theorizing of human beings about their action means that just as social theory was not an invention of professional social theorists, so the ideas produced by those theorists inevitably tend to be fed back into social life itself. One aspect of this is the attempt to monitor, and thereby control, highly generalized conditions of system reproduction — a phenomenon of massive importance in the contemporary world. To grasp such monitored processes of reproduction conceptually, we have to make certain distinctions relevant to what social systems 'are' as reproduced practices in interaction settings. The relations implied or actualized in social systems are, of course, widely variable in terms of their degree of 'looseness' and permeability. But, this being accepted, we can recognize two levels in respect of the means whereby some element of 'systemness' is achieved in interaction. One is that generally prominent in functionalism, as referred to earlier, where interdependence is conceived of as a homeostatic process akin to mechanisms of self-regulation operating within an organism. There can be no objection to this as long as it is acknowledged that the 'looseness' of most social systems makes the organic parallel a very remote one and that this relatively 'mechanized' mode of system reproduction is not the only one found in human societies. Homeostatic system reproduction in human society can be regarded as involving the operation of causal loops, in which a range of unintended consequences of action feed back to reconstitute the initiating circumstances. But in many contexts of social life there occur processes of selective 'information filtering' whereby strategically placed actors seek reflexively to regulate the overall conditions of system reproduction either to keep things as they are or to change them.[30]

The distinction between homeostatic causal loops and reflexive self-regulation in system reproduction must be complemented by one further, and final, one: that between social and system integration.[31] 'Integration' may be understood as involving reciprocity of practices (of autonomy and dependence) between actors or collectivities.[32] Social integration then means systemness on the level of face-to-face interaction. System integration refers to connections with those who are physically absent in time or space. The mechanisms of system integration certainly presuppose those of social integration, but such mechanisms are also distinct in some key respects from those involved in relations of co-presence.

Social Integration	*System Integration*
Reciprocity between actors in contexts of co-presence	Reciprocity between actors or collectivities across extended time-space

Forms of Institution

The division of rules into modes of signifying or meaning constitution and normative sanctions, together with the concept of resources — fundamental to the conceptualization of power — carries various implications which need to be spelled out.[33] What I call the 'modalities' of structuration serve to clarify the main dimensions of the duality of structure in interaction, relating the knowledgeable capacities of agents to structural features. Actors draw upon the modalities of structuration in the reproduction of systems of interaction, by the same token reconstituting their structural properties. The communication of meaning in inter-action, it should be stressed, is separable only analytically from the operation of normative sanctions. This is obvious, for example, in so far as language use is itself sanctioned by the very nature of its 'public' character.[34] The very identification of acts or of aspects of interaction — their accurate description, as grounded hermeneutically in the capability of an observer to 'go on' in a form of life — implies the interlacing of meaning, normative elements and power. This is most evident in the not infrequent contexts of social life where what social phenomena 'are', how they are aptly described, is contested. Awareness of such contestation, of divergent and overlapping characterizations of activity, is an essential part of 'knowing a form of life', although this is not made clear in the writings of authors such as Winch, who treat forms of life as both unified and consensual.[35]

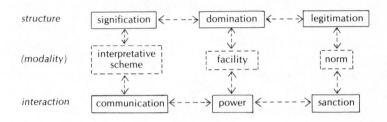

Figure 2

The dimensions of the duality of structure are portrayed in figure 2.[36] Human actors are not only able to monitor their activities and those of others in the regularity of day-to-day conduct; they are also able to 'monitor that monitoring' in discursive consciousness. 'Interpretative schemes' are the modes of typification incorporated within actors' stocks of knowledge, applied reflexively in the sustaining of communication. The stocks of knowledge which actors draw upon in the production and reproduction of interaction are the same as those whereby they are able to make accounts, offer reasons, etc.[37] The communication of meaning, as with all aspects of the contextuality of action, does not have to be seen merely as happening 'in' time-space. Agents routinely incorporate temporal and spatial features of encounters in processes of meaning constitution. Communication, as a general element of interaction, is a more inclusive concept than communicative intent (i.e. what an actor 'means' to say or do). There are once more two forms of reductionism to be avoided here. Some philosophers have tried to derive overall theories of meaning or communication from communicative intent; others, by contrast, have supposed that communicative intent is at best marginal to the constitution of the meaningful qualities of interaction, 'meaning' being governed by the structural ordering of sign systems. In the theory of structuration, however, these are regarded as of equivalent interest and importance, aspects of a duality rather than a mutually exclusive dualism.

The idea of 'accountability' in everyday English gives cogent expression to the intersection of interpretative schemes and norms. To be 'accountable' for one's activities is both to explicate the reasons for them and to supply the normative grounds whereby they may be 'justified'. Normative components of interaction always centre upon relations between the rights and obligations 'expected' of those participating in a range of interaction contexts. Formal codes of conduct, as, for example, those enshrined in law (in contemporary societies at least), usually express some sort of claimed symmetry between rights and obligations, the one being the justification of the other. But no such symmetry necessarily exists in practice, a phenomenon which it is important to emphasize, since both the 'normative functionalism' of Parsons and the 'structuralist Marxism' of Althusser exaggerates the degree to which normative obligations are 'internalized' by the members of societies.[38] Neither standpoint incorporates a theory of action which recognizes human beings as knowledgeable agents, reflexively monitoring the flow of interaction with one another. When social systems are conceived of primarily from the point of view of the 'social object', the emphasis comes to be placed upon the pervasive influence of a normatively co-ordinated legitimate order as an overall determinant or 'programmer' of social conduct. Such a perspective masks the fact that the normative elements of social systems are contingent claims which have to be sustained and 'made to count' through the effective mobilization of sanctions in the contexts of actual encounters. Normative sanctions express structural asymmetries of domination, and the relations of those nominally subject to them may be of various sorts other than expressions of the commitments those norms supposedly engender.

Concentration upon the analysis of the structural properties of social systems, it should be stressed, is a valid procedure only if it is recognized as placing an *epoché* upon — holding in suspension — reflexively monitored social conduct. Under such an *epoché* we may distinguish three structural dimensions of social systems: signification, domination and legitimation. The connotations of the analysis of these structural properties are indicated in the table below. The theory of coding presumed in the study of structures of signification must look to the extraordinary advances in semiotics which have been pioneered in recent decades. At the same time we have to guard against the association of semiotics with structuralism and with the shortcomings of the latter in respect of the analysis of human agency. Signs 'exist' only as the medium and outcome of communicative processes in interaction. Structuralist conceptions of language, in common with similar discussions of legitimation, tend to take signs as the given properties of speaking and writing rather than examining their recursive grounding in the communication of meaning.

Structure(s)	Theoretical Domain	Institutional Order
Signification	Theory of coding	Symbolic orders/modes of discourse
Domination	Theory of resource authorization Theory of resource allocation	Political institutions Economic institutions
Legitimation	Theory of normative regulation	Legal institutions

Structures of signification always have to be grasped in connection with domination and legitimation. Once more this bears upon the pervasive influence of power in social life. There are certain positions which have to be carefully skirted here. Thus some relevant issues have been brought to the fore by Habermas's critique of Gadamer and ensuing debates.[39] Among other things, Habermas criticized Gadamer's conception of linguistically saturated 'traditions' for failing to demonstrate that frames of meaning incorporate differentials of power. The criticism is valid enough, but Habermas sought to develop the point in the direction of showing the significance of 'systematically distorted' forms of communication. He has not been able on this basis, however, satisfactorily to integrate the concept of power with an institutional theory. 'Domination' is not the same as 'systematically distorted' structures of signification because domination — as I conceive of it — is the very condition of existence of codes of signification.[40] 'Domination' and 'power' cannot be thought of only in terms of asymmetries of distribution but have to be recognized as inherent in social association (or, I would say, in human action as such). Thus — and here we must also reckon with the implications of the writings of Foucault — power is not an inherently noxious phenomenon, not just the capacity to 'say no'; nor can domination be 'transcended' in some kind of putative society of the future, as has been the characteristic aspiration of at least some strands of socialist thought.

What are the connotations of the claim that the semantic has priority over the semiotic rather than vice versa? They can be spelled out, I think, through a comparison of structuralist and post-structuralist conceptions of meaning on the one hand, and that which can be derived from the later Wittgenstein on the other.[41] The foundation of a theory of meaning in 'difference' in which, following Saussure, there are no 'positive values' leads almost inevitably to a view accentuating the primacy of the semiotic. The field of signs, the grids of meaning, are created by the ordered nature of differences which comprise codes. The 'retreat into the code' — whence it is difficult or impossible to re-emerge into the world of activity and event — is a characteristic tactic adopted by structuralist and post-structuralist authors. Such a retreat, however, is not necessary at all if we understand the relational character of the codes that generate meaning to be located in the ordering of social practices, in the very capacity to 'go on' in the multiplicity of contexts of social activity. This is a discovery which Wittgenstein himself surely made, albeit against a very different philosophical backdrop, when he abandoned some of the main parameters of his early writings. Whereas his earlier analysis of language and meaning terminates in paradox — a sort of Indian rope trick, pulling up the ladder after it has been climbed — his later view hugs the ground of routine social practices. Even the most complicated semiotic relations have a grounding in the semantic properties generated by the rule-governed properties of daily activities.

In the terminology indicated in the table above the 'signs' implied in 'signification' should not be equated with 'symbols'. Many writers treat the two terms as equivalent, but I regard symbols, interpolated within symbolic orders, as one main dimension of the 'clustering' of institutions.[42] Symbols coagulate the 'surpluses of meaning' implied in the polyvalent character of signs; they conjoin those intersections of codes which are especially rich in diverse forms of meaning association, operating along the axes of metaphor and metonymy. Symbolic orders and associated modes of discourse are a major institutional locus of ideology. However, in the theory of structuration ideology is not a particular 'type' of symbolic order or form of discourse. One cannot separate off 'ideological discourse' from 'science', for example. 'Ideology' refers only to those asymmetries of domination which connect signification to the legitimation of sectional interests.[43]

We can see from the case of ideology that structures of signification are separable only analytically either from domination and from legitimation. Domination depends upon the mobilization of two distinguishable types of resource. Allocative resources refer to capabilities — or, more accurately, to forms of transformative capacity — generating command over objects, goods or material phenomena. Authoritative resources refer to types of transformative capacity generating command over persons or actors. Some forms of allocative resources (such as raw materials, land, etc.) might seem to have a 'real existence' in a way which I have claimed that structural properties as a whole do not. In the sense of having a time-space 'presence', in a certain way such is obviously the case. But their 'materiality' does not affect the fact that such phenomena become resources, in the manner in which I apply that term here, only when incorporated within processes of structuration. The transformational character of resources is logically equivalent to, as well as inherently bound up with the instantiation of, that of codes and normative sanctions.

The classification of institutional orders offered above depends upon resisting what has sometimes been called 'substantivist' concepts of 'economic', 'political' and other institutions. We can conceive of the relationships involved as follows:

S-D-L	Symbolic orders/modes of discourse
D (auth)-S-L	Political institutions
D (alloc)-S-L	Economic institutions
L-D-S	Legal institutions

where S = signification, D = domination, L = legitimation

'Substantivist' conceptions presume concrete institutional differentiation of these various orders. That is to say, it is held, for example, that 'politics' exists only in societies having distinct forms of state apparatus and so on. But the work of anthropologists demonstrates effectively enough that there are 'political' phenomena — to do with the ordering of authority relations — in all societies. The same applies to the other institutional orders. We have to be particularly careful in conceptualizing the 'economic', even having made the point that this does not presuppose the existence of a clearly differentiated 'economy'. There has been a strong tendency in some of the literature of economics to 'read back' into traditional cultures concepts that have meaning only in the context of market economies. The 'economic' cannot properly be defined, in a generic way at least, as concerning struggles for scarce resources.[44] This is somewhat like defining power solely by reference to sectional struggles. It is not scarcity of resources as such, far less struggles or sectional divisions centred upon distribution, that is the main feature of the 'economic'. Rather, the sphere of the 'economic' is given by the inherently constitutive role of allocative resources in the structuration of societal totalities. Other cautionary notes should be added here. If it is held that all societies are haunted by the possibility of material scarcity, it is only a short step to the supposition that conflicts over scarce resources make up the fundamental motor of social change, as is presumed in at least some versions of historical materialism and in many non-Marxist theories also. But this presumption is both logically wanting, usually depending upon a specious form of functional reasoning, and empirically false.[45]

Time, the Body, Encounters

In concluding this abbreviated opening exposition, we may return to the theme of time and history. As the finitude of *Dasein* and as 'the infinity of the emergence of being from nothingness', time is perhaps the most enigmatic feature of human experience. Not for nothing (sic) was that philosopher who has attempted to grapple in the most fundamental way with the problem, Heidegger, compelled to use terminology of the most daunting obscurity. But time, or the constitution of experience in time-space, is also a banal and evident feature of human day-to-day life. It is in some part the lack of 'fit' between our unproblematic coping with the continuity of conduct across time-space, and its ineffable character when confronted philosophically, that is the very essence of the puzzling nature of time. I make no particular claim to elucidate this matter, 'St Augustine's problem'. But the fundamental question of social theory, as I see it — the 'problem of order' conceived of in a way quite alien to Parsons's formulation when he coined the phrase — is to explicate how the limitations of individual 'presence' are transcended by the 'stretching' of social relations across time and space.

The *durée* of daily life, it is not too fanciful to say, operates in something akin to what Lévi-Strauss calls 'reversible time'. Whether or not time 'as such' (whatever that would be) is reversible, the events and routines of daily life do not have a one-way flow to them. The terms 'social reproduction', 'recursiveness' and so on indicate the repetitive character of day-to-day life, the routines of which are formed in terms of the intersection of the

durée of day-to-day experience: 'reversible time'

life span of the individual: 'irreversible time'

longue durée of institutions: 'reversible time'

passing (but continually returning) days and seasons. Daily life has a duration, a flow, but it does not lead anywhere; the very adjective 'day-to-day' and its synonyms indicate that time here is constituted only in repetition. The life of the individual, by contrast, is not only finite but irreversible, 'being towards death'. 'This is death, to die and know it. This is the Black Widow, death' (Lowell). Time in this case is the time of the body, a frontier of presence quite different from the evaporation of time-space inherent in the duration of day-to-day activity. Our lives 'pass away' in irreversible time with the passing away of the life of the organism. The fact that we speak of the 'life cycle' implies that there are elements of repetition here too. But the life cycle is really a concept that belongs to the succession of generations and thus to the third dimension of temporality indicated above. This is the 'supra-individual' *durée* of the long-term existence of institutions, the *longue durée* of institutional time.

The reversible time of institutions is both the condition and the outcome of the practices organized in the continuity of daily life, the main substantive form of the duality of structure. It would not be true, however, as I have already mentioned, to say that the routines of daily life are the 'foundation' upon which institutional forms of societal organization are built in time-space. Rather, each enters into the constitution of the other, as they both do into the constitution of the acting self. All social systems, no matter how grand or far-flung, both express and are expressed in the routines of daily social life, mediating the physical and sensory properties of the human body.

These considerations are of very considerable importance for the ideas set out in the succeeding parts of this book. The body is the 'locus' of the active self, but the self is obviously not just an extension of the physical characteristics of the organism that is its 'carrier'. Theorizing the self means formulating a conception of motivation (or so I shall argue) and relating motivation to the connections between unconscious and conscious qualities of the agent. The self cannot be understood outside 'history' — 'history' meaning in this case the temporality of human practices, expressed in the mutual interpolation of the three dimensions I have distinguished.

I earlier introduced the notion of co-presence, with specific reference to social integration. The study of interaction in circumstances of co-presence is one basic component of the 'bracketing' of time-space that is both condition and outcome of human social association. 'Systemness' here is achieved largely through the routine reflexive monitoring of conduct anchored in practical consciousness. Relations in conditions of co-presence consist of what Goffman has aptly called *encounters,* fading away across time and space. No one has analysed encounters more perceptively than Goffman himself, and I shall draw heavily upon his work in part of what follows. The importance of Goffman's work is due in no small degree to his preoccupation with the temporal and spatial ordering of social activity. He is one of the few sociological writers who treat time-space relations as fundamental to the production and reproduction of social life, rather than as making up 'boundaries' to social activity which can be safely left to 'specialists' — geographers and historians. But those working in the nominally separate subject area of geography have made their own independent contributions. Thus I shall propose not only that the time-geography of Hägerstrand (with appropriate critical emendation) offers forms of analysis of significance for structuration theory but also that some of the ideas involved complement Goffman's conceptions rather directly.

Relations with those who are physically absent, as I have said, involve social mechanisms distinct from what is involved in contexts of co-presence. We have to deal here with some basic questions about the structuring of institutions. These have a 'lateral' aspect to them — particularly in the modern world, given the tremendous expansion of the time-space distanciation of social activity in the contemporary era. But they also raise once more the problem of 'history', since the absent others include past generations whose 'time' may be very different from that of those who are in some way influenced by residues of their activities. These matters will be my concern in the concluding chapters.

References

1 For more detailed discussions of the basic concepts of structuration theory, the reader should turn to *NRSM,* especially chapters 2 and 3; *CPST:* and *CCHM,* chapters 1 and 2.
2 *CPST,* pp. 56—7.
3 *CPST,* chapter 1.
4 Donald Davidson, 'Agency', in *Essays on Actions and Events* (Oxford: Clarendon Press, 1980), p. 45.
5 *NRSM,* chapter 2.
6 Joel Feinberg, 'Action and responsibility', in Max Black, *Philosophy in America* (Ithaca: Cornell University Press, 1965). On the problem of what are 'consequences', see Lars Bergström, *The Alternatives and Consequences of Actions* (Stockholm: Almqvist, 1966).
7 Thomas Schelling, 'On the ecology of micromotives', *The Public Interest,* vol. 25, 1971; 'Dynamic models of segregation', *Journal of Mathematical Sociology,* vol. 4, 1971. See also the discussion in Raymond Boudon, *The Unintended Consequences of Social Action* (London: Macmillan, 1982), pp. 43ff.
8 *NRSM,* p. 76.
9 Merton, however, favours the term, 'unanticipated' rather than unintended consequences. In my analysis 'intention' presumes

knowledge of the likely consequences of action and therefore anticipation. Of course, one can anticipate that something will happen without intending it to happen, but one cannot intend something to happen without anticipating that it might happen. R. K. Merton, 'The unanticipated consequences of purposive social action', *American Sociological Review,* vol. 1, 1936; idem, 'Manifest and latent functions', in *Social Theory and Social Structure* (Glencoe: Free Press, 1963).

10   Merton, 'Manifest and latent functions', p. 51.

11   Ibid., pp. 64—5.

12   For a fuller discussion, see *CPST,* chapter 6.

13   Max Weber, *The Methodology of the Social Sciences* (Glencoe: Free Press, 1949).

14   Mancur Olson, *The Logic of Collective Action.* (Cambridge, Mass.: Harvard University Press, 1965); Boudon, *The Unintended Consequences of Social Action;* Jon Elster, *Logic and Society, Contradictions and Possible Worlds* (Chichester: Wiley, 1978); Jon Elster, *Ulysses and the Sirens* (Cambridge: Cambridge University Press, 1979).

15   Boudon, *The Unintended Consequences of Social Action,* chapter 2.

16   For a further development of this point, see 'Power, the dialectic of control and class structuration', in Anthony Giddens and Gavin Mackenzie, *Social Class and The Division of Labour* (Cambridge: Cambridge University Press, 1982).

17   Peter Bachrach and Morton S. Baratz, 'The two faces of power', *American Political Science Review,* vol. 56, 1962; *Power and Poverty* (New York: Oxford University Press, 1970); Steven Lukes, *Power, a Radical View* (London: Macmillan, 1974). For further discussion of these points, cf. *CPST,* pp. 88—94.

18   John R. Searle, *Speech Acts* (Cambridge: Cambridge University Press, 1969), pp. 34—5.

19   Ludwig Wittgenstein, *Philosophical Investigations* (Oxford: Blackwell, 1972), p. 59.

20   Ibid., p. 81.

21   Ibid.

22   Ibid.

23   *CPST,* pp. 80ff.

24   Harold Garfinkel, 'A conception of, and experiments with, "trust" as a condition of stable concerted actions', in O. J. Harvey, *Motivation and Social Interaction* (New York: Ronald Press, 1963).

25   Erving Goffman, *Frame Analysis* (New York: Harper, 1974), p. 5.

26   In *NRSM* I had not appreciated the need to distinguish

'structure' from 'structures' and used the latter term too casually as synonymous with the former.

27   *CPST*, pp. 195—6.
28   Cf. Roy Bhaskar, *The Possibility of Naturalism* (Brighton: Harvester, 1979), chapter 2.
29   Ibid., p. 48.
30   Cf. ibid., pp. 78—9. There I distinguished three levels of 'systemness' which here, for purposes of simplification, are reduced to two.
31   This distinction was introduced into the literature by David Lockwood who, however, employed it rather differently from the way I do: David Lockwood, 'Social integration and system integration', in George Z. Zollschan and W. Hirsch, *Explorations in Social Change* (London: Routledge, 1964).
32   My formulation of the concept of 'system integration' in *CPST*, p. 77, was ambiguous. I did not make it clear whether the separation of social from system integration depended upon a distinction between co-presence and absence in social relations, or between the ties linking actors as contrasted with those linking collectivities. As I use it now, the notion refers to the first of these two sets of contrasts, but they are in any case closely overlapping, so the fault was not too consequential.
33   *CPST*, chapter 2.
34   Cf. Paul Ziff, *Semantic Analysis* (Ithaca: Cornell University Press, 1960).
35   Cf. Hanna F. Pitkin, *Wittgenstein and Justice* (Berkeley: University of California Press, 1972), pp. 241—64.
36   For this style of representing these relations I am indebted to Derek Gregory; see his *Regional Transformation and Industrial Revolution* (London: Macmillan, 1982), p. 17.
37   Peter Marsh *et al.*, *The Rules of Disorder* (London: Routledge, 1978), p. 15 and *passim*.
38   *NRSM*, pp. 108—10.
39   Jürgen Habermas, *Zur Logik der Sozialwissenschaften* (Tübingen; Siebeck & Mohr, 1967); 'On systematically distorted communication', *Inquiry*, vol. 13, 1970.
40   Cf. my 'Habermas's critique of hermeneutics', in *SSPT*.
41   See *CPST*, pp. 33—8.
42   Paul Ricoeur, 'Existence and hermeneutics', in *The Conflict of Interpretations* (Evanston: Northwestern University Press, 1974).
43   For an elaboration of this position, see *CPST*, chapter 5. Symbolic orders and modes of discourse constitute the 'cultural' aspects of social systems. But, as with 'society' and 'history', I call upon the term 'culture' to fulfil a double duty. Thus I shall speak of 'cultures'

in a general way, as a term interchangeable with 'societies', although in some contexts these terms have to be accorded more precision.

44   Cf. Karl Polanyi *et al., Trade and Market in the Early Empires* (New York: Free Press, 1957), pp. 243—70 and *passim.*

45   My reasons for making these claims are given at some length in *CCHM,* especially in the introduction and in chapter 3.

2
Consciousness, Self and Social Encounters

In this chapter I shall seek to fulfil several objectives. First of all, I shall discuss some basic conceptual problems posed by connecting the main concepts of structuration theory to an interpretation of the nature of the unconscious. This turns upon questions of how the self, especially the 'I' of the reflexive agent, should best be conceptualized. I shall then move on to a portrayal of how the psychological foundations of the interweaving of conscious and unconscious can be represented, utilizing in particular the writings of Erikson. But it will be a major part of my argument that such a portrayal immediately raises questions of a social nature to do with the routinized character of day-to-day life. Via an analysis of 'critical situations', in which routines are radically disrupted, I shall try to indicate how the reflexive monitoring of encounters in circumstances of co-presence ordinarily co-ordinates with unconscious components of personality. This will lead directly through to an examination of some of the insights which can be drawn from Goffman about interaction between co-present agents. Concern with the body, as the locus of the acting self and as positioned in time-space, is the key linking theme of the material discussed and analysed.

Reflexivity, Discursive and Practical Consciousness

Freud divides the psychic organization of the individual into three, divisions represented in English by the unfortunate terms 'id', 'ego' and 'super-ego'. I do not believe these terms are particularly useful and shall instead substitute the threefold division suggested in the stratification model: basic security system, practical and discursive consciousness. I do not mean these to parallel the Freudian notions directly. The intersecting planes of the interpretative schemes and norms which actors utilize in the constitution of their conduct are embedded in all three dimensions of personality. But certainly the 'I' (*das Ich*) is at the core of what is involved in discursive consciousness and demands considerable attention conceptually. We can approach the issues involved by tracing some of the difficulties posed by Freud's division of the personality, especially in so far as these bear upon problems of agency.[1]*

Freud, of course, regarded the individual as an agent but also often spoke of the id, ego and super-ego as agencies within the individual. In his writings prior to the 1920s Freud frequently used the term *das Ich* to refer to the whole person, as well as to designate a part of the mind. These shifts of usage also apply to 'super-ego', sometimes differentiated from another notion, that of 'ego-ideal'. Terminological inconsistencies and transitions seem to indicate here some rather more significant conceptual troubles. Suppose *das Ich* is a subdivision of mind. How can Freud then say such things as that the ego 'decides on the repudiation of the incompatible idea'?[2] Is the ego's deciding some sort of process in miniature of the agent's deciding? This, surely, does not make much sense. Freud also writes, for example, of the ego's 'wish to sleep', although while sleep occurs it 'stays on duty' to protect against the worst emanations of the unconscious, 'guarding' the sleep of the dreamer. The same sort of questions arise. Whose sleep is it that the ego desires? The agent's? Its own? Whose waking does the 'guard' protect? And so on. Consider, finally, Freud's most general characterization of the tasks of the ego. The ego has the task of 'self-preservation', which it executes 'by learning to bring about changes in the external world to its own advantage'.[3] But which 'self' does the ego defend? Is its advantage also my advantage?

Now one traditional tactic among interpreters of Freud is to accept that there are misleading anthropomorphic usages in Freud's writings, but to claim that these can be dispelled if we understand id, ego and super-ego as referring to 'processes' or 'forces'. But this is not really very much help, for such concepts do not allow us properly to grasp the nature of human agency.

*References may be found on pp. 105—9.

Freud, of course, does himself speak of hydraulic flows, blockages of energy and so on. But these then conjure up the sort of mechanical conception of the origins of human conduct associated with the most naive forms of objectivism. Part of the problem is the use of the terms ego, super-ego and id (whether in their original German formulation or in their English version), each of which has some connotation of agency; each is a mini-agent within the agent as such. Discarding the terms 'id' and 'super-ego' helps, but this has to be complemented by recognition of the distinctive character of *das Ich,* the 'I'.

We might suppose that the 'I' is the agent. However, this is surely mistaken, even though it figures as the central assumption or proposition of whole schools of philosophy, including Cartesianism and the latter-day philosophy of G. H. Mead. Mead's writings certainly help to elucidate the processes leading to the emergence of a 'self' as a 'me'. But the 'I' appears in Mead's writings as the given core of agency, and its origins hence always remain obscure. To relate the 'I' to agency, it is necessary to follow the detour suggested by structuralists in respect of the decentring of the subject, without reaching conclusions which treat the subject simply as a sign within a signification structure. The constitution of the 'I' comes about only via the 'discourse of the Other' — that is, through the acquisition of language — but the 'I' has to be related to the body as the sphere of action. The term 'I' is in linguistic terms a 'shifter': the contextuality of social 'positioning' determines who is an 'I' in any situation of talk. Although we might tend to think of 'I' as bearing upon the richest and most intimate aspects of our experience, it is in a way one of the emptiest terms in language.[4] For the 'I' refers only to who is speaking, the 'subject' of a sentence or utterance. An agent who has mastered the use of 'I', as Mead says, has also mastered the use of 'me' — but only via concomitant mastery of a syntactically differentiated language. For I have to know that I am an 'I' when I speak to 'you', but that you are an 'I' when you speak to 'me', and that I am a 'you' when you speak to me. . . . and so on. The point is not just that these usages presume linguistic skills of a very complicated kind but also that they entail a ramified control of the body and a developed knowledge of how to 'go on' in the plurality of contexts of social life.

Recognition of the essential importance of the reflexive

monitoring of conduct in the day-to-day continuity of social life does not mean disavowing the significance of unconscious sources of cognition and motivation. But it does involve giving some attention to the differentiation which separates 'conscious' from 'unconscious'.

Ordinary English usage gives us at least a general guide to this. Sometimes we speak of consciousness as equivalent to what might be called 'sensibility'.[5] Thus someone who falls asleep or is knocked over the head 'lapses into unconsciousness' or is 'rendered unconscious'. 'Unconscious' here means something different from its orthodox Freudian usage, and the 'consciousness' with which it is contrasted has a very broad sense. To be 'conscious' in this meaning is to register a range of surrounding stimuli. There is nothing specifically reflexive about consciousness understood in this way. The sense in which human beings 'lose' and 'regain' consciousness is directly applicable to the higher animals also. This notion of consciousness evidently refers to the sensory mechanisms of the body and to their 'normal' modes of operation and is presupposed by the concepts of both practical and discursive consciousness.

'Conscious' is sometimes used to refer to circumstances in which people pay attention to events going on around them in such a way as to relate their activity to those events. In other words, it refers to the reflexive monitoring of conduct by human agents, largely in the sense of what I have called practical consciousness. Thus, for example, a school teacher may be 'conscious' of what the children in the front rows of the classroom are doing but 'unconscious' of others near the back who have started gossiping with one another. The teacher may be being inattentive, but is not unconscious in the same sense as an individual who has 'lost consciousness'. If this sense of 'conscious' has its counterpart among animals, it is not as unambiguously defined as in the more elemental sense of consciousness noted above. A third sense of 'conscious', labelled by Toulmin 'articulateness', corresponds roughly to discursive consciousness.[6] To use Toulmin's example, a businessman who obtains money on false pretences from a client can be said to have engaged in 'conscious and deliberate fraud'. On the other hand, if the same consequence follows quite inadvertently from the activities of the businessman, without his being unaware of it, he 'unconsciously' becomes the instrument of the other's financial discomfiture. Here the agent has to 'think' about what he or she is doing for that activity to be carried out 'consciously'. 'Consciousness' in this sense presumes being able to give a coherent account of one's activities and the reasons for them.

The Unconscious, Time, Memory

It is clear that the psychoanalytic sense of 'unconscious' has something to do with a contrast drawn between it and this third meaning of 'conscious', a contrast with what I have termed discursive consciousness. Discursive consciousness means being able to put things into words. The 'unconscious' in psychoanalytic theory has reference to the opposite of this — not being able to give verbal expression to the promptings of action.

To further explicate the notion of 'unconscious' as 'the unconscious', however, it is necessary to make some comments on memory, since memory and language are patently very close. I propose to argue that 'the unconscious' can be understood only in terms of memory and that this in turn means examining rather carefully what memory is. Here all the issues of theorizing temporality whose significance I have insisted upon before reappear.

(1) *Prima facie,* one might suppose that memory refers simply to the past — to past experiences, traces of which somehow remain in the organism. Action then occurs in the spatiality of the present, drawing upon memories of the past whenever such are needed or desired. A moment's reflection will demonstrate the inadequacy of such a view. 'Present' cannot be said or written without its fading into the past. If time is not a succession of 'presents' but 'presencing' in the sense attributed to this by Heidegger, then memory is an aspect of presencing.

(2) One might imagine that memory is above all a recall device — a mode of retrieving information or 'remembering'. Such a view is quite consistent with the idea that the past is clearly severed from the present because memory can then be seen as the recall of the past into the present. But once we discard such a standpoint, it is no longer plausible to define memory

as the remembrance of things past. Proust's title should surely be read as an ironic comment on just this type of naive conception. Recall is obviously not irrelevant to memory, but it does not designate what memory is.

These observations indicate that memory and perception are very closely linked. It is of some interest to point out that theories of perception tend to divide around an axis of subjectivism versus objectivism. One type of standpoint tends to emphasize, in quasi-Kantian fashion, the role of the perceiver as the processor of what would otherwise be a formless void.[7] An opposing view holds that perception is organized by the pre-given form of the object-world.[8] Attempts to overcome this division have stressed the importance of time, and of spatial differentiation, in perception. Like intentions, reasons, etc., perception is not an aggregate of discrete 'perceptions' but a flow of activity integrated with the movement of the body in time-space. Perception is organized via anticipatory schemata whereby the individual anticipates new incoming information while simultaneously mentally digesting old. Perception normally involves the continued active movement of the eyes, and usually of the head, even when the body is at rest. Because schemata are anticipations, they are, as one another puts it, 'the medium whereby the past affects the future', which is 'identical with the underlying mechanisms of memory'.[9] It may very well be that touch, ordinarily regarded as the most humble of the senses, and certainly the least studied, provides most clues for understanding perception in general. Touch has no clear-cut perceptual locus, like the eye; incoming haptic information is not ordered through any single mechanism within the nervous system; the use of touch is self-evidently part of the manipulatory movement of the body in the contexts of its action. A striking feature of most of the literature on perception, moreover, is that it treats the senses as though they operated in separation from one another. It has been observed that virtually all experimental studies of perception have involved only a single sense.[10] That this is artificial is shown by the most cursory examination of the nature of day-to-day life, in which the continuity of activities persistently integrates the various senses.

Perception, then, depends upon spatial and temporal continuity, actively organized as such by the perceiver. The main point of reference has to be neither the single sense nor the contemplative perceiver but the body in its active engagements with the material and social worlds. Perceptual schemata are neurologically based formats whereby the temporality of experience is continually processed. Such processing may in turn be understood as inherently involved with the reflexive monitoring of action in general. It seems impossible to deny that the new-born infant possesses an innate perceptual equipment. In other words, it has not only the sense organs but also neurologically established schemata that allow it to respond selectively to the surrounding world, even if that selectivity is relatively gross compared with what is developed later. A good deal of evidence exists to the effect that infants respond with movements of the head towards the direction of sounds, follow moving objects visually and reach out towards them. 'Looking towards sounds', of course, already involves integration of the senses.[11] Neonates already assess this in terms of a time difference between acoustic responses in the two ears, leading to the movement of the head in one direction or the other. Such responses do, of course, become more precise with further psychological and motor development; it takes a long while for children to learn the arts of coping conceptually with objects that have gone out of sight. Naming or identifying objects is evidently not just a matter of attaching a label to phenomena whose qualities are already known. To name something correctly is to be able to talk about it correctly, which means typifying its properties: relating it to a class of comparable objects differentiating it from other classes.[12] In this respect we can see both the attractions and the limitations of Gibson's concept of 'affordance'. According to Gibson, all the uses or activities which objects make possible — which they afford to the human actor — are directly perceivable. Such a view has the advantage of stressing the practical character of perceptual activities, but it does not indicate their connection with conceptual designations of objects, which are likely to be culturally variable.

If perception be understood as a set of temporal ordering devices, shaped by, yet shaping, the movements and orientations of the body in the contexts of its behaviour, we can understand thereby the significance of selective attention in day-to-day conduct. In every context of activity there is far more going on than the actor actually attends to, events or qualities that remain unnoticed. How does this happen? The usual answer is that redundant material is filtered out. But this is quite misleading, for it suggests an active attempt to reject redundant material. Selection is, however, a positive rather than a negative process; it expresses the active engagements of agents with their environments. Consider the following much debated experiment.[13] Tape recordings of two separate and different spoken messages were played simultaneously to experimental subjects, one in each ear and at equal volume. Subjects were instructed to listen to only one message and to repeat it as they heard it. They experienced no difficulty in doing this and by and large did not 'hear' the alternative message at all. The experimental situation is an interesting one because it mirrors what agents do most of the time when co-present with others in situations where more than one conversation is going on. The experimental results have been widely interpreted in terms of negative information filters.[14] Redundant information, in other words, is supposedly blocked off from reaching the higher cortical centres — definite neural mechanisms have been suggested as controlling such a process. But this type of theory not only treats the individual as essentially a passive receiver of input; it also depends upon an untenable dissociation between perception and memory. For it is supposed that while we perceive everything in our environment at any given moment, much of what is perceived is 'blocked off' — very rapidly 'forgotten'.[15] As Neisser has pointed out, the assumption is that any use of information a few milliseconds after it has been registered is dependent upon memory rather than perception. Such a view is neither conceptually compelling nor empirically plausible. If perception is regarded as what agents do, as part of their temporally and spatially situated activities, there is no need to posit any blocking mechanisms at all.

> Organisms are active: they do some things and leave others undone. To pick one apple from a tree you need not filter out all the others; you just don't pick them. A theory of apple picking would have much to explain (How do you decide which one you want? Guide your hand to it? Grasp it?) but it would not have to specify a mechanism to keep unwanted apples out of your hand.[16]

If the 'present' is not cut off from the flow of action, 'memory' can be nothing other than a way of describing the knowledge-ability of human agents. If memory does not designate 'past experience', neither does consciousness (in any of the three senses mentioned above) express the 'present'. What a person is 'aware of' cannot be fixed at a particular point in time. We need to distinguish, therefore, between consciousness as sensory aware-ness (the first and most general sense of the term mentioned above); memory, as the temporal constitution of consciousness; and recall, as the means of recapitulating past experiences in such a way as to focus them upon the continuity of action. If memory refers to this temporal mastery so inherent in human experience, then discursive and practical consciousness refer to *psychological mechanisms of recall,* as utilized in contexts of action. Discursive consciousness connotes those forms of recall which the actor is able to express verbally. Practical consciousness involves recall to which the agent has access in the *durée* of action without being able to express what he or she thereby 'knows'. The unconscious refers to modes of recall to which the agent does not have direct access because there is a negative 'bar' of some kind inhibiting its unmediated incorporation within the reflexive monitoring of conduct and, more particularly, within discursive consciousness. The origins of the 'bar' are of two related sorts. First, since the earliest experiences of the infant, shaping the basic security system whereby anxiety is canalized or controlled, predate differentiated linguistic competence, they are likely to remain thereafter 'outside the bounds' of discursive consciousness. Second, the unconscious contains repressions which inhibit discursive formulation.

As a matter of conceptual definition, these remarks are moderately consonant with Freud's characteristic usage of the 'conscious' and 'the unconscious'. But the thesis that most day-to-day activities are not directly motivated means placing in question the model of motivation with which Freud characteristically operated. For Freud all human activities are motivated, including (for example) apparent triviata or 'errors' such as slips of the tongue. Freud was often concerned precisely to demonstrate that phenomena which might be supposed to be 'accidental' do, in fact, have their origin in (unconscious) motives. There is no particular reason to question the illuminating quality of Freud's insights in such matters. But it makes no more sense to claim that every act or gesture is motivated — meaning that a definite 'motive' can be attached to it — than it does to treat action as involving a string of intentions or reasons. There is a logical flaw here in the simplified view of the nature of human action. Action, as I have said often, cannot satisfactorily be conceptualized as an aggregate of acts. Concentrating mainly upon specific demarcated 'segments' of behaviour (neurotic symptoms), Freud's writings inevitably tend to express such a deficient conception of action. But rather than supposing that every 'act' has a corresponding 'motive', we have to understand the term 'motivation' to be a processual one. What this means concretely is that the unconscious only rarely impinges directly upon the reflexive monitoring of conduct. Nor are the connections involved solely dependent upon psychological mechanisms within the personality of the individual actor; they are mediated by the social relations which individuals sustain in the routine practices of their daily lives.

Elaborating a little on this point provides something of a transition between the discussion so far in this chapter and that which follows later. The main theorems I wish to propose run as follows. Ordinary day-to-day life — in greater or less degree according to context and the vagaries of individual personality — involves an *ontological security* expressing an *autonomy of bodily control* within *predictable routines*. The psychological origins of ontological security are to be found in basic anxiety-controlling mechanisms (as indicated by Erikson, whose ideas I discuss in what follows), hierarchically ordered as components of personality. The generation of feelings of trust in others, as the deepest-lying element of the basic security system, depends substantially upon predictable and caring routines established by parental figures. The infant is very early on both a giver as well as a receiver of trust. As he or she becomes more autonomous, however, the child learns the importance of what are in Goffman's term 'protective devices', which sustain the mutuality implied in trust via tact and other formulae that preserve the face of others. Ontological security is protected by such devices but maintained in a more fundamental way by the very predictability of routine, something which is radically disrupted in critical situations. The swamping of habitual modes of activity by anxiety which cannot be adequately contained by the basic security system is specifically a feature of critical situations.

Criticizing Freud's terminology of agency and self carries with it several implications. The 'I' is an essential feature of the reflexive monitoring of action but should be identified neither with the agent nor with the self. By the 'agent' or 'actor' I mean the overall human subject located within the corporeal time-space of the living organism. The 'I' has no image, as the self does. The self, however, is not some kind of mini-agency within the agent. It is the sum of those forms of recall whereby the agent reflexively characterizes 'what' is at the origin of his or her action. The self is the agent as characterized by the agent. Self, body and memory are therefore intimately related.

Erikson: Anxiety and Trust

Theories which give prominence to unconscious elements of human behaviour often tend to go along with objectivist perspectives. It is not too difficult to see why. For objectivism, like many accounts of the unconscious, treats the reflexive monitoring of action as mere froth on the surface of human activity, whose true origins lie elsewhere. In setting out an account of (a few features of) the unconscious and social relations, I shall not follow those versions of structuralist psychoanalysis, associated particularly with Lacan, that are currently fashionable in some quarters. Although Lacan's writings undeniably contain some ideas of great interest, in my opinion they express an impoverished conception of the agent similar to that generated by 'structuralist Marxism'.[17] Lacan has been one of the figures in the forefront of the attacks upon the work of the so-called 'ego psychologists' within psychoanalysis. These polemics have been in substantial degree successful, since the work of Sullivan, Horney, Erikson, Kardiner and others now lies under something of a shadow. I consider that some of the contributions of these authors, however, retain a very considerable importance and shall draw upon them in some part here.

Critiques, 'revisionisms' and self-professed 'orthodoxies' have been as prolific in psychoanalytic theory since the early years of this century as they have been within Marxism. The ego psychologists, however, have been associated with two principal

F

lines of development as regards the 'classical' formulations of psychoanalysis in Freud's writings. On the one hand, they have taken up the perspective fostered by Anna Freud. That is to say, they have argued that Freud's preoccupation with repression and the unconscious led him to underplay the more cognitive, rational components of the agent. On the other hand, they have been influenced by the writings of social analysts, especially anthropologists, which demonstrate the sheer diversity of human modes of social life. Freud's cultural writings — however much they may retain their importance in some ways — were essentially bound up with the evolutionism of nineteenth-century anthropology. Being aware of this diversity means also acknowledging the variety of different forms of family organization, and hence of early socialization, that exist. Recognition of these two sets of factors, taken together, means making substantial departures from more traditional views of psychoanalytic theory, although it does not entail adopting a full-blown cultural relativism; there are processes of child development and adult personality common to all human societies. Erikson expresses this in *Childhood and Society* in the following way:

> Psychoanalysis today is implementing the study of the ego. . . . It is shifting its emphasis from the concentrated study of the conditions which blunt and distort the individual ego to the study of the ego's roots in social organization. . . . Long childhood makes a technical and mental virtuoso out of man, but it also leaves a lifelong residue of emotional immaturity in him.[18]

Erikson, together with Sullivan, are perhaps the two outstanding figures among those writers who have preserved certain universal elements of Freud's original account of the stages of psychosexual development, while at the same time adopting contributions from the social sciences. I shall draw — although sparingly and critically — upon their ideas in what follows. On the basis of both his clinical work and the study of a range of cultures, Erikson has distinguished a series of stages of personality development over the period from infancy to adulthood. His discussion of the nature of the motivational inclinations and mental capacities of the infant is extremely persuasive. But I do not think he brings out sufficiently the essential threshold in child development that derives from the phase of the syntactical mastery of language, a transition in the life of the individual, as Chomsky has demonstrated, whose consequences can be fairly readily identified but the origins of which remain tantalizingly obscure.

In all societies the early nurture of the infant is dominated by a single mothering agent, nearly always the biological mother of the child. The initial phases of personality development may be characteristically associated with resolutions of needs or tensions deriving from the physical traits of the organism. But it seems almost certain that Freud squeezed these into too deterministic a scheme, and a more flexible one is required to make sense of variations between and within societies. We may say that the earliest interaction between infant and mother is layered into the development of the 'unconscious': neither 'bodily movement' nor 'bodily control' is very similar to the senses in which they are involved in 'action' in the case of the adult member of society. If we follow Erikson, we can distinguish three successive polarities associated with the transformation of the body into an instrument of acting-in-the-world. The first, and earliest, is that of 'basic trust' versus 'basic mistrust'. The new-born infant is a bundle of impulses, which have certain genetically given homeostatic mechanisms of adjustment, existing in an alien environment; the activities of the mother provide care and protection. 'Trust' (here conceived of as a trait of personality) is understood as psychologically 'binding' time-space by the initial awakening of a sense that absence does not signify desertion. The psychological dyamics underlying the intersection of presence and absence have their point of origin in the body, bodily needs, their modes of satiation and control.

As Erikson comments, 'The infant's first social achievement, then, is his willingness to let the mother out of sight without undue anxiety or rage, because she has become an inner certainty as well as an outer predictability.' Predictability, continuity, sameness, provide 'a rudimentary sense of ego identity which depends . . . on the recognition that there is an inner population of remembered and anticipated sensations and images which are firmly correlated with the outer population of familiar and predictable things and people'.[19] 'Trust' here equals confidence, and very early on, Erikson suggests, it has a definite mutuality to it; there is at least an incipient feeling of 'being trustworthy' associated with the generalized extension of trust to the other.

Not, of course, that the initial formation of trust occurs without conflict or strain. On the contrary, it operates against the background of diffuse anxiety, control of which suggests itself as the most generalized motivational origin of human conduct. The interaction between infant and mother embeds the growing human individual in a nexus from which, for better or for worse, there is thereafter no escape. The mother is an agent (already a representative of the 'generalized other') who, in caring for the infant, lays a social claim upon it that presages the normative sanctions associated with the later formation of social relationships. The anxiety of absence is defused through the rewards of co-presence, setting the ground for the dialectic of engagement and disengagement on which the diversity of encounters is based. The expansion of the autonomy of the infant, anchored in control of the body as a medium of action (which undergoes a massive transformation with the mastery of language), simultaneously widens and integrates this dialectic. Each individual has the right — varying in content in manifold ways in different contexts — to maintain a distance from others by preserving bodily privacy and an integrity of self. But the self has to submit to social engagement, given that this is done with proper deference to the tactful recognition of the needs of others. The infant does not yet know this, nor its connection with face. Face, as Becker puts it, is 'the positive feeling of self-warmth turned to the world for others' scrutiny and potential sabotage'.[20]

As the foundation of a tension-management system, the trust/mistrust polarity is organized around relations between projection and introjection as mechanisms of personality. Infantile introjection, as Freud holds, assimilates outer goodness and inner certainty; projection treats an inner harm as external malevolence.[21] Themselves based on identification, these mechanisms become overlain by a variety of more mature psychic forms. But they come to the fore again in situations of extreme threat or crisis. The physical maturation of the body subsequently sets the stage for the transition to a new phase of development. Erikson suggests that this is not best understood in terms of a shift between pleasure zones on the surface of the body, as Freud holds, although fixations may become centred on these. 'Holding on' and 'letting go' are obviously applicable to control of the waste products of the body but are expressed in a much more generic way through the hands and arms. Holding on and letting go are the behavioural correlates of the main polarity on which this stage is centred, autonomy versus doubt or shame. As with the prior phase, with which it can stand in a relation of generalized tension, the polarity can be resolved in a relatively benign or more disruptive way. To hold on as a greedy mode of retention can represent a cruel self-absorption or can be a pattern of care expressing autonomy. Letting go can similarly be a hostile expression of aggressive impulses or a more relaxed attitude to 'letting things pass'. It seems important to emphasize the significance of the psychodynamics of shame as contrasted with guilt. Many psychoanalysts, following hints given by Freud, have treated shame as specifically connected to fear of genital exposure. This certainly helps to indicate one aspect of anxiety, about bodily 'appearance', which (as will shortly be indicated) Goffman shows to be so important. But the phenomenon of shame is surely much more pervasive than Freud's comments would lead us to believe.[22]

The prevalence of feelings of shame or self-doubt is indicated by the frequency with which being 'ashamed' and comparable terms ('mortified', 'humiliated', etc.) appear in ordinary talk. The idea, suggested by some writers, that guilt is 'private' while shame is 'public' seems difficult to sustain. Shame bites at the roots of self-esteem and clearly is closely related to the rather milder experience of 'embarrassment'. Both shame and embarrassment are located psychologically in the intersection of engagement and disengagement, the failure to 'bring off' certain aspects of performance through being 'caught out' in various ways. Unlike 'guilt', 'shame' and 'embarrassment' capture both sides of encounters: that is to say, the latter two terms can be used by the individual about his or her own conduct or that of others. I can be ashamed of myself, of something which I have done, or embarrassed about it. But I can also be ashamed of the conduct of someone else, as well as embarrassed for him or her. Here we seem to detect a difference between the two emotions. To be ashamed of somebody else's behaviour indicates a tie with that other, signalling a certain recognition of association with, or even responsibility for, the other. To be embarrassed for someone, rather than expressing an alienation from his or her conduct, reveals a certain complicity with it, a sympathy for someone who has been unnecessarily 'exposed'.

It is especially interesting, in the light of Goffman's pre-occupation with like happenings, to note that Erikson links shame in the infant (having strong residual traces in the security system of the adult) to bodily posture and to 'front' and 'back' regions of the body. Here we can see a mode in which Freud's theory of anal retention can be expressed in a much more socialized form. The 'front' and 'back regions' in which encounters occur, and in the context of which social occasions are staged, perhaps relate directly to the more primal experience of the front/back regionalization of the body. To sustain 'front' in social life is to avoid the anxieties provoked by shame, and loss of front leads precisely to shame or embarrassment. For the infant 'behind' means 'the behind':

> the small being's dark continent, an area of the body which can be magically dominated and effectively invaded by those who would attack one's power of autonomy . . . This stage, therefore, becomes decisive for the ratio of love and hate, co-operation and wilfulness, freedom of self-expression and its suppression. From a sense of self-control without loss of self-esteem comes a lasting sense of good will and pride; from a sense of loss of self-control and of foreign overcontrol comes a lasting propensity for doubt and shame.[23]

The third phase, the one that culminates in, and coincides with, the mastery of syntactically developed language, focalizes a polarity of initiative versus guilt. This is the phase of Oedipal transition which, whatever its obscurities and complexities, appears as a universal crisis phase in human psychological development. So far as the body is concerned, it is marked by the mastery of an upright stance and ambulatory movement in that stance, and by the maturation of infantile genitality. The dramatic potential of this phase for later personality development is given by the conjunction of the demand for repression of early attachment to the mother (in both boys and girls), coupled with the capabilities that become part of this process as it coincides with a vast leap forward in linguistic skills. It is a phase of initiative because the accomplishment of the Oedipal transition allows the child the internal control necessary to venture forth from the immediate confines of the family into peer relationships.

But this is purchased at the price of repression, which in some individuals and in some circumstances can have crippling costs in forms of anxiety stemming from guilt.

> For here the child becomes forever divided in itself. The instinct fragments which before had enhanced the growth of his infantile body and mind now become divided into an infantile set which perpetuates the exuberance of growth potentials, and a parental set which supports and increases self-observation, self-guidance, and self-punishment.[24]

Put together, the three phases represent a progressive movement towards autonomy, which should be understood as the foundation of the capability for the reflexive monitoring of conduct. But 'autonomy' does not mean the shedding of the anxiety-provoking stimuli or the modes of coping with anxiety which comprise the security system of the adult personality. The motivational components of the infantile and the adult personality derive from a generalized orientation to the avoidance of anxiety and the preservation of self-esteem against the 'flooding through' of shame and guilt. We may presume that the mechanisms of the security system remain on an unconscious level because they are pre-linguistic — although the Oedipal phase is the very time at which the child learns to constitute itself as an 'I'.

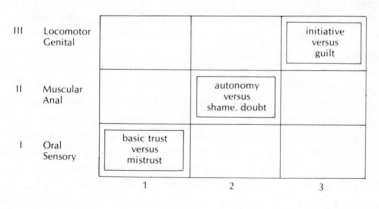

Figure 3

Figure 3 indicates that the successive phases presume varying ratios of independence and dependence, combinations of bodily modes and psychological mechanisms. If tracing out individual differences were at issue, it would imply thinking through the empty boxes, which would become filled in so far as infantile fixations or modes of regression exert a pervasive influence over the motivation of behaviour.

Research into child development suggests rather strongly that the formation of capabilities for autonomous action meshes closely with understanding others to be agents. Three main steps in the formation of concepts of agency can be distinguished, coinciding with the stages described by Erikson. One is the recognition of what has been called 'simple agency' — that others can causally intervene in a sequence of events to as to change them.[25] The infant's awareness that its body is a locus of action goes along with the attribution of like qualities to the bodies of others. At quite an early age infants react differently in their interaction with 'agent-like' others, although the aspects of the conduct of such figures to which response is made are relatively simple and clear-cut.[26] Other agents are, however, still treated instrumentally, as a special type of object in the environment, rather than as physically separate beings from the self, who can go away and return. The emotional competence associated with trust seems closely connected with the cognitive understanding of agency as a property of distinct beings. But specifically 'human' properties, generalized to human agents rather than attributed to particular parental figures, mark a transition to a third stage.

Vygotsky, among others, has demonstrated the close relation between locomotor skills (the mastery of the body as a locus of action) and the syntactical mastery of language. His work scarcely answers the 'Chomskyan problem' — how does the child, relatively suddenly, manage successfully to co-ordinate syntactic structures? — but it does elucidate important aspects of the association of agency and speech. Language use, in differentiated form, depends upon the expansion of the 'practical intelligence' of the child — in other words, upon definite aspects of practical consciousness.[27] The development of 'practical intelligence' accelerates, it can be suggested, from the period of the resolution of the third phase in Erikson's scheme, since it involves the exploration of the body as a medium of action. But the initial emergence of 'practical intelligence' dates from the first exploratory movements of the very young infant; mastery of syntactical speech *converges* with the growth of practical mastery at the key phase of development. It is striking how closely some of Vygotsky's observations about what to an adult would appear to be a 'dissociation' between speech and conduct resemble those made by Merleau-Ponty in respect of brain-damaged patients (see pp. 65—7). For instance, a child may be able to carry out a fairly complex task only on condition that it verbally describes each movement as it goes along. Children, like many of the 'mentally ill', are not reluctant to talk to themselves in public — a phenomenon which has to be distinguished from Piaget's identification of 'egocentric speech'.

Having appealed to Erikson a good deal, I should perhaps make it clear that my appropriation of some of his ideas is intended to be strictly limited and qualified. I consider the least interesting areas of Erikson's work to be those for which he is probably most famed — to do with the formation of 'ego-identity' and with the importance of developmental stages in personality that stretch up to adolescence and beyond. Erikson is critical of Freud's formulations about the 'ego' and its relations to society.[28] This is partly because of their sociological inadequacies. Freud drew upon highly inadequate sociological texts (such as contemporary discussions of crowd psychology) in his writings. At the same time, psychoanalytic method was based on individual case histories. Between these there is a large gap. No satisfactory account of a differentiated society was worked out by Freud or many of his epigones; 'the concept of social *organization* and its bearing on the individual ego' was 'shunted off by patronizing tributes to the existence of "social factors"'.[29] The concept of the ego was thus established by Freud, Erikson points out, in relation to its opposites in the lawless nature of the crowd and the primeval instincts of the id. In order to try to take account of the embattled moral sensibility of human beings, Freud introduced the super-ego or ego-ideal — also, however, thinking of it in terms primarily of a burden which the ego has to bear. Erikson wants to compensate for this one-sided emphasis. Rather than concentrating upon what is denied to the infant by social organization, we should be concerned also with how the child benefits from it, and we should give greater consideration to the influence of differentiated types of social organization. Erikson's notion of ego-identity is intended to complement the traditionally established psychoanalytic concepts.[30]

I am largely in accord with Erikson's critical comments on

Freud. But the term 'ego-identity' is not a satisfactory one. The term 'ego', as I have indicated, does too much conceptual work in psychoanalytic theory. That of 'ego-identity' tends only to compound the confusions that already exist. Even Erikson admits that it has at least four connotations. Sometimes it refers to a 'conscious' sense of individual identity. It can also mean 'an unconscious striving for a continuity of personal character'. A third meaning is 'a criterion for the silent doings of ego synthesis'. A fourth sense is 'a maintenance of an inner solidarity with a group's ideals and identity'.[31] None of these single uses, it might be remarked, is particularly lucid, let alone the concept that embraces them all!

Routinization and Motivation

Rather than employing the concept of ego-identity, in what follows I shall make use of Erikson's ideas of the origins and nature of bodily autonomy and of trust. A sense of trust in the continuity of the object-world and in the fabric of social activity, I shall suggest, depends upon certain specifiable connections between the individual agent and the social contexts through which that agent moves in the course of day-to-day life. If the subject cannot be grasped save through the reflexive constitution of daily activities in social practices, we cannot understand the mechanics of personality apart from the routines of day-to-day life through which the body passes and which the agent produces and reproduces. The concept of *routinization,* as grounded in practical consciousness, is vital to the theory of structuration. Routine is integral both to the continuity of the personality of the agent, as he or she moves along the paths of daily activities, and to the institutions of society, which *are* such only through their continued reproduction. An examination of routinization, I shall claim, provides us with a master key to explicating the characteristic forms of relation between the basic security system on the one hand and the reflexively constituted processes inherent in the episodic character of encounters on the other.

We can probe the psychological nature of the routine by considering the results of situations where the established modes of accustomed daily life are drastically undermined or shattered — by studying what may be called 'critical situations'. There is a sense in which critical situations, for specific individuals or clusters of individuals, are themselves built into the regularity of social life by the very nature of the intersection between the life process or 'cycle' of the individual, the *durée* of activity on the one hand and the *longue durée* of institutions on the other. These are the crises typically marked by rites of passage, beginning for the individual with birth and terminating in death. However, forming as they do an intrinsic part of the continuity of social life, even though they are discontinuities for individuals, such situations tend themselves to have a definitely routinized character.

By 'critical situations' I mean circumstances of radical disjuncture of an unpredictable kind which affect substantial numbers of individuals, situations that threaten or destroy the certitudes of institutionalized routines. I am concerned at this point not with analysing the social origins of such circumstances but with their psychological consequences, and with what those consequences indicate about the generality of routine social life. Since I have discussed critical situations in a certain amount of detail elsewhere,[32] I shall mention here only one — a famous portrayal of a wholly infamous episode in recent history. This is Bettelheim's discussion in *The Informed Heart,* a description and analysis of the experiences of the author and others in Dachau and Buchenwald. In the camps, he writes, 'I . . . saw fast changes taking place, and not only in behaviour but personality also; incredibly faster and often much more radical changes than any that were possible by psychoanalytic treatment.'[33] The concentration-camp experience was marked not only by confinement but also by extreme disruption of accustomed forms of daily life, deriving from the brutalized conditions of existence, ever-present threat or actuality of violence from the camp guards, scarcity of food and other elementary provisions for the sustenance of life.

The changes in personality described by Bettelheim — experienced by all prisoners who were interned in the camp over a period of years — followed a certain sequence of stages. The sequence was quite evidently a regressive one. The very process of initial imprisonment was traumatic for most of the inmates. Torn away from family and friends, usually with little or no prior warning, many prisoners were subjected to torture during their transportation to the camps. Those from middle-class or professional backgrounds, who mostly had had no previous contact with the police or the prison system, experienced the greatest dislocation in the initial stages of transportation and 'initiation' into camp life. According to Bettelheim, the suicides that took place in prison and transportation were confined mainly to this group. The vast majority of new prisoners, however, sought to distance themselves psychologically from the dreadful pressures of camp life and tried to maintain the modes of conduct associated with their previous lives. But this proved impossible to do. The 'initiative' of which Erikson writes as lying at the core of human autonomy of action was very rapidly corroded; the Gestapo in some degree deliberately forced the prisoners to adopt childlike behaviour.

> The vast majority of prisoners went through the camp without a public flogging, but the screamed threat that they were going to get twenty-five on the behind rang in their ears several times daily. . . . Threats like these, and also the curses thrown at prisoners by both the SS and prisoner foremen, were almost exclusively connected with the anal sphere. 'Shit' and 'asshole' were so standard that it was rare when a prisoner was addressed otherwise.[34]

The guards exerted strict but wilfully erratic control over toilet, in the sense both of elimination and of general cleanliness. All these activities were carried on in public. The camps destroyed virtually all differentiation between 'front' and 'back regions', making the latter physically and socially a central preoccupation of camp life.

Bettelheim places particular emphasis upon the general unpredictability of events in the camps. The feeling of autonomy of action that individuals have in the ordinary routines of day-to-day life in orthodox social settings was almost completely dissolved. The 'futural' sense in which the *durée* of social life ordinarily occurs was destroyed by the manifestly contingent character of even the hope that the next day would arrive. The prisoners, in other words, lived in circumstances of radical ontological insecurity: 'it was the senseless tasks, the lack of almost any time to oneself, the inability to plan ahead because of sudden changes in camp policies, that was so deeply destructive.'[35] Some prisoners became 'walking corpses' (*Muselmänner*, so-called) because they surrendered fatalistically to whatever the future might hold. They no longer behaved as though they were human agents, avoiding eye contact with others, making only gross movements of the body and shuffling their legs when they walked. These men and women soon died. Only prisoners who managed to maintain some small sphere of control in their daily lives, which they still regarded as their 'own', were able to survive. They preserved, as Bettelheim says, 'the mainstay of a radically reduced but still present humanity'. None the less, they were unable to avoid a range of childlike attitudes, a very marked diminution in time sense, in the capacity to 'think ahead', and volatile mood swings in response to entirely trivial happenings.

All these things refer to the behaviour of prisoners who had been in the camps for no more than a year (which included Bettelheim). The 'old prisoners', those who had survived in the camps for several years, behaved differently. They had lost altogether any orientation to the world outside and had, as it were, reconstituted themselves as agents by integrating themselves into camp life as participants in the very rituals of degradation which, as new prisoners, they had found so offensive. They were often unable to recall names, places and events in their previous lives. The end result, found in most but not all old prisoners, was a reconstructed personality based upon identification with the oppressors themselves, the camp guards. Old prisoners aped the activities of their captors, not merely to curry favour with them but also, Bettelheim suggests, because of an introjection of the normative values of the SS.

How should we interpret these events? The sequence of stages seems fairly clear (although not set out in this way by Bettelheim himself). The disruption and the deliberately sustained attack upon the ordinary routines of life produce a high degree of anxiety, a 'stripping away' of the socialized responses associated with the security of the management of the body and a predictable framework of social life. Such an upsurge of anxiety is expressed in regressive modes of behaviour, attacking the foundation of the basic security system grounded in trust manifested towards others. Those who are ill-equipped to face these pressures succumb and go under. Some are able to sustain a minimal sphere of control and self-esteem that allows them to survive for a longer period. But eventually, in most of the old prisoners at least, a process of 'resocialization' takes place in which an attitude of trust (limited and highly ambivalent),[36] involving identification with authority figures, is re-established. Such a sequence of heightened anxiety, regression, followed by a reconstruction of typical patterns of action, appears in a range of critical situations in otherwise very different contexts, such as responses to being under fire on the battlefield for prolonged periods of time, forced interrogation and torture in prisons and other conditions of extreme stress.[37]

Ordinary day-to-day social life, by contrast — in greater or lesser degree, according to context and the vagaries of individual personality — involves an ontological security founded on an autonomy of bodily control within predictable routines and encounters. The routinized character of the paths along which individuals move in the reversible time of daily life does not just 'happen'. It is 'made to happen' by the modes of reflexive monitoring of action which individuals sustain in circumstances of co-presence. The 'swamping' of habitual modes of activity by anxiety that cannot be adequately contained by the basic security system is specifically a feature of critical situations. In ordinary social life actors have a motivated interest in sustaining the forms of tact and 'repair' which Goffman analyses so acutely. However, this is not because social life is a kind of mutually protective contract into which individuals voluntarily enter, as Goffman on occasion suggests. Tact is a mechanism whereby agents are able to reproduce the conditions of 'trust' or ontological security within which more primal tensions can be canalized and managed. This is why one can say that many of the specific features of day-to-day encounter are not directly motivated. Rather, there is a generalized motivational commitment to the integration of habitual practices across time and space.

Presence, Co-Presence and Social Integration

The routines of day-to-day life are fundamental to even the most elaborate forms of societal organization. In the course of their daily activities individuals encounter each other in situated contexts of interaction — interaction with others who are physically co-present.

The social characteristics of co-presence are anchored in the spatiality of the body, in orientation to others and to the experiencing self. Goffman has devoted considerable care to analysing this phenomenon, particularly with regard to 'face', but perhaps the most telling reflections on the matter are to be found in Merleau-Ponty. I shall begin by considering these; they lead us directly into Goffman's observations. The body, Merleau-Ponty points out, does not 'occupy' time-space in exactly the same sense as material objects do. As he puts it, 'The outline of my body is a frontier which ordinary spatial relations do not cross.' [38] This is because the body, and the experience of bodily movement, is the centre of forms of action and awareness which really define its unity. The time-space relations of presence, centred upon the body, are geared into not a 'spatiality of position', in Merleau-Ponty's words, but a 'spatiality of situation'. The 'here' of the body refers not to a determinate series of coordinates but to the situation of the active body oriented towards its tasks. Much as Heidegger says: 'if my body can be a "form" and if there can be, in front of it, important figures against indifferent backgrounds, this occurs in virtue of its being polarized by its tasks, of its *existence towards* them, of its collecting together of itself in pursuit of its aims; the body image is finally a way of stating that my body is in-the-world.'[39]

The observations of Goldstein and others on brain-damaged patients provide graphic illustration of how this is so.[40] Thus some such individuals are not able to carry out movements which abstract from the visually present *milieu*. A person can point to a part of the body only if he or she is able to watch the movement carried out and actually touch that part of the body. From observations such as these it becomes apparent that, while both are seemingly 'positional' phenomena, 'touching' is not the same as 'pointing'. The difference indicates the importance of bodily space as an extraordinarily complex field of matrices of habitual action. The brain-damaged patient, asked to perform a given movement of the body, assumes a general position of the whole body to carry out the task. It is not cut down, as in the normal individual, to a minimal gesture. Thus, asked to salute, the patient takes up a formal stance of the whole body — the individual manages to make the gesture only by adopting the generalized situation to which the movement corresponds. The normal individual, by contrast, sees the situation as a test or as play. He or she is, as Merleau-Ponty says, 'using the body as a means to play acting'.[41] It is the dilemma of the patient which provides most insight into the ordinary integration of the body into the *durée* of activity. For the body operates, and is understood as a 'body' by its owner, only in the contextualities of action. Wittgenstein's question, 'What is the difference between my raising my arm and my arm going up?', has here created many difficulties, whatever he may have wanted the inquiry to draw our attention to. For it seems to treat as typical just that case of a test or a playful command; and the theory of action then can be taken, misleadingly, to hinge on contrasts between 'movements' and 'actions', as discrete operations, rather than on the time-space contextuality of bodily activity in the flow of daily conduct.

Such activity of the body, in the flow of action, is immediately involved in the ontological security or attitude of 'trust' towards the continuity of the world and of self implicated in the *durée* of day-to-day life. For the brain-damaged patient a thorough physical examination of an object is required before it can be identified as, say, a 'key'. Normal individuals would engage in such a scrutiny of an object only in unusual circumstances — where, for example, they were playing a party game in which there were definite reasons to suppose that objects might not be as they appear. The continuity of ordinary life would be impossible were we to attempt to submit all objects to such detailed inspection. From this we see that Garfinkel's 'etcetera clause' applies not just to language or conversation but also to bodily activities in physical relation to the external world. All this is in turn intrinsically involved with time and time-sense. Let me quote again from Merleau-Ponty:

> Whereas in the normal person every event related to movement or sense of touch causes consciousness to put up a host of intentions which run from the body as the centre of potential action either towards the body itself or towards the object, in the case of the patient, on the other hand, the tactile impression remains opaque and sealed up. . . . The normal person *reckons with* the possible, which thus, without shifting from its position as a possibility, acquires a sort of actuality. In the patient's case, however, the field of actuality is limited to what is met with in the shape of a real contact or is related to these data by some explicit process of deduction. [42]

The body, of course, is not an undifferentiated unity. What Gehlen calls the 'eccentric' posture of human beings — standing upright and 'outward' towards the world — is no doubt the result of biological evolution. We need not transpose biological into a presumptively parallel form of social evolution to see the implications of this for human social processes in circumstances of co-presence. In human beings the face is not simply the proximate physical origin of speech but the dominant area of the body across which the intricacies of experience, feeling and intention are written. In banal but very significant ways the face in human social relationships influences the spacing of individuals in circumstances of co-presence. Positioning 'facing' the other or others who are being addressed assumes a distinctive importance as compared with positioning in most animal societies. The numbers of people who can directly participate in face-to-face encounters is inherently strictly limited, save in those types of situation where one or a few individuals address a crowd or an audience facing them. But such circumstances, of course, demand that those in the crowd or audience sacrifice continuous face-to-face contact with one another. The primacy of the face as a medium of expression and of communication has moral implications, many of which are very acutely teased out by Goffman. To turn one's back on another while the other is speaking is in most (perhaps all?) societies a gesture of indifference or contempt. Moreover, most (all?) societies tend to recognize a linguistic similarity between the face as a term referring to physiognomy and face as concerning the maintenance of self-esteem. No doubt there are a range of cultures, such as traditional Chinese culture or sectors of it, which place an especial emphasis upon the preservation of face in most settings. No doubt also this may have something to do with the famous differentiation made by Benedict and others between 'shame' and 'guilt' cultures, even if this differentiation seems to have been drawn much too crudely. But aspects of the preservation and 'saving' of face are almost certainly generic to a whole diversity of transcultural contexts of social encounters.

The twin themes of the control of the body in fields of action in co-presence and the pervasive influence of face are essential to the whole of Goffman's writings. How should we understand the term 'co-presence'? As Goffman uses it, and as I employ it here also, co-presence is anchored in the perceptual and communicative modalities of the body. What Goffman calls 'the full conditions of co-presence' are found whenever agents 'sense that they are close enough to be perceived in whatever they are doing, including their experiencing of others, and close enough to be perceived in this sensing of being perceived'.[43] Although the 'full conditions of co-presence' exist only in unmediated contact between those who are physically present, mediated contacts that permit some of the intimacies of co-presence are made possible in the modern era by electronic communications, most notably the telephone.[44] In contemporary societies, and in differing formats in other cultures, the space contained in a room — with exceptions, such as parties, in which the whole house may be 'opened up' — ordinarily defines expected boundaries of co-presence. Of course, there are many 'public places', in jostling crowds on the streets and so on, in which there is no clear physical circumscribing of the conditions of co-presence.

Goffman: Encounters and Routines

Because Goffman has so persistently devoted himself to analysing the routines of day-to-day life, his writings offer many illuminations about the character of social integration. Several misunderstandings about Goffman's writings need to be countered before these insights can most profitably be developed. He has to be rescued here from the importunate embrace of his admirers. Goffman is often thought of as an idiosyncratic observer of social life, whose sensitivity to the subtleties of what I have called practical and discursive consciousness derives more from a combination of an acute intelligence and a playful style than from a co-ordinated approach to social analysis.[45] This is very misleading and one reason why Goffman has not generally been recognized as a social theorist of considerable stature. I want to say, in any case, that Goffman's writings have a highly systematic character, and this is in no small degree what gives them their intellectual power. Another misunderstanding, which Goffman himself has hardly been concerned to forestall, is that his writings are relevant only to a form of 'microsociology', which can be cleanly severed from 'macrosociological' issues. A much more interesting way to approach Goffman's works is treat them as being concerned to map out the intersections of presence and absence in social interaction. The mechanisms of social and system integration, to repeat, necessarily interlace with one another. Goffman's writings are certainly relevant to both, even if he has had a guarded stance towards problems of long-term institutional process or development.

Finally, it is frequently supposed that not only are Goffman's writings confined in their relevance to contemporary societies but they directly express features of conduct which are peculiarly modern, even distinctively American. Thus Gouldner, commenting upon Goffman's work, says:

> it dwells upon the episodic and sees life only as it is lived in a narrow interpersonal circumference, ahistorical and non-institutional, an existence beyond history and society. . . . [It] reflects the new world, in which a stratum of the new middle class no longer believes that hard work is useful or that success depends upon diligent application. In this new world there is a keen sense of the irrationality of the relationship between individual achievement and the magnitude of reward, between actual contribution and social regulation. It is the world of the high-priced Hollywood star and of the market for stocks, whose prices bear little relation to their earnings.[46]

Gouldner explicitly contrasts this standpoint with what he calls a 'structural' approach, to the detriment of the former. The social world Goffman portrays is not simply highly culturally specific but deals only with the transient, not with the enduring institutional forms that mould people's lives. One could not say that such an indictment of Goffman — in so far as it is an indictment — is wholly unjustified. But Gouldner's critique also reveals once more just that dualism which I have previously suggested is so pervasive in the social sciences. The fixity of institutional forms does not exist in spite of, or outside, the encounters of day-to-day life but *is implicated in those very encounters*.

The evanescence of encounters expresses the temporality of the *durée* of daily life and the contingent character of all structuration. But Goffman makes a very persuasive case for arguing that the 'fading away' inherent in the syntagmatic ordering of social interaction is consistent with a very marked fixity of form in social reproduction. Although he does not, to my knowledge, anywhere claim this, I think that his writings disclose features of co-presence that are found in all societies, however relevant those same writings indeed may be to identifying novel characteristics of the contemporary era. Goffman's work holds up a mirror to many worlds, not just to one. In using ideas formulated therein, nevertheless, I do not want to endorse all of Goffman's own emphases.

Goffman's writings comprise a major contribution to an exploration of the relations between discursive and practical consciousness in the contexts of encounters. However, he has little to say about the unconscious and may, indeed, reject the idea that such a phenomenon has any importance at all in social life. Moreover, Goffman's analyses of encounters presume motivated agents rather than investigating the sources of human motivation, as many of his critics have complained. The lack is a serious one and one of the main reasons (the other being a disinterest in long-term processes of institutional transformation) why Goffman's work has something of an 'empty' feel to it. For why do the agents whose reflective monitoring of conduct is described with so much subtlety follow the routines that they do? The question could be answered, up to a point, if it were the case that the individuals portrayed by Goffman were represented in a voluntaristic fashion as cynical agents who adapt to given social circumstances in a purely calculated and tactical way. But although many have interpreted Goffman in such a fashion, this is not the main implication which I wish to draw from the terrain of study which he has opened up. A stress upon the prevalence of tact in social encounters, the repair of strains in the social fabric and the sustaining of 'trust' suggest, rather, a predominant concern with the protection of social continuity, with the intimate mechanics of social reproduction.

Goffman develops a typology of the contours of interaction, and I shall employ several of his concepts, modifying them somewhat, in what follows. The range of concepts can be set out as follows:

[co-presence]

gatherings

social occasions

unfocused interaction

focused interaction: encounters   (face engagements)

                             routines   (episodes)

Gatherings refer to assemblages of people comprising two or more persons in contexts of co-presence. By the term 'context' (Goffman prefers that of 'situation') I mean those 'bands' or 'strips' of time-space within which gatherings take place. Anyone entering such a band of time-space makes himself or herself 'available' for moving into that gathering or may actually form it if it is dyadic in character. Gatherings presume the *mutual* reflective monitoring of conduct in and through co-presence. The contextuality of gatherings is vital, in a very intimate and integral fashion, to such processes of monitoring. Context includes the physical environment of interaction but is not something merely 'in which' interaction occurs (see pp. 118). Aspects of context, including the temporal order of gestures and talk, are routinely drawn upon by actors in constituting communication. The importance of this for the formulation of 'meaning' in gestures and in talk, as Garfinkel has done more than anyone else to elucidate, can scarcely be exaggerated.[47] Thus linguists have very often sought to analyse semantic problems either in terms of the 'internal' linguistic competence of individual speakers or by examining the properties of isolated speech acts. But the 'closure of meaning' of the polyvalent terminologies of everyday language achieved in discourse can be grasped only by studying the contextual ordering of whole conversations.

Gatherings may have a very loose and transitory form, such as that of a fleeting exchange of 'friendly glances' or greetings in a hallway. More formalized contexts in which gatherings occur can be called social occasions. Social occasions are gatherings which involve a plurality of individuals. They are typically rather clearly bounded in time and space and often employ special forms of fixed equipment — formalized arrangements of tables and chairs and so on. A social occasion provides the 'structuring social context' (Goffman's term) in which many gatherings 'are likely to form, dissolve and re-form, while a pattern of conduct tends to be recognized as the appropriate and (often) official or intended one'.[48] A whole variety of routinized aspects of daily life, such as the work day in a factory or office, are of this sort. But there are also many more irregular social occasions, including parties, dances, sports events and a diversity of other examples. Of course, a sector of physical space may simultaneously be the site or locale of several social occasions, each involving multiple gatherings. But more often than not there is a normatively sanctioned 'overriding social occasion' to which others are supposedly subordinated in a particular sector of time-space.

The contextual characteristics of gatherings, whether or not these occur on social occasions, can be divided into two main forms. Unfocused interaction relates to all those gestures and signals which can be communicated between individuals simply because of their co-presence within a specific context. The physical properties of the body and the limited scope of the positioning of the face are major constraints here. Actors' generalized awareness of the presence of others may range subtly over a wide spatial extension, even including those standing behind them. But such 'cueings of the body' are very diffuse compared with those that are possible, and are chronically utilized, in face-to-face interaction. Focused interaction occurs where two or more individuals co-ordinate their activities through a continued intersection of facial expression and voice. However much the participants might monitor whatever else is going on in the wider gathering, focused interaction in some part introduces an enclosure of those involved from others who are co-present. A unit of focused interaction is a face engagement or an encounter. Encounters are the guiding thread of social interaction, the succession of engagements with others ordered within the daily cycle of activity. Although Goffman does not include this formally within his schema of concepts, I think it highly important to emphasize the fact that encounters typically occur as routines. That is, what from the angle of the fleeting moment might appear brief and trivial interchanges take on much more substance when seen as inherent in the iterative nature of social life. The routinization of encounters is of major significance in binding the fleeting encounter to social reproduction and thus to the seeming 'fixity' of institutions.

I have defined social integration as systemness in circumstances of co-presence. Several phenomena suggest themselves as being most immediately relevant to the constitution of social integration thus defined. First, in order to grasp the connection of encounters with social reproduction stretching away over time and space, we must emphasize how encounters are formed and reformed in the *durée* of daily existence. Second, we should seek to identify the main mechanisms of the duality of structure whereby encounters are organized in and through the intersections of practical and discursive consciousness. This in turn has to be explicated in terms both of the control of the body and of the sustaining or rules or conventions. Third, encounters are sustained above all through *talk,* through everyday conversation. In analysing the communication of meaning in interaction via the use of interpretative schemes, the phenomenon of talk has to be taken very seriously, as constitutively involved in encounters. Finally, the contextual organization of encounters must be examined, since the mobilization of time-space is the 'grounding' of all the above elements. I shall undertake this latter task in terms of several basic notions, those of 'presence-availability', 'locale' and the relation of 'enclosure/disclosure'. Rather than discussing these latter three concepts in this chapter, however, I shall defer them until later.

Seriality

Encounters are sequenced phenomena, interpolated within, yet giving form to, the seriality of day-to-day life. The systematic properties of encounters can be traced to two principal characteristics: opening and closing, and turn-taking. Let me look briefly at each of these. The *durée* of daily life, as lived by each individual, is a continuous flow of activity, broken only (but regularly) by the relative passivity of sleep. The *durée* of activity can be 'bracketed' or 'conceptually segmented', as Schutz says, by a reflexive moment of attention on the part of the subject. This is what happens when someone is asked by another to supply 'a reason' or 'reason' for, or otherwise to explicate, certain features of his or her activity. But the *durée* of daily life is also 'bracketed' by the opening and closing of encounters. In Goffman's words, 'One may speak, then, of opening and closing temporal brackets and bounding spatial brackets.'[49] Fond as he is of dramaturgical metaphors and analogies, Goffman gives as an example the devices which are employed in the opening and closing of theatrical spectacles. To signal the opening of a play, a bell rings, the lights go down and the curtain is raised. At the conclusion the auditorium lights go on again as the curtain falls. Most social occasions use some type of formal cueing devices for opening and closing — a characteristic of ritual occasions as much in traditional cultures as in the variety of more secular social occasions characteristic of contemporary societies. The bracketing of initiation ceremonies, for example, typically cues a dramatic change in the manner of conduct within the frame of the occasion — markers indicating, as it were, a shift from the profane to the sacred. Caillois has demonstrated in this regard the parallels between, as well as the directly historical influences upon, the spheres of religion and 'play'.[50]

One might hazard the guess that bracketing markers tend to be regarded by everyday actors as particularly important when the activities that occur during the encounter, or upon a social occasion, are treated by the parties involved as particularly divergent from the normal expectations of everyday life. Goffman gives this example. In a medical examination of the naked body, or in the drawing of the same object in an art class, the individual does not usually shed his or her clothes in the presence of the other or others, or dress again in their presence at the conclusion of the encounter. Undressing and dressing in private allow the body to be suddenly exposed and hidden, both marking the boundaries of the episode and conveying that the actions stand separate from sexual or other connotations that might otherwise be read into them. This is part of what Goffman calls the 'keying' of encounters and suggests a close connection with Wittgenstein's discussions of the interweaving of forms of life. The occurrence of encounters, marked and given a definite social 'hue' or 'ethos', allows for transformations of a multiplicity of episodes into divergent 'types'.

> We (and a considerable number of theys) have the capacity and inclination to use concrete, actual activity — activity that is meaningful in its own right — as a model upon which to mark transformations for fun, deception, experiment, rehearsal, dream, fantasy, ritual, demonstration, analysis and charity. These lively shadows of events are geared into the ongoing world but not in quite the close way that is true of ordinary, literal activity.[51]

Most of the encounters that comprise the seriality of social life take place either outside (in time-space) or against the backdrop of the gatherings found on social occasions. Face engagements in many of these contexts do not involve clear enclosures which cut off the interaction from non-participants. In such circumstances the reflexive monitoring of the body, of gesture and positioning, are characteristically used to produce a 'conventional engagement closure'.[52] That is to say, a normatively sanctioned 'barrier' separates those engaged in the encounter from others who are co-present. This is a collaborative work, in which participants in the face engagement and bystanders — often, of course, involved in their own engagements with other parties — sustain a sort of 'civil inattention' towards one another. Goffman indicates various ways in which this may be achieved and how it may be dislocated. As in all areas of the mutual monitoring of interaction, there are extraordinarily complex features even to the manifestation of 'inattention'. Thus bystanders are usually expected not only not to exploit a situation of proximity of presence, whereby they could follow what is going on in other face engagements, but also actively to demonstrate inattention. This can be problematic. For if inattention is too studied, the effect may be to suggest that the individual is in fact eavesdropping.

All sorts of complications of these phenomena are possible. There may be many circumstances in which an individual may be interested in overhearing the content of an encounter and may very deliberately simulate inattention. However, this runs the risk of being noticed because of an artificiality of posture or because of a host of other traits that can give away what is going on. The point of this should not be taken to suggest, as many interpreters of Goffman have tended to do, that most of the marvelously subtle intricacies of interaction are studied or cynically manipulative. The opposite is the case. What is striking about the interaction skills that actors display in the production and reproduction of encounters is their anchoring in practical consciousness. Tact rather than cynicism is inherent in the structuration of encounters. While the content of what counts as 'being tactful' may vary widely, the significance of tact in otherwise very different societies or cultures is impossible to dispute. Tact — a latent conceptual agreement among participants in interaction contexts — seems to be the main mechanism that sustains 'trust' or ontological security over long time-space spans. Tact in the sustaining of conventional engagement enclosure becomes clearly pointed up in circumstances which threaten to fracture such closure. Thus in very constricted spaces, such as lifts, it is virtually impossible to sustain a posture of not listening. In Anglo-American society, at least, the tendency in such a situation is to suspend communication, with perhaps only the occasional comment that indicates that an encounter is suspended rather than broken off. Similarly, if three people are talking and one is interrupted to take a phone call, the others cannot feign complete inattention and may carry on a sort of hesitant, limp conversation.[53] Contexts of encounters such as these may directly express asymmetries of power. Thus if, say, two individuals in a lift continue to carry on their talk regardless of their surroundings of overly close proximity to others, it may very well be that they thereby demonstrate to those who are their subordinates or inferiors their indifference to the sustaining of civil inattention in such a context. However, they may nevertheless betray a certain concern about deviating from a norm that ordinarily would be observed, and hence they may talk even more loudly than they would in other circumstances.

Encounters involve 'spacing', as regards both the position of bodies in relation to one another, inside and outside the region of face engagement, and the serial spacing of contributions to the encounter in terms of seriality or turn-taking. Collaborative spacing within locales is obviously relevant to the bracketing of encounters (and, I shall try to indicate later, is subject to what Hägerstrand calls 'coupling constraints' and 'packing constraints'). The generalized normative sanctions influencing acceptable proximity of individuals in public places does vary cross-culturally, as do sanctions affecting the limits of acceptable bodily contact between persons in varying contexts. [54] But spacing can be effectively organized only within the limits of 'easy talk' — not so far apart that participants have to shout and not so close that the ordinary cues of facial expression, which help to monitor the sincerity and authenticity of what is said, cannot be observed. Face engagements, when others are co-present, are almost always carried on with some turning of the body away from those who are not party to the engagement, and the arrangement of bodies is such that there is no physical barrier to the free exchange of glances or visual contact. This may be difficult to achieve in crowded situations in which there is quite a lot of movement — at a party, for instance, or in a crowded train. In such contexts there may be some transitory relaxation of the sanctions which ordinarily control excessive mobility of the limbs. A person may quite acceptably sway the body about in this situation, if at the same time it is made clear to others that this is in order to sustain eye contact in an engagement where the positioning of others threatens to block the view. Such movements may be carried on in an exaggerated fashion, in fact, thus indicating to others that the actor making them is aware that such body motion would usually be looked upon as odd.

Turn-taking in encounters has been much studied by writers of an ethnomethodological bent.[55] Their work is often decried as trivial. But this is a short-sighted assessment indeed. For turn-taking is rooted in the most general properties of the human body and hence expresses fundamental aspects of the nature of interaction. Moreover, turn-taking is one major feature of the serial character of social life, hence connecting with the overall character of social reproduction. Turn-taking is one form of 'coupling constraint', deriving from the simple but elemental fact that the main communicative medium of human beings in situations of co-presence — talk — is a 'single-order' medium. Talk unfolds syntagmatically in the flow of the *durée* of interaction, and since only one person can speak at one time if communicative intent is to be realized, contributions to encounters are inevitably serial. It should be said that the empirical study of conversations shows that they have a much less symmetrical form than might be supposed. The managing of turn-taking rarely happens in such a way that participants finish sentences. There is a plethora of hesitation phenomena; speakers break into what another is saying, such that there are no clear divisions in the taking of turns and so on.[56]

Turn-taking may apply to the seriality of encounters as well as to the interaction between agents within encounters and may be again closely bound up with differentials of power. All organizations involve the co-ordination of interaction in flows of time-space relations 'channelled' through regularized contexts and locales (see pp. 119ff). Thus the process of organizing trials in the daily life of the courtroom has a formalized serial character, in which one case is heard, and bracketed as a definite social occasion, while the parties involved in the next are lined up in the adjoining waiting room. There are very many similar examples in societies of broad time-space distanciation. Sartre's discussion of seriality here has a direct connection with the seeming triviata of conversational turn-taking. Sartre points out that a banal example of seriality, a queue for a bus, can be used to demonstrate the mutual coupling of time-space relations of presence and absence:

> these separate people form a group, *in so far as* they are all standing on the same pavement, which protects them from the traffic crossing the square, *in so far as* they are grouped around the same bus stop, etc. . . . . They are all, or nearly all, workers, and regular users of the bus service; they know the timetable and frequency of the buses; and consequently they all wait for the *same* bus: say, the 7.49. This object in so far as they are dependent upon it (breakdowns, failures, accidents) *is in their present interest.* But this present interest — since they all live in the district — refers back to fuller and deeper structures of their general interest: improvement of public transport, freezing of fares, etc. The bus they wait for unites them, being their interest as individuals who *this morning* have business on the *rive droite*; but, as the 7.49, it is *their interest as commuters*; everything is temporalized: the traveller recognizes himself as a *resident* (that is to say, he is referred to the five or ten previous years), and then the bus becomes characterized by its daily eternal return (it is actually *the very same* bus, with the same driver and conductor). The object takes on a structure which overflows its pure inert existence; as such it is provided with a passive future and past, and these make it appear to the passengers as a fragment (an insignificant one) of their destiny.[57]

Talk, Reflexivity

Goffman's most telling contributions to understanding the sustaining and reproduction of encounters are to do with the relation between the reflexive control of the body — that is to say, the reflexive self-monitoring of gesture, bodily movement and posture — and the mutual co-ordination of interaction through tact and respect for the needs and demands of others. The prevalence of tact, trust or ontological security is achieved and sustained by a bewildering range of skills which agents deploy in the production and reproduction of interaction. Such skills are founded first and foremost in the normatively regulated control of what might seem, even more than turn-taking, to be the tiniest, most insignificant details of bodily movement or expression. This is readily demonstrated when these are lacking or are compromised, in a generic way among the 'mentally ill' and transitorily in bodily and verbal lapses or slips.

For Goffman 'mental illness', even the most serious forms of 'psychotic disturbance', are exemplified above all in inability, or unwillingness, to accept the diversity of minute (although wholly untrivial) forms of monitoring of bodily movement and gesture which are the normative core of day-to-day interaction. Madness is a cluster of 'situational improprieties'.[58] Psychotic behaviour diverges from, or actively clashes with, the public ordering of time-space relations, via the body and its media, whereby human beings 'get on with one another' in circumstances of co-presence. The 'mentally ill' do not conform to the extremely tight (and continuous) bodily control demanded of 'normal individuals'; they do not respect the intricacies of the formulae governing the formation, maintenance, breaking off or suspension of encounters; and they fail to contribute the manifold forms of tact that sustain 'trust'.[59] Individuals are very rarely expected 'just' to be co-present in gatherings and never are permitted to act thus in encounters. The reflexive monitoring of action, in contexts of co-presence, demands a sort of 'controlled alertness': as Goffman expresses it, actors have to 'exhibit presence'. This is exactly what many 'mental patients' — from those in a state of apparent catatonic stupor to those who move only mechanically, as if driven by some force, rather than being ordinary human agents — do not do.[60]

The exhibiting of presence takes quite artfully deliberate forms but is undeniably exemplified first and foremost in practical consciousness. Consider personal appearance and the visible marks of dress and bodily adornment. Concern with appearance is manifest, for example, in the care with which an individual selects and arranges types of clothing or adornment in relation to participation in particular contexts of activity. But it would be very misleading to suppose that such care is the prototypical mode of sustaining bodily idiom. More basic, more complex, is the chronic monitoring of the arrangement of clothing, in relation to bodily posture, in the presence of others. Thus 'mental patients' may sit slackly, their clothing disarranged or crumpled; women may not observe the usual expectation in Western societies, to keep the legs closely together when wearing skirts, and so on. There is a fundamental difference between bohemians or hobos, who flout the conventions of the wider society in their modes of dress and other modes of conduct, and the 'mentally ill'. For the normative expectations in which bodily control and appearance are grounded concern not merely the trappings of adornment or gross parameters of motor behaviour but precisely the kind of 'sustained control' which simultaneously 'carries' and demonstrates agency.

That such chronic self-monitoring is not undemanding is indicated by the pervasive importance of 'back regions' — found in varying contexts in all societies — in which control of bodily posture, gesture and apparel can be in some degree relaxed. But even when alone an individual may maintain presentability. For someone who is discovered inadvertently 'unassembled' cedes to others aspects of self that are perhaps only visible at such moments.[61] The point is that the sustaining of 'being seen as a capable agent' is intrinsic to what agency is, and that the motives which prompt and reinforce this connection as inherent in the reproduction of social practices are the *same* as those which order such reproduction itself. The strongly sanctioned character of these phenomena is well brought out in the following observations:

> Bodily idiom, then, is conventionalized discourse. We must see that it is, in addition, a normative one. That is, there is typically an obligation to convey certain information when in the presence of others and an obligation not to convey other impressions . . . Although an individual can stop talking, he cannot stop communicating through body idiom . . . Paradoxically, the way in which he can give least information about himself — although this is still appreciable — is to fit in and act as persons of his kind are expected to act.[62]

Many 'mental patients' have difficulty with, or flout, the norms associated with the opening and closing of encounters. Thus a person on the ward of an asylum may hold one of the staff in an encounter no matter how many indications the staff member may give that he or she wishes to move on. The patient may pursue the other closely, regardless of how rapidly the person walks, and might then try to accompany the orderly through the door at the end of the ward, even if it is a locked ward. At such a point the staff member may have physically to restrain the patient from following, perhaps tearing himself or herself away from the other's grasp. Such events, which are characteristic features of daily life on the wards, tend to run counter to the presumption of general communality of interest which staff ordinarily wish to foster. The final precipitous departure of the staff member exemplifies circumstances which, in the world outside, are likely to occur only where the individual attempting to leave in such a manner is demonstrating rejection of a strong moral tie — e.g. a love relationship — to which the pursuer lays claim. Such an implication, of course, is not necessarily lost upon the 'mental patient' on the ward of a hospital. Indeed, many apparently bizarre elements of encounters between the sane and the mad seem to represent 'experiments' which the latter carry out upon the usual frameworks of encounters. 'Schizophrenics', as Laing says, are perhaps aptly regarded as taking seriously, on the level of practical consciousness and in their actual conduct, some of the questions that philosophers pose hypothetically in the solitude of their studies. They really worry about, and build their activities around, heterodox solutions to questions such as 'In what sense am I a person?', 'Does the world only exist in so far as I perceive it?' and so on.[63] But most of the 'experimental activities' of the mad, significantly, are to do with the cueings and the normative sanctions associated with the complexities of bodily control within the immediacies of encounters. Garfinkel's 'experiments with trust' duplicate some of the jarring feelings of disquietude which 'normal' individuals experience when the routines of daily life are called in question.[64]

Many of these considerations apply to talk as the discursive medium of communicative intent in contexts of co-presence. Discussion of 'response cries' (forms of utterance that are not talk) can provide an appropriate transition to the study of talk. Such cries demonstrate once more that what may seem entirely trivial and wholly 'spontaneous' characteristics of human conduct are tightly ordered nomatively. Response cries transgress the normative sanctions against not talking to oneself in public. Consider 'Oops!'[65] 'Oops!' might be thought of as a pure reflex, a mechanical response like blinking the eyes when someone moves a hand sharply towards another's face. But this seemingly involuntary reaction lends itself to detailed analysis in terms of agency and the body. When someone exclaims 'Oops!' on dropping something or knocking something over it might appear at first sight as if the sound advertises a loss of control, thus drawing attention to an inference which the person would wish to avoid, a dislocation in the routine forms of control that indicate reflexively monitored agency. But the exclamation in fact shows to others that the occurrence in question is a mere accident, for which the individual cannot be held responsible. 'Oops!' is used by the agent to display that the lapse is only that, a momentary and contingent event, rather than a manifestation of either a more generalized incompetence or some opaque intent. But this also hides a range of other subtle shadings and possibilities. Thus, for example, 'Oops!' is used — and is known to be used — only in situations of minor failure rather than in those of major calamity. Hence 'Oops!', spontaneous and immediate though it may be, demonstrates care and attention to the implications of the sudden occurrence and therefore indicates overall competence which overrides what is thereby exhibited to be only a minor slip.

There is more. 'Oops!' can be construed as a warning to others. A hazard exists in the *milieu* of co-presence, and others in the vicinity would do well to take care. When someone has a minor mishap the exclamation 'Oops!' may sometimes be offered by a participant rather than by the individual experiencing it. The 'Oops!' perhaps sounds a warning to the other at the same time as conveying the assurance that the slip will not be treated by the observer as compromising the other's competence as a responsible agent. 'Oops!' is normally a curt sound. But the 'oo' in it may be more prolonged in some situations. Thus someone may extend the sound to cover a part of a task or enterprise in which a particular hazardous moment has to be overcome for its successful execution. Or a parent may utter an extended 'Oops!' or 'Oopsadaisy!' when playfully tossing a child in the air, the sound covering the phase when the child may feel a loss of control, reassuring it and perhaps at the same time helping to facilitate a developing understanding of the nature of response cries.[66]

'Oops!' thus turns out to be not as distant from talk as might initially be supposed, since it participates in that very public character of communication, intersecting with practices, which Wittgenstein identifies as the foundation of language use. In the light of the preceding discussion in this chapter, it should be clear that the indexicality of ordinary language is a 'problem' neither for lay speakers nor for philosophical analysis. 'Indexicality' means 'contextuality': the contextuality of talk, like the contextuality of bodily posture, gesture and movement, is the basis upon which such phenomena are co-ordinated as encounters extending in time-space. Talk is an intrinsic feature of nearly all encounters and also displays similarities of systemic form. Talk ordinarily manifests itself as conversation. 'Conversation' admits of a plural, which indicates that conversations are episodes having beginnings and endings in time-space. Norms of talk pertain not only to what is said, the syntactical and semantic form of utterances, but also to the routinized occasions of talk. Conversations, or units of talk, involve standardized opening and closing devices, as well as devices for ensuring and displaying the credentials of speakers as having the right to contribute to the dialogue. The very term 'bracketing' represents a stylized insertion of boundaries in writing. Let me give Goffman the last word in the bracketing that constitutes this section. What is talk, viewed interactionally? 'It is an example of that arrangement by which individuals come together and sustain matters having a ratified, joint, current, and running claim upon attention, a claim which lodges them together in some sort of intersubjective, mental world.'[67]

Positioning

Social systems, I have emphasized, are organized as regularized social practices, sustained in encounters dispersed across time-space. The actors whose conduct constitutes such practices are 'positioned', however. All actors are positioned or 'situated' in time-space, living along what Hägerstrand calls their time-space paths, and they are also positioned relationally, as the very term 'social position' suggests. Social systems only exist in and through the continuity of social practices, fading away in time. But some of their structural properties are best characterized as 'position-practice' relations.[68] Social positions are constituted structurally as specific intersections of signification, domination and legitimation which relates to the typification of agents. A social position involves the specification of a definite 'identity' within a network of social relations, that identity, however, being a 'category' to which a particular range of normative sanctions is relevant.

Since Linton the concept of social position has ordinarily been associated with that of role, and the latter has received far more

G

discussion and analysis than the former.[69] I do not intend to survey this discussion, only to emphasize some reservations about the notion of role. The concept is connected with two apparently opposed views, about each of which I have some unease. One is that of Parsons, in whose theory role is fundamental as the point of connection between motivation, normative expectations and 'values'. This version of the role concept is much too closely bound up with the Parsonian theorem of the dependence of societal integration upon 'value consensus' to be acceptable. The other is the dramaturgical viewpoint fostered by Goffman, about which more will be said in the next chapter, for here we reach the limits of his views. The two conceptions might seem to be contrary to one another but actually have a definite affinity. Each tends to emphasize the 'given' character of roles, thereby serving to express the dualism of action and structure characteristic of so many areas of social theory. The script is written, the stage set, and actors do the best they can with the parts prepared for them. Rejecting such standpoints does not mean dispensing with the concept of role entirely, but it does imply regarding the 'positioning' of actors as a more important idea. For definitional purposes I shall adopt the formulation I have offered in a previous work. A social position can be regarded as 'a social identity that carries with it a certain range (however diffusely specified) of prerogatives and obligations that an actor who is accorded that identity (or is an "incumbent" of that position) may activate or carry out: these prerogatives and obligations constitute the role-prescriptions associated with that position.[70]

'Position' is best understood as 'positioning', allowing the second of these terms to mine a rich vein of meanings. Actors are always positioned in respect of the three aspects of temporality around which the theory of structuration is built. The positioning of agents in circumstances of co-presence is an elemental feature of the structuration of encounters. Positioning here involves many subtle modalities of bodily movement and gesture, as well as the more general motion of the body through the regional sectors of daily routines. The positioning of actors in the regions of their daily time-space paths, of course, is their simultaneous positioning within the broader regionalization of societal totalities and within intersocietal systems whose broadcast span is convergent with the geopolitical distribution of social systems on a global scale. The significance of positioning in this most rudimentary sense is obviously closely bound up with the level of time-space distanciation of societal totalities. In those societies in which social and system integration are more or less equivalent, positioning is only thinly 'layered'. But in contemporary societies individuals are positioned within a widening range of zones, in home, workplace, neighbourhood, city, nation-state and a worldwide system, all displaying features of system integration which increasingly relates the minor details of daily life to social phenomena of massive time-space extension.

Positioning in the time-space paths of day-to-day life, for every individual, is also positioning within the 'life cycle' or life path. The formation of an 'I' is perhaps founded on the original narcissism of a 'mirror phase' in personality development. The child forms the capability of becoming a reflexive agent through the positioning of the body in relation to its image. The very connotation of 'I' as a shifter necessarily relates self to positioning within the seriality of discourse and action. Positioning along the life path, of course, is always closely related to the categorizing of social identity. 'Childhood' and 'adulthood', among a number of other possible forms of age grading, always mingle biological and social criteria of ageing. Differential positioning on the life path is the major constraining condition influencing the fundamental significance of the family in conjoining physical and social reproduction. A human society in which all members were born as a single age cohort would be impossible, since the human infant has such a long period of more or less complete dependency upon the ministrations of its elders.[71]

But it is the intersection between these forms of positioning and that within the *longue durée* of institutions which creates the overall framework of social positioning. Only in the context of such intersection within institutionalized practices can modes of time-space positioning, in relation to the duality of structure, be properly grasped. In all societies it seems to be the case that age (or age grade) and gender are the most all-embracing criteria of attributes of social identity. But although it is common in the sociological literature to speak of age roles, gender roles and so on in a generic way, I shall not follow such usage. Social identity conferred by age or gender — and other supposedly 'ascriptive' characteristics, such as skin pigmentation — tend to be the focus of so many aspects of conduct that to employ the term 'role' to describe them is both misleading and superficial.[72] The notion of role, as many critics of its profligate use in the social sciences have pointed out, has some conceptual precision only if applied in contexts of social interaction in which the normative rights and obligations associated with a specific identity are relatively clearly formulated. As its dramaturgical origins indicate, it is useful to speak of role only when there are definite settings of interaction in which in the normative definition of 'expected' modes of conduct is particularly strongly pronounced. Such settings of interaction are virtually always provided by a specific locale or type of locale in which regularized encounters in conditions of co-presence take place.[73] Settings of this sort tend to be associated with a more clear-cut closure of relationships than is found in social systems as a whole.

'Positioning' gets at what I shall call the contextualities of interaction and allows us to spell out, in a direct way, the relevance of Goffman's work for structuration theory. All social interaction is *situated* interaction — situated in space and time. It can be understood as the fitful yet routinized occurrence of encounters, fading away in time and space, yet constantly reconstituted within different areas of time-space. The regular or routine features of encounters, in time as well as in space, represent institutionalized features of social systems. Routine is founded in tradition, custom or habit, but it is a major error to suppose that these phenomena need no explanation, that they are simply repetitive forms of behaviour carried out 'mindlessly'. On the contrary, as Goffman (together with ethnomethodology) has helped to demonstrate, the routinized character of most social activity is something that has to be 'worked at' continually by those who sustain it in their day-to-day conduct. One of the most striking gaps in Goffman's writings is the absence of an account of motivation. In the preceding sections I have sought to remedy this by suggesting that trust and tact, as basic properties which participants bring to encounters, can be interpreted in terms of the relation between a basic security system, the sustaining (in *praxis*) of a sense of ontological security, and the routine nature of social reproduction which agents skilfully organize. The monitoring of the body, the control and use of face in 'face work' — these are fundamental to social integration in time and space.

It is of the first importance to emphasize that a theory of routine is not to be equated with a theory of social stability. The concern of structuration theory is with 'order' as the transcending of time and space in human social relationships; routinization has a key role in the explication of how this comes about. Routine persists through social change of even the most dramatic type, even if, of course, some aspects of taken-for-granted routines may be compromised. Processes of revolution, for example, no doubt usually dislocate the daily activities of multitudes of people who either are caught up in the fervour of revolt or are the luckless victims of social events which they have had no part in initiating. But it is in circumstances in which the texture of day-to-day life is attacked frontally and systematically deformed — as in the concentration camps — that the hold of routine is more substantively broken. Even here, as Bettelheim demonstrates so well, routines, including those of an obnoxious sort, are re-established.

It is instructive to see the rules implicated in encounters, as Goffman suggests, as being clustered in frameworks or 'frames'. Framing may be regarded as providing the ordering of activities and meanings whereby ontological security is sustained in the enactment of daily routines. Frames are clusters of rules which help to constitute and regulate activities, defining them as activities of a certain sort and as subject to a given range of sanctions. Whenever individuals come together in a specific context they confront (but, in the vast majority of circumstances, answer without any difficulty whatsoever) the question 'What is going on here?' 'What is going on?' is unlikely to admit of a simple answer because in all social situations there may be many things 'going on' simultaneously. But participants in interaction address this question characteristically on the level of practice, gearing their conduct to that of others. Or, if they pose such an question discursively, it is in relation to one particular aspect of the situation that appears puzzling or disturbing. Framing as constitutive of, and constricted by, encounters 'makes sense' of the activities in which participants engage, both for themselves and for others. This includes the 'literal' understanding of events but also the criteria by which it is made plain that what is going on is humour, play, theatre and so on.

Primary frameworks of daily activity can be seen as those

generating 'literal' languages of description both for lay participants in encounters and for social observers. Primary frameworks vary widely in their precision and closure. Whatever its level of organization, a primary framework allows individuals to categorize an indefinite plurality of circumstances or situations so as to be able to respond in an appropriate fashion to whatever is 'going on'. Someone who finds that what is going on at a particular time and place is, say, a party, may be able to bring into play conduct of an apposite kind even if some aspects of the contexts are unfamiliar. Most of Goffman's work is to do with rules which allow for transitions to be made between primary and secondary frameworks. Thus the 'keys' in transformations are the formulae whereby an activity that is already meaningful in a primary framework is given a meaning in a secondary one[74] For example, a fight can be 'play', an apparently serious comment a joke. But exactly the same kind of analysis could be carried out to indicate the rules involved in transitions between different primary frameworks.

It would not be relevant to pursue the detail of Goffman's analysis of framing any further in this context. Let me instead briefly consider the significance which the discursive formulation of rules can have by taking a different piece of work, that of Wieder on 'telling the code'.[75] Wieder's research reports the results of a participant observation study in a residential unit for rehabilitating paroled prisoners. The inmates spoke of the existence of rules of conduct which they called the 'code'. The code was explicitly verbalized but not, of course, formalized in written form as it was established and co-ordinated by inmates, not the staff. No inmate could apparently recite all the maxims making up the code, but all could mention some, and the code was frequently discussed. It was made up of such rules as: do not 'snitch' (inform about other inmates to staff); do not 'cop out' (i.e., admit guilt or responsibility for an act defined by staff as illegitimate); do not steal from other inmates; share with others any unexpected gifts or benefits which might be received; and so on. Staff knew the code too and made use of it in their dealings with inmates. As Wieder says, 'It was used as a wide-reaching scheme of interpretation which "structured" their environment.'[76] But, as he also points out, its verbalization meant that it was invoked in ways that implicitly formulated rules cannot be. It formed a 'vocabulary of motive' whereby both staff and inmates interpreted actions, especially deviant or problematic ones. It was not treated simply as a description of what was tacitly acknowledged; rather, the circumstances in which the code was called upon could be altered by the fact of invoking it. 'Telling the code' meant, as the phrase sounds, not only reporting upon what the code is but reprimanding those who contravened it; it exhibited the code as a control device, that exhibiting being part of how it in fact operated as such. I would suggest that this is characteristic of 'rule interpretations' discursively offered in many social contexts.

Rules applied reflexively in circumstances of co-presence are never limited in their implications to specific encounters but apply to the reproduction of the patterning of encounters across time and space. The rules of language, of primary and secondary framing, of the conduct of interpersonal interaction all apply over large arenas of social life, although they cannot be taken as necessarily coextensive with any given 'society'. Here we have to give some attention to conceptually differentiating between 'social interaction' and 'social relations' (although I shall not always be particularly careful to separate them subsequently). Social interaction refers to encounters in which individuals engage in situations of co-presence, and hence to social integration as a level of the 'building blocks' whereby the institutions of social systems are articulated. Social relations are certainly involved in the structuring of interaction but are also the main 'building blocks' around which institutions are articulated in system integration. Interaction depends upon the 'positioning' of individuals in the time-space contexts of activity. Social relations concern the 'positioning' of individuals within a 'social space' of symbolic categories and ties. Rules involved in social positions are normally to do with the specification of rights and obligations relevant to persons having a particular social identity, or belonging in a particular social category. The normative aspects of such rules, in other words, are particularly pronounced, but all the previously stated characteristics of rules apply to them too. They may, for example, be tacitly followed rather than discursively formulated. There are many such cases in the anthropological literature. An instance is cultures in which there is unilateral cross-cousin marriage. Although the members of these cultures obviously have some ideas which they put into effect about who marries who, the rules of eligibility that they are in fact following in their behaviour are tacit rather than explicit.

Goffman demonstrates that social integration depends upon the reflexively applied procedures of knowledgeable agents, but he does not indicate in any effective way what are the limits or the bounds of such knowledgeability, nor does he indicate the forms which such knowledgeability takes. I want to pose such a question here: in what sense are agents 'knowledgeable' about the characteristics of the social systems they produce and reproduce in their action?

Let us presume that 'knowledge' equals accurate or valid awareness — I do not say 'belief', because beliefs are only one aspect of knowledgeability. It does not make sense to treat practical consciousness as exhaustively constituted by propositional beliefs, although some elements could in principle be thus formulated. Practical consciousness consists of knowing the rules and the tactics whereby daily social life is constituted and reconstituted across time and space. Social actors can be wrong some of the time about what these rules and tactics might be — in which cases their errors *may* emerge as 'situational improprieties'. But if there is any continuity to social life at all, most actors must be right most of the time; that is to say, they know what they are doing, and they successfully communicate their knowledge to others. The knowledgeability incorporated in the practical activities which make up the bulk of daily life is a constitutive feature (together with power) of the social world. What is known about the social world by its constituent actors is not separate from their world, as in the case of knowledge of events or objects in nature. Testing out just what it is that actors know, and how they apply that knowledge in their practical conduct (which lay actors engage in as well as social observers), depends upon using the same materials — an understanding of recursively organized practices — from which hypotheses about that knowledge are derived. The measure of their 'validity' is supplied by how far actors are able to co-ordinate their activities with others in such a way as to pursue the purposes engaged by their behaviour.

There are, of course, potential differences between knowledge of the rules and tactics of practical conduct in the *milieux* in which the agent moves and knowledge about those which apply

[margin note: In a secular age]

in contexts remote from his or her experience. How far the agent's social skills allow immediate ease in culturally alien contexts is obviously variable — as, of course, is the meshing of different forms of convention expressing divergent boundaries between cultures or societies. It is not just in knowledge — or belief claims — which agents are able to formulate discursively that they display awareness of broader conditions of social life over and above those in which their own activities take place. It is often in the manner in which routine activities are carried on, for example, that actors in circumstances of marked social inferiority make manifest their awareness of their oppression. Goffman's writings are replete with commentaries on this type of phenomenon. But in other respects when we speak of 'the knowledge actors have of the societies of which they are members' (and others of which they are not), the reference is to discursive consciousness. Here there is no logical difference between the criteria of validity in terms of which belief-claims (hypotheses, theories) are to be judged in respect of lay members of society and social observers.

What — on a general plane, at any rate — are the types of circumstance that tend to influence the level and nature of the 'penetration' actors have of the conditions of system reproduction? They include the following factors:

(1) the means of access actors have to knowledge in virtue of their social location;
(2) the modes of articulation of knowledge;
(3) circumstances relating to the validity of the belief-claims taken as 'knowledge';
(4) factors to do with the means of dissemination of available knowledge.

Of course, the fact that all actors move in situated contexts within larger totalities limits the knowledge they have of other contexts which they do not directly experience. All social actors know a great deal more than they ever directly live through, as a result of the sedimentation of experience in language. But agents whose lives are spent in one type of *milieu* may be more or less ignorant of what goes on in others. This applies not only in a 'lateral' sense — in the sense of spatial separation — but also in a 'vertical' one in larger societies. Thus those in elite groups may know very little about how others in less privileged sectors live, and vice versa. However, it is worth mentioning that vertical segregation of *milieux* is nearly always also a spatial segregation. In category (2) above I mean to refer both to how far belief claims are ordered in terms of overall 'discourses' and to the nature of different discourses. Characteristic of most common-sense, everyday claims to knowledge is that they are formulated in a fragmentary, dislocated way. It is not only the 'primitive' who is a *bricoleur*: much day-to-day talk among lay members of all societies is predicated upon claims to knowledge that are disparate or left unexamined. The emergence of discourses of social science, however, clearly influences all levels of social interpretation in societies where it has become influential. Goffman has a large audience, not limited to his professional sociological colleagues.

So far as (3) is concered, it is enough to point out that individuals may operate with false theories, descriptions or accounts both of the contexts of their own action and of the characteristics of more encompassing social systems. There are obvious sources of possible tension here between practical and discursive consciousness. These can have psychodynamic origins, in repressions which separate off or muddle the reasons why people act as they do and what they are inclined or able to say about those reasons. But obviously there can be more systematic social pressures that can influence how far false beliefs are held by the members of a society about features of that society. Particularly influential in respect of (4), it is almost needless to say, are the relations, historically and spatially, between oral culture and the media of writing, printing and electronic communication. All of the latter have made a difference not only to stocks of available knowledge but also to types of knowledge produced.

Critical Notes: Freud on Slips of the Tongue

As an example of some of the notions analysed in this chapter I propose to consider interpretations of slips of the tongue in discourse. What Freud calls 'parapraxes' (*Fehlleistungen*) refer not just to verbal infelicities but to miswriting, misreading, mishearing and to the temporary forgetting of names and other items. Freud treats these as belonging together in some part because the terms designating them have a similar root in German, all beginning with the syllable *Ver-* (*Versprechen, Verlesen, Verhören, Vergessen*). All parapraxes involve errors, but most refer to seemingly unimportant ones which are without lasting significance in the activities of the individuals who commit them. 'Only rarely', Freud writes, 'does one of them, such as losing an object, attain some degree of practical importance. For that reason, too, they attract little attention, give rise to no more than feeble emotions, and so on.'[1]* In fact, he tries to demonstrate, these minor infractions supply clues to key characteristics of the psychodynamics of personality.

Whether or not parapraxes do actually form a single class of errors I shall not be concerned to discuss here. I shall concentrate only upon slips of the tongue. Employing a classification established by the linguist Meringer and by Mayer, a psychiatrist (with whose views he otherwise disagrees), Freud mentions the following types of verbal error: *transpositions* (the 'Milo of Venus' instead of the 'Venus of Milo'); *pre-sonances* or *anticipations* ('es war mir auf der Schwest . . . auf der Brust so schwer' — 'Schwest' is a nonexistent word); *post-sonances* or *perseverations* ('ich fordere Sie *auf, auf* das Wohl unseres Chefs aufzutossen', rather than 'anzustossen'); *contaminations* ('er setzt sich auf den Hinterkopf', a combination of 'er setzt sich einen Kopf auf' and 'er stellt sich auf die Hinterbeine'); and *substitutions* ('ich gebe die Präparate in den Briefkasten', instead of 'Brütkasten').[2]

Meringer tried to explain these in terms of phases of neutral

*References may be found on p. 109.

excitation. When a speaker utters the first word of a sentence, a process of excitation, connected with anticipating the form of the utterance, is set in being. This process sometimes has the effect of disturbing later sounds in the utterance. Some sounds are physically more intense than others, and these can affect other sounds or words. To discover the source of slips of the tongue we therefore have to look for those sounds or verbalizations which have the highest physical valence. One way of doing this, according to Meringer, is to consider what is involved in searching for a forgotten word, such as someone's name. The first sound to come back into consciousness is always the one of greatest intensity before the word was forgotten. This is often, for example, the critical sound in the word or the vowel which is particularly accentuated. Freud will have little of this. In the case of forgotten words it is very rarely true that either the initial sound or the accentuated vowel is the first to be recalled. Speakers may sometimes believe this to be the case but in fact are usually wrong; Freud asserts that in the vast majority of instances the initial sound which the speaker utters in attempted recall is the wrong one.

As an instance of the latter phenomenon Freud's famous discussion of his own lapse of memory about the name of the painter Signorelli can be mentioned. Talking about the frescoes of the 'Four Last Things', Death, Judgement, Hell and Heaven, in Orvieto Cathedral. Freud found himself unable to recall the name of the artist. Rather than finding the name he was trying to remember, he could think only of the names 'Botticelli' and 'Boltraffio'. On being told the correct name by another person, he recognized it without any hesitation. The forgetting is not to be explained in terms of anything distinctive about the painter's name itself or any definite psychological aspect of the context in which Freud was trying to recall it. Freud was as familiar with one of the substitute names, 'Botticelli', as with 'Signorelli', and more familiar with 'Signorelli' than with the other mistaken name that occurred to him, 'Boltraffio'. Freud's inability to recall the word happened in the course of a casual conversation with a stranger while driving from Ragusa in Dalmatia to a place in Herzegovina.

Freud offers the following analysis of the phenomenon. The forgetting of the name was connected with the preceding topic which had been discussed in the conversation. Just prior to mentioning Orvieto, Freud and his travelling companion had been talking about the customs of the Turkish people living in Bosnia and Herzegovina. Freud was telling the other of the fatalistic attitude with which the Turks approach sickness and death. If a doctor tells them nothing can be done to save someone who is ill, their response is 'Herr [Sir], what is there to be said? If he could be saved, I know you would have saved him.'³ The words 'Bosnia', 'Herzegovina' and 'Herr' have an unconsciously charged association with 'Signorelli', 'Botticelli' and 'Boltraffio'. A second anecdote lay close to the first in Freud's mind. In contrast to their quiescence in the face of death, the Turkish people in question display great agitation when afflicted by sexual disorders. Thus one said: 'Herr, you must know that if *that* comes to an end, then life is of no value.' Freud had suppressed this anecdote from his account, since he was talking to a stranger. He thereby diverted his attention from thoughts which might have been provoked in his mind by the themes of death and sexuality. He had recently received an unfortunate piece of news while staying at Trafoi, a small village in the Tyrol. One of his patients, to whom Freud had devoted considerable attention and who was suffering from what Freud refers to as an 'incurable sexual disorder',⁴ had committed suicide. The similarity of the words 'Trafoi' and 'Boltraffio' indicated that this event had made itself felt psychologically in spite of Freud's decision not to mention it.

Having established this resemblance, Freud asserts, it is no longer possible to regard the forgetting of 'Signorelli' as a chance event; it was something that was (unconsciously) motivated. The item which Freud deliberately chose not to mention became displaced on to another element, the painter's name.

The connections established here⁵ indicate that the name 'Signorelli' became divided in two. One of the pairs of syllables, 'elli' occurs in unaltered form in one of the two names which came to Freud's mind. The other has become involved in a network of connections by means of the translation of 'Signor' into 'Herr'. A displacement has occurred between the names '*Her*zegovina and *Bos*nia — two places often spoken of together in the same phrase. Most of the connections which produced the forgetting have been forged below the level of consciousness. The suppressed topic and the factors that have brought to mind the substitute names do not have any manifest connections. The

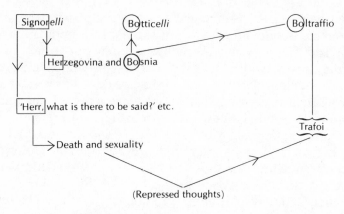

Figure 4

similarities involved do depend partly upon common sounds which the words possess, but these can be pieced together only when we understand that the forgetting is a result of repression. Not all instances of the forgetting of names, of course, are of this sort: 'By the side of simple cases where proper names are forgotten there is a type of forgetting which is motivated by repression.'[6]

A mechanism similar to his, Freud goes on to argue, exists in instances of slips of the tongue. Verbal errors may be of the type analysed by Meringer and Mayer, where one component of an utterance influences another, or they may be like the 'Signorelli' example, where the influences that produce the error come from outside the utterance and the immediate circumstances in which it is made. Both have their origins in a kind of 'excitation', but in the one case this is internal to the utterance or to the situation in which the words are said; in the other it is external to them. Only in the first type is there any possibility of explaining slips of the tongue in terms of a mechanism linking sounds and words to one another so that they influence articulation. Moreover, subjected to further scrutiny, the first type in fact evaporates. Slips of the tongue that seem at first blush to be simply the result of a 'contact effect of sounds' actually turn out on further investigation to depend upon outside (that is, motivated) influences.

Freud lists many examples of slips of the tongue, including the following:

(1) On the part of a woman patient: 'I shut up like a

Tassenmescher [a nonexistent word] — I mean *Taschen-messer* (pocket-knife).' Freud recognizes that there are difficulties of articulation with the word, but he points out the error to the patient and associates it with a name that impinges on unconscious anxieties.

(2) Another woman patient, asked how her uncle is, answers: 'I don't know. Nowadays I only see him *in flagrante*.' The phrase she meant to use is *en passant*. The term said in error is shown to relate to an episode in the patient's past.

(3) A young man addresses a woman in the street with the words: 'If you will permit me, madam, I should like to *begleit-digen* you.' He wants to accompany (*begleiten*) her but fears his offer would insult (*beleidigen*) her. As in the 'Signorelli' case, a concealed intention — the request not being a wholly innocent one on the man's part — leads to an unconsciously motivated slip of the tongue.

(4) During a disputatious meeting the chairman says: 'We shall now *streiten* (quarrel, instead of *schreiten*, proceed) to point four on the agenda.' The speaker's true view, which he intends to suppress, manifests itself in his verbal mistake.

(5) Someone is asked, 'What regiment is your son with?' The answer given is: 'With the 42nd Murderers' (*Mörder,* instead of *Mörser*, 'Mortars').

(6) A guest at a social occasion advances the opinion: 'Yes a woman must be pretty if she is to please men. A man is much better off; as long as he has his five straight limbs he needs nothing more!' This is one of numerous examples of what Meringer and Mayer called contaminations but which Freud regards as instances of the psychological process of condensation. The utterance is a fusion of two turns of phrase resembling each other in meaning: 'as long as he has his four straight limbs' and 'as long as he has his five wits about him'. Freud notes that, as in many slips of the tongue, the remark could pass as a joke. The difference lies simply in whether or not the speaker consciously intended the words to come out as they did.

(7) Reanalysis of one of the Meringer and Mayer examples: 'Es war mir auf der Schwest . . . auf der Brust so schwer.' This cannot be adequately explained by the anticipation of sounds. The slip of the tongue is probably to be interpreted

in terms of an unconscious association between 'Schwester' (sister), 'Bruder' (brother) and perhaps 'Brust der Schwester' (sister's breast).

Freud concludes: 'There must be a reason for every mistake in speaking.'[7] This includes other forms of speech disturbance besides slips of the tongue, such as stammering or stuttering. These phenomena are all symptoms of internal conflict which manifests itself as deformations of speech. Speech disturbances, Freud claims, do not appear in circumstances in which an individual is heavily engaged, such as a well-prepared address or a declaration of love.

> Ce qu'on conçoit bien
> S'annonce clairement
> Et les mots pour le dire
> Arrivent aisément.[8]

Does unconscious motivation exist in all cases of slips of the tongue? Freud believes such to be the case, for 'every time one investigates an instance of a slip of the tongue an explanation of this kind is forthcoming.'[9]

Let me now compare Freud on slips of the tongue with Goffman on radio talk[10] — a comparison which might seem unpromising but is actually very instructive for structuration theory. Goffman's concerns in his discussion are quite divergent from those of Freud, and rather than following the themes of his own argument I shall try to tease out its implications for assessing Freud's views on errors of speech. Radio and TV announcing is substantially different from ordinary conversation but just for that reason allows considerable insight into those circumstances. Announcers are not the authors of the scripts they read out. Their talk occurs as part of pre-planned sequences, from which they are not free to depart in anything save minor ways. At the same time announcers are expected to convey an impression of 'fresh talk' and to keep alive a sense of spontaneity in what they do. Meeting these inconsistent requirements is difficult, since they have to deliver their lines in a technically error-free way. The broadcaster's task is 'the production of seemingly faultless fresh talk'.[11]

Yet announcers do, of course, make slips of the tongue. Among the examples given by Goffman it is easy to find instances of the errors listed by Meringer and Mayer:

(1) 'In closing our TV Church of the Air, let me remind all of

our listeners that time wounds all heals' (transposition or Spoonerism).

(2) 'You are listening to the mucous of Clyde Lucas' (presonance).

(3) 'And now coming into the ball game for the Reds is number forty-four, Frank Fuller, futility infielder' (perseveration).

(4) 'This is the Dominion network of the Canadian Broad Corping Castration' (contamination).

(5) 'Word has just reached us that a home-made blonde exploded in the Roxy Theatre this morning' (substitution).

There are also numerous examples close to those listed by Freud, such as:

(1) 'Viceroys — if you want a good choke.'

(2) 'Beat the egg yolk and then add the milk, then slowly blend in the sifted flour. As you do you can see how the mixture is sickening.'

(3) 'And now, audience, here is our special TV Matinee guest that we've all been waiting for — world-famous author, lecturer and world traveller, a man about town. Mr, er, Mr. . . . . Oh! What the hell is his name?'

(4) 'So, friends, be sure to visit Frankie's restaurant for elephant food and dining.'

Most of these slips are humorous[12] and aptly reinforce Freud's point that joking and slips of the tongue have a close affinity. Although it is not possible to demonstrate this directly, such examples fit quite closely with Freud's interpretation of verbal parapraxes. The mispronounced or substituted words do not look simply like non-specific alternatives to those which should have been uttered. They are embarrassing in respect of the view that the broadcaster is supposed to convey; some have the 'only too true' connotations to them to which Freud calls attention; and others have a self-evidently sexual character. But consider two other forms of slips in radio talk:

(1) 'Ladies who care to drive by and drop off their clothes will receive prompt attention.'

(2) 'Folks, try our comfortable beds. I personally stand behind every bed we sell.'

(3) 'The loot and the car were listed as stolen by the Los Angeles Police Department.'

(4)   'And here in Hollywood it is rumoured that the former movie starlet is expecting her fifth child in a month.'

(1)   'Tums will give you instant relief and assure you no indigestion or distress during the night. . . . So try Tums and go to sleep with a broad . . . [turns page] smile.'

(2)   'It's time now, ladies and gentlemen, for our featured guest, the prominent lecturer and social leader, Mrs Elma Dodge. . . [Superman cut-in] who is able to leap buildings in a single bound.'

(3)   A local TV station showing a boxing match from Madison Square Garden interrupted the programme to report the death of a local politician. On cutting back to the fight, the announcer was saying: 'That wasn't much of a blow, folks!'

In these cases no slip of the tongue is involved, but they do otherwise take the form of parapraxes. Something has gone awry with what the speaker intended to convey. The second set of examples is interesting because if we did not know the circumstances in which they occurred, it would seem as though they contain typical 'only too true' utterances. No motive for them can be imputed, unless the producers responsible for cutting from one programme to the other somehow (consciously or otherwise) organized the sequencing to have the effects noted. The first category of slips are more difficult to interpret. It may be the case that these are unconsciously motivated ambiguities. But this seems unlikely. It is more probable that their ambiguous character would pass unnoticed by speakers and listeners alike if they were uttered within ordinary, everyday conversations. The point is not just that their ambiguous meanings are not immediately apparent but also that in everyday talk meanings other than those intended by speakers tend to be ruled out by contextual features of the conversation. Speakers are able to address themselves to the specific people with whom they are engaged, pre-selecting words and phrases so that possible alternative readings are excluded. Radio or TV announcers cannot do this because they speak to a generalized audience, that audience not being co-present with them.

Now, it would clearly be mistaken to regard radio talk as typical of talk in general. There are two reasons why slips of the tongue stand out much more prominently in radio talk than in day-to-day conversations. First, the discourse does not take place between co-present communicants. Disentangled from other cues, what is said becomes a more 'witnessable' phenomenon than it is when embedded in everyday activities. This is also true of many of Freud's examples of slips of the tongue, culled as they are from the therapeutic situation. The therapeutic encounter, after all, hardly exemplifies ordinary talk any more than broadcasting does. The words of the patient are treated as having a special significance, to be carefully scrutinized. Second, announcers are specialists in the production of flawless speech and are expected to be such by the nature of their profession. The main task of the performer is to present the script fluidly and clearly. It is only when we recognize how distinctive and unusual this relatively flawless speech mode is that we can begin to appreciate the contingencies of ordinary day-to-day talk. Both lay participants and linguists usually regard everyday talk as much more 'perfected' and 'ordered' than in fact it is. Summarizing recent work on the empirical study of conversations, Boomer and Laver comment:

> It is important to recognize that in speech 'normal' does not mean 'perfect'. The norm for spontaneous speech is demonstrably imperfect. Conversation is characterized by frequent pauses, hesitation sounds, false starts, misarticulations and corrections. . . . In everyday circumstances we simply do not hear many of our own tongue-slips nor those made by others. They can be discerned in running speech only by adopting a specialized 'proof-reader' mode of listening.[13]

In most circumstances of day-to-day conversations it is, in fact, very difficult indeed to distinguish slips of the tongue from the fragmented nature of virtually *all* the talk that goes on. As Goffman points out, for a particular utterance to be tested as a slip or as 'faulty', it has to be of a sort which the speaker would alter were he or she to begin the utterance again (or, of course, one that actually is altered or 'remedied'). It will not do to identify slips of the tongue by reference to an idealized model of enunciation or discourse. Moreover, to understand the character of day-to-day talk, we have to look at the other types of fault that may intrude. What are the implications of this?

First, as regards slips of the tongue, it may be argued that Meringer and Mayer were not as far off the mark as Freud tended to argue. Fromkin has demonstrated that mispronunciation of words manifests properties similar to those characteristic of 'correct' word production.[14] This does not show that such faults are not brought about by unconscious promptings, but it does suggest that there is usually no 'interruption' in the reflexive monitoring of speech production that necessarily needs to be invoked to explain slips of the tongue. The phenomena of pre-sonances and perseverations are also presumably directly bound up with the reflexive monitoring of speech. Words must characteristically be transferred from the brain to speech as syntagmatically ordered groupings, or else such speech distur-bances would not occur at all.

A second large category of faults concerns not individual speech production as such but turn-taking. A speaker may begin to talk before the utterance of another is concluded, either 'overlapping' with or directly interrupting the other; two participants might begin speaking simultaneously; each may 'back off' from speaking, producing an unwanted gap in the conventional flow. Just as in the case of individual speech faults, most such disjunctions pass completely unnoticed by speakers engaged in ordinary conver-sation. They are 'heard' only when, for example, a strip of speech is recorded so that they can be deliberately attended to. Here again day-to-day talk is not like radio talk, where overlaps, double uptakes, etc., are very noticeable. It is more often than not the case in conversations that overlap occurs, so that one speaker is beginning an utterance while another is finishing. But participants filter these out so that contributions to the conversation are heard as separate strips of talk.

Third, faulty talk which is recognized as such usually involves remedial procedures initiated either by the speaker or by the listeners. Correction by others seems relatively rare, partly because many imperfections which are phonological or syntactical slips when judged against an idealized grammatical model are not heard as such, but partly also because tact is exercised in respect of what might be taken to be the incompetencies of speakers. Remedial work done by speakers nearly always concerns turn-taking difficulties rather than slips of the tongue.

These observations tell us a good deal about what everyday

speech is like and confirm that verbal parapraxes cannot be interpreted against an idealized conception of 'correct' speech. Announcers' talk differs from the day-to-day use of language in so far as it does approximate to such a conception. The talk and the activities of announcers when they are on set in fact comes close to how human social life would be if it were actually like the portrayals given by objectivist social scientists. Most of what is said is programmed prior to transmission or screening and can be modified only in marginal ways by the agent following the script. The actor here does appear merely as a 'bearer' of pre-given patterns of social organization — or, as Goffman puts it, an 'animator', a 'sounding box from which utterances come'.[15] The vast majority of situations of talk (and of interaction) are simply not like this. The 'loose' or flawed character of day-to-day talk, or what appears as such when compared with an idealized model, is actually generic to its character as enmeshed in human *praxis*. What is remarkable, to put it another way, is not lack of technical polish in talk but the fact that conversations and the (always contingent) reproduction of social life have any symmetry of form at all. In day-to-day interaction the normative elements involved in communication in talk as the production of 'good speech' are hardly ever the main impelling interest of participants. Rather, talk is saturated with the practical demands of the routine enactment of social life.

Accepting this means recasting Freud's view. According to Freud, every slip of the tongue has a motivated origin and could in principle be explained if sufficient knowledge of the psychological make-up of the individual in question were available. Here we clearly discern an implied picture of well-ordered speech, from which slips of the tongue lead the speaker to depart. The standpoint I am advocating in effect turns this around. 'Well-ordered' speech, in the context of day-to-day conversations at least, is geared to the overall motivational involvements which speakers have in the course of pursuing their practical activities. 'Correct speech', in common with many other aspects of such activities, is not usually directly motivated — unless one is an announcer. It should be pointed out in parenthesis that on occasion disturbed speech may be so motivated. Thus in circumstances of mourning, a bereaved person who maintained ordinary standards of speech production might be thought hard-hearted and unfeeling. Where there are sanctions implying that people should manifest emotional agitation, speech disturbances, or alterations in normal modes of speech, may be one way of 'bringing off' such states.[16]

If most particular forms of language use are not directly motivated, then it follows that most slips of the tongue cannot be traced to unconscious motivation. Where does this leave us, then, as regards Freud's theory of verbal parapraxes? I would make the following suggestion. Freud's interpretation probably applies only in circumstances rather different from those he had in mind when formulating it. In Freud's view, slips of the tongue tend to be made above all in casual or routine situations, where nothing much hangs on what is said. On such occasions, the unconscious is likely to 'break through', as it were, and disturb the utterances that a speaker produces. I would hold that on these occasions — which make up most of social life — unconscious elements are actually least prone to influencing directly what is said. Routinization, involving the continual 'regrooving' of the familiar in circumstances of substantial ontological security, is the main condition of the effective reflexive monitoring by human beings of their activities. Anxiety concerning the actual form of speech will be heightened only when the actor has a specific interest in getting what he or she says 'exactly right'. This is what radio and TV announcers have to do. It is likely to be the case in a declaration of love, contrary to Freud's supposition. We can also readily make sense of the 'Signorelli' example and the forgetting of proper names generally as a motivated phenomenon. Proper names have a special significance which other words do not. To mispronounce someone's name or to call someone by the wrong name causes personal affront in a way that other vagaries of pronunciation do not. There is thus a special premium on getting names right, which perhaps means that the recall of names impinges more immediately on sources of anxiety than do other linguistic items. As I have pointed out, something similar applies to the therapeutic encounter as well.

References

Consciousness, Self and Social Encounters

1 A particularly useful discussion of these difficulties is to be found in Irving Thalberg, 'Freud's anatomies of the self', in Richard Wollheim, *Freud, A Collection of Critical Essays* (New York: Doubleday, 1974). A revised version of this essay appears in Wollheim and James Hopkins, *Philosophical Essays on Freud* (Cambridge: Cambridge University Press, 1982).

2 Quoted in Thalberg, 'Freud's Anatomies of the self', p. 156.

3 Freud, *An Outline of Psychoanalysis* (London, Hogarth, 1969), pp. 56–7.

4 P. F. Strawson, *The Bounds of Sense* (London: Methuen, 1966), pp. 162–70; G. E. M. Anscombe, 'The first person', in Samuel Guttenplan, *Mind and Language* (Oxford: Blackwell, 1972); J. L. Mackie, 'The transcendal "I"', in Zak Van Straaten, *Philosophical Subjects* (Oxford: Clarendon Press, 1980).

5 Stephen Toulmin, 'The genealogy of "consciousness"', in Paul F. Secord, *Explaining Human Behaviour* (Beverly Hills: Sage, 1982), pp. 57–8.

6 Ibid., pp. 60–1.

7 See J. S. Bruner, *Beyond the Information Given* (New York: Norton, 1973).

8 J. S. Gibson, *The Ecological Approach to Visual Perception* (Boston: Houghton Mifflin, 1979).

9 Ulric Neisser, *Cognition and Reality* (San Francisco: Freeman, 1976), p. 22. See also idem, *Memory Observed* (San Francisco: Freeman, 1982); John Shotter, '"Duality of structure" and "intentionality" in an ecological psychology', *Journal for the Theory of Social Behaviour*, vol. 13, 1983.

10 Neisser, *Cognition and Reality*, p. 29.

11 M. Wertheimer, 'Psychomotor coordination of auditory and visual space at birth', *Science*, vol. 134, 1962.

12 Neisser, *Cognition and Reality*, p. 72.

13 E. C. Cherry, 'Some experiments on the recognition of speech, with one and two ears', *Journal of the Acoustical Society of America*, vol. 25, 1953.

14 A. M. Treisman, 'Strategies and models of selective attention', *Psychological Review*, vol. 76, 1969.

15 J. A. Deutsch and D. Deutsch, 'Attention': some theoretical considerations', *Psychological Review*, vol. 70, 1963.

16 Neisser, *Cognition and Reality*, pp. 84–5.

17   *CPST*, pp. 120—3.
18   Erik H. Erikson, *Childhood and Society* (New York: Norton, 1963), pp. 15—16.
19   Ibid., p. 247.
20   Ernest Becker, *The Birth and Death of Meaning* (New York: Free Press, 1962), p. 95.
21   See also Erikson, *Childhood and Society*, p. 249; Harry Stack Sullivan, *The Interpersonal Theory of Psychiatry* (London: Tavistock, 1955), chapter 4. I do not accept Erikson's claim that these psychological phenomena can be directly related to the form of social institutions.
22   G. Piers and M. B. Singer, *Shame and Guilt* (Springfield: Addison, 1963). Here I repeat some observations originally made in relation to the theory of suicide; cf. *SSPT*, p. 393, footnote 32.
23   Erikson, *Childhood and Society,* p. 251.
24   Ibid., p. 256.
25   Dennie Wolf, 'Understanding others: a longitudinal case study of the concept of independent agency', in George E. Forman, *Action and Thought* (New York: Academic Press, 1982).
26   T. B. Brazelton *et al.,* 'The origins of reciprocity', in M. Lewis and L. Rosenblum, *The Infant's Effects on the Caregiver* (New York: Wiley, 1974).
27   L. S. Vygotsky, *Mind in Society* (Cambridge: Harvard University Press, 1978), pp. 20ff.
28   Erik H. Erikson, *Identity, Youth and Crisis* (London: Faber & Faber, 1968), chapter 5; idem, *Identity and the Life Cycle* (New York: International Universities Press, 1967).
29   Erikson, *Identity and the Life Cycle,* p. 19.
30   See ibid., chapter 3, 'The problem of ego-identity'.
31   Ibid., p. 102.
32   See *CPST,* pp. 123—8.
33   Bruno Bettelheim, *The Informed Heart* (Glencoe: Free Press, 1960), p. 14. Goffman's work on 'total institutions' overlaps at many points with the analysis given by Bethelheim: Goffman, *Asylums* (Harmondsworth: Penguin, 1961).
34   Bettelheim, *The Informed Heart,* p. 132.
35   Ibid., p. 148.
36   'Since old prisoners had accepted, or been forced to accept, a childlike dependency on the SS, many of them seemed to want to feel that at least some of the people they were accepting as all-powerful father images were just and kind', ibid., p. 172.
37   See the examples collected in William Sargant, *Battle for the Mind* (London: Pan, 1959).

38 M. Merleau-Ponty, *Phenomenology of Perception* (London: Routledge, 1974).

39 Ibid., p. 101.

40 L. Goldstein, *Language and Language Disturbances* (New York: Grune and Stratton, 1948).

41 Merleau-Ponty, *Phenomenology of Perception,* p. 104.

42 Ibid., p. 109.

43 Erving Goffman, *Behaviour in Public Places* (New York: Free Press, 1963), p. 17; idem, *Interaction Ritual* (London: Allen Lane, 1972), p. 1.

44 Cf. Ithiel De Sola Pool, *The Social Impact of the Telephone* (Cambridge, Mass.; MIT Press, 1981).

45 This seems to be the prevalent notion, for instance, in most of the contributions to Jason Ditton, *The View from Goffman* (London: Macmillan, 1980). See also Alasdair MacIntyre, *After Virtue* (London: Duckworth, 1981), pp. 108−9. Cf. R. Harré and P. F. Secord, *The Explanation of Social Behaviour* (Oxford: Blackwell, 1972), chapter 10.

46 Alvin W. Gouldner, *The Coming Crisis of Western Sociology* (London: Heinemann, 1971), pp. 379−81.

47 *CPST,* pp. 83−4, and *passim.*

48 Goffman, *Behaviour in Public Places,* p. 18.

49 Erving Goffman, *Frame Analysis* (New York: Harper, 1974), p. 252.

50 Roger Caillois, *Man, Play and Games* (London: Thames & Hudson, 1962); see also the famous work by Jan Huizinga, *Homo Ludens* (London: Routledge, 1952).

51 Goffman, *Frame Analysis,* p. 560. I shall not discuss here the epistemological questions which are broached, but hardly resolved, in Goffman's discussion in this book. They share a good deal in common with Schutz's ponderings over the nature of 'multiple realities', and with many other currents in modern philosophy concerned with the apparently relativistic implications of the mediation of frames of meaning. See *NRSM,* chapter 4.

52 Goffman, *Behaviour in Public Places,* pp. 156ff.

53 Ibid.

54 This theme, of course, has been much explored. The best-known work is Edward T. Hall, *The Silent Language* (New York: Doubleday, 1959); see also the same author's *The Hidden Dimension* (London: Bodley Head, 1966).

55 Harvey Sacks and Emmanuel A. Schegloff, 'A simplest systematics for the organisation of turn-talking in conversation', *Language,* vol. 50, 1974.

56   Cf. George Psathas, *Everyday Language: Studies in Ethnomethodology* (New York: Irvington, 1979).
57   Jean-Paul Sartre, *Critique of Dialectical Reason* (London: New Left Books, p. 259).
58   Goffman, *Interaction Ritual,* pp. 141ff.
59   Habermas, *Theorie des kommunikativen Handelns* (Frankfurt: Suhrkamp, 1981), vol. I, section 3.
60   Goffman, *Behaviour in Public Places,* p. 25.
61   Cf. the general discussion of politeness in Penelope Brown and Stephen Levinson, 'Universals in language use: politeness phenomena', in Esther N. Goody, *Questions and Politeness* (Cambridge: Cambridge University Press, 1978).
62   Goffman, *Behaviour in Public Places,* p. 35. cf. John Blacking: *The Anthropology of the Body.* (London: Academic Press, 1977).
63   'I take many bodily feelings to be private. If I have a burn on my arm, I take the pain to be private, the sight to be public. This is not always so. Some people feel that they can actually *feel* another person's pain, or think directly another's thoughts, and may feel that other people can feel their bodily feelings, or actually be thinking their thoughts', R. D. Laing, *Self and Others* (London: Penguin, 1971), p. 34.
64   Harold Garfinkel, 'A conception of, and experiments with, "trust" as a condition of stable concerted actions', in O. J. Harvey, *Motivation and Social Interaction* (New York: Ronald Press, 1963).
65   Erving Goffman, *Forms of Talk* (Oxford: Blackwell, 1981), pp. 101ff.
66   Ibid., p. 103.
67   Ibid., pp. 70−1.
68   Roy Bhaskar, *The Possibility of Naturalism* (Brighton: Harvester, 1979), pp. 51−2.
69   For a recent example − among very many others − see Bruce J. Biddle, *Role Theory* (New York: Academic Press, 1979).
70   *CPST,* p. 117.
71   Ibid.
72   A point often made in the controversy over role theory in Germany some two decades ago. A contribution that retains its interest is F. H. Tenbrük: 'Zur deutschen Rezeption der Rollenanalyse', *Kölner Zeitschrift fur Soziologie,* vol. 3, 1962.
73   Cf. Nigel Thrift, 'Flies and germs: a geography of knowledge', in Derek Gregory and John Urry, *Social Relations and Spatial Structures* (London: Macmillan, 1984).
74   Cf. William Labov, 'Rules for ritual insults', in David Sudnow, *Studies in Social Interaction* (New York: Free Press, 1972).

75   D. Lawrence Wieder, 'Telling the code', in Roy Turner, *Ethnomethodology* (Harmondsworth: Penguin, 1974).

76   Ibid., p. 149.

Critical Notes: Freud on Slips of the Tongue

1   Sigmund Freud, *Introductory Lectures on Psychoanalysis* (Harmondsworth: Penguin, 1974), p. 51.

2   R. Meringer and C. Mayer, *Versprechen und Verlesen* (Vienna, 1895).

3   Freud, *The Psychopathology of Everyday Life* (Harmondsworth: Penguin, 1975), p. 39.

4   Ibid., p. 40.

5   Originally published in Freud's article, 'The physical mechanism of forgetfulness' (1890); see the Standard Edition, vol. 3.

6   Freud, *The Psychopathology of Everyday Life*, p. 44.

7   Ibid., p. 135.

8   Boileau, *Art poétique*, quoted in ibid., p. 148.

9   Freud, *Introductory Lectures on Psychoanalysis*, p. 71.

10   Erving Goffman, 'Radio talk: a study of the ways of our errors', in *Forms of Talk* (Oxford: Blackwell, 1981).

11   Ibid., p. 242.

12   They were no doubt selected for this reason. Most of Goffman's material comes from collections of 'bloopers' edited by Kermit Schafer, such as *Prize Bloopers* (Greenwich: Fawcett, 1965).

13   Donald S. Boomer and John D. M. Laver, 'Slips of the tongue', *British Journal of Disorders of Communication*, vol. 3, 1968, p. 2.

14   Victoria A. Fromkin, 'The non-anomalous nature of anomalous utterances', *Language*, vol. 47, 1971.

15   Goffman, *Forms of Talk*, p. 226.

16   As indicated by Goffman. ibid., pp. 223ff.

3
Time, Space and Regionalization

Time-Geography

I have concentrated in the preceding chapter upon specifying certain psychological qualities of the agent and upon analysing interaction in situations of co-presence. The positioning of actors in contexts of interaction, and the interlacing of those contexts themselves, is elemental to such concerns. But to show how these matters relate to broader aspects of social systems it is necessary to consider how social theory should confront — in a concrete rather than an abstractly philosophical way — the 'situatedness' of interaction in time and space.

Most social analysts treat time and space as mere environments of action and accept unthinkingly the conception of time, as mensurable clock time, characteristic of modern Western culture. With the exception of the recent works of geographers — of which more in a moment — social scientists have failed to construct their thinking around the modes in which social systems are constituted across time-space. As I have indicated earlier, investigation of this issue is one main task imposed by the 'problem of order' as conceptualized in the theory of structuration. It is not a specific type or 'area' of social science which can be pursued or discarded at will. It is at the very heart of social theory, as interpreted through the notion of structuration, and should hence also be regarded as of very considerable importance for the conduct of empirical research in the social sciences.

Fortunately, we do not need to tackle these issues *de novo*. Over the past few years there has taken place a remarkable convergence between geography and the other social sciences, as a result of which geographers, drawing upon the various

established traditions of social theory, have made contributions to social thought of some significance. Most such writings, I think it would be true to say, remain unknown to the majority of those working in the rest of the social sciences, although they contain ideas of very general application. Some of these contributions are to be found in the work of Hägerstrand, but they are by no means confined to his writings and those of his immediate colleagues.[1]*
In previous analyses of the theory of structuration I have mentioned the significance of this approach without confronting it directly or trying to point out its limitations. But in this expanded exposition I shall do so.

Time-geography, as formulated by Hägerstrand, takes as its starting-point the very phenomenon which I have much stressed — the routinized character of daily life. This is in turn connected with features of the human body, its means of mobility and communication, and its path through the 'life-cycle' — and therefore with the human being as a 'biographical project'. As I have mentioned before, Hägerstrand's approach is based mainly upon identifying sources of constraint over human activity given by the nature of the body and the physical contexts in which activity occurs. Such constraints provide the overall 'boundaries' limiting behaviour across time-space. Hägerstrand has formulated these in various different ways, but his characteristic emphasis is upon the following factors.[2]

(1) The indivisibility of the human body, and of other living and inorganic entities in the *milieux* of human existence. Corporeality imposes strict limitations upon the capabilities of movement and perception of the human agent.

(2) The finitude of the life span of the human agent as a 'being towards death'. This essential element of the human condition gives rise to certain inescapable demographic parameters of interaction across time-space. For this reason if no other, time is a scarce resource for the individual actor.

(3) The limited capability of human beings to participate in more than one task at once, coupled with the fact that every task has a duration. Turn-taking exemplifies the implications of this sort of constraint.

*References may be found on pp. 158—61.

(4)   The fact that movement in space is also movement in time.
(5)   The limited 'packing capacity' of time-space. No two human bodies can occupy the same space at the same time; physical objects have the same characteristic. Therefore any zone of time-space can be analysed in terms of constraints over the two types of objects which can be accommodated within it.

These five facets of 'time-geographic reality', according to Hägerstrand, express the material axes of human existence and underlie all contexts of association in conditions of co-presence.[3] Examined as resources (and thus, I would say, implicated in both the generation and the distribution of power), such factors condition the webs of interaction formed by the trajectories of the daily, weekly, monthly and overall life paths of individuals in their interactions with one another. The trajectories of agents, as Hägerstrand puts it, 'have to accommodate themselves under the pressures and the opportunities which follow from their common existence in terrestrial space and time'.[4]

Hägerstrand's generalized conception of time-geography originated in a long-term series of studies of a local parish in Sweden. The area in question boasted comprehensive population statistics, enabling him to trace all the individuals who had lived there, and had moved in and out of the area, for a period of something like a hundred years. Ordering these data as lifetime biographies, he sought to analyse them as composing life paths in time-space that could be charted using a particular form of notation. The typical patterns of movement of individuals, in other words, can be represented as the repetition of routine activities across days or longer spans of time-space. Agents move in physical contexts whose properties interact with their capabilities, given the above constraints, at the same time as those agents interact with one another. Interactions of individuals moving in time-space compose 'bundles' (encounters or social occasions in Goffman's terminology) meeting at 'stations' or definite time-space locations within bounded regions (e.g. homes, streets, cities, states, the outer limit of terrestrial space being the earth as a whole — save for the odd space traveller or two in the current age of high technology). Hägerstrand's dynamic 'time-space maps' are of definite interest and provide a graphic form that has relevance to situations well beyond those for which they have been used so far.

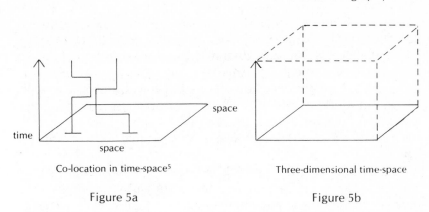

Co-location in time-space[5]	Three-dimensional time-space
Figure 5a	Figure 5b

Figures 5a and 5b show this in its simplest guise. Two individuals, say, live a mile apart in a neighbourhood; their time-space paths across the course of the day bring them into contact in an encounter of short duration in, say, a coffee house or restaurant, following which their activities again diverge. If the daily activities of a specific individual are recorded, it is easy to build up a gross characterization of his or her routine activities, in so far as these comprise trajectories in time and space. As a portrayal of a life path, this would involve generalized patterns of time-space movement within the 'life-cycle'. A person may live in the house of his or her parents, for example, until establishing a new residence on marriage. This may be associated with a change of job, such that both home and workplace, as 'stations' along the daily trajectory, become altered. Mobility within the housing market, marital separation or career progression, amid a host of other possible factors, may influence typical life paths.

The encounters into which individuals enter in the trajectories of daily life are subject to constraints deriving from the list indicated above. Hägerstrand acknowledges, of course, that agents are not merely mobile bodies but intentional beings with purposes, or what he calls 'projects'. The projects which individuals seek to realize, if they are to be actualized, have to utilize the inherently limited resources of time and space to overcome constraints which they confront. 'Capability constraints' are those of the sort listed above. Some affect primarily time distribution: for example, the need for sleep or for food at regular intervals ensures certain limits to the structuration of daily activities. 'Coupling constraints' refer to those that condition activities undertaken jointly with others. The volume of time-space available to an individual in a day is a prism bounding the pursuance of projects. Prisms of daily conduct are not just geographical or physical boundaries but have 'time-space walls on all sides'. The size of such prisms, of course, is also very strongly influenced by the degree of time-space convergence in the means of communication and transformation available to agents.

The notion of time-space convergence was introduced by another geographer, Janelle, to refer to the 'shrinking' of distance in terms of the time needed to move between different locations.[6] Thus the time taken to travel from the East Coast to the West Coast of the United States, in terms of available media, can be calculated as follows. On foot the journey would take more than two years; on horseback eight months; by stagecoach or wagon, four months; by rail in 1910, four days; by regular air services today, five hours; by the fastest jet transport, just over two hours. Time-space convergence can be plotted to describe the outer bounds of daily prisms. However, it is obvious that there are major discrepancies between and within social communities in terms of the constraints on mobility and communication affecting different groups and individuals. Seriality and turn-taking are built into most forms of transportation. Thus, for instance, an express train may connect two cities in a time of three hours. But the availability of seats may be limited, even for those able and willing to pay. Moreover, if a person misses the train, there may be only local trains for several hours until the next express, giving time-space convergence a 'palpitating' character.[7] Finally, for those in most societies, and for most of the days in an individual's life, mobility takes place within relatively constricted time-space prisms.

Palm and Pred provide one example, among many that exist in the literature, of an application of Hägerstrand's ideas: to the daily prism of 'Jane', an unmarried mother.[8] Figure 6 offers a representation of the prism of Jane's day-to-day activities. Jane cannot leave home for work before a certain hour of the day because of her child's dependence on her for feeding and other needs, and because the sole accessible nursery is not yet open. Jane has no car and hence is faced with severe capability and coupling constraints in reaching the two 'stations' of the nursery (N₁), and her place of work (W₁). Her choice of jobs is restricted by these constraints, and reciprocally the fact that she has little chance of acquiring or holding down a well-paid occupation reinforces the other constraints she faces in the trajectory of her

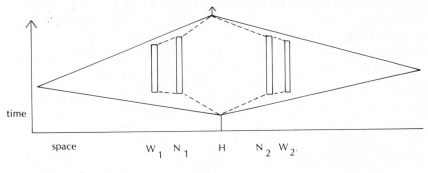

Figure 6

path through the day. She has to collect her child in mid-afternoon, before the nursery closes, and is thus effectively restricted to part-time employment. Suppose she has a choice of two jobs, one better-paid and offering the chance to run a car (W₂), making it possible for her to take her child to a nursery (N₂) further away from her home. On taking the more remunerative job, she finds that the time expended in driving to the nursery, to and from work and then back home (H) again does not allow her time to do other necessary tasks, such as shopping, cooking and housework. She may therefore feel herself 'forced' to leave the job for a low-paid, part-time alternative nearer home (W₁).

Hägerstrand has made a particular effort to employ time-geography to grasp the seriality of the life paths or 'life biographies' of individuals. A life biography, he says, is made up of 'internal mental experiences and events', 'related to the interplay between body and environmental phenomena'.[9] The conduct of an individual's day-to-day life entails that he or she successively associates with sets of entities emanating from the settings of interaction. These entities are: other agents, indivisible objects (solid material qualities of the *milieu* of action), divisible materials (air, water, minerals, foodstuffs) and domains. Domains

H

refer to what I prefer to call the regionalization of time-space: the movement of life paths through settings of interaction that have various forms of spatial demarcation. But the properties of domains can be subjected to direct study in terms of the coupling constraints which a given distribution of 'stations' and 'activity bundles' creates for the overall population whose activities are concentrated within those domains. Thus the nature of interacting social patterns within domains of time-space is limited by the overall organization of capability and coupling constraints. There are 'ecological' constraints which, as Carlstein has tried to show in detail, derive from three modes of 'packing':

(1)   the packing of materials, artefacts, organisms and human populations in settlement space-time;
(2)   the packing of time-consuming activities in population time-budgets;
(3)   the packing of bundles of various sizes, numbers and durations in the population system, i.e. group formation because of the indivisibility and continuity constraints of individuals.[10]

Critical Comments

The interest of time-geography to the theory of structuration is surely evident.[11] Time-geography is concerned with the constraints that shape the routines of day-to-day life and shares with structuration theory an emphasis upon the significance of the practical character of daily activities, in circumstances of co-presence, for the constitution of social conduct. We are able to begin to flesh out the time-space structuring of the settings of interaction which, however important Goffman's writings may be, tend to appear in those writings as given *milieux* of social life. Hägerstrand's concentration upon everyday social practices is very pronounced and clear; he wishes to use time-geography, he insists, to understand 'the impact of the ordinary day of the ordinary person' upon the overall organization of social systems.[12] But time-geography has some very distinct shortcomings, some of which, I hope, are apparent from the preceding discussion in this book.

The main reservations one must have about time-geography are the following. First, it operates with a naive and defective conception of the human agent. In stressing the corporeality of the human being in structured time-space contexts, Hägerstrand's ideas accord closely with those I have sought to elaborate previously. But he tends to treat 'individuals' as constituted independently of the social settings which they confront in their day-to-day lives. Agents are regarded as purposive beings in the sense that their activities are guided by 'projects' which they pursue. But the nature and origin of projects is left unexplicated. Second, Hägerstrand's analyses therefore tend to recapitulate the dualism of action and structure, albeit in rather novel form because of his pre-eminent concern with time and space. 'Stations', 'domains', etc., are themselves taken as givens, the outcome of uninterpreted processes of institutional formation and change. Unsurprisingly, in this type of viewpoint little emphasis is placed on the essentially transformational character of all human action, even in its most utterly routinized forms. Third, concentration solely upon constraining properties of the body, in its movement through time-space, is unwarranted. All types of constraint, as I have said, are also types of opportunity, media for the enablement of action. The specific way in which Hägerstrand tends to conceptualize 'constraint', moreover, betrays a certain culture-bound element in his views. For capability constraints, coupling constraints and so on are typically discussed by him in terms of their operation as scarce resources. It is not difficult to see here once more a possible link with a version of historical materialism. There is more than a hint in Hägerstrand's writings of the notion that allocation of scarce resources of the body and its media has some sort of determining effect upon the organization of social institutions in all types of society. Such is a feasible proposition, I think, only in the case of contemporary societies, in which a premium is placed upon the 'efficient' use of resources.[13] Finally, time-geography involves only a weakly developed theory of power. Hägerstrand does talk of 'authority constraints', which he links to capability and coupling constraints. But these are both vaguely formulated and invoke a zero-sum conception of power as a source of limitations upon action. If power is conceived of as generative, on the other hand, the 'constraints' of which Hägerstrand speaks are all modalities for the engendering and sustaining of structures of domination.

In order to develop such ideas more adequately in respect of considerations explored earlier in this book we have to look again at the notion of 'place' as ordinarily used by geographers. Hägerstrand's time-geography suggests a very effective critique of 'place' in respect of demonstrating the significance, in studying human social conduct, of analysing the organization of time-space. But his emphasis is very much upon integrating temporality into social theory. He does not subject the notions of place or location to a close conceptual scrutiny and uses such terms in a relatively unexamined fashion. The term 'place' cannot be used in social theory simply to designate 'point in space', any more than we can speak of points in time as a succession of 'nows'. What this means is that the concept of presence — or, rather, of the mutuality of presence and absence — has to be explicated in terms of its spatiality as well as its temporality. In developing the theory of structuration I have introduced two notions that are of some relevance here: the concepts of *locale* and of *presence availability* as involved in the relations between social and system integration.[14]

Locales refer to the use of space to provide the *settings* of interaction, the settings of interaction in turn being essential to specifying its *contextuality*. The constitution of locales certainly depends upon the phenomena given pride of place by Hägerstrand: the body, its media of mobility and communication, in relation to physical properties of the surrounding world. Locales provide for a good deal of the 'fixity' underlying institutions, although there is no clear sense in which they 'determine' such 'fixity'. It is usually possible to designate locales in terms of their physical properties, either as features of the material world or, more commonly, as combinations of those features and human artefacts. But it is an error to suppose that locales can be described in those terms alone — the same form of error made by behaviourism with regard to the description of human action. A 'house' is grasped as such only if the observer recognizes that it is a 'dwelling' with a range of other properties specified by the modes of its utilization in human activity.

Locales may range from a room in a house, a street corner, the shop floor of a factory, towns and cities, to the territorially demarcated areas occupied by nation-states. But locales are typically internally *regionalized*, and the regions within them are of critical importance in constituting contexts of interaction. Let me develop a little further the notion of context. One of the reasons for using the term 'locale' rather than 'place' is that properties of settings are employed in a chronic way by agents in the constitution of encounters across space and time. An obvious element of this is the physical aspect of what Hägerstrand calls 'stations' — i.e. 'stopping places', in which the physical mobility of agents' trajectories is arrested or curtailed for the duration of encounters or social occasions — as locales in which the routine activities of different individuals intersect. But the features of settings are also used, in a routine manner, to constitute the meaningful content of interaction: demonstration of the manifold ways in which this occurs ranks among the major contributions of Garfinkel and of Goffman. Context thus connects the most intimate and detailed components of interaction to much broader properties of the institutionalization of social life.

Modes of Regionalization

'Regionalization' should be understood not merely as localization in space but as referring to the zoning of time-space in relation to routinized social practices. Thus a private house is a locale which is a 'station' for a large cluster of interactions in the course of a typical day. Houses in contemporary societies are regionalized into floors, halls and rooms. But the various rooms of the house are zoned differently in time as well as space. The rooms downstairs are characteristically used most in daylight hours, while bedrooms are where individuals 'retire to' at night. The division between day and night in all societies used to be perhaps the most fundamental zoning demarcation between the intensity of social life and its relaxation — ordered also, obviously, by the need of the human organism for regular periods of sleep. Night time was a 'frontier' of social activity as marked as any spatial frontiers have ever been. It remains a frontier, as it were, that is only sparsely settled. But the invention of powerful, regularized modes of artificial lighting has dramatically expanded the potentialities of interaction settings in night hours. As one observer has remarked:

> The last great frontier of human immigration is occurring in time: a spreading of wakeful activity throughout the twenty-four hours of the day. There is more multiple shift factory work, more police

coverage, more use of the telephone at all hours. There are more hospitals, pharmacies, aeroplane flights, hostels, always-open restaurants, car rental and gasoline and auto repair stations, bowling alleys, and radio stations, always active. There are more emergency services such as auto-towing, locksmiths, bail bondsmen, drug and poison and suicide, gambling 'hot lines' available incessantly. Although different individuals participate in these events in shifts, the organizations involved are continually active.[15]

Zerubavel's study of the temporal organization of a modern hospital, where zoning is very tightly controlled, is relevant here. Most of the services of medical care in the hospital he studied are provided by rotating nursing staff. The majority of nurses work for set periods on different wards, moving around the different sectors of the hospital, and they also are called upon to alternate day and night shift work. The cycle of movement between wards coincides with that between day and night work, so that when someone 'goes to days' he or she also changes to another sector. The scheduling of these activities is complex and detailed. While nurses' work is regulated in standardized four-weekly periods, the rotation of interns and residents is variable. Nurses' rotations always begin on the same day of the week, and since they are of twenty-eight days, they do not coincide with calendar months. The activities of house staff, on the other hand, are organized in terms of calendar months and hence begin on different days of the week.

Weekly and daily zones are also punctiliously categorized. Many routines occur at precise, seven-day intervals, especially those involving nurses. Nurses' 'time off' is also counted against a weekly schedule. Time off can be split into a number of segments taken separately, but each segment has to be a multiple of seven days, and each has to begin on Sunday and to end on Saturday to co-ordinate with the rotations of work activities. 'Weekdays' are not identical to 'weekend' days, however, because although operating upon a continuous basis, various kinds of services are restricted in the hospital during the weekend. As laboratories are closed, for example, the hospital staff know that they cannot get certain sorts of tests carried out. They try to admit as few new patients as possible at weekends and to avoid initiating new treatment programmes for existing inmates. Saturdays and Sundays are usually 'quiet' days; Monday is the busiest day of the week. In day-to-day life in the hospital the alternation of 'day' and 'night' resembles the division of the week into weekdays and weekends. As the author notes, the fact that working at nights is still considered unusual, and unusually demanding, is indicated by the term used to refer to it: 'night duty'. There is no corresponding term 'day duty'.[16]

A useful classification of modes of regionalization might be offered by figure 7. By the 'form' of regionalization I mean the

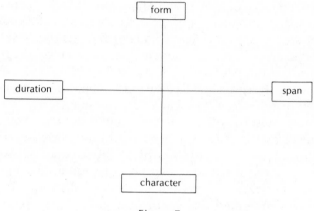

Figure 7

form of the boundaries that define the region. In most locales the boundaries separating regions have physical or symbolic markers. In contexts of co-presence these may allow a greater or lesser number of the features of 'presencing' to permeate adjoining regions. As has been mentioned, in social gatherings the regionalization of encounters is usually indicated only by body posture and positioning, tone of voice and so on. In many such gatherings, as regionally bounded episodes, encounters may be nearly all of very short duration. Walls between rooms, on the other hand, may demarcate regionalization in such a way that none of the ordinary media of co-presence can penetrate. Of course, where walls are thin various kinds of interruptions or embarrassments to the closure of encounters can occur. Ariès, Elias and others have pointed to the ways in which the internal differentiation of the houses of the mass of the population since the eighteenth century has been interrelated with changing aspects of family life and sexuality.[17] Prior to the eighteenth century in Western Europe the homes of the poor frequently had only one or two rooms, in which various communal living and sleeping arrangements were found. The grander houses of the aristocracy had many rooms, but these usually connected directly with one another, without the hallways which in modern houses permit types of privacy that were formerly difficult to achieve for all classes of society.

Regionalization may incorporate zones of great variation in span or scale. Regions of broad spans are those which extend widely in space and deeply in time. Of course, the intersection of 'spans' of space and time may vary, but regions of considerable span necessarily tend to depend upon a high degree of institutionalization. All regions, as defined here, involve extension in time as well as space. 'Region' may sometimes be used in geography to refer to a physically demarcated area on a map of the physical features of the material environment. This is not what I mean by the term, which as used here always carries the connotation of the structuration of social conduct across time-space. Thus there is a strong degree of regional differentiation, in terms of class relationships and a variety of other social criteria, between the North and the South in Britain. 'The North' is not just a geographically delimited area but one with long-established, distinctive social traits. By the 'character' of regionalization I refer to the modes in which the time-space organization of locales is ordered within more embracing social systems. Thus in many societies the 'home', the dwelling, has been the physical focus of family relationships and also of production, carried on either in parts of the dwelling itself or in closely adjoining gardens or plots of land. The development of modern capitalism, however, brings about a differentiation between the home and the workplace, this differentiation having considerable implications for the overall organization of production systems and other major institutional features of contemporary societies.

Front Regions, Back Regions

One aspect of the character of regionalization is the level of presence-availability associated with specific forms of locale. The notion of 'presence-availability' is an essential adjunct to that of co-presence. The 'being together' of co-presence demands means whereby actors are able to 'come together'. Hägerstrand's time-geography draws our attention to some of the factors typically involved here. Communities of high presence-availability in *all* cultures, prior to only some hundred years ago, were groupings of individuals in close physical proximity to one another. The corporeality of the agent, the limitations upon the mobility of the body in the trajectories of the *durée* of daily activity, together with the physical properties of space, ensured that this was so. The media of communication were always identical to those of transportation. Even with the use of fast horses, ships, forced marches, etc., long distance in space always meant long distance in time. The mechanization of transport has been the main factor leading to the dramatic forms of time-space convergence noted previously as characteristic of the modern age. But the most radical disjuncture of relevance in modern history (whose implications today are very far from being exhausted) is the separation of media of communication, by the development of electronic signalling, from the media of transportation, the latter always having involved, by some means or another, the mobility of the human body. Morse's invention of the electromagnetic telegraph marks as distinctive a transition in human cultural development as the wheel or any other technical innovation ever did.

The different aspects of the regionalization of locales indicated above shape the nature of presence-availability in varying ways. Thus the rooms of a dwelling may ensure that encounters can be sustained in different parts of the building without intruding upon one another, providing a particular symmetry, perhaps, with the routines of the day for its incumbents. But living in close proximity within the house also means, of course, high presence-availability: co-presence is very easily secured and sustained. Prisons and asylums are often associated with enforced continuity of co-presence among individuals who are not ordinarily accustomed to such routines of daily life. Prisoners who share the same cell may rarely be out of each other's presence for the whole of the day and night. On the other hand, the 'disciplinary power' of prisons, asylums and other types of 'total institution' is based upon disrupting the gearing of presence-availability into the routines of daily trajectories 'outside'. Thus the very same inmates

who are forced into continuous co-presence are denied the
avilability of easy encounters with other groups in the prison,
even though those others may be physically only on the other side
of the walls of the cell. The enforced 'sequestration' of prisoners
from the 'outside world', limiting the possibilities of co-presence
to those within a single locale, is, of course, a defining feature of a
'total institution'.

We can further draw out the relevance of regionalization to the
structuration of social systems by considering how zoning is
accomplished in different settings. 'Face' and 'front' are related

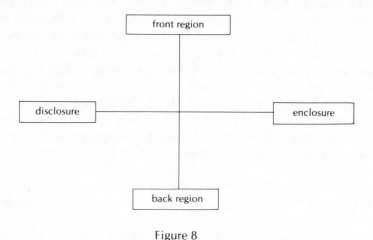

Figure 8

first of all to the positioning of the body in encounters. The
regionalization of the body, so important to psychoanalysis —
which, in Lacan's phrase, explores 'openings on the surface' of
the body — has a spatial counterpart in the regionalization of the
contexts of interaction. Regionalization encloses zones of time-
space, enclosure permitting the sustaining of distinctive relations
between 'front' and 'back' regions, which actors employ in
organising the contextuality of action and the sustaining of
ontological security. The term 'façade' in some part helps to
designate the connections between face and front regions.[18] It
hints, however, that frontal aspects of regionalization are
inherently inauthentic, and that whatever is real or substantial is
hidden behind. Goffman's discussion of front and back regions
also tends to have the same implication: that whatever is 'hidden

away' expresses the real feelings of those who enact role performances 'up front'. While obviously this may often be the case, I think here we come up against the limitations of the dramaturgical model that Goffman employs, especially in his earlier writings, and we see again the consequences of the lack of a general interpretation of the motivation of the routines of daily life. If agents are only players on a stage, hiding their true selves behind the masks they assume for the occasion, the social world would indeed be largely empty of substance. Why, in fact, should they bother to devote the attention they do to such performances at all? Players in genuine theatre, after all, have a motivation to impress the audience with the quality of their performances, since they are specialists in those very performances as professionals. But this is a very particular situation, not in fact one generic to social life. To regard it as such is to make something of the same mistake which Goffman himself identifies in analysing talk. The 'faultless speech' of the newscaster is exceptional, and bound up with the presumed expertise of one who is a specialist in the production of smooth talk; in most contexts of day-to-day life agents are not motivated to produce this kind of speech.

The sustaining of ontological security could not be achieved if front regions were no more than façades. The whole of social life would be, in Sullivan's phrase, a desperate search to put on 'security operations' to salvage a sense of self-esteem in the staging of routines. Those who *do* feel this way characteristically display modes of anxiety of an extreme kind. It is precisely because there is generally a deep, although generalized, affective involvement in the routines of daily life that actors (agents) do not ordinarily feel themselves to be actors (players), whatever the terminological similarity between these terms. Theatre can challenge social life by its very mimicry in pantomime. This is presumably what Artaud means in saying, 'The true theatre has always seemed to me the exercise of a terrible and dangerous act, in which, moreover the idea of theatre and performance is eradicated. . . .'[19] Consider also Laing's discussion of the hysteric:

Unless one is depressed, it is the others who complain of self's lack of genuiness or sincerity. It is regarded as pathognomic of the hysteric's characteristic strategy that his or her actions should be false, that they should be histrionic, dramatized. The hysteric, on the other hand, often insists that his feelings are real and genuine. It is we who feel they are unreal. It is the hysteric who insists on the seriousness of his intention of committing suicide while we speak of a mere 'gesture' towards suicide. The hysteric complains that he is going to pieces. It is just in so far as we feel that he is not going to pieces, except in that he is pretending or making believe that he is, that we call him an hysteric. . . .[20]

Thus the differentiation between front and back regions by no means coincides with a division between the enclosure (covering up, hiding) of aspects of the self and their disclosure (revelation, divulgence). These two axes of regionalization operate in a complicated nexus of possible relations between meaning, norms and power. Back regions clearly often do form a significant resource which both the powerful and the less powerful can utilize reflexively to sustain a psychological distancing between their own interpretations of social processes and those enjoined by 'official' norms. Such circumstances are likely to approximate most closely to those in which individuals feel themselves to be playing parts in which they do not really 'believe'. But it is important to separate out two types of situation in which this may hold, because only one approximates at all closely to the dramaturgical metaphor. In all societies there are social occasions which involve ritual forms of conduct and utterance, in which the normative sanctions regulating 'correct performance' are strong. Such episodes are usually set apart regionally from the rest of social life and differ from it specifically in requiring homology of performance from occasion to occasion. It seems especially in these circumstances that individuals are likely to feel they are 'playing roles' in which the self is only marginally involved. Here there is likely to be tension in the style and continuity of performance, and style may be accentuated much more than in most day-to-day social activity.

Disclosure and Self

Back regions involved in ritualized social occasions probably often do quite closely resemble the 'backstage' of a theatre or the 'off-camera' activities of filming and television productions. But this backstage may very well be 'on stage' so far as the ordinary routines of social life, and the ordinary proprieties, go. For these sorts of occasion do involve fixed performances for audiences, though there is no necessary implication that those in the back regions are able to relax the usual courtesies of tact or 'repair'. The level of enclosure between front and back regions is nevertheless likely to be very high, since it often holds that the more ritualized the occasion, the more it has to be presented as an autonomous set of events, in which the backstage props are kept entirely out of view of audiences or observers. It is worth pointing out that there is much more to the distinction between 'public' and 'private' activities than might appear from the seemingly mutually exclusive nature of these categories. Ceremonial occasions are distinctively, prototypically public events, often involving 'public figures'. But the backstage of such occasions is not a 'private sphere': the chief figures in the drama may be able to relax even less when, leaving the ceremonial arena, they move among their inferiors, the individuals who are merely 'behind the scenes'.

Ritual occasions seem for the most part distinctively different from the range of circumstances in which back regions are zones within which agents recover forms of autonomy which are compromised or treated in frontal contexts. These are often situations in which sanctions are imposed upon actors whose commitment to those norms is marginal or nonexistent. The forms of enclosure and disclosure which allow agents to deviate from, or flout, those norms are important features of the dialectic of control in situations involving surveillance. Surveillance, as I have pointed out elsewhere, connects two related phenomena: the collation of information used to co-ordinate social activities of subordinates, and the direct supervision of the conduct of those subordinates. In each respect the advent of the modern state, with its capitalist-industrial infrastructure, has been distinguished by a vast expansion of surveillance.[21] Now 'surveillance', by its very nature, involves disclosure, making visible. The garnering of information discloses the patterns of activity of those to whom that information refers, and direct supervision openly keeps such activity under observation in order to control it. The minimization or manipulation of conditions of disclosure is thus ordinarily in the interests of those whose behaviour is subject to surveillance — the more so according to how far what they are called upon to do in such settings is regarded as uninteresting or noxious.

Back regions in, say, settings of the shop floor include 'odd corners' of the floor, tea rooms, toilets and so on, as well as the intricate zonings of displacement of contact with supervisors which workers can achieve through bodily movement and posture. Descriptions of the use of such zoning in order to control properties of the setting (and thereby to sustain modes of autonomy in power relationships) are legion in the literature of industrial sociology. For instance, here is a worker talking about a characteristic incident on the floor of a car factory:

> I was working on one side of the car and the boot lid dropped. It just grazed the head of the fella working opposite me. I can see it now. He stopped working, had a look round to see if anyone was watching. I was pretending not to look at him — and then he held his head. He'd had enough like. You could see him thinking, 'I'm getting out of this for a bit.' He staggered, I could see him looking round. You know what it was like in there. Paint everywhere. He wasn't going to fall in the paint . . . so he staggered about ten yards and fell down with a moan on some pallets. It was bloody funny. One of the lads saw him there and stopped the line. The supervisor came chasing across. 'Start the line . . . start the line. . . .' He started the line and we had to work. We were working one short as well. It took them ages to get him out of there. They couldn't get the stretcher in. It must have been half an hour before they got him. Him lying there, y'know, with his one eye occasionally opening for a quick look round: 'What's happening?'[22]

Derogation of those in authority is obviously extremely common in such situations. The incident described here, however, emphasizes the fact that defamatory action of this sort is not always kept confined to the back region, to activities closed off from the presence of those who are the targets.

The regional zoning of activities in many contexts of this sort connects closely, of course, with the seriality of encounters in time-space. But again it does not clearly converge with a division between public and private activity. The worker makes no attempt to disguise to his workmate that the act of malingering is directed towards temporarily escaping from the pressures of the assembly line. Such front/back differentiations — ordinarily occurring in circumstances of marked imbalances of power — can in a general way be distinguished from those in which the situational proprieties of interaction are weakened or allowed to lapse. These are situations in which front, the details of bodily control and some 'repair' procedures of care for others can all be relaxed. At least one connotation of 'privacy' is the regional isolation of an individual — or of individuals, for privacy does not seem inevitably to imply solitude — from the ordinary demands of the monitoring of action and gesture, whereby 'infantile' types of conduct are permitted expression. The zoning of the body seems in most (all?) societies to be associated with the zoning of activities in time-space in the trajectories of the day within locales. Thus eating usually occurs in definite settings at definite times, and is usually also 'public' in the restricted sense of involving gatherings of family members, friends, colleagues and so on. The dressing or adornment of the body may not be universally treated as 'private' but at least in most cultures seems to be so regarded. In spite of Elias's claims that sexual activity was carried on in an unconcealed way in medieval Europe,[23] genital sexuality seems everywhere to be zoned as a back-region phenomenon, with many variations, of course, in intersecting modes of public and private behaviour.

It seems plausible to suppose that the intersections between regionalization and the expressions of bodily care are intricately bound up with the sustaining of the basic security system. Back regions which allow the individual complete solitude from the presence of others may be less important than those which allow the expression of 'regressive behaviour' in situations of co-presence. Such regions may permit

> profanity, open sexual remarks, elaborate griping . . . rough informal dress, 'sloppy' sitting and standing posture, use of dialect or substandard speech, mumbling and shouting, playful aggressivity and 'kidding', inconsiderateness for the other in minor but potentially symbolic acts, minor physical self-involvements such as humming, whistling, chewing, nibbling, belching and flatulence.[24]

Far from representing a diminution of trust, these types of behaviour might help to reinforce the basic trust in the presence of intimates originally built up in relation to the parental figures. They are marked not by the sort of upsurge of anxiety brought about by critical situations but the reverse — a dissipation of tensions deriving from the demands of tight bodily and gestural control in other settings of day-to-day life.

Regionalization as Generic

The differentiations between enclosure, disclosure, back and front regions, apply across large spans of time-space, not only in the contexts of co-presence. These are, of course, unlikely to be as directly monitored reflexively by those whom they affect, although such may be the case. Regionalization within urban areas in contemporary societies has been much studied since the early work of the Chicago sociologists Park and Burgess. In most Western societies, the zoning of cities into neighbourhoods with markedly different social characteristics is strongly influenced by the operation of housing markets, and by separations between individually owned homes and state-operated housing sectors. Neighbourhoods may not be zoned as symmetrically as some of the 'ecological' urban analysts suggested, but their distribution has the consequence of creating various sorts of front/back contrasts. Industrial areas in northern towns and cities in England were once the most visible features of the built environment — factories and mills, as it were, proudly displayed. But the tendency in urban planning in recent years has been to treat such areas as unsightly, as back regions to be hidden away in enclosed enclaves, or transferred to the edge of town. Examples can easily be multiplied. The access of those in more affluent sectors of housing markets to relatively easy transfer of property underlies the 'flight to the suburbs', changing city centres from regions of frontal display to back regions of urban decay, which the 'respectable classes' avoid. Ghetto areas may be rendered 'invisible' by their regional enclosure in neighbourhoods having very low rates both of property transfer and of daily mobility in and out of those neighbourhoods. As always, various types of time-series phenomena underlie such spatial regionalization.

Regionalization across long spans of time-space has been analysed by many writers in terms of familiar notions such as 'uneven development' and distinctions between 'centre' (or 'core') and 'periphery'. These notions, however, can be applied across the whole range of the settings of locales, from large to small. Rather than discussing the theme of uneven development here, I shall develop the differentiation of centre and periphery by relating it to embeddedness in time. If the world economy has its centres, and cities have their centres, so too do the daily trajectories of individual actors. In modern societies, for the majority of males at least, the home and workplace form the two main centres in which the day's activities tend to be concentrated. Locales also tend to be centred regionally. Some rooms in a house, such as spare bedrooms, for example, may be used only 'peripherally'.

Centre/periphery distinctions tend frequently to be associated with endurance over time.[25] Those who occupy centres 'establish' themselves as having control over resources which allow them to maintain differentiations between themselves and those in peripheral regions. The established may employ a variety of forms of social closure[26] to sustain distance from others who are effectively treated as inferiors or outsiders.

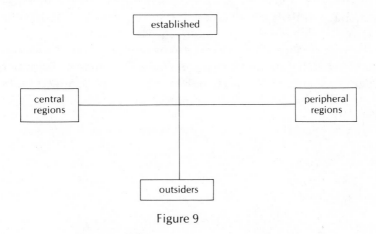

Figure 9

The 'established' industrial nations of the Western 'core' maintain a central position in the world economy on the basis of their temporal precedence over the 'less developed' societies. The geopolitical regionalization of the world system may be changing — with, for example, shifts in centres of manufacturing production to erstwhile peripheral zones in the East — but the factor of priority in time has so far decisively influenced preeminence in space. Within nation-states centre/periphery regionalization seems everywhere to be associated with the existence of 'establishments' that lie at the core of the structuration of dominant classes.[27] Of course, there are a variety of complex relations involved in these phenomena, and I offer these examples as purely illustrative.

Time, Space, Context

Let me at this point offer a summary of the main points in this chapter so far. The discussion has been concerned with the *contextuality* of social life and social institutions. All social life occurs in, and is constituted by, intersections of presence and absence in the 'fading away' of time and the 'shading off' of space. The physical properties of the body and the *milieux* in which it moves inevitably give social life a serial character, and limit modes of access to 'absent' others across space. Time-geography provides an important mode of notation of the intersection of time-space trajectories in day-to-day activity. But it has to be inserted within a more adequate theorization both of the agent and of the organization of the settings of interaction. In proposing the ideas of locale and of regionalization I want to formulate a scheme of concepts which help to categorize contextuality as inherently involved in the connection of social and system integration.[28]

daily time-space paths

distribution of encounters

regionalization of locales

contextuality of regions

intersection of locales

The graphic techniques developed in time-geography have already proved their fruitfulness in several areas of research. There is no reason at all why those working in a range of fields in the social sciences should not adopt, and adapt, Hägerstrand's method of notation. But the limitations of time-geography, as indicated above, must certainly also be borne in mind. Moreover, 'clock time' should not be accepted simply as an unquestioned dimension of the construction of topographical models, but must be regarded as itself a socially conditioned influence upon the nature of the time-space paths traced out by actors in modern societies. The point may, on the face of things, appear to be a banality but is actually very far from being so. What is at issue is not just different means of reckoning time, but divergent forms of the structuration of daily activities.

Consider, for instance, Bourdieu's well-known discussion of time and time-reckoning in Kabylia. Here the year is considered to run from autumn towards summer and the day from evening towards noon. This scheme expresses, however, a conception of time as eternal recurrence, which is in turn part of the basic composition of day-to-day activities. Night is symbolically a time of death, marked by regular taboos — against bathing, coming into contact with stretches of water, looking in a mirror, anointing the hair or touching ashes.[29] The morning is not just 'daybreak' but a triumph in the struggle between day and night: to be 'in the morning' is to be open to the light, to the beneficence that is associated with it. The 'opening' of the day is thus a time for going out, when people pour from their houses to their work in the fields. Getting up early means putting oneself under favourable auspices, to 'do honour to the angels'. It is not just a transition in time but a keying of events and practices. Nevertheless, the creative potential of the day must be fostered by magic or other malignant forces can intervene, particularly following the zenith of the sun's rise. For after this the day goes into decline, signalling the imminent return of the decadence and decay of night, 'the paradigm of all forms of decline'.[30]

Bearing this example in mind, let me develop some of the main notions considered in this chapter, taking as an illustration schooling in contemporary societies. There is no doubt that mapping the time-space patterns followed by pupils, teachers and other staff in a school is a useful topological device with which to begin to study that school. Rather than using the exact forms of representation formulated by Hägerstrand and his co-workers, however, I propose to emphasize the 'reversible time' of day-to-day routine conduct. Hägerstrand usually portrays time-space paths as having a 'linear' movement through the day. But a more accurate representation of the repetitive character of day-to-day social life is given if we see that most daily time-space paths involve a 'return'. Instead of adopting the form of figure 10a we might take as examplary that of figure 10b.

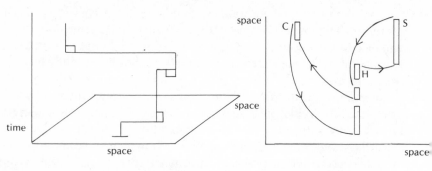

Figure 10a   Figure 10b

Figure 10a is of the sort favoured by Hägerstrand, in which we look at time-space 'laterally' and the 'time' arrow makes out a specific temporal sequence (usually equivalent to the working day). I propose not to abandon this type of notation but to supplement it — certainly conceptually, if not figuratively — with figure 10b, in which we are looking 'down', as it were, rather than laterally. The lines marked with the arrows represent paths of time-space movement. The length of the lines refers to the amount of time, measured chronologically, spent moving between 'stations' in the course of a particular day by a particular or typical individual; the degree of elongation of the boxes indicates how long is spent within a specific locale. Thus a child's day in school term looks something like the scheme indicated in the diagram. The child may spend three discrete periods in the home (H) per day — sleeping there from the middle of the evening until the early morning, returning there from school (S) in the late afternoon and coming back again after having been out to the cinema (C) in the evening. Some aspects of the child's day are no doubt strongly routinized (the journey to school and back), whereas others (going out to the cinema) may be less so. The most routinized types of activity can be represented as a profile of time-space paths embedded in reversible time.

A school, in Hägerstrand's terms, is a 'station' along the converging paths traced by clusters of individuals in the course of the day. He is right to point out that the conditions which make it possible for individuals to come together within a single locale cannot be taken for granted but have to be examined directly. But a locale is, of course, more than a mere stopping-point.

'Stations' tend to be black boxes, as it were, in time-geography, because the main focus is upon movement between them. As a type of social organization, concentrated upon a locale having definite physical characteristics, the characteristics of a school can be understood in terms of three features: the distribution of encounters across time and space occurring within it, the internal regionalization that it displays, and the contextuality of the regions thus identified.

Modern schools are disciplinary organizations, and their bureaucratic traits clearly both influence and are influenced by the regions they contain. Like all forms of disciplinary organization, the school operates within closed boundaries, its physical borders being cut off rather clearly from day-to-day interaction outside. A school is a 'container', generating disciplinary power. The enclosed nature of school life makes possible a strict co-ordination of the serial encounters in which inmates are involved. The segments of children's time that are spent in school are spatially and temporally sealed off from potentially intrusive encounters outside. But this is also true, usually at least, of the divisions between different classes. Schools are internally partitioned. There may be some areas in a school, and some times, when heterogeneous or unfocused forms of interaction tend to occur — e.g. at the beginning and end of classes. But for the most part the distribution of encounters within a school contrasts dramatically with sectors of social life in which the normative regulation of activity is looser. Disciplinary spacing is part of the architectural character of schools, both in the separation of classrooms and in the regulated spacing of desks that is often found inside them. There is no doubt that spatial divisions of this sort facilitate the routinized specification and allocation of tasks.

The school timetable is fundamental to the mobilization of space as co-ordinated time-space paths. School administrators normally do not face the same problems of 'packing' as their counterparts in hospitals do. But, like all disciplinary organizations, schools operate with a precise economy of time. It is surely right to trace the origins of school discipline in some part to the regulation of time and space which a generalized transition to 'clock time' makes possible. The point is not that the widespread use of clocks makes for exact divisions of the day; it is that time enters into the calculative application of administrative authority.

The contextual features of classrooms, as the main 'areas of application' of disciplinary power, obviously vary widely. But in more severe forms of classroom spacing the specification of bodily positioning, movement and gesture is usually tightly organized. The spatial positioning of teacher and pupils in the context of a class is quite different from that of most other situations in which face engagements are carried on. Indeed, it usually signals a collapse of the teacher's control if such situations come into being. The seeming minutiae of bodily posture and mobility to which Goffman draws attention are once more far from incidental here.

The classroom, like the school, is a 'power container'. But it is not one that merely churns out 'docile bodies'. Contexts of co-presence, as I have emphasized, can be described as settings, and settings have to be reflexively activated by authority figures in the course of making that authority count. Discipline through surveillance is a potent medium of generating power, but it none the less depends upon the more or less continuous compliance of those who are its 'subjects'. The achievement of such compliance is itself a fragile and contingent accomplishment, as every teacher knows. The disciplinary context of the classroom is not just a 'backdrop' to what goes on in the school class; it is mobilized within the dialectic of control. A school class is a face engagement which has to be reflexively managed, like any other.

Consider the following strip of interaction, described and discussed by Pollard:

> Bell for 9. 0 a.m. goes, about half class in, mostly reading books. Teacher enters breezily: 'Morning — ah, that's good, getting those books out.' Teacher sits at desk, tidies up, gets register out. Meanwhile most of the other children have come into the classroom. The later arrivals talk, swap some football cards, occasionally glance at the teacher.

> TEACHER: Right, let's do the register, then, hurry up and sit down you football maniacs — I see that Manchester United lost again.
> MANCHESTER UNITED SUPPORTERS: Oh yeah, well they're still better than Liverpool.
> TEACHER: (Jokey sarcasm in voice) Really? It must be all the spinach they don't eat. Now then . . . Martin . . . Doreen . . . Alan . . . Mark (calls register and children answer).

A child comes in late, looking sheepish, and walks to his seat. Other children point and laugh.

CHILD: Hey, Duncan, what are you doing?
TEACHER: Duncan, come here. You're late *again*, three minutes late to be exact. Why?
DUNCAN: Sorry, sir.
TEACHER: I said, 'Why?'
DUNCAN: I slept in, sir.
TEACHER: Well, are you awake now?
   (Other children laugh.)
DUNCAN: Yes, sir.
TEACHER: Well you'd better stay behind for three minutes at 4 o'clock and don't go to sleep again after that.

More laughter, Duncan sits down. Teacher finishes register.[31]

What is going on here? We have to recognize, as the teacher does, that registration has a particular significance for the ordering of the day's activities. It is a marker that signals the opening of the brackets in an encounter, and it is the first salvo fired in a battle that is joined daily between teacher and pupils. The teacher recognizes it as the first occasion to test the mood of the children, as the children do in respect of the teacher. The teacher's maintenance of directive control depends upon ensuring that the children assume the routines involved in the classroom setting. On entry to the classroom in the morning the children are expected to sit in their assigned places, get out their reading books and answer to their names when they are called out. Pollard interprets the teacher's joking and teasing as a front performance, which is intended to set the tone of the day as one of co-operative work. However, this strategy has its risks, as is indicated by the response to a late arrival of one of the children. Another feels able to tease the latecomer. The teacher at once recognizes this as the first test case of the day, in respect of which his superior authority must be demonstrated. His bantering rebuke to Duncan mixes appeal with firmness, a tactic shown to be successful by the laughter of the children. Thus the events of the day move on. If the teacher had been more overtly disciplinarian and had sent the miscreant to the head, the response could have been judged too severe by the rest of the children. The result then might have been an escalation of threat and punishment less effective in sustaining routine than the 'effort bargain' which teacher and pupils have implicitly concluded as part of a more co-operative atmosphere.

The very nature of classrooms, in which most things both teachers and children do are visible each to the other, means that back regions usually have a strong temporal as well as spatial definition. For children these lie in some part along the narrow temporal boundaries between classes, whether or not they involve physical movement from one classroom to another. Although the weight of discipline normally bears down most on the children, it is sometimes felt more oppressively by teachers. Teachers usually have a back region to which they can retreat, the staff room, which children ordinarily do not enter. The staff room is no doubt a place for unwinding and relaxation. But it is also somewhere in which tactics of coping with teaching tend endlessly to be discussed, formulated and reformulated.

It is in the nature of disciplinary organizations that the intensity of surveillance inside inhibits direct control from outside. This is a phenomenon which can be seen both in the internal regionalization of the school and in its situation as a locale within other locales. Inside the school the concentration of disciplinary authority in separately partitioned classrooms is the condition of the high level of control over bodily positioning and activity which can be achieved. But this circumstance also acts against the direct supervision of the supervisor. The head is 'in authority' over the teaching staff, but such authority cannot be exercised in the same way as teachers endeavour to control the conduct of children in their classes. Schools therefore tend to have a rather sharply opposed 'double line' of authority. The control which teachers seek to exercise over their pupils is immediate, involving the teacher's continuous face-to-face presence with the children. Supervision of the activity of teachers, however, is necessarily indirect and proceeds by other means. One might hazard a guess that it is only in organizations in which a considerable amount of autonomy from direct supervision is given that a graduated line of authority can be achieved. The enclosed nature of the school, and its clear separation in time and space from what goes on in surrounding locales, also inhibits supervisory control from the outside, however. Thus inspectors may visit schools regularly to check upon their operation; boards of governors and parents' associations may make their power felt in influencing policies that help to shape the life of the school. But it is intrinsic to disciplinary power that what goes on in the 'power container' of the school has a significant degree of autonomy from the very outside agencies whose ethos it expresses.

Against 'Micro' and 'Macro': Social and System Integration

The foregoing considerations are of some importance in examining the relations between social and system integration. I do not employ the more familiar terms, 'micro-' and 'macrosociological' study, for two reasons. One is that these two are not infrequently set off against one another, with the implication that we have to choose between them, regarding one as in some way more fundamental than the other. In Goffman's studied refusal to be concerned with issues of large-scale social organization and history, for example, there seems to lurk the idea that in what he sometimes calls microsociology is to be found the essential reality of social life. On the other hand, advocates of macrosociological approaches are prone to regard studies of day-to-day social activity as concerned with trivia — the most significant issues are those of broader scope. But this sort of confrontation is surely a phoney war if ever there was one. At any rate, I do not think that there can be any question of either having priority over the other. A second reason why the micro/macro division tends to conjure up unfortunate associations is that, even where there is no conflict between the two perspectives, an unhappy division of labour tends to come into being between them. Microsociology is taken to be concerned with the activities of the 'free agent', which can safely be left to theoretical standpoints such as those of symbolic interactionism or ethnomethodology to elucidate; while the province of macrosociology is presumed to be that of analysing the structural constraints which set limits to free activity (see pp. 211). I have made it clear previously that such a division of labour leads to consequences that are at best highly misleading.

Why should the issue of the relation between 'micro-' and 'macrosociological' study be seen as so problematic by many writers? The conceptual division of labour just referred to is presumably the main reason. Reinforced by a philosophical dualism, it demands a more thoroughgoing reformulation of social theory than most authors are able or willing to contemplate. It will help to develop this point to look briefly at one of the more interesting recent discussions of the issue, that offered by Collins.[32] Collins points out that the schism between micro- and macro-sociological approaches, as these terms are ordinarily understood, has become accentuated over the past decade or so. While social theory was dominated by functionalism and Marxism, or some combination of the two, social relations in situations of co-presence were typically regarded as substantially determined by broader, 'structural' factors. However, as led especially by ethnomethodology, microsociology has become a burgeoning field of interest and one in which the presumptions of the above approaches have been taken to task in a fairly radical fashion. In Collins's view, 'the newer, radical microsociology is epistemologically and empirically much more thorough than any previous method. . . . I would suggest that the effort coherently to reconstitute macrosociology upon radically empirical micro-foundations is the crucial step toward a more successful sociological science.'[33]

According to Collins, the proper way forward is via a programme of the 'microtranslation' of 'structural phenomena'. Such translation is likely to eventuate in theories which have a stronger empirical basis than existing macrosociological theories. Those who are concerned with macrosociological issues are called upon not to abandon their endeavours but to recognize that their work is theoretically incomplete. There are, in Collins's eyes, only three 'pure macrovariables': time, space and number. Thus a concept such as 'centralization of authority' can be translated into accounts of microsituations — how situated actors actually exert authority in describable contexts. However the 'pure macrovariables' enter in as the number of situations of such a sort, in time and in space. 'Hence structural variables often turn out to be sheer numbers of people in various kinds of micro-situations.'[34] 'Social reality', then, is 'micro-experience'; it is the numerical temporal and spatial aggregations of such experience which make up the macrosociological level of analysis. The 'structural' qualities of social systems are the 'results' Collins says, of conduct in microsituations, in so far as they do not depend upon number, time and space.

Although Collins's concept of 'structural variables' is somewhat similar to that advocated by Blau (see pp. 208—10), Collins quite rightly questions the sort of version of 'structural sociology' which Blau and many others propose. But in other respects, Collins's view is wanting. As I have consistently stressed, to treat time and space as 'variables' is to repeat the characteristic error of most forms of orthodox social science. Moreover, why should we assume that 'structure' is relevant only to macrosociological issues? Both in the more precise and in the vaguer senses of the term I have distinguished activity in microcontexts has strongly defined structural properties. I take this, in fact, to be one of the main claims which ethnomethodological research has successfully sustained. Moreover, why hold that time as a 'variable' is relevant only to macrosociological concerns? Temporality is as inseparable from a small strip of interaction as it is from the longest of *longues durées*. Finally, why propose that structural properties consist only of three dimensions, time, space and number? The reason, I assume, is that Collins still has in mind that 'structure' must refer to something 'outside' the activities of social agents if it is to have any sense at all in social science. Dispersion in time and space seems the only phenomenon left, given that Collins accepts a good deal of the criticisms that have been levelled by those whom he calls 'radical microsociologists' against the collective concepts with which their macrosociological antagonists usually operate.

But the most important confusion in Collins's account is the assumption that 'macroprocesses' are the 'results' of interaction in 'microsituations'. According to Collins, the 'macrolevel' consists only of 'aggregations of micro-experiences'. Now, it can be agreed that generalizations in the social sciences always presuppose — and make at least implicit reference to — the intentional activities of human agents. However, it does not follow from this that what is described as the 'macrolevel' has a rather sham existence. This only takes us back to the phoney war. Social institutions are not explicable as aggregates of 'microsituations', nor fully describable in terms that refer to such situations, if we mean by these circumstances of co-presence. On the other hand, institutionalized patterns of behaviour are deeply implicated in even the most fleeting and limited of 'microsituations'.

Let us pursue this thought by indicating why the micro/macro distinction is not a particularly useful one. What is a 'micro-situation'? The response might be: a situation of interaction confined in space and time — seemingly Collins's view. But this is not very helpful. For not only do encounters 'slide away' in time but also once we start being concerned with how encounters are carried on by their participating actors, it becomes clear that no strip of interaction — even if it is plainly bracketed, temporally and spatially — can be understood on its own. Most aspects of interaction are sedimented in time, and sense can be made of them only by considering their routinized, repetitive character. Moreover, the spatial differentiation of the micro and macro becomes imprecise once we start to examine it. For the forming and reforming of encounters necessarily occurs across tracts of space broader than those involved in immediate contexts of face-to-face interaction. The paths traced by individuals in the course of the day break off some contacts by moving spatially to form others, which are then broken off and so on.

What is normally talked about under the heading of micro/macro processes is the positioning of the body in time-space, the nature of interaction in situations of co-presence, and the connection between these and 'absent' influences relevant to the characterization and explanation of social conduct. These phenomena — the anchoring concerns, in fact, of structuration theory — are better dealt with as concerning the relations between social and system integration. Now, some of the questions at issue in the micro/macro debate are conceptual problems to do with the long-standing controversy over methodological individualism. These I shall leave aside until the next chapter. Other aspects, however, do not rest upon solely conceptual considerations. They can be resolved only by directly analysing particular types of society. Because societies differ in their modes of institutional articulation, the modes of intersection of presence and absence that enters into their constitution can be expected to vary. I shall indicate this briefly here, introducing at the same time material to be expanded upon in the next chapter.

Social integration has to do with interaction in contexts of co-presence. The connections between social and system integration can be traced by examining the modes of regionalization which channel, and are channelled by, the time-space paths that the members of a community or society follow in their day-to-day activities. Such paths are strongly influenced by, and also reproduce, basic institutional parameters of the social systems in which they are implicated. Tribal societies (see pp. 182—3) tend to have a heavily segmental form, the village community being overwhelmingly the most important locale within which encounters are constituted and reconstituted in time-space. In these societies relations of co-presence tend to dominate influences of a more remote kind. It makes sense to say that in them there is something of a fusion of social and system integration. But obviously such a fusion is never complete: virtually all societies, no matter how small or seemingly isolated, exist in at least loose connection with wider 'intersocietal systems'.

Since we now live in a world where electronic communication is taken for granted, it is worth emphasizing what is otherwise a self-evident feature of traditional societies (of all societies, in fact, up to a little over a century ago). This is simply that all contacts between members of different communities or societies, no matter how far-flung, involve contexts of co-presence. A letter may arrive from an absent other, but of course it has to be taken physically from one place to another. Very long journeys were made by specialized categories of people — sailors, the military, merchants, mystics and diverse adventurers — in the traditional world. Nomadic societies would roam across vast tracts of land. Population migrations were common. But none of these phenomena alters the fact that contexts of co-presence were always the main 'carrying contexts' of interaction.

What made possible the larger time-space 'stretch' involved in what I shall call class-divided societies was above all the development of cities. Cities establish a centralization of resources — especially administrative resources — that makes for greater time-space distanciation than is typically the case in tribal orders. The regionalization of class-divided societies, however complicated it may be in detail, is always formed around the connections, of both interdependence and antagonism, between city and countryside.

We tend to use the term 'city' in an encompassing fashion to refer both to urban settlements in traditional societies and to those convergent with the formation and spread of capitalist-industrialism. But this is an obfuscating usage if it is taken to imply that in modern times we merely have more of the same — that today's urbanism is only a denser and more sprawling version of what went before. The contextualities of traditional cities are in many respects different from those of modern urbanism. Rykwert, for example, points out the symbolic form that many cities had, in widely removed parts of the world, prior to modern times:

> It is difficult [for us today] to imagine a situation where the formal order of the universe could be reduced to a diagram of two intersecting coordinates in one place. Yet this is exactly what did happen in antiquity: the Roman who walked along the *cardo* knew that his walk was the axis around which the sun turned, and that if he followed the *decumanus*, he was following the sun's course. The whole universe and its meaning could be spelled out of his civic institutions — so he was at home in it.[35]

Such cities, we could say, do not yet exist in commodified time and space.[36] The buying and selling of time, as labour time, is surely one of the most distinctive features of modern capitalism. The origins of the precise temporal regulation of the day may perhaps be found in the chime of the monastery bell, but it is in the sphere of labour that its influence became embedded in such a way as to spread throughout society as a whole. The commodification of time, geared to the mechanisms of industrial production, breaks down the differentiation of city and countryside characteristic of class-divided societies. Modern industry is accompanied by the spread of urbanism, but its operation is not necessarily fixed in any particular type of area. The traditional city, on the other hand, is both the main locus of disciplinary power in class-divided societies and, as such, set off from the countryside — very often, physically and symbolically, by the city walls. Together with the transformation of time, the commodification of space establishes a 'created environment' of a very distinctive character, expressing new forms of institutional articulation. Such new forms of institutional order alter the conditions of social and system integration and thereby change the nature of the connections between the proximate and remote in time and space.

Critical Notes: Foucault on Timing and Spacing

Foucault's various discussions of the origins of disciplinary power demonstrate a persistent concern with temporal and spatial distribution. According to Foucault, disciplinary power has as its focus the manipulation of the body, regarded essentially as a machine that can be finely tuned. The forms of administration associated with the disciplinary organizations which have mushroomed from the eighteenth century onwards are different from the mass mobilization of labour power found in large-scale projects in agrarian civilizations. Such projects — road-building, the construction of temples, public monuments and so on — often involved large numbers of people. But their activities were co-ordinated only in a gross fashion. The new forms of discipline are tailored precisely to movements, gestures and attitudes of the individual body. Unlike monastic discipline, which is one of its main historical forerunners, the new techniques of power connect discipline directly with utility. The control of the body is part of the novel 'political anatomy' and as such, Foucault says, increases the output of the body while also reducing its independence of orientation.

Discipline can proceed only via the manipulation of time and of space. It ordinarily requires enclosure, a sphere of operations closed off and closed in upon itself. Foucault makes a great deal of the concept of 'confinement', the more or less forcible separation of individuals from the rest of the population in the early hospitals, in mental asylums and in prisons. However, other less embracing disciplinary organizations also involve enclosure. The factors leading to the establishment of closed areas may vary, but the end result is similar in all of them, in some degree because similar models were followed by the individuals and authorities responsible for setting them up. Enclosure is a generalized basis of disciplinary power, but taken alone it is not enough to permit the detailed management of the movements and activities of the body. This can be achieved only through internal regional division or 'partitioning'. Each individual has his or her 'proper place' at any particular time of the day. The partitioning of disciplinary time-space has at least two consequences. It helps to avoid the formation of large groups which might be a source of independent will formation or of opposition, and it allows for the direct manipulation of individual activities, avoiding the flux and indeterminacy which casual encounters tend to have. What is involved here, according to Foucault, is an 'analytical space', in which individuals can be watched and assessed, their qualities measured. The partitioning of disciplinary space may have been influenced by the example of the monastic cell, but often originated also in architectural forms that were established for purely practical purposes. In France the naval hospital at Rochefort served as a model. It was set up as part of an attempt to cope with the contagious disorders rife in a port teeming with numerous disparate groupings of people engaged in war or trade. Controlling the spread of disease involved other kinds of supervisory regulation of transient populations — that of the military over deserters and of the local administration over the flow of goods, rations and raw materials. This led to pressure for the rigorous control of space, which first involved caring for valuable commodities rather than organizing human beings. But the practice of tagging goods, categorizing and controlling their distribution was later applied to patients. Case records began to be kept. The overall number of patients was carefully regulated; restrictions were placed on their movement and the times at which they were visited. The emergence of 'therapeutic spacing' thus was developed from 'administrative and political' spacing.[1]*

The partitioning of space came about in rather different circumstances in factories in the late eighteenth century. Here the tendency was also to distribute individuals in demarcated space, but this distribution had to be directed towards the co-ordination of machinery. Thus the arrangement of bodies in space had to correspond to the technical demands of production. But this 'articulation of production space' can also be shown to have been infused with disciplinary power. Foucault quotes the Oberkampf manufactory at Jouy as an example. The manufactory was constructed of a series of workshops identified according to the type of production operation. Toussaint Barré designed the

*References may be found on pp. 160—1.

largest of the buildings, which was 110 metres long, with three storeys. On the ground floor block printing was carried out. There were 132 tables, set up in two rows running the length of the workshop; two employees worked at each table. Supervisors would walk up and down the central aisle, being thereby able to supervise the labour process in general and the activities of each individual worker in particular. Workers could be compared for their speed and productivity and their activities correlated with one another. By assorting workers according to strict principles of classification, each element of the labour task could be characterized and related to discrete motions of the body. The doctrines of Frederick Taylor are not much more than a late formulation of the disciplinary power that accompanied the rise of large-scale industry over a century earlier.

The character of disciplinary space, according to Foucault, derives primarily not from the association of an organization with a specific piece of territory but from the farming of space. Lines, columns, measured walled intervals are its distinguishing features. It is not any particular part of the building that matters, but its overall relational form. The classroom exemplifies this phenomenon. In the eighteenth century, in France and elsewhere, classes come to be divided intervally into clearly delimited rows, externally separated by a connecting system of corridors. These are curricular as well as spatial divisions. Individuals move through such partitions not only in the course of the day but also during their educational careers.

> In organizing 'cells', 'places' and 'ranks', the disciplines create complex spaces that are at once architectural, functional and hierarchical. It is spaces that provide fixed positions and permit circulation; they carve out individual segments and establish operational links; they mark places and indicate values; they guarantee the obedience of individuals, but also a better economy of time and gesture.[2]

Discipline depends upon the calculative division of time as well as space. The monastery, after all, was one of the first places in which the day was temporally regulated in a precise and ordered fashion. The religious orders were the masters of the methodical control of time, and their influence, diffuse or more direct, was felt everywhere. As in most aspects of disciplinary power, the

J

army provides an apt illustration. Soldiers had long been trained to march in regular formations. The Dutch were the early pioneers of the precise timing of military manoeuvres.[3] By the end of the sixteenth century a method had been developed in the Dutch army whereby troops were trained programmatically to manoeuvre in an ordered way while maintaining a steady and continuous rate of fire. This was accomplished by timing the various movements of the body. The method was later applied to the gestures involved in loading, firing and reloading weapons and to many other aspects of military organization. It was in relation to such developments, in fact, that the term 'discipline' underwent a change in meaning. In its original sense it referred to a learning process and was regarded as a trait of the 'disciplined'. However, in the armed forces it came to be applied as ordinarily it is today, as to do with an overall mode of regulation rather than with the process of instruction itself.[4]

The timing of activities is more than their subordination to measured temporal intervals. It is perhaps the most basic condition of the 'co-ordination of the body and the gesture'. Disciplinary power does not consist only in the imposition of control over specific gestures, but is maximized where gestures are related to the positioning of the body as a whole. The efficient use of the body means that nothing remains idle or unused; attention must be focused wholly upon the act with which the individual is concerned. A disciplined body is a trained body: in this, one might say, the traditional sense of 'discipline' persists. The positioning of the body is the main mediating factor between two temporally articulated sequences. One is the disaggregation of the gesture into a timed series of movements, specifying the parts of the body to be used. Thus Maurice of Orange broke down the handling of the musket into a series of forty-three separate movements, that of the pike into twenty-three, co-ordinated within a formation of soldiers in a battle unit.[5] However, the parts of the objects handled are also specified and integrated with the gesture. Precise timing is essential for this, since weaponry and machinery have increasingly become designed to operate in a sequential way, each step in its operation being a prerequisite to what is done next. Disciplinary power depends upon not just the exploitation of pre-given materials but also the establishment of a 'coercive link with the apparatus of production'.

Timing also stretches across the progression of careers. Foucault compares two phases in the development of the manufactory school of the Gobelins. The manufactory was established by royal edict in 1667; a school for apprentices was planned as part of the scheme. The superintendent of royal buildings was to select sixty scholarship children for participation in the school, the educational process being organized along the typical lines of guild apprenticeship. The pupils were first of all the responsibility of a master, later serving six years' apprenticeship. Following further service lasting four years and the successful passing of an examination, they were able to set up their own workshops. Here there was a diffuse process of transmission of knowledge, involving an exchange of services between masters and apprentices. The temporal organization of the apprentices' lives — by the standards of what was to follow — was lax. Some seventy years after the school was set up, a new type of training was initiated for the apprentices; it was first of all complementary to the existing modes of procedure. Unlike those modes of procedure, it was based on the careful serial arrangement of time. The children attended the school for two hours a day. Classes were divided according to ability and previous experience. Allotted tasks were carried out in a regular fashion, appraised by the teacher and the most able rewarded. Progression between classes was governed by the results of tests administered to all pupils. Day-to-day behaviour was recorded in a book kept by teachers and their assistants; it was periodically looked at by an inspector.

The Gobelins school was one instance of a general trend in eighteenth-century education, in Foucault's words an expression of a 'new technique for taking charge of the time of individual existences'. Disciplines 'which analyse space, break up and rearrange activities' have to be concentrated also in ways which make possible 'adding up and capitalizing time'.[6] Four methods can be used to effect this.

(1) The division of lives chronologically, such that phases of development are specifically timed. Thus the period of training can be separated out in a clear fashion from a career proper. Within the training period steps in attainment can be demarcated, and all those receiving instruction can be

made to move sequentially through all of them.

(2)   The separate phases of training and the subsequent 'career' — a word which thereby attains only its modern sense — can be organized according to an overall plan. Education has to be freed from the personalized dependence entailed in the relation between master and apprentice. The educational plan has to be set out in impersonal terms, wherever possible dismembered into their most elementary operations, which are then readily learned by anyone undergoing instruction.

(3)   Each of the temporal segments has to be concluded with an examination, which not only guarantees that every individual will undergo the same process of instruction but also differentiates each in terms of his or her relative capabilities. The various examinations involved in the pursuit of a career are graded so that they each have to be successfully undertaken before the novitiate can move on to another.

(4)   Different forms or levels of training can be designated for the achievement of ranked offices. At the conclusion of each series some individuals can be hired off and allocated to a particular grade, while others continue to higher grades. Every individual is involved in a temporal series by means of which his or her office or rank is defined.

The 'seriation' of successive activities makes possible a whole investment of duration by power: the possibility of a detailed control and a regular intervention (of differentiation, correction, punishment, elimination) in each moment of time; the possibility of characterizing, and therefore of using individuals according to the level in the series that they are moving through; the possibility of accumulating time and activity, of rediscovering them, totalized and usable in a final result, which is the ultimate capacity of an individual. Temporal dispersal is brought together to produce a profit, thus mastering a duration that would otherwise elude one's grasp. Power is articulated directly on to time; it assures its control and guarantees its use.[7]

Thus disciplinary methods reflect a specific understanding of time, one which is an equal-interval scale. In the seriation of time, Foucault proposes, there is a procedure corresponding to the mapping of partitioned space on to bodily activities: this is 'exercise'. Exercise is the imposition of regular and graduated physical training of the body, with an end state of fitness in view — 'fitness' referring to the preparedness of the body but also to a generalized capacity to carry out designated tasks. The idea and practice of exercise had religious origins but became a secular theme of most of the disciplinary organizations. Exercise demands regular participation over time and works on specific parts of the body. It expresses in a direct fashion the significance of control of the body, in relation to other bodies, which is essential to discipline as a whole. The body is treated as a moving part in a larger composite. Discipline, in sum, demonstrates the following main characteristics. It is 'cellular' (in terms of spatial distribution); it is 'organic' (coding activities according to programmed procedures); it is 'genetic' (in respect of serial phases); and it is 'combinatory' (uniting human activities as the paths of a social machine). Foucault quotes Guibert:

> The state that I depict will have a single, reliable, easily controlled administration. It will resemble those large machines, which by quite uncomplicated means produce great effects; the strength of this state will spring from its own strength, its prosperity from its own prosperity. It will disprove that vulgar prejudice by which we are made to imagine that empires are subjected to an imperious law of decline and ruin.

There is an obvious similarity between Foucault's discussion of disciplinary power and Max Weber's analysis of modern bureaucracy. To be sure, the focus of their respective writings is different. Weber concentrates upon the 'heartland' of bureaucracy — the state and its administrative offices. In Foucault's work, on the other hand, the mechanisms of the state are rarely analysed directly; the state is examined 'symptomatically', via seemingly more marginal forms of organization, hospitals, asylums and prisons. However, in each author there is a stress upon the emergence of novel types of administrative power, generated by the concentrated organization of human activities through their precise specification and co-ordination. At first sight the theme of the transformation of time and space seems lacking in Weber's writings, and it is worth indicating how Weber's ideas can be shown to incorporate such a theme. Admittedly, it is latent rather than manifest. Consider first Weber's treatment of the nature of modern capitalist enterprise. What differentiates 'rational capitalism' from preceding forms? Above all, it is its stable, regular character. Pre-existing types of capitalistic enterprise take place in sporadic, stuttering fashion across time and space. Rational capitalism involves the forging of regularized market relationships across space, something that can only become well-developed with the formation of a bureaucratic state, which guarantees not only property rights but also other essential institutions, most notably a regularized form of paper money exchange.

But control of time is equally necessary. The rational capitalist enterprise is one that is able to operate in a stable, orderly fashion. Weber's emphasis upon the significance of double-entry book-keeping for the development of modern capitalism is readily understandable in these terms. Double-entry book-keeping makes possible continuous capital accounting over long periods of time. Capital accounting is the valuation and verification of profit-making opportunities. This means making a valuation of total assets at the beginning of a transaction or venture and comparing it with assets at a later date. Profitability depends, among other factors, upon being able to predict future events and subject them to calculation. Double-entry book-keeping is a kind of time-machine, because it both expresses and allows the quantification of units by reference to which the performance of an enterprise can be judged in 'ordered time'.[8]

Control of time is characteristic of bureaucracy in general, not just of capital enterprises. Double-entry book-keeping is a device which 'stacks' past events as well as anticipating future ones. Bureaucratic rules are also a way of doing this. Modern bureaucracies, Weber asserts, could not exist without the collation of documents which are both records of the past and prescriptions for the future — the 'files'. The files are not only documents of bureaucratic procedure; they exemplify that procedure and make possible the continuous and regular operation upon which bureaucratic discipline depends. Files are usually organized within definite offices and are part of what gives each office in a bureaucracy its distinctiveness. An 'office' is a physical setting as well as a level in an administrative hierarchy. Although Weber barely touches upon the point, the physical distribution of offices in bureaucracies is a distinctive feature of such organizations. The physical separation of offices insulates each from the other and gives a measure of autonomy to those within them, and also serves as a powerful marker of hierarchy.

Weber also stresses the importance of the separation of the office from the domicile of the worker.[9] One of the main characteristics of bureaucracy is that the vocational life of the official is segregated from home and family life. Impersonal formulae of bureaucratic discipline can be much more effectively applied when corporate monies and equipment can be kept separate from the private possessions of officials, when personal or kin ties are not the basis upon which decisions are concluded or appointments made and when matters concerning the household are distinguished from business affairs. The thoroughgoing separation of the home from the workplace, Weber makes clear, is found only in the modern West. But we might also note the importance of differentiation of locales in distinguishing between the spheres of operation of varying types of bureaucratic organization. Anyone who doubts the influence of the differentiation of space and setting in shaping and reflecting social patterns should ponder the position of the 'City' in Britain. Its spatial districtiveness from centres of 'industry', and its sheer concentration in one area, express major institutional characteristics of the society of which it is a part (see pp. 319—26).

Here we might return to Foucault. In this brief excursus I am not interested in assessing the historical rights and wrongs of his exposition, or in probing the theoretical shortcomings which might be discerned in the general views upon which it draws. I want only to add a point or two to his interpretation of the relation of disciplinary power to modalities of time and space. Let me begin with the discussion given in reference to Weber in the preceding paragraph. Foucault treats disciplinary organizations as epitomized by the prison and the asylum — 'total institutions' in Goffman's phrase, 'complete and austere institutions' in the characterization Foucault adopts from Beltard. 'The prison', as Foucault remarks, 'has neither exterior nor gap; it cannot be interrupted, except when the task is totally completed; its action on the individual must be uninterrupted: an increasing discipline . . . it gives almost total power over the prisoners; it has its internal mechanisms of repression and punishment: a despotic discipline.'[10] Factories, offices, schools, barracks and other contexts where surveillance and disciplinary power are brought into play are mostly not like this, as Foucault admits, without developing the point. It is an observation of some significance, however, because 'complete and austere institutions' are the exception rather than the rule within the main institutional sectors of modern societies. It does not follow that because prisons and asylums maximize disciplinary power, they express its nature more clearly than the other, less all-embracing organizations.

The journey to work (or school) probably indicates as much about the institutional character of modern societies as do carceral organizations. The time-space separation of different sectors of social life may indeed be the condition of the large-scale operation of disciplinary power. Most children attend schools only for part of the day and at certain periods of the year. Moreover, within the school day discipline is often observed in its stricter forms only within the definite timed periods that count as 'lessons'. There is no doubt that disciplinary power can be systematically generated only by the 'packing' of human beings into specific physically demarcated settings. But Weber is surely right to say that administrative discipline is most effective precisely when other aspects of individuals' lives are separated out from it. For it involves the regularized application of criteria of conduct that do not accord with the enactment of activities in other spheres of life. This is not solely because of the factors that Weber mentions but also because of the 'machine-like' nature of discipline. Foucault is led into difficulties in this regard. The point is not just that human beings resist being treated as automata, something which Foucault accepts; the prison is a site of struggle and resistance. Rather, it is that Foucault's 'bodies' are not agents. Even the most rigorous forms of discipline presume that those subject to them are 'capable' human agents, which is why they have to be 'educated', whereas machines are merely designed. But, unless subjected to the most extreme deprivation of resources, capable agents are likely to submit to discipline only for parts of the day — usually as a trade-off for rewards that derive from being freed from such discipline at other times.

In this respect reading Goffman on 'total institutions' can be more instructive than reading Foucault. For Goffman stresses that entry to prisons or asylums is demonstratively different from moving between other settings in which individuals may spend part of their day. 'Total institutions', by virtue of their all-embracing character, impose a totalizing discipline upon those who are placed within them. 'Adjustment' to these circumstances implies, and usually directly leads to, a process of degradation of self, by which the inmate is stripped of tokens of self-identity at the same time as the ordinary components of autonomy of action are heavily constricted. 'Total institutions', it may be said, both express aspects of surveillance and discipline found in other contexts in modern societies and yet also stand out in relief against those other contexts. 'Total institutions' ordinarily involve what Goffman calls 'civil death' — the loss of the right to vote and to engage in other forms of political participation, of the right to will money, write cheques, contest divorce or adopt children. But in addition inmates simply do not have separate spheres of activity where rewards denied in one sector can be pursued in another. Goffman's comment on such matters is very relevant:

> There is an incompatibility, then, between total institutions and the basic work-payment structure of our society. Total institutions are also incompatible with another crucial element of our society, the family. Family life is sometimes contrasted with solitary living, but in fact the more pertinent contrast is with batch living, for those who eat or sleep at work, with a group of fellow workers, can hardly sustain a meaningful domestic existence.[11]

Foucault treats the investigative procedures of criminal law, psychiatry and medicine as illustrating the nature of disciplinary power in general, especially as these are applied within carceral organizations. But again 'total institutions' stand out in this respect as different from the daily life paths of those outside. What Goffman calls the 'territories of the self' are violated there in ways which do not apply to those not within their walls. Four distinctive features of 'total institutions' can be mentioned in this respect.

(1) Interrogative procedures frequently transgress what for most of the population are regarded as legitimate 'information preserves' about the self and about the body. In other words, data about inmates' characteristics and past conduct — which would often be regarded as discreditable by them and by others and protected by suppression or tact — are collected in dossiers available to staff.

(2)   There is a dissolution of the boundaries between enclosure and disclosure that ordinarily serve to protect a sense of ontological security. Thus it may be the case that excretion, the maintenance of hygiene and appearance not only have to be carried out publicly but are subjected to regimentation by others.

(3)   There are often forced and continual relations with others. Hence just as there are no back regions for toilet activities, there are no back regions in which sectors of social life can be kept free from the disciplinary demands made elsewhere. Like Bettelheim, Goffman notes that in 'total institutions' human beings are reduced to states of childlike dependence.[12]

(4)   The temporal seriation of activities, in the short and long term, is specified and controlled. Inmates do not have 'free time' or 'their own time', as workers do. Moreover, those who undertake serial examinations or pass through serial stages of a career in the outside world are normally also able to counterpose these to other temporal units which have a different pattern. The temporal distribution of marriage and raising children, for example, is initiated separately from those pertaining in other spheres of life.

In carceral organizations the significance of the dialectic of control is still considerable. There are contexts in which that autonomy specifically characteristic of the human agent — the capability to 'have acted otherwise' — is severely reduced. The forms of control which inmates seek to exert over their day-to-day lives tend to be concentrated above all upon protection against degradation of the self. Resistance is certainly one of these and no doubt is an important consideration that in some degree imposes itself, whatever policies the administrative staff might follow in the implementation of disciplinary procedures. But various other forms of reaction can be readily identified. These include what Goffman calls 'colonization', the construction of a tolerable world within the interstices of managed time and space, and 'situational withdrawal', refusing, as it were, any longer to behave as a capable agent is expected to do. But probably the most common among prisoners, as among the 'mentally ill', is simply 'playing it cool'. This Goffman aptly describes as 'a somewhat opportunistic combination of secondary adjustments, conversion, colonization, and loyalty to the inmate group. . . .'[13]

There is no doubt, as many sociological studies have demonstrated, that such inmate groups can exert considerable control over day-to-day activities even in the most stringently disciplined carceral organizations. But the modes of control exerted by subordinates in other contexts, such as that of work, is likely to be greater because of a further way in which these contexts contrast with carceral ones. This is that superordinates have an interest in harnessing the activities of those subject to their authority to the enactment of designated tasks. In prisons or asylums the 'disciplining of bodies' comes close to describing what goes on; the administrative staff are not concerned with producing a collaborative endeavour at productive activity. In workplaces and schools, on the other hand, they are. Managers have to coax a certain level of performance from workers. They are concerned not only with the time-space differentiation and positioning of bodies but also with the co-ordination of the conduct of agents, whose behaviour has to be channelled in definite ways to produce collaborative outcomes. Foucault's bodies do not have faces. In circumstances of surveillance in the workplace — where surveillance means direct supervision, at any rate — discipline involves a great deal of 'face work' and the exercise of strategies of control that have in some part to be elaborated by agents on the spot. The time-space 'packing' of groupings of individuals in confined locales, where continuous supervision in circumstances of co-presence can be carried on, is obviously highly important to the generation of disciplinary power. But the demand that agents work together to effect some sort of productive outcome gives those agents a basis of control over the day-to-day operation of the workplace which can blunt supervisory efficacy. Supervisors and managers are as aware of this as anyone, and often build that awareness into the type of disciplinary policies they follow.[14] Some of the forms of control open to workers in a tightly integrated disciplinary space (e.g., the possibility of disrupting or bringing to a halt an entire production process) do not exist where a workforce is disaggregated in time and space.

Let me offer one final comment on Foucault and Goffman. Both writers have as one of the leading themes in their work the positioning and disciplining of the body. Like Foucault, Goffman has also pursued at some length questions of the nature of 'madness'. Their common concern with carceral organizations might lead one to overlook the differences in their respective views of madness. Goffman's perspective actually places that of Foucault radically in question in respect of the relations between 'insanity' and 'reason'. Foucault argues that what we call 'madness' — or, following the triumph of the medical metaphor, 'mental illness' — has been created in relatively recent times. Madness is the suppressed, sequestered, dark side of human awareness and passion, which Enlightenment and modern thought is unable to conceive of in any other way save as 'unreason'. In traditional cultures, or at least in medieval Europe, folly/*folie* encapsulated its own reason, permitting something of a direct access to God. But by the middle of the seventeenth century and thereafter, 'Madness has ceased to be, at the margins of the world, of man or death, an eschatological figure; the darkness on which the eyes of madness were trained, out of which the forms of the impossible were born, has evaporated. . . .'[15] But perhaps this view invests madness with a grandeur which it does not have and has never had? In seeing madness as the other face of reason it may express just those Enlightenment claims it affects to disparage. It may very well be that the clues to the character of madness or, in its modern guise, 'mental illness' are to be found not in the extravagance of delusions, visions of other worlds, but in much more mundane features of bodily and gestural impropriety. Social disability, not a mysterious access to a lost continent of unreason, may express its real nature.

References

Time, Space and Regionalization

1   See T. Hägerstrand, 'Space, time and human conditions', in A. Karlqvist, *Dynamic Allocation of Urban Space* (Farnborough: Saxon House, 1975); Derek Gregory, *Ideology, Science and Human Geography* (London: Hutchinson, 1978), and 'Solid geometry: notes on the recovery of spatial structure', in T. Carlstein *et al.*, *Timing Space and Spacing Time* (London: Arnold, 1978); T. Carlstein, *Time Resources, Society and Ecology* (Lund: Department of Geography, 1980); Alan Pred, 'The choreography of existence:

comments on Hägerstrand's time-geography', *Economic Geography,* vol. 53, 1977; Don Parkes and Nigel Thrift, *Times, Spaces and Places* (Chichester: Wiley, 1980); Nigel Thrift, 'On the determination of social action in space and time', *Society and Space,* vol. 1, 1982.

2 Hägerstrand: 'Space, time and human conditions', cf. also Parkes and Thrift, *Times, Spaces and Places,* pp. 247—8.

3 Alan Pred, 'The impact of technological and institutional innovations of life content: some time-geographic observations', *Geographical Analysis,* vol. 10, 1978.

4 Hägerstrand, *Innovation as a Spatial Process* (Chicago: Chicago University Press, 1967), p. 332. Cf. also Amos H. Hawley, *Human Ecology* (New York: Ronald Press, 1950), chapters 13—15; E. Gordon Ericksen, *The Territorial Experience* (Austin: University of Texas Press, 1980).

5 After Parkes and Thrift, *Times, Spaces and Places,* p. 245.

6 D. G. Janelle, 'Spatial reorganisation: a model and concept', *Annals of the Association of American Geographers,* vol. 58, 1969, and other articles by the same author.

7 P. Forer, in Carlstein *et al., Timing Space and Spacing Time.*

8 R. Palm and A. Pred, 'A time-geographic perspective on problems of inequality for women', in D. A. Lanegran and R. Palm, *An Invitation to Geography* (New York: McGraw-Hill, 1978).

9 Hägerstrand: 'Survival and arena: on the life-history of individuals in relation to their geographical environment', in Carlstein *et al., Timing Space and Spacing Time,* vol. 2, p. 123.

10 Carlstein, 'Innovation, time-allocation and time-space packing', ibid., p. 159; Carlstein, *Time Resources, Society and Ecology.*

11 Cf. T. Carlstein, 'The sociology of structuration in time and space: a time-geographic assessment of Giddens's theory', *Swedish Geographical Yearbook* (Lund: Lund University Press, 1981).

12 T. Hägerstrand, 'What about people in regional science?', *Papers of the Regional Science Association,* vol. 24, 1970, p. 8.

13 *CCHM,* chapter 5.

14 Ibid., pp. 161ff.; *CPST,* pp. 206—10.

15 M. Melbin, 'The colonisation of time', in Carlstein *et al., Timing Space and Spacing Time,* vol. 2, p. 100.

16 Evitar Zerubavel, *Patterns of Time in Hospital Life* (Chicago: University of Chicago Press, 1979), p. 22; cf. also P. A. Clark, 'A review of the theories of time and structure for organisational sociology', *University of Aston Management Centre Working Papers,* no. 248, 1982; Zerubavel, *Hidden Rythms* (Chicago: University of Chicago Press, 1981). One might point out that while

the 'year', 'month' and 'day' have links with natural events, the 'week' does not; cf. F. H. Colson, *The Week* (Cambridge: Cambridge University Press, 1926).

17   P. Ariès, *Centuries of Childhood* (Harmondsworth: Penguin, 1973); Norbert Elias, *The Civilising Process* (Oxford: Blackwell, 1978).

18   Edward T. Hall, *The Hidden Dimension* (London: Bodley Head, 1966), p. 98.

19   Antonin Artaud, *Le théâtre et la science* (Paris: Seuil, 1947), p. 98.

20   R. D. Laing, *Self and Others* (Harmondsworth: Penguin, 1971), p. 52.

21   *CCHM*, p. 169.

22   Huw Benyon, *Working for Ford* (London: Allen Lane, 1973), p. 76.

23   Elias, vol. 1.

24   Erving Goffman, *The Presentation of Self in Everyday Life* (New York: Doubleday, 1959), p. 128.

25   Cf. N. Elias and J. Scotson, *The Established and the Outsiders* (Leicester: University of Leicester Press, 1965).

26   Max Weber, *Economy and Society* (Berkeley: University of California Press, 1978), vol. 1, pp. 341—4.

27   *CSAS*, chapter 9.

28   *CCHM*, chapter 5, and *passim.*

29   Pierre Bourdieu, *Outline of a Theory of Practice* (Cambridge: Cambridge University Press, 1977), pp. 143—52.

30   Ibid., p. 153.

31   Andrew Pollard, 'Teacher interests and changing situations of survival threat in primary school classrooms', in Peter Woods, *Teacher Strategies* (London: Croom Helm, 1980).

32   Randall Collins, 'Micro-translation as a theory-building strategy', in K. Knorr-Cetina and A. V. Cicourel, *Advances in Social Theory and Methodology* (London: Routledge, 1981). See also idem, 'On the micro-foundations of macro-sociology', *American Journal of Sociology*, vol. 86, 1981. For Goffman's thoughts on the matter — given in a lecture which, sadly, he did not live to deliver — see 'The interaction order', *American Sociological Review*, vol. 48, 1973.

33   Ibid., p. 82.

34   Ibid., p. 99.

35   Joseph Rykwert, *The Idea of a Town* (London: Faber & Faber, 1976), p. 202.

36   *CCHM*, chapter 5.

Critical Notes: Foucault on Timing and Spacing

1   Michel Foucault, *Discipline and Punish* (Harmondsworth: Penguin, 1979), pp. 143—4.

2 Ibid., p. 148.
3 Cf. Maury D. Feld, *The Structure of Violence* (Beverly Hills: Sage, 1977), pp. 7ff.
4 Ibid., p. 7.
5 Jacques van Doorn, *The Soldier and Social Change* (Beverly Hills: Sage, 1975), p. 11.
6 Foucault, *Discipline and Punish*, p. 157.
7 Ibid., p. 160.
8 Max Weber, *Economy and Society* (Berkeley: University of California Press, 1978), pp. 86–94.
9 Ibid., p. 957.
10 Foucault, *Discipline and Punish*, pp. 235–6.
11 Erving Goffman, *Asylums* (Harmondsworth: Penguin, 1961), p. 22.
12 Ibid., p. 33.
13 Ibid., p. 64.
14 Cf. Andrew L. Friedman, *Industry and Labour* (London: Macmillan, 1977).
15 Foucault, *Folie et déraison* (Paris: Plon, 1961), p. 51. Foucault's preoccupation with exclusion, sequestration, etc., is not accompanied by a concern with the excluded themselves, who appear only as shadowy figures. Thus in his analysis of the case of the murderer Pierre Rivière the character himself barely emerges from the testimony discussed, which is treated only as a 'discursive episode'. Carlo Ginzburg's description of the cosmology of Mennochio, a sixteenth-century heretic, offers a telling comparison in this respect. See Foucault *et al.*, *Moi, Pierre Rivière . . .* (Paris: Plon, 1973); Carlo Ginzburg, *The Cheese and the Worms* (London: Routledge, 1980), pp. xvii–xviii, and *passim*.

4
Structure, System, Social Reproduction

Let me at this point try to ensure that the main threads of the discussion do not become too disaggregated in the reader's mind by summarizing the overall thrust of the preceding sections of the book. In structuration theory a range of dualisms or oppositions fundamental to other schools of social thought are reconceptualized as dualities. In particular, the dualism of the 'individual' and 'society' is reconceptualized as the duality of agency and structure. Thus far I have concentrated mainly upon developing a series of concepts which serve to elucidate what the 'individual' is as a reflexive agent, connecting reflexivity with positioning and co-presence. The discussion of regionalization, however, begins to point the way towards showing how these concerns intersect with the study of social systems stretched across large spans of time-space. The next step, therefore, is to look in more detail at the concept of society, taken by many to be the main unit of analysis in the social sciences. The term needs to be examined carefully, and I shall propose that some usages are best avoided altogether.

In certain traditions of social theory the concept of society is characteristically linked in a direct way with that of constraint. The advocates of structural sociology have, in fact, tended to regard constraint as in some way the defining characteristic of social phenomena. In rejecting such a view, I shall try to clarify the contention that the structural properties of social systems are both enabling and constraining, and shall specify how 'structural constraint' should be understood. This in turn involves indicating how a number of concepts associated with that of 'structure' might best be formulated. Such a formulation cannot be developed wholly on a conceptual level, however. Just as I gave some substance to the discussion of agency and self in the shape of an account of motivation, so I shall introduce a classification and interpretation of societal types to give flesh to the analysis of structural properties. This will in turn lead back again to questions of 'history', which will prepare the way for a consideration of problems of analysing social change in the following chapter.

A book has a sequential form, which can be overcome to some degree by 'circulating in and out' of a range of connected issues but which inevitably has its own presentational spacing. In the light of my discussion in chapter 1 I take it that, while the sections on the agent and upon co-presence precede in the text those on larger social systems, it will not be presumed that I am conceptually 'starting with the individual', or that I hold that individuals are real in some way in which societies are not. I do not accept any such views, as the Critical Notes appended to this chapter should make clear.

Societies, Social Systems

It is easy to see that in ordinary usage the term 'society' has two main senses (among others, such as 'society' in the sense of 'high society'). One is the generalized connotation of 'social association' or interaction; the other is the sense in which 'a society' is a unity, having boundaries which mark it off from other, surrounding societies. The ambiguity of the term in respect of these two senses is less unfortunate than it looks. For societal totalities by no means always have clearly demarcated boundaries, although they are typically associated with definite forms of locale. The tendency to suppose that societies, as social wholes, are easily definable units of study has been influenced by several noxious presumptions in the social sciences. One is the tendency to understand 'social systems' in close conceptual relation to biological systems, the bodies of biological organisms. There are few today who, as Durkheim, Spencer and many others in nineteenth-century social thought were prone to do, use direct organic analogies in describing social systems. But implicit parallels remain very common, even among those, for instance, who talk of societies as 'open systems'. A second factor is the prevalence of what I call 'endogenous' or 'unfolding models' in the social sciences.[1]* Such models presume that the main structural features of a society, governing both stability and change, are internal to that society. It is fairly evident why this is frequently connected to the first type of view: societies are imagined to have properties analogous to those which control the form and development of an organism. Finally one should mention the widespread proclivity to generalize to all forms of societal totality features that are in fact specific to modern societies as nation-states. Nation-states have clearly and precisely delimited territorial boundaries, but other types of society, by far the more numerous in history, do not.[2]

Resisting these presumptions can be facilitated if we recognize that societal totalities are found only within the context of *intersocietal systems* distributed along *time-space edges* (see pp. 244—6). All societies both are social systems and at the same time are constituted by the intersection of multiple social systems. Such multiple systems may be wholly 'internal' to societies, or they may cross-cut the 'inside' and the 'outside', forming a diversity of possible modes of connection between societal totalities and intersocietal systems. Intersocietal systems are not cut of whole cloth and characteristically involve forms of relation between societies of differing types. All these can be studied as systems of domination in terms of relations of autonomy and dependence which pertain between them. 'Time-space edges' refer to interconnections, and differentials of power, found between different societal types comprising intersocietal systems.

'Societies' then, in sum, are social systems which 'stand out' in bas-relief from a background of a range of other systemic relationships in which they are embedded. They stand out because definite structural principles serve to produce a specifiable overall 'clustering of institutions' across time and space. Such a clustering is the first and most basic identifying feature of a society, but others also have to be noted.[3] These include:

(1) An association between the social system and a specific locale or territory. The locales occupied by societies are not necessarily fixed areas. Nomadic societies roam across time-space paths of varying types.

*References may be found on pp. 221—4.

(2) The existence of normative elements that involve laying claim to the legitimate occupation of the locale. The modes and styles of such claims to legitimacy, of course, may be of many kinds and may be contested to greater or lesser degree.

(3) The prevalence, among the members of the society, of feelings that they have some sort of common identity, however that might be expressed or revealed. Such feelings may be manifest in both practical and discursive conscious-ness and do not presume a 'value consensus'. Individuals may be aware of belonging to a definite collectivity without agreeing that this is necessarily right and proper.

It is important here to re-emphasize that the term 'social system' should not be understood to designate only clusters of social relations whose boundaries are clearly set off from others. The degree of 'systemness' is very variable. 'Social system' has tended to be a favoured term of functionalists, who have rarely abandoned organic analogies altogether, and of 'system theorists', who have had in mind either physical systems or, once more, some kinds of biological formation. I take it to be one of the main features of structuration theory that the extension and 'closure' of societies across space and time is regarded as problematic.

The tendency to take nation-states as 'typical' forms of society, by reference to which others can be assessed, is so strong in the literature of social theory that it is worth developing the point. The three criteria mentioned above apply differentially in varying societal contexts. Consider, for instance, traditional China at a relatively late date, about AD 1700. It is common amongst Sino-logists to speak of 'Chinese society' at this period. Under this label scholars discuss such phenomena as state institutions, the gentry, economic units, family patterns and so on, regarding these as convergent with a specifiable overall social system, 'China'. But 'China' as designated in this way refers to only a small segment of the territory that a government official would have regarded as the land of the Chinese. According to his perspective, only one society existed on earth, centred upon 'China' as the capital of cultural and political life but stretching away to include a diversity of barbarians on the outer edges. Although the latter acted as though they were social groupings distinct from the Chinese, they were regarded in the official view as belonging to China. The Chinese of 1700 included Tibet, Burma and Korea within their concept of 'China', as these were in certain ways connected with the centre. There is some basis for the more restricted notion of 'China' espoused by Western historians and social scientists. But even acceptance that there was a distinct 'Chinese society' in 1700, separate from Tibet, etc., usually means including under that designation several million ethnically distinct groups in South China. These tribes regarded themselves as independent and as having their own organs of government. They were, however, continuously molested by representatives of Chinese officialdom, who treated them as belonging to the central state.

Modern Western nation-states are highly internally co-ordinated administrative unities compared with larger-scale agrarian societies. Let us shift the example somewhat further back, to fifth-century China, and ask what social ties might exist between a Chinese peasant farmer in Ho-nan province and the T'o-pa ruling class. From the point of view of the members of the dominant class, the farmer was at the lowest level of the hierarchical order. But the social relations of the farmer were quite discrete from the social world of the T'o-pa. Most of the farmer's contacts would be with others in the nuclear and extended family: many villages were composed only of lineage members. The fields were usually so arranged that members of lineage groups rarely met anyone other than kin in the course of the working day. The farmer would have visited neighbouring villages only on two or three occasions in the year, and perhaps a local town as infrequently. In the market-place of a nearby village or town he would have encountered other classes or ranks of people — craftsmen, artisans, traders, and a low-ranking official of the state administration, to whom he would pay taxes. Over his lifetime he would in all probability never see a T'o-pa. Local officials who visited the village would have to be given deliveries of grain or cloth. But the villager would probably avoid any other contacts with higher officialdom if they were ever imminent. For they could potentially mean brushes with the courts, imprisonment or enforced military service.

The borders recognized by the T'o-pa administration would not have coincided with the span of activities of the farmer if he were in certain areas in Ho-nan. Throughout the T'o-pa period many farmers had sustained contacts with members of their clan groups living on the other side of the border, in the southern states. A farmer who did not have such contacts would none the less have treated someone from beyond the border as a member of his own people rather than as a foreigner from another state. Suppose, however, he encountered someone from Kan-su province, in the north-west of the T'o-pa state. Such a person would have been treated as a complete stranger, even if that individual were working alongside him in the fields. The stranger would have spoken a different language (probably a Mongolian or Tibetan dialect), dressed differently and practised different customs. Neither the farmer nor the visitor may have been aware that they were both 'citizens' of the T'o-pa empire.

The Buddhist priests of the time were a different matter again. But with the exception of a small minority who were directly appointed by T'o-pa gentry to serve in their official temples, they also had little contact with the dominant class. Their locale, in which their lives were concentrated, was the monastery, but they had networks of social relationships which ranged from Central Asia to the south of China and Korea. The monasteries contained people of quite different ethnic and linguistic origin, brought together by their common religious pursuits. Their scholarship distinguished them from other social groupings. They travelled across state frontiers without restriction, regardless of those to whom they were nominally 'subject'. They were not, however, regarded as 'outside' Chinese society, as was the Arab community in Canton of the T'ang period. The state administration treated that community in some ways as belonging within its jurisdiction, requiring taxes from them and setting up special offices to deal with them. But it was also recognized that they belonged to a separate social order and therefore were not on a par with others within the realm of the state. One final example:

> In the nineteenth century we find in Yun-nan province a political rule of a bureaucracy which was controlled by Peking and represented the 'Chinese' government; there were villages and cities in the plains, inhabited by other Chinese who interacted with the government representatives and to some degree identified with that government. But on the slopes of the mountains there were other groups, in theory also subjects of China, yet living their own life, as far as they were allowed, and having their own values and institutions, even their own economic system. Interaction with the

valley-living Chinese was minimal and restricted to the sale of fire-wood and buying of salt or textiles. Finally, there was often a third group on the top of the mountains, again with its own institutions, language, values, religion. We can, if we like, bypass such conditions by calling these people 'minorities'. Yet the earlier the periods we study, the more such apparent minorities were truly self-contained societies, linked sometimes loosely by economic ties, and by occasional interaction; the relationship of such a society to the ruling power was typically that of subject to conqueror at the end of a war, with contacts held to a minimum from both sides.[4]

In thinking of units larger than imperial states, we have to avoid the tumble into ethnocentrism which it is so easy to make. We are prone today to speak readily of 'Europe' as a distinct sociopolitical entity, for example, but this is often a result of reading history backwards. As many historians interested in perspectives wider than those concentrated within nations or even 'continents' have pointed out, if the complex of societies stretching across Afro-Eurasia were to be divided into two, a cleavage between Europe as one portion (the 'West') and the rest as the 'East' would not make much sense. The Mediterranean Basin, for instance, was an historical unity both before the Roman Empire and for hundreds of years subsequently. India marked a greater cultural disjunction, travelling eastwards, than did the various Mid-Eastern lands with those bordering in 'Europe'; and there was yet greater discontinuity with China. As one historian has laconically expressed it, 'The Himalayas were more effective even than the Hindu-Kush.'[5] The differences between major 'culture areas' were often not much less marked than those between the units we would ordinarily recognize as 'societies'. Regionalization of wide scope should not be treated as composed simply of aggregate relations between 'societies'. Such a view has some validity when applied to the modern world of internally centralized nation-states but not when speaking of previous eras. Thus, for some purposes, the whole Afro-Eurasian zone can be treated as a unity. 'Civilization', from 6000 BC onwards, did not develop just as the creation of divergent centres; it was in some ways a continuous expansion 'outwards' of the Afro-Eurasian zone as a whole.[6]

Structure and Constraint: Durkheim and Others

Most forms of structural sociology, from Durkheim onwards, have been inspired by the idea that structural properties of society form constraining influences over action. In contrast to this view, structuration theory is based on the proposition that structure is always both enabling and constraining, in virtue of the inherent relation between structure and agency (and agency and power). All well and good, a critic may say — and some indeed have said[7] — but does not this conception in fact sacrifice anything akin to structural 'constraint' in Durkheim's sense? Does not speaking of structure as both constraining and enabling pay only lip service to the former? For in structuration theory 'structure' is defined as rules and resources. It is perhaps easy to see how structure in this sense is implicated in the generation of action but not so apparent where constraint enters in. For there seems to be no way in which the 'externality' of social phenomena to individual activity is sustained. Such a notion must be defended, it might be suggested, whatever the flaws in the writings of those mainly responsible for advocating it. Thus Carlstein remarks:

> a major drawback in Gidden's paradigm is that the *enabling* aspects of structure are not sufficiently balanced by *constraining* ones. There are too few principles of limitation, and by this I do not simply mean the moral-legal-normative social constraints empha- sized by Durkheim and Parsons, i.e. structures of legitimation. I am referring to *basic constraints of mediation and resource limitation* rooted in certain biotic-cum-physical realities of existence. Surely, structure must also imply limits to variation and to contingency in social systems (socio-environmental systems). Of course there is room for variation and human creativity. History has proven over and over again how the application of ideas and inventions in all realms of practice alters the received structure. But the latter is heavily biased towards the past, and imposes hard screening on things that are produced and reproduced. . . .[8]

I shall argue here, however, that the theory of structuration in no way minimizes the significance of the constraining aspects of structure. But 'constraint' as discussed in structural sociology tends to have several senses (Durkheim's terminology, for what it is worth, actually oscillated between the terms '*contrainte*' and '*coercition*'); and 'constraint' cannot be taken as a uniquely defining quality of 'structure'.

In structuration theory structure has always to be conceived of as a property of social systems, 'carried' in reproduced practices embedded in time and space. Social systems are organized hierarchically and laterally within societal totalities, the institutions of which form 'articulated ensembles'. If this point is ignored, the notion of 'structure' in the theory of structuration appears more idiosyncratic than it really is. One of the circumstances which Durkheim usually associates with constraint (also hinted at in the quotation from Carlstein) depends upon the observation that the *longue durée* of institutions both pre-exists and outlasts the lives of individuals born into a particular society. This is not only wholly compatible with structuration theory but is also inherent in its very formulation — although the 'socialization' of the individual into society should be understood as involving mutual time process, connecting the 'life-cycles' of both infant and parental figures. In his earlier writings Durkheim heavily emphasized the constraining elements of socialization, but later he in fact came to see more and more clearly that socialization fuses constraint and enablement. This is easily demonstrated in the instance of learning a first language. No one 'chooses' his or her native language, although learning to speak it involves definite elements of compliance. Since any language constrains thought (and action) in the sense that it presumes a range of framed, rule-governed properties, the process of language learning sets certain limits to cognition and activity. But by the very same token the learning of a language greatly expands the cognitive and practical capacities of the individual.

A second context in which Durkheim tends to speak of constraint also offers no logical difficulties for structuration theory. However, we have to be careful to avoid some of the dilemmas to which Durkheim's own analyses at this point give rise. Societal totalities, Durkheim points out, not only pre-exist and post-date the lives of the individuals who reproduce them in their activities; they also stretch across space and time away from any particular agent considered singly. In this sense the structural properties of social systems are certainly exterior to the activities of 'the individual'. In structuration theory the essentials of this point can be put as follows. Human societies, or social systems, would plainly not exist without human agency. But it is not the case that actors create social systems: they reproduce or transform them, remaking what is already made in the continuity of *praxis*.[9] The span of time-space distanciation is relevant here. In general (although certainly not universally) it is true that the greater the time-space distanciation of social systems — the more their institutions bite into time and space — the more resistant they are to manipulation or change by any individual agent. This meaning of constraint is also coupled to enablement. Time-space distanciation closes off some possibilities of human experience at the same time as it opens up others.

Durkheim's own formulation of this issue, however, is wanting, because it is couched in the terminology of what has come to be called by many writers 'emergent properties'. Thus Durkheim remarks:

> The hardness of bronze lies neither in the copper, nor in the tin, nor in the lead which have been used to form it, which are all soft and malleable bodies. The hardness arises from the mixing of them. The liquidity of water, its sustaining and other properties, are not in the two gases of which it is composed, but in the complex substance which they form by coming together. Let us apply this principle to sociology. If, as is granted to us, this synthesis *sui generis*, which constitutes every society, gives rise to new phenomena, different from those which occur in consciousnesses in isolation, one is forced to admit that these specific facts reside in the society itself that produces them and not in its parts — namely its members. In this sense therefore they lie outside the consciousness of individuals as such, in the same way as the distinctive features of life lie outside the chemical substances that make up a living organism.[10]

I have quoted this passage at some length just because it is so well-known and has been referred to so often as a particularly persuasive formulation. Social systems do have structural properties that cannot be described in terms of concepts referring to the consciousness of agents. But human actors, as recognizable 'competent agents', do not exist in separation from one another as copper, tin and lead do. They do not come together *ex nihilo* to form a new entity by their fusion or association. Durkheim here confuses a hypothetical conception of individuals in a state of nature (untainted by association with others) and real processes of social reproduction.

A third circumstance in which 'constraint' appears in Durkheim's writings is in juxtaposition to the scope of action of the agent. Durkheim gives the following among other examples:

> When I perform my duties as brother, husband, or citizen, and carry out the commitments I have entered into, I fulfil obligations which are defined in law and custom which are external to myself and my actions. Even if they conform to my own sentiments and I feel their reality within me, that reality does not cease to be objective, for it is not I who have prescribed those duties. . . .[11]

The point here is that 'social facts' have properties that confront each single individual as 'objective' features which limit that individual's scope of action. They are not just external but also externally defined, incorporated in what others do or in what they consider right and proper to do.

There is surely something correct about this claim, but Durkheim was prevented from spelling it out satisfactorily because of ambiguities about the notion of externality. In linking externality and constraint, especially in his earlier writings, he wanted to reinforce a naturalistic conception of social science. In other words, he wanted to find support for the idea that there are discernible aspects of social life governed by forces akin to those operative in the material world. Of course, 'society' is manifestly not external to individual actors in exactly the same sense as the surrounding environment is external to them. The parallel thus turns out to be at best a loose one, and a concern with it rests uneasily in Durkheim's later work alongside a recognition that the 'facticity' of the social world is in certain basic respects a very different phenomenon from the 'giveness' of nature.

Durkheim concentrated mostly upon social constraints in his various discussions of the nature of sociology. However, as Carlstein quite rightly points out — and as I have accentuated earlier, drawing upon the time-geography of which he himself is an expositor — fundamental constraints upon action are associated with the causal influences of the body and the material world. I have already indicated that these are regarded as of essential importance in structuration theory. Capability and coupling constraints, within definite material settings, do indeed 'screen' (as he puts it) the possible forms of activity in which human beings engage. But these phenomena are also at the same time enabling features of action. Moreover, as I have pointed out, there are major shortcomings in the usual formulations of time-geography.

The above aspects of constraint/enablement are not the same as, and are not to be reduced to, the operations of power in social life. Durkheim's sociology, in fact, may be seen as irremediably flawed in respect of the absence of a conception of power distinguished from the generalized constraining properties of 'social facts'. Consider one final celebrated passage from Durkheim. Constraint, he says, is

> intrinsically a characteristic of [social] facts. . . . the proof of this is that it asserts itself as soon as I try to resist. If I attempt to violate the rules of law, they react against me so as to forestall my action, if there is still time. Alternatively, they annul it or make my action conform to the norm if it is already accomplished but capable of being reversed; or they cause me to pay the penalty for it if it is irreparable. . . . In other cases the constraint is less violent; nevertheless, it does not cease to exist. If I do not conform to ordinary conventions, if in my mode of dress I pay no heed to what is customary in my country and in my social class, the laughter I provoke, the social distance at which I am kept, produce, although in a more mitigated form, the same results as any real penalty.[12]

Constraint here refers to the structuration of social systems as forms of asymmetrical power, in conjunction with which a range of normative sanctions may be deployed against those whose conduct is condemned, or disapproved of, by others. As Durkheim's statement indicates, the constraints generated by different types of resource may range from naked physical coercion to much more subtle ways of producing compliance. But it does no good at all to collapse this meaning of constraint into the others. Moreover, as I have strongly underlined, power is never merely a constraint but is at the very origin of the capabilities of agents to bring about intended outcomes of action.

Each of the various forms of constraint are thus also, in varying ways, forms of enablement. They serve to open up certain possibilities of action at the same time as they restrict or deny

others. It is important to emphasize this point because it shows
that those, (including Durkheim and many others) who have
hoped to find a distinctive identity for 'sociology' in the
identification of structural constraint are embarked on a vain
enterprise. Explicitly or otherwise, such authors have tended to
see in structural constraint a source of causation more or less
equivalent to the operation of impersonal causal forces in nature.
The range of 'free action' which agents have is restricted, as it
were, by external forces that set strict limits to what they can
achieve. The more that structural constraint is associated with a
natural science model, paradoxically, the freer the agent appears
— within whatever scope for individual action is left by the
operation of constraint. The structural properties of social
systems, in other words, are like the walls of a room from which
an individual cannot escape but inside which he or she is able to
move around at whim. Structuration theory replaces this view
with one which holds that structure is implicated in that very
'freedom of action' which is treated as a residual and unexplicated
category in the various forms of 'structural sociology'.

Three Senses of 'Constraint'

Let me first of all consider the meaning of constraint in respect of
material constraint and constraint associated with sanctions, then
move to structural constraint. What is constraint when we speak
of the constraining aspects of the body and its location in contexts
of the material world? It evidently refers here to limits which the
physical capacities of the human body, plus relevant features of
the physical environment, place upon the feasible options open
to agents. The indivisibility of the body, finitude of the life span
and 'packing' difficulties in time-space emphasized by Hägerstrand
are all examples of such limits. The sensory and communicative
capabilities of the human body are others. We are so used to
treating these as enabling qualities that it is necessary to make
something of a conceptual switch to stress that they are
constraining also. Of course, these constraints are not wholly
'given', once and for all; the invention of electronic communication, for example, has altered the pre-existing relation between
presence and the sensory media of the body. Alone among the
categories mentioned above, constraint in this sense does not

derive from the impact which the activities or social ties of actors have upon those of other actors. Physical capability and coupling constraints are limits to the feasible social lives that people can lead.

The time-geographic approach of beginning social analysis from identifying physical constraints is surely useful if certain qualifications are borne in mind. One, as I have said, is that the physical properties of the body and its material *milieux* of action are enabling as well as constraining, and these two aspects have to be studied together. Another is that the identification of physical constraints provides no particular fuel to defend a materialist interpretation of social life. All human beings have to cope with the constraints of the body, its media of mobility and communication. But it does not follow that the modes of coping with such constraints have somehow a more fundamental influence over social activity than do other types of constraint.

Turning to power as a source of constraint, again it needs to be stressed that power is the means of getting things done, very definitely enablement as well as constraint. The constraining aspects of power are experienced as *sanctions* of various kinds, ranging from the direct application of force or violence, or the threat of such application, to the mild expression of disapproval. Sanctions only very rarely take the shape of compulsion which those who experience them are wholly incapable of resisting, and even this can happen only for a brief moment, as when one person is physically rendered helpless by another or others. All other sanctions, no matter how oppressive and comprehensive they may be, demand some kind of acquiescence from those subject to them — which is the reason for the more or less universal purview of the dialectic of control. This is familiar enough ground. Even the threat of death carries no weight unless it is the case that the individual so threatened in some way values life. To say that an individual 'had no choice but to act in such and such a way', in a situation of this sort evidently means 'Given his/her desire not to die, the only alternative open was to act in the way he or she did.' Of course, where the threat offered by a sanction is not as lethal, compliance may depend more on mechanisms of conscience than on fear of any sanction — something, in fact, upon which Durkheim laid considerable emphasis in talking of 'moral sanctions'. In the case of sanctions there are obviously major asymmetries in the constraint/enablement relation. One person's constraint is another's enabling. However, as critiques of zero-sum theories of power have shown, such asymmetries by no means exhaust the scope of the concept of power.

We should bear in mind both the rather vague sense which terms like 'acquiescence' or 'compliance' tend to have, and the fact that by no means all 'acquiescence' in a given set of power relations is directly motivated. To acquiesce in a particular course of action might be thought to suggest conscious acceptance of that course of action and even 'voluntary' acceptance of the broader power relations in which it is enmeshed. Understood in such a fashion, acquiescence would cover only a small and relatively marginal proportion of instances in which the conduct of one actor or aggregate of actors conforms to what others want, or what is in their interests. Sanctions are usually very 'visible' only where some sort of designated transgression actually occurs or is perceived as likely to occur. Power relations are often most profoundly embedded in modes of conduct which are taken for granted by those who follow them, most especially in routinized behaviour, which is only diffusely motivated.

Material constraint	*(Negative) sanction*	*Structural constraint*
Constraint deriving from the character of the material world and from the physical qualities of the body	Constraint deriving from punitive responses on the part of some agents towards others	Constraint deriving from the contextuality of action, i.e., from the 'given' character of structural properties *vis-à-vis* situated actors

What, then, of structural constraint? Once constraint deriving from sanctions is separated off, Durkheim's other points collapse into one if scrutinized at all closely. To say that society pre-exists the lives of each of its individual members at any given moment is only to identify a source of constraint in so far as its pre-existence in some way limits possibilities open to them. To emphasize that individuals are contextually situated within social relations of greater or lesser span is similarly only to identify a source of constraint if it is shown how this limits their capabilities. In each case constraint stems from the 'objective' existence of structural properties that the individual agent is unable to change. As with the constraining qualities of sanctions, it is best described as

placing limits upon the range of options open to an actor, or
plurality of actors, in a given circumstance or type of circumstance.

Take the example given by Durkheim, that of the enactment of
contractual obligations, or one particular type of contract, the
labour contract. Contract, of course, involves strongly defined
legal sanctions, but let us conceptually filter them out. The
contractual relations of modern industry face the individual with
a set of circumstances which limit available options of action.
Marx says that workers 'must sell themselves' — or, more
accurately, their labour power — to employers. The 'must' in the
phrase expresses a constraint which derives from the institutional
order of modern capitalist enterprise that the worker faces. There
is only one course of action open to the worker who has been
rendered propertyless — to sell his or her labour power to the
capitalist. That is to say, there is only one feasible option, given
that the worker has the motivation to wish to survive. The
'option' in question could be treated as a single one or as a
multiple set of possibilities. That is to say, a worker may have a
choice of more than one job opening in the labour market.
Marx's point, however, is that these options effectively are of a
single type. In respect of the rewards they offer to the worker,
and of other features of the worker—employer relationship, all
wage labour is effectively the same — and supposedly becomes
even more so with the further development of capitalism.

All structural properties of social systems have a similar
'objectivity' *vis-à-vis* the individual agent. How far these are
constraining qualities varies according to the context and nature
of any given sequence of action or strip of interaction. In other
words, the feasible options open to agents may be greater than in
the case of the labour contract example. Let me reaffirm once
more the theorem that all structural properties of social systems
are enabling as well as constraining. The conditions of the
capitalist labour contract may heavily favour employers as
compared with workers. But once they have become propertyless,
workers are dependent upon the resources that employers
provide. Both sides derive their livelihood from the capital/wage-
labour relation, heavily asymmetrical though it may be.

This analysis does not invalidate the sorts of claim that social
scientists or historians make when they talk of 'social forces'
without reference to agents' reasons or intentions. In institutional

analysis it is permissible to establish regularized connections which are set out in an 'impersonal' manner. Suppose, by way of illustration, we isolate a relation between technological change and patterns of managerial organization in business firms. The expanding use of microchip technology, let us say, might be shown to be associated with a partial dissolution of more rigid forms of hierarchical authority. The 'social force' involved here is not like a force of nature. Causal generalizations in the social sciences always presume a typical 'mix' of intended and unintended consequence of action, on the basis of the rationalization of conduct, whether 'carried' on the level of discursive or of practical consciousness. Technological change is not something that occurs independently of the uses to which agents put technology, the characteristic modes of innovation, etc. It is odd that many structural sociologists who are perfectly able to accept this — that technology does not change in and of itself (how could it?) — do not seem to see that exactly the same applies to the social forces linking technological change with such a phenomenon as managerial hierarchies. Somehow, whether mainly as a result of conscious planning or in a fashion more or less completely unintended by any of those involved, actors modify their conduct and that of others in such a way as to reshape modes of authority relations — presuming that the connection is indeed a genuinely causal one.

Why is it that some social forces have an apparently 'inevitable' look to them? It is because in such instances there are few options open to the actors in question, given that they behave rationally — 'rationally' in this case meaning effectively aligning motives with the end-result of whatever conduct is involved. That is to say, the actors have 'good reasons' for what they do, reasons which the structural sociologist is likely to assume implicitly rather than explicitly attributing to those actors. Since such good reasons involve a choice from very limited feasible alternatives, their conduct may appear to be driven by some implacable force similar to a physical force. There are many social forces that actors, in a meaningful sense of that phrase, are 'unable to resist'. That is to say, they cannot do anything about them. But 'cannot' here means that they are unable to do anything other than conform to whatever the trends in question are, given the motives or goals which underlie their action.

I take it as one of the main implications of the foregoing points that there is no such entity as a distinctive type of 'structural explanation' in the social sciences; all explanations will involve at least implicit reference both to the purposive, reasoning behaviour of agents and to its intersection with constraining and enabling features of the social and material contexts of that behaviour. Two qualifications require to be added to this observation, one to do with the historically shifting character of constraint, the other associated with the phenomenon of reification.

Constraint and Reification

The nature of constraint is historically variable, as are the enabling qualities generated by the contextualities of human action. It is variable in relation to the material and institutional circumstances of activity, but also in relation to the forms of knowledgeability that agents possess about those circumstances. To have understood this is one of the main achievements of Marxist thought where it has not relapsed into objectivism. When it has done so, it has become methodologically just another version of a structural sociology, insensitive to the multiple meanings which constraint must be recognized as having in social analysis. Why should such insensitivity exist? The answer, I think, is fairly clear. It is usually associated with those types of social thought which suppose that the aim of the social sciences is to uncover laws of social activity which have a status similar to that of natural scientific laws. To look for sources of 'structural constraint' is presumed to be more or less the same as looking for the law-governed conditions that put limits on the bounds of free action. This, for many writers, is exactly where 'sociology' finds its role as a distinctive endeavour among the other social sciences. But according to the view suggested here, it produces a form of reified discourse not true to the real characteristics of human agents.

'Reification' has been understood in a variety of different ways in literature of social theory. Among those divergent uses three characteristic senses can be most commonly discerned. One is an animistic sense, where social relations become attributed with personified characteristics. A version of this is to be found in Marx's celebrated discussion of the 'fetishism of commodities', in which he compares commodity relations to the 'mist-enveloped regions of the religious world'. Just as in religion 'the productions of the human brain appear as independent beings endowed with life, and entering into relation both with one another and the human race', so it is in the 'world of commodities' with the 'products of men's hands'.[13] Another sense in which the term reification is often employed is to refer to circumstances in which social phenomena become endowed with thing-like properties which they do not in fact have. Again there is a reputable ancestry for this coinage in Marx: 'In exchange value, the social connection between persons is transformed into a relation between things. . . .'[14] Finally, 'reification' is sometimes used to designate characteristics of social theories which treat concepts as though they were the objects to which they referred, as attributing properties to those concepts.

The second of these senses is the one I shall adopt, but it is not acceptable as it stands because it implies that the quality of being 'thing-like' does not need further explication and because it does not make it clear that reification is a discursive notion. The concept should not be understood simply to refer to properties of social systems which are 'objectively given' so far as specific, situated actors are concerned. Rather, it should be seen as referring to forms of discourse which treat such properties as 'objectively given' in the same way as are natural phenomena. That is to say, reified discourse refers to the 'facticity' with which social phenomena confront individual actors in such a way as to ignore how they are produced and reproduced through human agency.[15] Reification thus should not be interpreted to mean 'thing-like' in such a connotation; it concerns, rather, the consequences of thinking in this kind of fashion, whether such thinking is done by those who would call themselves social scientists or by lay members of society. The 'reified mode' should be considered a form or style of discourse, in which the properties of social systems are regarded as having the same fixity as that presumed in laws of nature.

The Concept of Structural Principles

The implications of the foregoing sections of this chapter can be described as follows. Structural constraint is not expressed in terms of the implacable causal forms which structural sociologists have in mind when they emphasize so strongly the association of 'structure' with 'constraint'. Structural constraints do not operate independently of the motives and reasons that agents have for what they do. They cannot be compared with the effect of, say, an earthquake which destroys a town and its inhabitants without their in any way being able to do anything about it. The only moving objects in human social relations are individual agents, who employ resources to make things happen, intentionally or otherwise. The structural properties of social systems do not act, or 'act on', anyone like forces of nature to 'compel' him or her to behave in any particular way. (For further discussion in relation to problems of empirical research, see pp. 304—10.)

However, there is a range of further notions relevant to speaking of 'structure' in social analysis, and these require special consideration. I shall discuss them in the following order. First, how should the concept of 'structural principle' be developed? Second, what levels of abstraction can be distinguished in studying the structural properties of social systems? Third, how are diverse social systems articulated within societal totalities?

In identifying structural principles the discussion has to move back from the formal to the rather more substantive. Let me recall, to begin with, a main strand of structuration theory, introduced in the first chapter. The 'problem of order' in the theory of structuration is the problem of how it comes about that social systems 'bind' time and space, incorporating and integrating presence and absence. This in turn is closely bound up with the problematic of time-space distanciation: the 'stretching' of social systems across time-space. Structural principles can thus be understood as the principles of organization which allow recognizably consistent forms of time-space distanciation on the basis of definite mechanisms of societal integration. Drawing upon a range of comparative and historical studies,[16] I propose a threefold classification of types of society as below:

TRIBAL SOCIETY (Oral cultures)	{ Tradition (communal practices) Kinship Group sanctions	(Fusion of social and system integration)

Dominant locale organization   Band groups or villages

CLASS-DIVIDED SOCIETY

$\left\{\begin{array}{l}\text{Tradition (communal}\\ \quad\text{practices)}\\ \text{Kinship}\\ \text{Politics—military power}\\ \text{Economic interdependence}\\ \quad\text{(low lateral and vertical}\\ \quad\text{integration)}\end{array}\right.$

STATE

(Differentiation
of social and
system integration)

Dominant locale organization   Symbiosis of city and
countryside

CLASS SOCIETY
(Capitalism)

$\left\{\begin{array}{l}\text{Routinization}\\ \text{Kinship (family)}\\ \text{Surveillance}\\ \text{Politics—military power}\\ \text{Economic interdependence}\\ \quad\text{(high lateral and vertical}\\ \quad\text{integration)}\end{array}\right.$

STATE

(Differentiation of
social and system
integration)

Dominant locale organization   The 'created environment'

This scheme is described in some detail in *A Contemporary Critique of Historical Materialism*, and I shall gloss it rather rapidly here.[17] In tribal societies or small oral cultures the dominant structural principle operates along an axis relating tradition and kinship, embedding themselves in time and space. In these societies the media of social and system integration are the same, depending overwhelmingly upon interaction in the settings of locales of high presence availability. Of course, a variety of different sub-types of society can be distinguished within this general category. I should emphasize that I do not intend to present this classification as a surreptitious evolutionary scheme. Oral cultures should not be understood as societies in which system integration has 'not yet' become disentangled from social integration. As Lévi-Strauss has done more than anyone else to make clear, tribal societies — in which humankind has lived out all but a small fraction of its history — are substantially divergent from 'civilizations', of whatever type. The invention of writing, so closely involved with the formation of states and classes, alters the character of time as lived experience, by the very means whereby it permits an expanding of time-space distanciation.

The dominant structural principle of class-divided society — which obviously also includes a range of sub-types — is to be found along an axis relating urban areas to their rural hinterlands. The city is far more than a mere physical *milieu*. It is a 'storage container' of administrative resources around which agrarian states are built. The differentiation of city and countryside is the means of the separation of social and system integration, although the two are not necessarily coincident, for the symbiotic relation of city and countryside may take various forms.[18] In class-divided societies traditional practices and kinship relations, even tribal identifications, remain very prominent. The state is unable to penetrate deeply into localized customs, and sheer military power is one of the principal foundations upon which government officialdom is able to 'contain' outlying regions where direct administrative control is particularly weak. Class-divided society is marked, however, by some disentangling of the four institutional spheres distinguished above (p. 33). The polity, with its officials, is separated in some part from the procedures of economic activity; formal codes of law and punishment exist; and modes of symbolic co-ordination, based in written texts, make their appearance.

Modern capitalism is not one type of 'civilization' among others, and it does not mark an evolutionary development 'out of' class-divided societies. The first genuinely global type of societal organization in history, it has its origins in a double discontinuity in the development of the West. There are long-term divergencies in the formation of the West, as compared with that of the other major 'civilizations', over a period of some two millennia; Europe remained a 'state system', and no dominant imperial centre was re-established in its midst after the disintegration of the Roman Empire. Within this broad divergence, however, a range of massive discontinuities from other types of society was introduced by the intertwining of political and industrial revolutions from the eighteenth century onwards. The distinctive structural principle of the class societies of modern capitalism is to be found in the disembedding, yet interconnecting, of state and economic institutions. The tremendous economic power generated by the harnessing of allocative resources to a generic tendency towards technical improvement is matched by an enormous expansion in the administrative 'reach' of the state. Surveillance — the coding of information relevant to the administration of subject populations, plus their direct supervision by officials and administrators of all sorts — becomes a key mechanism furthering a breaking away of system from social integration. Traditional practices are dispersed (without, of course, disappearing altogether) under the impact of the penetration of day-to-day life by codified administrative procedures. The locales which provide the settings for interaction in situations of co-presence undergo a major set of transmutations. The old city—countryside relation is replaced by a sprawling expansion of a manufactured or 'created environment'.

A categorization of intersocietal systems can be formulated — in a broad way at least — in terms of the above classification of society types as follows:

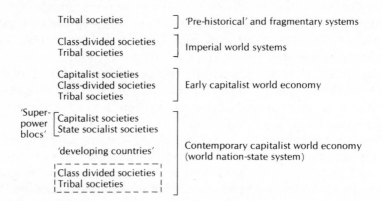

This categorization, it should be pointed out, is not at all symmetrical in respect of historical chronology. The smallest category figuratively — systems of tribal societies — is by far the largest in terms of span of time. Intersocietal systems involving tribal societies have always been relatively fragmentary, however, in the sense that they have been confined in respect of their configurations across time-space. They have dominated the world for most of human history, but they have not formed 'world systems' in Wallerstein's sense.[19] That is to say, 'civilizations' have developed centres of power which have influenced large segments of the globe, and they have fired the 'heat' of rapid social change. Imperial world systems, however, have existed only in uneasy relation to a diversity of forms of tribal societies and have frequently succumbed to attacks or pressures from such societies. The phase of the early capitalist world economy was a transitory one in history, lasting no longer than two centuries or so. Yet during that phase a greater variety of types of society existed in relation with one another than at any other period before or afterwards. For since that time the increasing ascendancy of Western capitalist societies, challenged only by the state socialist societies[20] in terms of their industrial and military power, has implacably destroyed or corroded tribal and class-divided societies, which perhaps are forever disappearing from the face of the earth. The contemporary world system is, for the first time in human history, one in which absence in space no longer hinders system co-ordination. Is it necessary to stress again that the development of the world nation-state system is not coeval with the expansion of cohesion or consensus? For the same developments which have created at once that distinctively modern form of society, the nation-state and its involvement in a global system of a new type, have at the same time brought into being schisms which, in the nuclear age, threaten the very survival of humanity as a whole.[21]

Structures, Structural Properties

As I have previously emphasized, the concept of structure may be used in a technical and in a more general way. Understood as rules and resources, structure is recursively implicated in the reproduction of social systems and is wholly fundamental to structuration theory. Used in a looser fashion, structure can be spoken of as referring to the institutionalized features (structural properties) of societies. In both usages 'structure' is a generic category involved in each of the structural concepts given below:

(1) *structural principles*: Principles of organization of societal totalities;
(2) *structures*: Rule-resource sets, involved in the institutional articulation of social systems;
(3) *structural properties*: Institutionalized features of social systems, stretching across time and space.

The identification of structural principles, and their conjunctures in intersocietal systems, represents the most comprehensive level of institutional analysis. That is to say, the analysis of structural principles refers to modes of differentiation and articulation of institutions across the 'deepest' reaches of time-space. The study of structural sets, or *structures*, involves the isolating of distinct 'clusterings' of transformation/mediation relations implied in the designation of structural principles. Structural sets are formed by the mutual convertibility of the rules and resources implicated in social reproduction. Structures can be analytically distinguished within each of the three dimensions of structuration, signification, legitimation and domination, or across these. I have offered elsewhere an illustration,[22] on which I shall comment at rather greater length here. This is the example of private property in Marx's analysis of modern capitalism.

Consider what is involved in the following structural set:

private property : money : capital : labour contract : profit

The structural relations indicated here mark out one of the most fundamental transmutations involved in the emergence of capitalism and hence contribute in a significant way to the overall structuration of the system. In feudalism (in my terminology, one among other types of class-divided society) private property in the means of production was based predominantly on ownership of land, and such ownership was hedged about with numerous qualifications upon alienability. In so far as these conversion relations pertained at all, they were confined to marginal sectors of the economy. In capitalism, by contrast, private ownership of the means of production takes on a different *form* — land becoming only one type among other resources mobilized within production — and a diversity of goods becomes freely alienable. Essential to this process, Marx demonstrates, is the universalizing of commodity form. The condition of such universalization is the development of a full-blown money economy. Money, Marx says, is 'the metamorphosed shape of all other commodities, the result of their general alienation'.[23] Money (M) represents, on the one side, a sold commodity (C) and, on the other, a commodity to be bought. M-C is a purchase but is at the same time C-M, a sale: 'the concluding metamorphosis of one commodity is the first metamorphosis of another' or, as Quesnay expressed the same thing in his *Maximes générales*, 'vendre est acheter.' The differentiation of commodities into commodities and money does not dissolve the material differences between commodities; it develops, Marx says, a *modus vivendi*, 'a form in which they can exist side by side'.[24]

C-M-C, the simplest form of the circulation of commodities, is the beginning point of capital. As contrasted with the landed property of feudalism, capital first takes the form of money — the capital of the merchant and the usurer. The first distinction between money and capital is simply a difference in the relation of transformation involved, expressed as M-C-M. This formula expresses the transformation of money into commodities and of commodities back into money — in other words, buying in order to sell. Money which has undergone this transformation has become capital. Like the other relation, M-C-M involves two linked phases of transmutation. In the first money is changed into a commodity; in the second the commodity is changed back again into money. But the combination of these phases, Marx argues, 'constitutes a single moment' whereby a commodity is bought in order to be sold. It might seem as though money has simply been exchanged for money — more or less, according to the success or otherwise of the transaction. But where money has been transformed into capital it has gone through a 'characteristic and original movement' quite distinct in type from that of, say, a peasant who sells corn and uses the money thus acquired to buy clothes. The transformations involved in M-C-M, as compared with C-M-C, differ more than in the mere difference in the 'direction' of change.

The difference is that in the C-M-C relation the money is converted into a use value, which is then 'consumed'. In the opposite form, M-C-M, the money is not spent; it is 'advanced' — the secret of the transformation of money into capital. In the C-M-C form the same element of money changes its place twice, completing the transaction. But the contrary is the case in the M-C-M relation: in this connection it is not the money that changes hands twice but the commodity. The transmutation of money into capital depends upon the renewal of the operation, its 'reflux', which only the M-C-M relation makes possible. M-C-M should thus more accurately be written as M-C-M^1, as an expansionary process. The circulation of commodities has here become separated off from a direct relation to use value. Capital trades not in use values but in exchange values.

M-C-M^1, however, can represent mercantile capital as well as industrial capital. It is therefore only the 'general formula for capital'. A further structural relation is implicated in the development of industrial or manufacturing capital, one which, like the altered nature of private property, presumes a major process of social change. This further relation is the possibility of the transformation of capital into labour and *vice versa*, something which presupposes a massive expropriation of workers from control of their means of production, such that they have to offer their labour power for sale on the market in order to attain a livelihood. Labour power is a commodity that has the peculiar feature, among others, of being a source of the creation of value. The capitalist labour contract is inherently involved with the transformation of money into an equivalent of labour power. 'This relation has no natural basis, neither is its social basis one that is common to all historical periods. It is clearly the result of a past historical development, the product of many economic revolutions, of the extinction of a whole series of older forms of social production.'[25] Thus the isolation of such a connection helps to diagnose one of the key structural features of the novel institutional form constituted by capitalism. That labour power is a commodity is not given in the 'general formula for capital'.

The capitalist labour contract presumes that employer and worker 'meet in the market' in circumstances in which each is 'formally free'. This is a basic aspect of the class relations of capitalism. One is a buyer of labour power, the other a seller. The 'owner' of labour power sells it only for a definite period, as does the employer who 'takes on' labour. Slavery, in which some persons are owned by others, does not permit the commodification of labour power. The value of labour power, in common with that of other commodities, is governed by the labour time involved in its production and therefore by what is demanded to ensure the physical survival of those who supply labour. The transformation of the hire of labour power into profit, of course, is dependent upon the generation of surplus value. 'Necessary labour time' is that given over to the sustaining of the source of labour power, the worker; surplus labour is the source of profit.

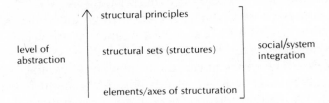

There is no definite cut-off point between the three levels of abstraction distinguished in the above diagram. The specification of structural sets, as indicated previously, is of basic importance to the elaboration of overall structural principles, but the one task obviously merges into the other. The same holds for the lowest level of abstraction, the isolating of elements or axes of structuration. Distinguishing elements of structuration preserves the *epoché* of institutional analysis, but brings the level of study closer to the direct examination of relations of co-presence. In order to preserve continuity with the preceding discussion, let me follow through Marx's discussion in respect of a major feature of capitalist production, the division of labour. It is an analysis with which I am largely in accord, although my main purpose here is an illustrative one.[26]

The division of labour, Marx seeks to show, is closely bound up with the nature of manufacture and therefore with the structural relations portrayed in the foregoing paragraphs of this chapter. The division of labour links the broader structural characteristics of capitalism, as identified previously, with the more proximate organization of the industrial enterprise. Manufacture, a pre-eminent feature of capitalism that has advanced beyond commerce, is associated with two modes of the emergence of workshops. One is the assembling, under the control of a particular employer, of workers with different craft skills in a specific locale. These are co-ordinated in the making of a single product. But such co-ordination tends also progressively to strip away aspects of the skills originally possessed by workers, leading to the splitting up of tasks into 'detailed' processes, 'each of which crystallizes into the exclusive function of a particular workman, the manufacture, as a whole, being carried on by the men in conjunction'.[27] A second way in which manufacture arises is something of the reverse of this. It is the assembling within one locale of a number of workers who all do the same task, each worker making the entire commodity. However, 'external circumstances', Marx says, lead to changes in much the same direction as those occurring in the first type of setting. Labour is therefore redistributed; instead of workers all occupied in the same way side by side, operations become broken down into detailed tasks, organized in a co-operative fashion. The final form is thus the same in both cases: 'a productive mechanism whose parts are human beings'.[28]

The detailed division of labour is of major importance to the organization of the capitalist enterprise in several ways. It enhances the opportunities for direct surveillance of the workforce and the consolidation of labour discipline. But it also both expresses and makes possible the connection of labour, as labour power, with the technology of machine production. For the 'detail labourer' carries out a circumscribed number of repetitive operations that can be co-ordinated with the movements of mechanized production processes. Division of labour within the enterprise is not simply an aspect or extension of the division of labour outside, the 'division of labour in society', but these none the less react upon one another. The 'division of labour in society' depends upon the purchase and sale of products of different sectors of industry; the division of labour within the enterprise derives from the sale of the labour power of a plurality of workers to an employer who applies it in a co-ordinated fashion.

> Division of labour within the workshop implies the undisputed authority of the capitalist over men, that are but parts of a mechanism that belongs to him. The division of labour within the society brings into contact independent commodity-producers, who acknowledge no other authority but that of competition. . . . It is very characteristic [Marx adds caustically] that the enthusiastic apologists of the factory system have nothing more damning to urge against a general organization of the labour of society than that it would turn all society into one immense factory.[29]

To analyse the division of labour in this way is to elucidate an axis of structuration connecting the internal form of the enterprise with broader aspects of the societal totality, indicating at the same time contrasts with the 'division of labour in society'. Of course, these relations could be spelled out in very much greater detail. In institutional analysis this involves detailing the transformation/mediation relations implicated in the 'clustering' of institutionalized practices across space and time. However, once we abandon the *epoché* of institutional analysis, all the structural relations indicated above, at whatever level, have to be examined as conditions of system reproduction. They help to pick out basic features of the *circuits of reproduction* implicated in the 'stretching' of institutions across space and time. Analysing circuits of reproduction, it should be clear, is not equivalent to identifying the sources of social stability alone. They serve indeed to indicate some of the main forms of change involved in the transition from one type of societal totality to another. What 'must happen' for certain conditions of system reproduction to occur is posed as a counterfactual question, not as a covert version of functionalism.

A reproduction circuit can be sketched in diagrammatic form (see figure 11):

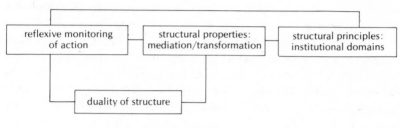

Figure 11

The reintroduction of the duality of structure means leaving the virtual time-space of institutional analysis, thereby re-entering 'history'. All structural properties of social systems, to repeat a leading theme of structuration theory, are the medium and outcome of the contingently accomplished activities of situated actors. The reflexive monitoring of action in situations of co-presence is the main anchoring feature of social integration, but both the conditions and the outcomes of situated interaction stretch far beyond those situations as such. The mechanisms of 'stretching' are variable but in modern societies tend to involve reflexive monitoring itself. That is to say, understanding the conditions of system reproduction becomes part of those conditions of system reproduction as such.

We can trace these observations through more concretely by returning to the structural set discussed previously. The two opposed but complementary transformations C-M and M-C occur, of course, only through the activities of buyers and sellers acting in a range of divergent settings. According to Marx, the C-M-C relation brings into co-relation three *'dramatis personae'*. The owner of a commodity comes into contact with a possessor of money, the money becoming, Marx's words, 'its transient equivalent-form'. Money, the 'final term of the first transmutation', is the origin of the third, the buying of another commodity.[30] But as Marx expresses it, this is unsatisfactory. For structural relations are not isomorphic to the acts of corresponding individuals who personify them. It is in just such tendencies of Marx's argument that one can see where Althusser derives textual corroboration for the view that human agents are no more than 'supports' for modes of production. Moreover, it is also easy to see how such a style of analysis slips over into functionalism. For if the relations between structural properties, once isolated, are treated as having their own 'inner dynamics', as functional necessities rather than as continually reproduced conditions, the activities of historically situated individuals do indeed seem rather redundant. The overall conditions of system reproduction are in no way 'guaranteed' by the structural relations upon which (counter-factually) they depend. Nor does analysing those relations in virtual time-space explain in any way why they came about. This means that it is highly important to shift conceptual gears when moving from such analysis to the study of the conditions of system reproduction.

By circuits of reproduction I mean fairly clearly defined 'tracks' of processes which feed back to their source, whether or not such feedback is reflexively monitored by agents in specific social positions. When Marx uses the term 'circuits of capital' he seems to have something of this sort in mind; however, I want to refer to actual conditions of social reproduction, while Marx sometimes uses the term in reference to what I have called structural sets. Reproduction circuits can always usefully be examined in terms of the regionalization of locales. There is no harm in thinking of such circuits as having something in common with electronic circuits, which can be traced out in a visual display — the graphic techniques of time-geography, in fact, might be relevant here. The reproduction circuits associated with the M-C-M^1 set — as Marx himself makes clear — actually depend upon vast processes of change not just within societies but on an international scale. The concentration of the population in newly expanding (and internally transformed) urban areas is one of these processes of change. Others concern the nature of the workplace. But as important as any of these is the mechanization of transportation, the tremendous expansion of means of communication from the late eighteenth century onwards and the development of electronic communication dating from the invention of the Morse Code.

Contradiction

It is commonly remarked that the concept of contradiction should remain a logical one rather than being applied to social analysis. One can indeed see considerable justification for such a judgement because the term is often employed so vaguely that it has no particular connection with contradiction in logic. Given that it is used with some care, however, I think the concept to be an indispensable one in social theory. I propose to use it in two senses: that of 'existential contradiction' and that of 'structural contradiction'. Each preserves some continuity with the logical usage of the term while not being a direct extension of that usage.

By existential contradiction I refer to an elemental aspect of human existence in relation to nature or the material world. There is, one might say, an antagonism of opposites at the very heart of the human condition, in the sense that life is predicated upon nature, yet is not of nature and is set off against it. Human beings emerge from the 'nothingness' of inorganic nature and disappear back into that alien state of the inorganic. This might seem to be an unabashedly religious theme and as such to be the proper province of theology rather than social science. But I think it to be in fact of great analytical interest, although I shall not attempt to develop that contention here.

Structural contradiction refers to the constitutive features of human societies. I suggest that structural principles operate in contradiction. What I mean by this is that structural principles operate in terms of one another but yet also contravene each other.[31] 'Contradiction' in this sense can be further divided into two. By primary contradictions I refer to those which enter into the constitution of societal totalities; by secondary contradictions I mean those which are dependent upon, or are brought into being by, primary contradictions. I do not intend by these simply an abstract series of distinctions; they have to be related to the study of the societal types described above. The concept of structural contradiction has reference to a specific characterization of the state. Except in the case of tribal society, the state is regarded as the focus (although not as such also the origin) of primary structural contradiction.

Of the three types of society I have distinguished, tribal societies exist in closest relation to nature. By this I do not refer to their technological development, or at least not to that alone. In tribal societies human beings live closely with each other in conditions of co-presence and within the rhythms of nature in their day-to-day conduct, but they also integrate the natural world cognitively with their activities. From the point of view of civilizations — especially that of the modern West — this is something to be seen only negatively, a failure to rise to a higher level on a cognitive scale. Lévi-Strauss expresses this very well when he comments: 'Anthropology, we are apt to say . . . is concerned with societies that are *non*-civilized, *without* a system of writing, and *pre-* or *non*-industrial in type.' In some respects, however, it is 'modern' societies that should be defined in negative terms. Our relations with one another are now only occasionally and fragmentarily based upon 'generic experience', the 'concrete "apprehension" of one person by another'.[32] The mythic 'world view' and the modes of representation that it employs serve to establish homologies between natural and social conditions or, more accurately, make it possible to equate significant contrasts found on different planes: the 'geographical, meteorological, zoological, botanical, technical, economic, social, ritual, religious and philosophical'.[33]

Myths mediate existential contradiction cognitively. That is to say, in myth themes of incest, of sexuality, of life and death are explored and 'explicated' for those who tell them and those who listen to them. If tribal societies are cold cultures — cultures which are not caught up in a flux of change to which their institutions are geared — it is not because they are poorly 'adapted' to nature, as evolutionary theories would have it. On the contrary, it is because those institutions intermingle with nature in an immediate and embracing fashion. Existential contradiction is directly expressed, as it were, in those institutions by virtue of the key role of kinship and of tradition. Kinship relations are the main format around which that 'concrete "apprehension"' of individuals of which Lévi-Strauss speaks is built. They are also the means whereby life is produced — or, in the original sense of the term, reproduced. Tradition, on the other hand, is the source of the injection of moral meaning into the reversible time of day-to-day life; immersed in it, the finitude of individual existence is interpolated within a dimension of moral timelessness. There is no need to portray such circumstances of social life as a Rousseauian idyll; the point is that whether pastoral and bucolic life 'red in tooth and claw', or in oral cultures expresses directly the proximity of humanity and nature.

TRIBAL SOCIETY (Oral cultures)	Pre-eminence of existential contradiction Absence of state
CLASS-DIVIDED SOCIETY	Structural contradiction/existential contradiction State form: city/countryside relation
CLASS SOCIETY (Capitalism)	Pre-eminence of structural contradiction State form: nation-state

Tribal cultures are segmented in character. That is to say, they consist of multiple centres of high presence availability, in which the boundaries between different 'societies' are usually not clearly marked. In such decentred systems structural contradiction is nonexistent. Existential contradiction traces out the contours of the natural world. Structural contradiction is signalled by the rise of the state, which is in turn associated above all with the formation of cities. I do not mean to say that the state is simply based 'in' the city. Rather, cities are power containers which, in conjunction with their relations to the countryside, generate the structural nexus of the state form. Existential contradiction is weakened by the introduction of structural contradiction but not dissolved altogether. The city is a *milieu* alien to that of nature and therefore helps to foster attitudes and symbolic systems discrepant from those that ally themselves with natural elements and events. The city wall may symbolically and materially seal off the urban *milieu* from the outside. But traditional cities could exist only through their transactions with their agrarian hinterlands. Their internal layout and architecture still maintained close connections with the natural environment, usually in conjunction with traditionally established symbols. In traditional cities, as has been mentioned previously, the distribution of areas and the alignment of buildings often expressed sacred cosmological distinctions.

I do not propose to offer a discussion of the state or the origins of state power here.[34] Suffice it to say that I hold the 'early state' to be a contradictory formation in the following sense. The state, expressing the city—countryside relation, represents a new type of structural principle that is counter to the old while still depending on it. The symbiotic/antagonistic relation of city and countryside is the specific form of this structural contradiction. As power containers, cities generate potential dynamism of a novel type in 'history'. That is to say, they break with the 'ahistorical' character of cold cultures. In class—divided societies 'economy' is typically not clearly distinct from 'polity', and the sense in which the state lodges claims to represent the society as a whole is minimal. State power has not lost its connection with existential contradiction and is symbolized in persistently religious form. The state may have escaped from tradition in the sense of being able to innovate through the use of consolidated power. But it must none the less continually yield to tradition in another way, because traditional beliefs and practices retain their hold everywhere outside the main centres of concentration of state agencies. In so far as the power of the state depends upon surveillance, this is centred primarily in the physical locales of the agencies of state: palace, temples and administrative buildings.

The emergence of state-based societies also alters the scope and pace of 'history' by stimulating secondary contradictions. States bring into being, or at least greatly accentuate, social relations across considerable reaches of time and space. That is to say, at the same time as they generate and consolidate centralized power, 'drawing in' various aspects of social activity within their scope, states stimulate the development of other ties and interconnections which cut across the social and territorial realms over which they claim sovereignty. Structural contradiction in this context concerns the sovereignty of the state over a given territorial area, which is antagonistic to and yet depends upon processes that cut across that sphere of jurisdiction and involve different mechanisms. These include external relations with other states but also the existence of cross-cutting trading enterprises, religious groups, intellectual communities and so on.

The secondary contradictions associated with the formation of modern nation-states, whose development is intertwined with that of industrial capitalism as a mode of economic enterprise, are substantially different from those of previous eras. The connection between capitalism and the nation-state, I have argued elsewhere,[35] is not merely a fortuitous one. Nation-states, to express the matter in an oversimplified way, are the new power containers that replace cities. The transformation of the city—countryside relation through the emergence of 'created environments' — exemplified by, but not limited to, the 'built environment' of modern urbanism — is part and parcel of the formation of the nation-state. The transmuted character of space and of time is essential to both the political formation of the state and the differentiated 'economy'. Such a process of transmutation severs structural from existential contradiction, and the former now becomes pre-eminent over the latter. Put in less wordy fashion, this means that human social organization no longer has any symmetry with nature; nature becomes a means to the expansion of production. The suppression of existential questions and problems is not, and cannot be, wholly complete. Indeed, they are fundamental to the structural contradictions introduced by capitalism and are part of what gives them their peculiarly explosive potential.[36]

The primary contradiction of the capitalist (nation-)state is to be found in the mode in which a 'private' sphere of 'civil society' is created by, but is separate from and in tension with, the 'public' sphere of the state. It is a mistake to suppose that civil society is everything that lies outside the scope of the state, if that is taken to mean institutions which precede, and are not incorporated within, the realm of state power. The origins of the modern state are also the origins of the sphere of civil society — so I wish to claim at any rate, although I shall leave it here as a bald assertion. Civil society is the sector within which capital accumulation occurs, fuelled by the mechanisms of price, profit and investment in labour and commodity markets. I therefore take the contradiction between civil society and state to be at least roughly parallel to the classical formulation of the capitalist contradiction between 'private appropriation' and 'socialized production'. The capitalist state, as a 'socializing' centre representing the power of the community at large, is dependent upon mechanisms of production and reproduction which it helps to bring into being but which are set off from and antagonistic to it.

Secondary contradiction in the novel global order ushered in by the advent of modern capitalism is concentrated upon the tension between the internationalizing of capital (and of capitalistic mechanisms as a whole) and the internal consolidation of nation-states. It is probably because these push in different directions that most schools of social theory have seen the connections between capitalism and the nation-state as no more than an accident of history. The dominant trend in social thought, in fact, has tended to see nation-states as little more than epiphenomena of, or as mere impediments to, the natural propensity of capitalist production to dissolve political and cultural differences. It is not hard to detect the origins of this type of view in nineteenth-century social thought. They lie in classical political economy and in its main opponent, Marxism. For both, in spite of their major divergencies in other respects, economic relationships disclose the true origin of political formations, and it is economic change which is the leading source of transforming the modern world. This view fails to see that the separation of the 'economic', as a sphere of continued and rapid change, has as its necessary condition the power of the modern state. The modern state is intrinsically, not just contingently, a nation-state, existing in a world of other nation-states.

What is the relation, analytically expressed, between contradiction and conflict, since the two terms are often used in the same breath?

Conflict	Struggle between actors or collectivities expressed as definite social practices
(Structural) contradiction	Disjunction of structural principles of system organization

By conflict I mean actual struggle between actors or groups, however such struggle may be carried on or through whatever sources it may be mobilized. Whereas contradiction is a structural concept, conflict is not. Conflict and contradiction tend to coincide because contradiction expresses the main 'fault lines' in the structural constitution of societal systems. The reason for this coincidence is that contradictions tend to involve divisions of interest between different groupings or categories of people (including classes but not limited to them). Contradictions express divergent modes of life and distributions of life chances in relation to possible worlds which the actual world discloses as immanent. If contradiction does not inevitably breed conflict, it is because the conditions under which actors not only are aware of their interests but are both able and motivated to act on them are widely variable. It is right to say, for example, that the existence of class division presumes opposition of interest (as well as common interests). But the conditions under which class conflict occurs are certainly not to be inferred directly from this observation. Thus in agrarian states or class-divided societies conflict between dominant and subordinate classes is relatively rare; this is mainly because there is very little contact between them which would supply the contexts in which conflict could actually occur.[37]

According to the conceptions I have outlined above, the pre-eminence of existential contradiction is characteristic of those societies immersed in traditionally sanctioned reversible time — societies which 'have no history'. The emergence of structural contradiction (the origins of which I am not concerned to try to explain here) 'heats up' processes of social change. But it is only with the development of modern capitalism that such processes become 'white-hot'. Compared with the modern world, with its extraordinary rates of prolonged social transformation, traditional empires and other types of state appear to be marked by an absence of change rather than the reverse. What Marx took to be characteristic of the 'Asiatic mode of production', and rather contemptuously referred to as social and economic stagnation, is in fact a distinguishing feature of all large-scale agrarian societies of whatever kind. As one observer has remarked, it is the 'relatively overwhelming absence of major social and economic change' that characterizes the variant forms of society that existed across the face of world history until some two or three centuries ago.[38]

Making History

I shall distinguish two main types of collectivity according to the form of the relations that enter into their reproduction. I shall call these *associations* and *organizations*, and I shall separate them from *social movements*. In associations, as in all social systems, social reproduction occurs in and through the regularized conduct of knowledgeable agents. The settings of interaction in which routine encounters occur are reflexively monitored by their constituent actors in the reproduction of mutually linked role relationships. But while such monitoring is the condition of their reproduction, it does not take the form of an active attempt to control or to alter the circumstances of reproduction. There tends to be a close connection between traditional modes of legitimacy and the prevalence of associations. Tradition is more than a particular form of the experience of temporality; it represents the moral command of 'what went before' over the continuity of day-to-day life. It is a mistake to suppose that tradition, even in the coldest of cold cultures, is wholly refractory to change or to diversification of conduct. Shils's characterization of tradition is probably very apt. Tradition is like 'the movement of raindrops on a windowpane. . . . A wavering stream of water slipping downward at an angle, comes into contact with another stream moving at a different angle. They fuse into a single stream for a brief moment, which then breaks into two streams, each of which might break apart again, if the window pane is large enough and the rain heavy enough.'[39] What the metaphor does not carry, however, is the very aspect of tradition which grounds the routine in 'traditional societies'. In this respect Lévi-Strauss is surely right to emphasize that tradition is *the* medium of the reversible time linking the *durée* of daily life with that of the *longue durée* of institutions.

The distinction between associations on the one side and organizations and social movements on the other coincides with a distinction in modes of reproduction that I drew in the first chapter. Organizations and social movements are collectivities in which the reflexive regulation of the conditions of system reproduction looms large in the continuity of day-to-day practices. Organizations and social movements are characteristically found in segments of class-divided societies — and, indeed, in some degree mark their separation from tribal societies. For reflexive self-regulation, as a property of collectivities, depends upon the collation of information which can be controlled so as to influence the circumstances of social reproduction. Information control, in turn, depends upon information *storage* of a kind distinct from that available in individual recollection, in myths or story-telling or in the practical consciousness of 'lived tradition'. The invention of writing, the prime mode of the collation and storage of information in class-divided societies, marks a radical disjuncture in history. This is true not only because the forms of storage and retrieval of information generated by writing allow an expansion of time-space distanciation but also because the nature of 'tradition' becomes altered, changing the sense in which human beings live 'in' history. Class-divided societies have always maintained a strongly traditional foundation, especially outside the relatively restricted sphere of cities. The works of philosophers of pre-Ch'in China conceived of the intersection of past and present as a mobile relation, in which not only does 'present' penetrate into 'past' and vice versa but also history is 'flat' rather than linear. That is to say, it runs laterally rather than 'backwards' into time. Life was represented as governed by the *li*, or traditional rituals, continuously transmitted. According to Hsun Tzu, 'Past and present are the same. Things that are the same in kind, though extended over a long period, continue to have the self-same principle.'[40] None the less, the introduction of writing means that tradition becomes visible *as* 'tradition', a specific way, among others, of doing things. 'Tradition' which is known as such is no longer a time-honoured basis of custom but a discursive phenomenon open to interrogation.

So far as 'history' is concerned, it is worth while at this point to return to Marx's dictum that human beings 'make history'. It was not merely whimsical to ask earlier what it is that is 'made' here, as the debate between Sartre and Lévi-Strauss shows. All human beings live in history in the sense that their lives unfold in time, but this they share in common with all things extant. As reflexively founded practice, human society is distinct from that of the animals, but this in and of itself hardly explains what 'history' is or what there is that is specific to human history. To suggest that a response to these issues has to be historical contains no paradox because, of course, 'history' trades on two meanings: the occurrence of events in the elapsing of time and the chronicling or explication of those events. The fact that today we tend to elide the two senses is expressive of some key features of the contemporary era and again indicates what extraordinary complexities underlie the innocent proposition that human beings 'make history'. For its elucidation presumes a philosophical account of time. We return here to some of the matters upon which I touched in the very first sections of this book in relation to structuration theory.

Lévi-Strauss's analysis of 'savage thought' perceptively identifies some of the relevant questions. In *Totemism* he shows a parallel between Bergson's concept of *durée* and ideas 'common to all the Sioux, from the Osage in the south to the Dakota in the north, according to which things and beings are nothing but materialized forms of creative continuity'.[41] Bergson's attempt to formulate a philosophy of time, like the more powerful notions of Heidegger, can be seen as an endeavour to escape from the 'linear' or 'unitary' view of time expressed in the world view of modern Western culture. Bergson wants to apprehend *durée* as fusing the continuous and the discontinuous, the order of differences that actually constitutes 'reality'. Similarly, in the cosmology of the Sioux, as one song describes it:

> Everything as it moves, now and then, here and there, makes stops. The bird as it flies stops in one place to make its nest and in another to rest in its flight. A man when he goes forth stops when he wills. So the god has stopped. The sun, which is so bright and beautiful, is one place where he has stopped. The moon, the stars, the minds, he has been with. The trees, the animals, are all where he has stopped. . . .[42]

In this version of 'history', as the explication of events, time is associated not with social change but with repetition, not with the capability of human beings to transform the world or themselves but with their involvement in nature.

If 'history', in the phrase human beings 'make history' means the conjunction of a linear view of time with the idea that, through expanding the knowledge of their past, agents can change their future, it is a conception that begins no earlier than Vico. Indeed, Vico's writings might be seen as bridging an older understanding of time and continuity and a newer, emergent one. Thus in a celebrated passage — quoted and endorsed by Thompson[43] — Vico asserts:

> It is true that men have themselves made this world of nations, although not in full cognizance of the outcomes of their activities, for this world without doubt has issued from a mind often diverse, at times quite contrary, and always superior to the particular ends that men had proposed to themselves. . . . That which did all this was mind, for men did it with intelligence; it was not fate, for they did it by choice; not chance, for the results of their always so acting are perpetually the same.[44]

Thompson is no doubt correct to see in this an anticipation of Marx, as many others have done. But regarding Vico as a direct forerunner of Marx means ignoring features of his thought which preserve a divergent view of time and of 'experience'. Thompson casually dismisses what he calls 'Vico's own attempt to attribute to process a cyclical intelligibility', concentrating instead upon 'his superb expression of process' arguing, 'this is the point from which all sustained historical thought must start.'[45] But 'cyclical intelligibility' is fundamental to Vico's views, and it is only relatively recent 'historical thought' that has taken as its point of departure 'history as process'.

Modern organizations and social movements operate in a social world in which the retreat of the gods and the dissolving of tradition create the conditions in which reflexive self-regulation is manifested as history — and as sociology. The modern era, dominated by the rise of capitalism in the West over a slim period of a few centuries, is one marked by the prevalence of *historicity*, awareness of the 'progressive movement' of society shaped by that very awareness, the 'feeling for world history' of which Spengler wrote. The collation, analysis and retrieval of information that both stimulates and expresses historicity is made possible, first, by the development of printing and mass literacy and, second, by the invention of electronic media of communication. Each expands time-space distanciation by an 'alienation' of communication in circumstances of co-presence. Any written text becomes distanciated from its author; printing is for the most part a quantitative extension of such distanciation. Electronic media separate presence in time from presence in space, a phenomenon of decisive significance for contemporary forms of collectivity.

Organizations and social movements are what Touraine calls 'decision-making units',[46] utilizing certain typical forms of resources (authoritative and allocative) within discursively mobilized forms of information flow. The study of social movements has been distinctly under-represented within the social sciences as compared with the vast literature given over to the numerous vying elaborations of 'organization theory'. There seems little justification for this in a century in which revolutions and the clash of rival doctrines oriented towards radical social change have been so prominent, and one must agree that Touraine and others are right to claim that the notions of organization and social movement are of equivalent importance in the modern era. Social movements can be conceptually differentiated from population movements, migrations, etc., precisely because they suppose a high degree of reflexive self-regulation. Social movements can be cogently defined as 'collective enterprises to establish a new order of life'.[47] Unlike organizations, social movements do not characteristically operate within fixed locales, and positioning within them does not have the clarity of definition associated with 'roles'.

Cohn's characterization of millennial movements in medieval Europe helps to indicate some of the distinctive elements of social movements in the modern period. As described by Cohn, millenarian movements are inspired by the phantasy of a salvation which is to be

(a) collective, in the sense that it is to be enjoyed by the faithful as a group;

(b) terrestrial, in the sense that it is to be realized on this earth and not in some other—worldly heaven;

(c) imminent, in the sense that it is to come both soon and suddenly;

(d) total, in the sense that it is utterly to transform life on earth, so that the new dispensation will be no mere improvement on the present but perfection itself;

(e) accomplished by agencies which are consciously regarded as supernatural.[48]

Cohn's work has been cited so often that some caution is necessary against over-generalization on the basis of it. Not all medieval social movements can readily be described in terms of the above features, and, of course, millennialism does not disappear with the closing of the Middle Ages. But we can say with some confidence that most latter-day social movements differ from all these characteristics of millennialism, with the exception of the second and, not infrequently, the third.[49] Modern social movements are almost exclusively this-worldly and are invariably oppositional in character. They are situated in the same 'fields of historicity' as the organizations and associations they confront.

The labour movement may not provide the solution to 'the riddle of history', as Marx foresaw. But it is in certain ways prototypical of contemporary social movements. In the circuit of capitalist reproduction discussed earlier 'labour power' appears as a commodity, to be 'translated' into other commodities. However, labour power, of course, is not a commodity like any other. Labour movements have their origin in the forms of 'defensive control' whereby workers seek to achieve some measure of mastery over circumstances in which they are denied rights of participation in decisions that affect them. In so far as labour movements have been infused with socialism, and more particularly with Marxism, they incorporate historicity in a direct fashion into the scope of their activities. Labour movements have been animated by much the same nexus of ideas as the capitalist organizations against which they have been pitted. Whether reformist or revolutionary, such movements have been concerned to foster, although in an egalitarian fashion, those very forces of production which their opponents seek to develop through the accumulation of capital. Here, however, is where the labour movement ceases to exemplify modern social movements in general. For Marx it was to carry the burden of a general reformation of the societal totality, acting in the general interest against the sectional interests expressed by class divisions. The limits of this vision have become increasingly apparent, not only because of the failure of the proletariat to make the revolution,[50] nor even because of the tendency to reduce all sectional interests to class interests, but exactly because of an uncovering of the historical roots of historicity itself. Our era is one which entertains radical doubts about the accomplishments of enlightenment guided by science and by technological innovation, one in which historicity loses its erstwhile unquestioned pre-eminence.

In a similar way the capitalist enterprise is in some respects both typical of modern organizations and one of the main sources of innovation generating the circumstances in which they have arisen. As analysed by Marx, capitalism is a mode of production in which reflexive self-regulation within the enterprise — a phenomenon clarified by Weber's demonstration of the significance of double-entry book-keeping to the capitalist firm — is not matched by reflexive control over economic life as a whole. However, as Weber has again done more than anyone else to make clear, reflexive self-regulation gains momentum in many sectors of social life. Herein lies one of the most profound issues which faces us today. Is the expansion of a diversity of different forms of organization — in which the conditions of reproduction are reflexively monitored — a medium of emancipation from pre-established modes of exploitative domination? There is no doubt that Marx believed such to be the case in the context of his anticipation of the revolutionary overthrow of capitalism by socialism. But Marx's critics and adversaries, from Weber to Foucault, have provided more than good cause to treat this basic tenet of Marxism with caution, if not with outright scepticism.

Critical Notes: 'Structural Sociology' and Methodological Individualism

Blau: a Version of Structural Sociology

There are strong connections between an emphasis upon a 'structural approach', as used by those writing outside traditions of structuralism, and objectivism in the social sciences. Some motifs continually crop up in the works of those who regard themselves as taking such an approach. These include particularly the Durkheimian ideas that 'societies are more than the sum of their constituent individuals' and (a conception I have already criticized) that structural properties are qualities of social systems which are to be defined solely in terms of their constraining influence over actors. 'Structural approaches' also tend to stress endurance in time and extension in space. Structures are 'supra-individual' in the sense that they outlive the individual agent and spread well beyond the scope of the activity of individual agents.[1]* These considerations obviously overlap considerably with themes of my preceding discussion in this book. But something of an epistemological element is often involved too. For it is frequently held, or assumed, that to examine structural features of social activity is to demonstrate causal influences over human conduct akin to those which operate in nature.

Thus Wallace identifies the 'crucial difference' between what he calls 'social structuralist theory' and 'social actionist theory' in the following way: 'social structuralist theory treats purposiveness and other subjective orientational factors as at least secondary and at most [?] irrelevant in explaining social phenomena. . . .'[2] The bluntness with which this view is expressed is not at all unusual. Consider a recent account on these lines set out by Mayhew. Mayhew identifies the proper concerns of sociology as 'structural'. Structures refer to networks of relations, and such networks can and should be analysed without any allusion to the characteristics of individuals: 'in structural sociology the unit of analysis', he says, 'is always the social network, never the individual.'[3] A 'structural approach' is here linked, as is very often the case, with an endorsement of a rather naive form of behaviourism. Mayhew argues that 'structuralists do not employ subjectivist concepts such as purpose or goals in their analysis.'[4]

Blau has developed a more sophisticated version of ideas such as these in a number of recent publications, and his views no doubt are representative of a substantial segment of sociological opinion.[5] Like most Anglo-Saxon sociological writers, he will have nothing to do with Lévi-Strauss's conception of structuralism or with kindred standpoints. He also, however, carefully separates himself from functionalism, proposing a notion of structure 'stripped of its broader cultural and functional connotations to its core properties'.[6] Accepting that 'structure' has been used variably by different authors, he points out that it is usually agreed that, in its most elemental sense, it refers somehow to social positions and relations between social positions. As specified by Blau, structural social science is concerned with parameters of population distributions, not with actors as such. A 'structural parameter' is any criterion of categorizing aggregates of individuals relevant to social positions which individuals might occupy. He explains this as follows:

> Thus, we speak of the age structure of a population, the kinship structure of a tribe, the authority structure of an organization, the power structure of a community, and the class structure of a society. These are not types of social structure but analytical elements of it distinguishing social positions in one dimension only. The different positions generated by a single parameter are necessarily occupied by different persons — an individual is either a man or a woman, old or young, rich or poor — but the case differs for positions generated by several parameters, because the same person simultaneously occupies positions on different parameters. . . . Social structures are reflected in diverse forms of differentiation, which must be kept analytically distinct.[7]

The task of studying structural parameters, according to Blau, delimits the distinctive concern of sociology.

Two types of structural parameter can be distinguished. 'Nominal parameters' are lateral, separating a given population into categories, such as gender, religion or race; 'graduated parameters' are hierarchical, differentiating individuals along a scale, and include, for example, wealth, income and education. One of the main objects of structural study is to examine the relation between these parameters, in so far as they are associated with clusters of interaction. Where there is considerable differentiation along either parameter, there will be less chance of such interaction clusters being formed. Parameters can thus be analysed so as to explain the forms and degrees of social differentiation and integration. Blau writes as a 'structural determinist', 'who believes that the structures of objective social positions among which people are distributed exert more fundamental influences on social life than do cultural values and norms'.[8] His aim is to explain variations in the structural features of societies, not factors relevant to individual attitudes, beliefs or motives. Structural analysis in his sense of the term, he notes, can be carried on without investigating overall characteristics of societies.

However, he does make claims relevant to those characteristics. Thus he remarks, for example, that in small oral cultures kinship is the main co-ordinating structural axis of differentiation and integration. Industrialized societies, by contrast, are characterized by 'multiform heterogeneity', the complex intersection of structural parameters, producing diverse forms of association and clusters of interaction. In the current era, he adds, a considerable structural consolidation is going on in Western societies — Blau's own version, in fact, of the looming threat of a 'one-dimensional' social order.[9]

On the basis of these concepts, Blau attempts to formulate what he calls a deductive theory of social structure. The theory begins from propositions involving very simple analytical terms (for example, the size of aggregates or groups) and builds up more complex generalizations on this foundation. Some of the assumptions involved, Blau says, depend upon 'essentially psychological principles'; he quotes as an example the generalization that people prefer to associate with others who have traits similar to their own. However, the structural properties analysed cannot be derived directly from such psychological theorems. Blau's deductive theory is a complicated affair, involving several dozen generalizations about 'structural effects', ranging from the marvellously trite ('people associate not only with members of their own groups but also with members of other groups'), through the mildly interesting although quite debatable ('decentralization of authority in an association increases informal association among administrative ranks') to the provocative but perhaps substantially mistaken ('high rates of mobility promote structural change'). 'The theory is sociological', according to Blau, 'in the specific sense that it explains patterns of social relations in terms of properties of social structure, not in terms of the assumptions made, whether or not these are derivable from psychological principles. The nature of the logical formulations employed makes the explanations structural.'[10]

Blau's views are in some ways idiosyncratic but for the most part exemplify the ambitions of 'structural sociology' in a general way. He expresses in a cogent fashion the persistent feeling shared by many that sociology can and must be clearly separated from other neighbouring disciplines, particularly psychology. The point is made forcibly that what gives sociology its distinctiveness is its specific concern not only with social structure but also with the ways in which the constraining properties of structure make themselves felt in regard of the conduct of individuals. According to Blau, neither the formulation of structural analysis nor structural explanation needs to make reference to 'values or norms'. In this latter respect he seems to diverge from Durkheim, but in other ways what he has to say could be taken as a latter-day version of a Durkheimian manifesto. Discussion of the shortcomings of his standpoint will both serve to reiterate features of structuration theory mentioned earlier and help to point up aspects of 'structure' and 'structural properties' as I want to understand those terms.

There are some interesting and instructive features of Blau's ideas. He skirts functionalism, and he avoids identifying structural analysis with some unexplicated influence which society 'as a whole' has over its individual members. He recognizes that societies are not all of a piece — that is to say, that one of the aims of structural study should be to show exactly what levels of integration can be discovered within and between social groupings. None the less, the limitations of such a conception of 'structural sociology' are marked.

Blau's approach confuses the demand to distinguish the influence of structural properties from psychological explanations of conduct on the one hand with the assertion that structural parameters can be defined independently of 'values', 'norms' or 'cultural traditions' on the other. His programme of discovering the 'independent influence the structure of social positions in a society or community exerts on social relations' is supposed to be accomplished 'independently of cultural values and psychological motives'.[11] But reduction to psychological generalizations is not the same as formulation in terms of cultural values or meanings. The latter have reference to the inevitably hermeneutic task of the generation of social descriptions, parasitic upon agents' concepts that help constitute them. A characteristic mistake of the advocates of structural sociology is to confuse two different senses in which the 'objective' nature of structural properties can be counterposed to 'subjectivity'. Structural parameters, as Blau defines them, are 'non-subjective' in the sense that they cannot be described in terms of individual predicates. But they *cannot* be 'non-subjective' in the sense that they cannot be characterized at all independently of 'cultural traditions', where this term refers to agents' meanings. Thus Blau regards kinship categories as 'structural'. But kinship categories patently depend upon concepts and discriminations employed by actors. The very term 'position', so basic to Blau's notion of structure, clearly involves agents' concepts. Social positions, like all other aspects of 'structural parameters', exist only in so far as actors make discriminations in their conduct based upon the attribution of certain identities to others.

The notion that the study of structural parameters is convergent with the distinctive character of sociology might be plausible if there were some definite causal properties associated with them, thus making 'sociological explanation' convergent with 'structural explanation'. But the causal relations supposedly at work are obscure — although evidently supposed to operate in some way outside the scope of the reasons that agents might have for what they do. Thus Blau proposes the generalization that an organization's increasing size produces greater internal differentiation and hence raises the proportion of administrative personnel it contains. According to him, this relationship can be grasped 'without investigating the motives of individuals in organizations'.[12] But, as Blau develops it, this proposition is false. If the implication were that certain typical motives can be assumed by the theorist, and could be spelled out if necessary, the statement could be

defended. But this is not what Blau has in mind. He makes it clear
that he thinks that the specification of motives (and reasons or
intentions) is actually *irrelevant* to the factors involved in the
generalization. And this is not so at all. It is, on the contrary,
necessary precisely to its causal explication. The increased
proportion of administrators will tend to come about as actors
respond to what they see to be new problems and issues which
increased organizational size presents.[13]

The 'structural' generalizations given by Blau may in fact on
closer inspection turn out to be *formulae which actors use to
produce the results indicated.* If we know nothing about what the
agents themselves believe they are doing — because this type of
information is thought to be distinct from the analysis of structural
effects — we cannot assess the likelihood that such may be the
case. Those who administer organizations have their own theories-
in-use about them and may, indeed, be well aware of the academic
literature on the subject. Consider the proposition that decentralization of authority in organizations increases informal associations
between administrative ranks. As with the generalization about
size and internal differentiation, this may presume intended
consequences which agents have reasons for bringing about, or,
alternatively, the outcome may be largely unintended. It is
essential for the social observer to know which is the case in
order to be able to elucidate what is going on. At least some of
the agents involved could be acting in the light of the very
generalization which Blau identifies. It might very well be that a
policy of decentralization is followed specifically in order to
increase certain sorts of informal association among different
ranks of administrators.

What these comments demonstrate is that a 'structural
approach' to the social sciences cannot be severed from an
examination of the mechanisms of social reproduction. It is
perfectly correct, of course, to emphasize that society is not a
creation of individual actors and that the structural properties of
social systems endure beyond the lifetimes of individuals. But
structure, or structural properties, or 'structural parameters', exist
only in so far as there is continuity in social reproduction across
time and space. And such continuity in turn exists only in and
through the reflexively monitored activities of situated actors,
having a range of intended and unintended consequences. Let me

repeat: *there is no such thing as a distinctive category of 'structural explanation'*, only an interpretation of the modes in which varying forms of constraint influence human action. There is nothing mysterious about what 'influence' means here. Take the generalization that high rates of mobility promote structural change. We can probably assume that high mobility rates are largely unintended and that the resultant changes they induce are also, although it may be the case, for example, that educational policies have been set up in order to enhance mobility and hence that what is going on is part of a reflexively monitored process. Suppose, however, that the mobility in question is unintended, is that of women, is upward occupational mobility, and that the 'structural change' it promotes is higher (or lower) divorce rates. We can probe what the causal influences might be, but only by knowing about the motives and reasons of those involved — wives, husbands and others. It could be that women who become successful in occupational careers spend less time at home than they would otherwise, leading to the (unintended) result of placing a strain on the marital relationship; that they see marriage as unimportant compared with success at work; that their husbands resent their success, etc.; or a combination of all of these for different individuals.

An Alternative? Methodological Individualism

Conceptions of distinctively 'structural explanation' in sociology have long had a natural enemy in methodological individualism. The debate between the two positions is in some part the methodological counterpart to the dualism of subject and social object that has characterized the ontology of the social sciences. Although Max Weber has frequently been adopted as a 'structural sociologist', he made his own preferences clear enough. In a letter which he wrote not long before his death he observed: 'if I have become a sociologist . . . it is mainly in order to exorcise the spectre of collective conceptions which still lingers among us. In other words, sociology itself can only proceed from the actions of one or more separate individuals and must therefore adopt strictly individualistic methods.'[14] Human action, as Weber says in *Economy and Society*, 'exists only as the behaviour of one or more *individual* human beings'.[15] The debate over what claims

Weber and other 'methodological individualists' might in fact be making has stretched far and wide, but there is no doubt a genuine difference of opinion between them and the 'structural sociologists'. The details may be complex, but the outline is relatively simple. The methodological individualists agree with the view I have stated above: the search for 'structural explanation' is futile and perhaps even harmful.

Let me follow through one of the more influential accounts of the issues raised by various versions of methodological individualism. Lukes discusses and seeks to 'render harmless' each of what he takes to be the main expressions of methodological individualism.[16] The doctrines that advocate methodological individualism involve one or more of the following theses.

(1)   'Truistic social atomism'. This is the view which holds that it is self-evident that social phenomena can be explained only in terms of the analysis of the conduct of individuals. Thus Hayek says: 'There is no other way toward an understanding of social phenomena but through our understanding of individual actions directed towards other people and guided by their expected behaviour'[17] (a formulation close to Weber's definition of 'social action', in fact).

(2)   The idea that all statements about social phenomena — such as Blau's exposition of structural parameters — can be reduced, without loss of meaning, to descriptions of the qualities of individuals. This view would deny that Blau's talk of 'structure' makes any sense; he is merely aggregating properties of individuals.

(3)   The assertion that only individuals are real. Thus it seems to be held by some writers that any concepts which refer to properties of collectivities or social systems (one might again instance 'structural parameters') are abstract models, constructions of the theorist, in some way that the notion of 'individual' is not.

(4)   The allegation that there cannot be laws in the social sciences, save in so far as there are laws about the psychological dispositions of individuals.[18]

All of these four elements would appear to be found in the much-quoted statement that Watkins gives of what he calls the 'principle of methodological individualism':

According to this principle, the ultimate constituents of the social world are individual people who act more or less appropriately in the light of their dispositions and understanding of their situation. Every complex social situation, institution or event is the result of a particular configuration of individuals, their dispositions, situations, beliefs, and physical resources and environment. There may be unfinished or half-way explanations of large-scale social phenomena (say, inflation) in terms of other large-scale phenomena (say, full employment); but we shall not have arrived at rock-bottom explanations of such large-scale phenomena until we have deduced an account of them from statements about the dispositions, beliefs, resources and inter-relations of individuals. (The individuals may remain anonymous and only typical dispositions, etc., may be attributed to them.)[19]

Lukes's bomb-disposal squad of arguments designed to defuse methodological individualism advances on two fronts. None of the claims mentioned under the four categories is in the least bit plausible when examined closely. Since the first is truistic (that is to say, trivially true), it is neither here nor there. That 'society consists of people' is a 'banal proposition about the world' which is 'analytically true, that is, in virtue of the meaning of words'.[20] The second, third and fourth points are demonstrably false. The fact that the description or analysis of kinship relations, such as those designated as 'cross-cousin marriage', cannot be accomplished without reference to the knowledgeability of human agents does not entail that such relations can be described solely in terms of predicates of individuals. If point (3) implies somehow that only individuals are directly observable, it is mistaken — although there is no reason in any case to support the proposition, associated with behaviourism, that only that which is observable is real. We may not be able to observe the elements Blau has in mind when he speaks of structural parameters, but we certainly can observe social phenomena in circumstances of co-presence, such as the formation and enactment of encounters. Finally, point (4) is covered by what I have said previously: there is no shortage of generalizations in the social sciences, although they do not have the same logical form as universal laws in natural science.

These arguments, Luke concedes, do not yet render methodological individualism harmless. They do not even attack its main strength, which is concerned with explanation. The most important assertion in the quotation from Watkins, and perhaps also that from Hayek, is to be found in the declaration that 'rock-bottom' explanations of social phenomena have to involve the 'dispositions, beliefs, resources and inter-relations of individuals'. It is here that Lukes feels the potentially explosive power of methodological individualism to lie, and from where the fuse has to be delicately removed. What are the 'dispositions, etc.' of individuals? And what, in any case, is 'explanation'? As regards the latter, Lukes is able to demonstrate rather easily that many proponents of methodological individualism have in mind an overly restricted notion of what explanation is (this is equally true of Blau and most of the structural sociologists). To explain is to answer a why question, and often this involves making a particular social phenomenon intelligible simply in the sense of providing an accurate characterization of it.[21] Explanation here operates, as it were, on or around the baseline of the necessarily hermeneutic nature of the social sciences. It is undeniably important to emphasize that 'explanation' partakes of the contextuality of all social activity, whether this be in respect of the inquiries of lay actors or those of sociological observers. However, let us concentrate upon the more confined meaning of 'explanation' as having to do with the formulation not just of generalizations but of causal generalizations — in other words, generalizations which do not simply assert that a relation of an abstract kind holds between two categories or classes of social phenomena but also identify the causal connections involved.

In what sense do these causal connections necessarily relate to individuals? According to Lukes, in some versions of methodo-logical individualism the qualities of individuals invoked in explanations are physiological traits of the organism or organically given needs. But these explanations turn out to be quite implausible. No one has been able to produce any accounts which reduce social phenomena to organic properties. So these forms of methodological individualism are at best hypothetical claims; they have no direct bearing upon the materials of study with which social scientists operate. In other interpretations of methodological individualism, however, either the characteristics attributed to individuals and incorporated in explanations do not exclude the possibility of more structural analyses, or these characteristics are covered by the rebuttal of (3) above and do, in fact, involve social (structural) characterizations anyway. Hence methodological individualism has been neutralized. Those who advocate a reductionism involving physiological characteristics of the organism cannot make their claim count for anything as regards the actual practice of the social sciences, but others cannot find any properties of individuals that are not irreducibly 'contaminated' by the social.

There Lukes leaves the matter. I do not think that this will do: we have to formulate the issues rather differently. However, before picking up some of the threads left dangling by Lukes's discussion, it will be instructive to refer to some quite similar problems raised from a different quarter — in interchanges between Thompson and Anderson about the character of Marxism.[22] Thompson has long regarded structural concepts as suspect, without rejecting them altogether, and has consistently emphasized the significance of studying the texture and variety of human agency. Thus in describing the views informing his analysis of class development in England in the eighteenth and nineteenth centuries, he comments, 'class is defined by men as they live their own history, and, in the end, this is its only definition.'[23] In the course of a sustained polemic against Althusser and those influenced by him — prompting a book-length reply from Anderson — Thompson spells out the implications of his standpoint in some detail. I shall make no attempt to characterize the debate as a whole but shall mention only a few aspects of it which are relevant here.

Althusser is taken to task by Thompson — rightly, in my opinion[24] — for offering a deficient account of human agency and a deterministic conception of structure. Human beings are regarded not as knowledgeable agents but only as the 'supports' for modes of production. This 'derogation of the lay actor', as I have called it, Thompson expresses in blunter fashion. Althusser, and most others associated with either structuralism or functionalism, 'proceed from the same "latent anthropology", the same ulterior assumption about "Man" — that all men and women (except themselves) *are bloody silly*'.[25] Social life, or human history, Thompson says, should be understood as 'unmastered human practice'. That is to say, human beings act purposively and knowledgeably but without being able either to foresee or to control the consequences of what they do. To understand how this happens we need a term which, Thompson says, goes missing in Althusser: it is what Thompson simply calls 'human experience'.[26] Experience is the connection between 'structure' and 'process', the real material of social or historical analysis. Thompson stresses that such a view does not bring him close to methodological individualism. In fact, he finds a certain affinity between methodological individualism and Althusser's Marxism. For Althusser believes that 'structures' exist only within theoretical domains, not in reality itself; hence this stance resembles the nominalism of the methodological individualists. But yet in the end it is not easy to see just how distinct Thompson's ideas are from methodological individualism. Many of the passages in his work where he characterizes his overall views resemble conceptions such as that of Watkins quoted above. Thus, talking again of the concept of class, he insists: 'When we speak of *a* class we are thinking of a very loosely defined body of people who share the same categories of interests, social experiences, tradition and value-system, who have a *disposition* to *behave* as a class, to define themselves in their actions and in their consciousness in relation to other groups of people in class ways.'[27]

There is much that is attractive about Thompson's views, but Anderson does not find it difficult to find some shortcomings in them. When Thompson writes of 'people' and of the primacy of 'experience', how are these seemingly transparent terms actually to be understood? In emphasizing them Thompson clearly means to accentuate the significance of human agency in making history. But what 'agency' is remains unexplicated, in spite of the profusion of historical examples Thompson offers in the course of his original works and by way of criticizing Althusser. 'Experience' — as we know from Dilthey's attempts to grapple with *Erlebnis* — is a notoriously ambiguous term. One use of the word, for example, connects directly with empiricism, in which experience is a passive registration of events in the world, something very far from the active connotations of the term which Thompson wishes to accentuate. Moreover, Thompson nowhere effectively teases out the relation between action and structure. This is even true of his major book, *The Making of the English Working Class*. The book opens with a celebrated paragraph: 'The working class did not rise like the sun at the appointed time. It was present at its own making' and its formation 'owes as much to agency as to conditioning'.[28] But in spite of the plaudits which the work has justly received, Anderson points out, it does not really resolve the issues thus raised.

> For if the claim for the co-determination of agency and necessity were to be substantiated, we would need to have at a minimum a conjoint exploration of the objective assemblage and transformation of a labour force by the Industrial Revolution, and of the subjective germination of a class culture in response to it. . . . [But] the advent of industrial capitalism in England is a dreadful backcloth to the book rather than a direct object of analysis in its own right. . . . The jagged temporal rhythms and breaks, and the uneven spatial distributions and displacements, of capital accumulation between 1790 and 1830 inevitably marked the composition and character of the nascent English proletariat. Yet they find no place in this account of its formation.[29]

The interchange between Thompson and Anderson is not at all conclusive, but it is useful to place it alongside the more abstract debate about methodological individualism. The latter debate seems largely played out, but the liveliness of the polemics between Thompson and Anderson graphically demonstrates that the issues are not dead. There is one very important sense in which they cannot be. Every research investigation in the social sciences or history is involved in relating action to structure, in tracing, explicitly or otherwise, the conjunction or disjunctions of intended and unintended consequences of activity and how these affect the fate of individuals. No amount of juggling with abstract concepts could substitute for the direct study of such problems in the actual contexts of interaction. For the permutations of influences are endless, and there is no sense in which structure 'determines' action or vice versa. The nature of the constraints to which individuals are subject, the uses to which they put the capacities they have and the forms of knowledgeability they display are all themselves manifestly historically variable.

Conceptual clarification can at least help in suggesting how these matters are best approached. What connects the arguments of Thompson with those of Watkins *et al.* is that both rest their cases too much upon an intuitive, untheorized conception of the 'individual' or agent. They are quite justified in being suspicious of the aspirations of 'structural sociology', whether it takes the form offered by Blau or that elaborated by Althusser. Methodological individualism is not, as Lukes suggests, harmless in respect of the objectives of 'structural sociologists'. The methodological individualists are wrong in so far as they claim that social categories can be reduced to descriptions in terms of individual predicates. But they are right to suspect that 'structural sociology' blots out, or at least radically underestimates, the knowledge-ability of human agents, and they are right to insist that 'social forces' are always nothing more and nothing less than mixes of intended or unintended consequences of action undertaken in specifiable contexts.

'Structural sociology' and methodological individualism are not alternatives, such that to reject one is to accept the other. In some respects, as Luke says, the debate between the two sides is an empty one. The point is to discard some of the terms of the debate while elaborating others further than any of its contributors have done. What the 'individual' is cannot be taken as obvious. The question here is not that of comparing predicates but of specifying what human agents are like — something I have tried to do in respect of the basic concepts of structuration theory. This presumes abandoning the equation of structure with constraint. The relation between enablement and constraint can be fairly easily set out on a logical level, given a beginning point in the notion of the duality of structure. History is not 'unmastered human practices'. It is the temporality of human practices, fashioning and fashioned by structural properties, within which diverse forms of power are incorporated — not by any means as neat a turn of phrase, but I think it is more accurately put.

A further question raised by the debate over methodological individualism is: are collectivities actors? What does it mean to say, for example, 'The government decided to pursue policy X'? or 'The government acted quickly in the face of the threat of rebellion'? Various distinctions need to be disentangled here. Action descriptions, as I have mentioned in a previous chapter, should not be confused with the designation of agency as such. Neither descriptions of action nor accounts of interaction can be given purely in terms of individual predicates. But only individuals, beings which have a corporeal existence, are agents. If collectivities or groups are not agents, why do we sometimes speak as though they were, as in the above examples? We tend to do so when there is a significant degree of reflexive monitoring of the conditions of social reproduction, of the sort associated especially with organizations, although not exclusive to them. 'The government decided to pursue policy X' is a shorthand description of decisions taken by individuals, but normally in some kind of consultation with one another, or where a resulting policy is normatively binding. Decisions that are taken by governments or other organizations may not represent the desired outcome of all, or the most desired outcome of any, of those who participate in making them. In such circumstances it makes sense to say that participants 'decide' (individually) 'to decide' (corporately) upon a given course of action. That is to say, individual members of a Cabinet may agree to be bound by the outcome of a meeting with which they disagree or a proposal which they voted against yet which found majority support. It is important to understand that 'The government decided . . .' or 'The government acted . . .' are shorthand statements because in some situations it may matter a great deal which individuals were the main initiators or executors of whatever decisions were taken (or not taken) and whatever policies followed.

References

Structure, System, Social Reproduction

1   *CPST*, pp. 222—5.
2   *CCHM*, chapter 8.
3   Ibid., pp. 45—6. My discussion here modifies my earlier version of this problem only slightly. For other sections drawn upon here, see pp. 157—64 and 166—9.
4   I have followed Eberhard's discussion closely in the preceding few paragraphs: Wolfram Eberhard, *Conquerors and Rulers* (Leiden: Brill, 1965), p. 9, and *passim.*
5   Marshall G. S. Hodgson, 'The interrelations of societies in history', *Comparative Studies in Society and History,* vol. 5, 1962—3, p. 233.
6   H. A. Gailey, *A History of Africa, 1800 to the Present* (New York: Houghton-Mifflin, 1970—2, 2 vols.; René Grousset, *The Empire of the Steppes* (New Brunswick: Rutgers University Press, 1970).
7   T. Carlstein, 'The sociology of structuration in time and space: a time-geographic assessment of Giddens's theory', *Swedish Geographical Yearbook* (Lund: Lund University Press, 1981); Derek

Layder, *Structure, Interaction and Social Theory* (London: Routledge, 1981); J. B. Thompson, *Critical Hermeneutics* (Cambridge: Cambridge University Press, 1981); Margaret S. Archer, 'Morphogenesis versus structuration: on combining structure and action', *British Journal of Sociology*, vol. 33, 1982.

8 Carlstein, 'The sociology of structuration in time and space', pp. 52—3. See also John Thompson, *Critical Hermeneutics* (Cambridge: Cambridge University Press, 1981), pp. 143—4.

9 Roy Bhaskar, *The Possibility of Naturalism* (Brighton: Harvester, 1979), p. 42.

10 Emile Durkheim, *The Rules of Sociological Method* (London: Macmillan, 1982), pp. 39—40.

11 Ibid., pp. 50 and 52.

12 Ibid., pp. 2—3.

13 Karl Marx, *Capital* (London: Lawrence & Wishart, 1970), p. 72. An instructive discussion of this issue appears in Gillian Rose, *The Melancholy Science* (London: Macmillan, 1978), chapter 3.

14 Karl Marx, *Grundrisse* (Harmondsworth: Penguin, 1976), p. 157.

15 See *CPST*, chapter 5.

16 Prepared for the writing of *CCHM* but not in the final version included therein.

17 The classfication also leaves open the possibility of other types — for example, state socialist society as distinct from capitalism, as well, of course, as other forms of societal organization that might conceivably develop in the future.

18 The view expressed in *CCHM*, p. 164, 'The city is the locus of the mechanisms which produce system integration', is rather inadequately formulated. Moreover, I do not want to convey that the city—countryside relation is a unitary or single one; it is heterogeneous and complex when considered across the generality of societies.

19 Immanuel Wallerstein, *The Modern World-System* (New York: Academic Press, 1974); cf. Spengler: 'Is it not ridiculous to oppose a "modern" history of a few centuries, and that history to all intents localized in West Europe, to an "ancient" history which covers as many millennia — incidentally dumping into that "ancient history" the whole mass of the pre-Hellenic cultures, unprobed and unordered, as mere appendix matter?' Oswald Spengler, *The Decline of the West* (London: Allen & Unwin, 1961), p. 38.

20 Cf. note 2 above.

21 Cf. my essay, 'The nation-state and violence'.

22 *CPST* pp. 104—5.

23   Marx, *Capital*, p. 110.
24   Ibid., pp. 110 and 103.
25   Ibid., p. 168.
26   For an earlier version of some of these points, see *CSAS*, chapter 6.
27   Marx, *Capital*, vol. 1, p. 337.
28   Ibid., p. 338.
29   Ibid., p. 356.
30   Marx, *Capital*, vol. 1, p. 111.
31   *CPST*, pp. 141ff.
32   Claude Lévi-Strauss, *Structural Anthropology* (London: Allen Lane, 1968), pp. 365—6.
33   Claude Lévi-Strauss, *The Savage Mind* (London: Weidenfeld & Nicolson, 1966), p. 93.
34   This is a major preoccupation of *Between Capitalism and Socialism.*
35   *CCHM*, chapters 7, 8 and 9. I also leave out of consideration here the very important question (also analysed in *CCHM*) of the relations between capitalism, the state and class divisions.
36   A theme more fully developed in *Between Capitalism and Socialism.*
37   See John H. Kautsky, *The Politics of Aristocratic Empires* (Chapel Hill: University of North Carolina Press, 1982): 'If a class is conceived of as a grouping in conflict with another class, then, indeed, aristocracies and peasantries are not classer at all' (p. 75).
38   Ibid., pp. 5—6. See also Henri J. M. Claessen and Peter Skalnik, *The Early State* (The Hague: Mouton, 1978).
39   Edward Shils, *Tradition* (London: Faber & Faber, 1981), p. 280.
40   Arthur Waley, *Three Ways of Thought in Ancient China* (London: Allen & Unwin, 1939), p. 38. For an extended discussion, see J. G. A. Pocock, 'The origins of the study of the past', *Comparative Studies in Society and History*, vol. 4, 1961—2.
41   Claude Lévi-Strauss, *Totemism* (London: Merlin, 1964), p. 98.
42   Ibid. Lévi-Strauss also remarks, 'The Dakota language possesses no word to designate time, but it can express in a number of ways modes of being in duration. For Dakota thought, in fact, time constitutes a duration in which measurement does not intervene: it is a limitless "free good"' (p. 99). Interesting observations relevant to these issues are made in Birgit Schintlholzer, *Die Auflösung des Geschichtbegriffs im Strukturalismus,* doctoral dissertation (Hamburg, 1973).
43   E. P. Thompson, *The Poverty of Theory* (London: Merlin, 1978), pp. 86 and 291.
44   G. Vico, *The New Science* (Ithaca: Cornell University Press, 1968), p. 382, para. 1108.
45   Thompson, *The Poverty of Theory*, p. 86.

46   Alain Touraine, *The Self Production of Society* (Chicago: University of Chicago Press, 1977), p. 238.
47   Herbert Blumer, 'Collective behaviour', in Alfred M. Lee, *Principles of Sociology* (New York: Barnes & Noble, 1951), p. 199.
48   Norman Cohn, 'Mediaeval millenarianism: its bearing upon the comparative study of millenarian movements', in Silvia L. Thrupp, *Millenial Dreams in Action* (The Hague: Mouton, 1962), p. 31.
49   Cf. J. A. Banks, *The Sociology of Social Movements* (London: Macmillan, 1972), pp. 20—1, and *passim*.
50   André Gorz, *Farewell to the Working Class* (London: Pluto, 1982).

Critical Notes: 'Structural Sociology'
and Methodological Individualism

1   Cf. Raymond Boudon, *The Uses of Structuralism* (London: Heinemann, 1971). Boudon categorizes a number of divergent uses of the concept. For a rather different set of approaches, see Peter M. Blau, *Approaches to the Study of Social Structure* (London: Collier-Macmillan, 1975).
2   Walter L. Wallace, 'Structure and action in the theories of Coleman and Parsons', in Blau, *Approaches to the Study of Social Structure*, p. 121.
3   Bruce H. Mayhew, 'Structuralism versus individualism', Parts 1 and 2, *Social Forces*, vol. 59, 1980, p. 349.
4   Ibid., p. 348.
5   Peter M. Blau, *Inequality and Heterogeneity* (New York: Free Press, 1977); 'Structural effects', *American Sociological Review*, vol. 25, 1960; 'Parameters of social structure', in Blau, *Approaches to the Study of Social Structure*; 'A macrosociological theory of social structure', *American Journal of Sociology*, vol. 83, 1977.
6   *Inequality and Heterogeneity*, p. ix.
7   'Parameters of social structure', p. 221.
8   *Inequality and Heterogeneity*, p. x.
9   'Parameters of social structure', pp. 252—3. 'What poses this threat is the dominant position of powerful organizations in contemporary society, such as the Pentagon, the White House, and huge conglomerates. The trend has been toward increasing concentration of economic and manpower resources and powers derived from them in giant organizations and their top executives, which implies a growing consolidation of major resources and forms of power. . . .'
10   *Inequality and Heterogeneity*, p. 246.
11   'A macrosociological theory of social structure', p. 28.

12 Peter M. Blau, 'A formal theory of differentiation in organizations', *American Sociology Review,* vol. 35, 1970, p. 203.

13 This point is made in Stephen P. Turner, 'Blau's theory of differentiation: is it explanatory?', *Sociological Quarterly,* vol. 18, 1977. Some of these issues are aired again in Blau: 'Comments on the prospects for a nomothetic theory of social structure', *Journal for the Theory of Social Behaviour,* vol. 13, 1983. See also an extraordinary piece by Mayhew, in the same volume on 'Causality, historical particularism and other errors in sociological discourse'. Blau's contribution continues to display the shortcomings I have indicated. (1) Hermeneutic elements in the formulation of concepts of social analysis are suppressed in favour of the view that 'the objective of sociology is to study the influence of the "social environment" on "people's observable tendencies"' (p. 268). (2) Reference to agents' motives, reasons and intentions is persistently equated with 'psychology', relegated to a realm separate from the concerns of 'sociology'. (3) A version of a discredited philosophy of natural science, in which 'explanation' is regarded as necessarily to do with 'nomothetic-deductive theorizing' (p. 265), is accepted unquestioningly. (4) No consideration is given to the possibility that even if the philosophy of natural science thus implied were acceptable, the character of 'laws' in social science might be fundamentally different from laws of nature. (5) The whole standpoint is wrapped up in the familiar but erroneous claim that social science, as compared with natural science, is in the early phases of its development. Blau accepts that there are, 'at least so far', 'no deterministic laws in sociology' (p. 266). But he expresses faith that these will one day be found — we certainly cannot write off the possibility because 'nomothetic theory of social structure is undoubtedly still in a most rudimentary stage' (p. 269).

14 Quoted in Wolfgang Mommsen, 'Max Weber's political sociology and his philosophy of world history', *International Social Science Journal,* vol. 17, 1965, p. 25. Of course, it is a moot point how far Weber's substantive writings were guided by this principle.

15 Max Weber, *Economy and Society* (Berkeley: University of California Press, 1978), vol. 1, p. 13.

16 Steven Lukes, 'Methodological individualism reconsidered', in *Essays in Social Theory* (London: Macmillan, 1977).

17 F. A. Hayek, *Individualism and Economic Order* (Chicago: University of Chicago Press, 1949). p. 6.

18 Lukes also identifies a further connotation of methodological individualism, a doctrine of 'social individualism' which '(ambiguously) asserts that society has as its end the good of individuals'. Lukes, 'Methodological individualism reconsidered', pp. 181−2.

19 J. W. N. Watkins, 'Historical explanation in the social sciences', in P. Gardiner, *Theories of History* (Glencoe: Free Press, 1959).
20 Lukes, 'Methodological individualism reconsidered', p. 178.
21 Cf. *NRSM,* chapter 4.
22 E. P. Thompson, *The Poverty of Theory* (London: Merlin, 1978); Perry Anderson, *Arguments within English Marxism* (London: Verso, 1980).
23 E. P. Thompson, *The Making of the English Working Class* (Harmondsworth: Penguin, 1968), p. 40.
24 *CPST*, chapter 1, and *passim.*
25 Thompson, *The Poverty of Theory*, p. 148.
26 Ibid., p. 30.
27 Ibid., p. 295. Italics in the original.
28 Thompson, *The Making of the English Working Class*, p. 9.
29 Anderson, *Arguments within English Marxism,* pp. 32—4.

5
Change, Evolution and Power

I want to argue in this chapter for a *deconstruction* of a whole range of theories of social change, particularly those of an evolutionary type, and for a *reconstruction* of the nature of power as inherent in the constitution of social life. To deconstruct theories of social change means to deny that some of the most cherished ambitions of social theory — including those of 'historical materialism' — can be realized. This does not imply making the relatively weak claim that such theories cannot be supported by the available evidence. It involves a much stronger and more controversial contention: that they are mistaken about the types of account of social change that are possible. A deconstruction of theories of social change can proceed through three sets of considerations of progressively diminishing generality, as below:

A great deal of social science, in academic sociology as well as Marxism, has been based upon the presumption that it is possible to formulate theorems of structural causation which will explain the determination of social action in general.[1]* Most versions of structural determination are linked to the thesis that the social sciences can uncover universal laws, these laws identifying the effects of structural constraints. A given occurrence or type of behaviour would be shown to be an instance of a general law,

*References may be found on pp. 274–9.

certain boundary conditions for the operation of the law having been specified. 'Determination' here equals a particular form of determinism. The so-called 'covering law' debate has explored these sorts of issues at some length, and without entering into it directly it is enough to say here that such a view is quite inconsistent with the character of generalizations in the social sciences as I have portrayed it previously (see also pp. 343—7).[2] To deny that a general account of structural determination can be achieved is to take a stance to which a great deal of this book is relevant.[3]

Some theories of social change are linked to the above conceptions. It has sometimes been thought, for example, that there are universal laws governing social change and that a theory of social change should be organized around such laws. But there are many attempts to explain change which, while they do not postulate laws, specify certain limited principles of determination of change which are held to apply in something like a universal fashion. Among these, evolutionary conceptions have been by far the most prominent.

'Evolutionism', of course, cannot be easily categorized, since a variety of different standpoints have been associated with the term, and the popularity of evolutionary conceptions has waxed and waned in the social sciences. The second half of the nineteenth century was certainly the high point of evolutionism in social theory, inspired in some considerable degree by the achievements of Darwin in biology.[4] Evolutionary notions subsequently tended to drop out of fashion, especially among anthropologists, who for the most part became strongly influenced by one or other interpretation of 'cultural relativism'. But such notions retained some defenders in anthropology, and in archaeology evolutionism has consistently remained dominant. In the Anglo-Saxon world the rise of functionalism, as led by Malinowski and Radcliffe-Brown in anthropology and subsequently in sociology by Merton and Parsons, was in some degree responsible for the eclipse of evolutionary thinking, although a revival of evolutionary theory was later initiated by Parsons himself.[5]

Evolutionism and Social Theory

Many theories of evolution form prime examples of what I have called 'endogenous' or 'unfolding' models of change, which I have criticized earlier. These sorts of evolutionary theory have in fact often been closely connected with functionalism — the works of Comte being a notable instance — and the separation between functionalism and evolutionism introduced by Malinowski and others should perhaps be regarded as something of an aberration rather than a natural state of affairs. Organic metaphors have often provided the relation between the two. A plant or an organism contains within itself a trajectory of growth, an unfolding of latent potentialities. Change here is understood as governed by the mechanisms involved in such unfolding, with societies being regarded as clearly bounded unities. External conditions are held to accentuate or hold back processes of growth, but they are really a background against which the mechanisms of change operate. Some evolutionary models have treated change as inherently slow and cumulative. Thus Durkheim regarded political revolution as agitation on the surface of social life, incapable of giving rise to major transformations of society because the evolution of basic social institutions is always necessarily slow.[6] But unfolding conceptions of change are certainly not alien to theories which propose that evolution proceeds through processes of revolutionary transition. Marx's views represent a case in point. The chief motor of social change, in the scheme Marx portrays in the 'Preface' to *A Contribution to the Critique of Political Economy*, is the expansion of the forces of production within a given type of society. At some point such an expansion can no longer be contained within the existing institutions of the society, leading to a process of revolution, following which the same process occurs all over again.[7] The sources of change are to be found in the tendential properties of class societies, which contain the 'seeds of their own transformation'.

How should the term 'evolution' be understood? The word itself comes from the Latin *evolutia*, derived from *e-* ('out of') and *volatus* ('rolled'). It was used to refer to the unrolling of parchment books. The concept was not applied in anything like its modern sense until the late seventeenth century, when it came to mean an orderly process of change, passing through discernible stages. Comte was one of the first leading social thinkers to make extensive use of the notion, and his formulation is not very different from those proposed by many subsequently (including Parsons, see pp. 263–74). The variation of societal types, their differentiation and synthesis, promoting 'order with continuity' — these were Comte's themes. 'Aucun ordre réel ne peut plus s'établir, ni surtout durer, s'il n'est pleinement compatible avec le progrès; aucun grand progrès ne saurait effectivement s'accomplir, s'il ne tend finalement a l'évidente consolidation de l'ordre.'[8]

Let me mention some latter-day definitions of social or cultural evolution, culled more or less at random:

> Whether the adjective 'biological' be used or not, the principle of evolution is firmly established as applying to the world of living things. . . . Such basic concepts of organic evolution or variation, selection, adaptation, differentiation, and integration belong at the centre of our concern, when appropriately adjusted to a social and cultural subject-matter. (Parsons)[9]

> Evolution can be considered as an interest in determining recurrent forms, processes and functions. . . . Cultural evolution may be regarded as either a special type of historical reconstruction or a particular methodology or approach. (Steward)[10]

> Evolution (both natural and social) is a self-maintaining, self-transforming and self-transcending process, directional in time and therefore irreversible, which in its course generates every fresh novelty, greater variety, more complex organization, higher levels of awareness, and increasingly conscious mental activity. (Huxley)[11]

> Evolution may be defined as a temporal sequence of forms: one form grows out of another; culture advances from one stage to another. In this process time is as integral a factor as change of form. The evolutionist process is irreversible and non-repetitive. . . . The evolutionist process is like the historical, or diffusionist, process in that both are temporal, and therefore irreversible and non-repetitive. But they differ in that the former is nomothetic in character, whereas the latter is idiographic. . . . To be sure, the evolutionist process always takes place somewhere and in a temporal continuum, but the particular time and the particular place are not significant. It is the temporal sequence of forms that counts. (White)[12]

> In both its biological and cultural spheres evolution moves simultaneously in two directions. On the one side, it creates diversity through adaptive modification: new forms differentiate

from old. On the other side, evolution generates progress: higher forms arise from, and surpass, lower. The first of these directions is Specific Evolution, and the second, General Evolution . . . a different taxonomy is required in examining these two aspects of evolution. Concerned with lines of descent, the study of specific evolution employs phylogenetic classification. In the general evolutionary outlook emphasis shifts to the character of progress itself, and forms are classed in stages or levels of development without reference to phylogeny. (Sahlins)[13]

There are significant points of variation between these formulations. What Sahlins calls 'specific evolution', for example, is the only sense of evolution recognized by Steward, who actually directly rejects 'general evolution'. But the definitions do tend to have certain common traits, stated or implied, and they can be utilized to characterize what a theory or approach has to be like to be worth calling 'evolutionary'. I shall take it for granted that 'evolution' is to be more than a casually applied term (to which there can be no objection), synonymous with 'development' or 'change'. For 'evolutionary theory' in the social sciences to have a distinctive meaning, I shall say, it should show the following characteristics. (I do not think these are arbitrary or overly strong.)

First, there must be at least some presumed conceptual continuity with biological evolution. As the above definitions make clear, this is a criterion which many but not all of those who regard themselves as evolutionary theorists are prone to emphasize. It is a claim that makes sense, for even if it originated primarily within social thought rather than in biology, it is the latter which has given 'evolution' a fairly precise designation and elaborated an account of evolutionary transformations — one which illuminates evolution without using any teleological notions at all. To use the term 'evolution' in the social sciences is rather gratuitous if it does not have at least some connections with the conceptual vocabulary which has become established in biology. It does not follow from this that a complete conceptual correspondence is either necessary or desirable. Evolutionism, or at any rate Darwinianism, has recently come under strong attacks within natural science, and it is conceivable, if not at all likely, that it may be discarded there while being sustained in the realm of social science.

Second, social evolutionism must specify something more than just a progression of change in respect of certain designated criteria, that something being a mechanism of change. This point needs looking at in a certain amount of detail, because it is important. Some evolutionists tend to believe that to defend the concept of evolution in social theory, it is enough to show that progression has occurred, in respect of a certain social item or items, over the course of history from the earliest period of which we have evidence of human society up to the modern era. Thus, for example, White has constructed an index of evolution on the basis of energy production. Societies, or in White's terminology, 'cultural systems', vary as means of harnessing energy. Some are more effective in this regard than others. Different cultural systems may therefore be ranked along a scale by comparing coefficients derived from relating the amount of energy harnessed and expended to the number of human beings involved in those systems.[14] From Comte and Spencer onwards, evolutionary thinkers have referred to increasing complexity, differentiation and so on. Of course, 'evolution' *could* be used just to refer to such progression, abstracted from time and space. It may be justifiable to say, for example, that small, oral cultures are at one end of a continuum of energy consumption and distribution (or time-space distanciation), with the modern, industrialized societies at the other. There is no difficulty, either, in sustaining the claim that certain technical developments, or forms of social organization, are prerequisites to others. 'Evolution' in this sense is uncontentious as a concept. But to use 'evolution' in this way is not to explain anything about social change and does not meet the criterion of having a reasonably close affinity to biological evolution.

Third, a sequence of stages of social development must be specified, in which the mechanism of change is linked to the displacement of certain types or aspects of social organization by others. These stages may be arranged in the form either of specific or of general evolution, or some kind of combination of the two. No presumption must be smuggled in such that progression up such an evolutionary scale means progress as judged in terms of moral criteria, save in so far as this is explicitly justified in some way. As I shall emphasize below, evolutionary theories are highly prone to merge 'progression' with 'progress' because of ethnocentric assumptions which, while probably not logically implied in evolutionism, are very difficult in practice to avoid.

Fourth, identifying a mechanism of social change means explaining change in some way which applies across the whole spectrum of human history, not as an exclusive mechanism of change but as the dominant one. There is no doubt about the prime candidate here, since it figures somewhere in virtually all evolutionary theories, however much they may differ in other respects. This is 'adaptation' — usually meaning adaptation to the material environment.

Not all accounts of social change which depend upon the concept of adaptation are evolutionary, since they may not conform to the first three criteria. But the notion of adaptation is so important in evolutionary theories that without it they lose most of their cogency.[15] It makes sense, therefore, to hold that if in the explication of social change the concept of adaptation turns out to be without value (as I shall claim), evolutionism is stripped of much of its appeal. But I shall also pursue two further critical avenues of attack upon evolutionary theories: they force human history into a mould which it does not fit descriptively, and they tend to be associated, although not inevitably, with a number of unfortunate corollaries.

Adaptation

The concept of adaptation, used in a social context, can be shown characteristically to be either (1) vacuous, i.e., so wide and vague in its meaning as to be more confusing than illuminating, or (2) implicated in a specious and logically deficient claim to functionalist explanation, or (3) involved in the predication of dynamic tendencies in human societies that are demonstrably false.

To address the first point: the notion of adaptation can be used in a fairly precise way in biology, whence it derives,[16] where its usual meaning is to refer to modes in which the gene pool of organisms is influenced by interaction with the environment as a result of selective survival traits. 'Adaptation' can perhaps be formulated in a cogent way in social science if it is taken as a general label referring to the gamut of processes whereby human

beings respond to and modify features of their physical environments. Thus Rappaport defines the term as 'the process by which
organisms or groups of organisms, through responsive changes in
their states, structures, or compositions, maintain homeostasis in
and among themselves in the face of both short-term environmental fluctuations and long-term changes in the composition or
structure of their environments'.[17] It is characteristic of evolutionary social thought, however, to extend this usage so much
that the term becomes irremediably amorphous. For instance,
Harding begins his discussion of adaptation by defining the
concept as 'the securing and conserving of control over the
environment', which is unobjectionable enough. But he then goes
on to say that in evolutionary theory adaptation concerns not just
the relation between societies and nature but 'the mutual
adjustment of societies'.

> Adaptation to nature will shape a culture's technology and
> derivatively its social and ideological components. Yet adaptation
> to other cultures may shape society and ideology, which in turn act
> upon technology and determine its future course. The total result
> of the adaptive process is the production of an organized cultural
> whole, an integrated technology, society, and ideology, which
> copes with the dual selective influence of nature on the one hand
> and the impact of outside cultures on the other.[18]

Adaptation here has simply become such a diffuse notion as to
include all possible sources of influence upon social organization
and transformation!

This sort of usage is entirely typical of evolutionary theories in
the social sciences (compare, for example, Parsons's usage of the
concept, discussed on pp. 270—1). The reasons for this are plain
enough. Where 'adaptation' is specified with some degree of
precision — as in the formulation by Rappaport — and where
what is adapted to is also clearly delimited, the notion is manifestly
inadequate as a general mechanism of social change. If environment means 'natural environment', and if 'adapting' to it means
responding to distinguishable changes in that environment in
ways which have this effect of modifying existing organic or
social traits, 'adaptation' simply is much too narrow to be a
credible candidate for such a mechanism. It can be made plausible
only by expanding one or both aspects of its meaning — by

including other societies (i.e., the 'social environment') within the term 'environment' and/or by including as 'adaptation' more or less any major social process which seems to further the changes of maintaining a society in something like a stable form. Once this has been done, however, the concept becomes so vague that it is useless as a means of explaining anything at all.

Second, it is often because of its vacuous character, as expressed in such formulations, that the notion of adaptation features so widely in spurious 'explanations'. It is if little value indeed to claim that those societies or types of society which have survived for a given period of time, because they survived, must have survived. But that is exactly what explanations which involve 'adaptation' frequently amount to. Thus it is common to propose that the survival of a social item can be explained in terms of its superior adaptive capacity. But how is adaptive capacity understood? In terms comparable with those above — all the elements which need to be invoked if that item is to endure while another does not. Where 'adaptation' is understood in a more limited way, however, proffered explanations tend to be equally defective, embodying versions of functionalism.[19] An example which is typical of much of the relevant literature and has had a great deal of substantive influence is the following, from G. H. Childe, who

> starts from the obvious fact that man cannot live without eating. So a society cannot exist unless its members can secure enough food to keep alive and reproduce. In any society approved beliefs or institutions that cut off the food supply altogether (if for instance all Egyptian peasants had felt obliged to work all year round building a superpyramid), or stopped reproduction (as a universal and fanatical conviction of the virtue of celibacy would do), the society in question would soon come to an end. In this limiting case it is quite obvious that the food supply must exercise a final control in determining even beliefs and ideals. Presumably, then, methods of getting a living in the end exercise a similar control more concretely. The way people get their living should be expected in the long run to 'determine' their beliefs and institutions.[20]

However, what is obvious to Childe does not follow at all from his premise. To identify a functional exigency of a society or social item carries no implication at all, in and of itself, about its actual influence upon the shaping of the institutions which meet it.

Turning to the last of the three charges, adaptation would be given explanatory force if a dynamic were found which successfully interpreted the diversity and the succession of the major types of human society in history. Here evolutionary theories show themselves to be empirically wanting. If it were the case that there were some sort of generalized motivational impulse for human beings progressively to 'adapt' more effectively to their material environments, there would be a basis for sustaining evolutionary theory. But there is not any such compulsion.[21] Alternatively, it might be supposed that some sort of equivalent to natural selection could be found in respect of human societies. This is certainly what many nineteenth-century evolutionists supposed. Spencer preferred his term, 'survival of the fittest', to 'natural selection', but the idea is the same. He interpreted 'survival' less as a result of meeting the material requirements of a given environment than of besting other societies militarily. The formation of larger and larger societies through war, Spencer says, 'is an inevitable process through which the varieties of men most adapted for social life supplant the less adapted varieties'.[22] But if this sort of view has become largely discarded today, even among evolutionists, it is for sound empirical reasons. The influence of war upon social change is real enough. But military strength simply does not have the overall explanatory value necessary to turn 'adaptation' into a viable evolutionary mechanism. Once we start adding in other factors, however, we are back to the situation where the concept explains everything and nothing.

Evolution and History

Human history does not have an evolutionary 'shape', and positive harm can be done by attempting to compress it into one. Here I shall list three reasons why human history does not resemble an evolutionary model of the species and four dangers to which evolutionary thought in the social sciences is prone. Most of the ground has been well-traversed by critics of evolutionism from the nineteenth-century onwards, but it is perhaps worth while spelling these items out. An evolutionary 'shape' — a trunk with branches, or a climbing vine, in which the elapsing of chronological time and the progression of the species are integrated — is an inappropriate metaphor by which to analyse human society.

Human beings make their history in cognizance of that history, that is, as reflexive beings cognitively appropriating time rather than merely 'living' it. The point is a hackneyed enough one, but usually figures in the discussions of evolutionists only in relation to the question of whether or not there is a distinctive break between proto-humans and *Homo sapiens*. That is to say, they regard it simply as something new added to existing evolutionary processes — another factor complicating natural selection. The nub of the matter, however, is that the reflexive nature of human social life subverts the explication of social change in terms of any simple and sovereign set of causal mechanisms. Getting to know what goes on 'in' history becomes not only an inherent part of what 'history' is but also a means of transforming 'history'.

Evolutionary theory in biology depends upon postulates of the independence of the origin of species and the unchangeability of species save through mutation. These conditions do not apply in human history. 'Societies' simply do not have the degree of 'closure' that species do. Biologists can fairly easily answer the question: what evolves? But there is no readily available 'unit of evolution' in the sphere of the social sciences.[23] I have already made this point (pp. 163—8), but it needs to be repeated here. Evolutionists usually speak of the evolution of either 'societies' or 'cultural systems', with the presumption that those which are most highly advanced are simply differentiated versions of the less advanced. But what constitutes a 'society' or 'culture' varies with the very traits upon which evolutionary thinkers tend to concentrate. The debate between evolutionists and 'diffusionists' helped only to conceal this problem because both tended to treat societies or cultures as discrete entities, differing primarily in respect of their divergent appraisals of the sources of change that affected them.

Human history is not, to use Gellner's term, a 'world-growth story'. As Gellner remarks, for two centuries it has been difficult for anyone from the West to

think about human affairs without the image . . . of an all-embracing upward growth. . . . It seemed a natural conclusion from the pattern of Western history, which was generally treated as *the* history of humanity. Western history seems to have a certain continuity and a certain persistent upward swing — or at any rate, so it seemed, and so it came to be taught. Emerging from the river valleys of the Middle East, the story of civilization seems one of continuous and in the main upward growth, only occasionally interrupted by plateaus or even retrogressions: history seemed to creep gently around the shores of the Mediterranean and then up the Atlantic coast, things getting better and better. Oriental empires, the Greeks, the Romans, Christianity, the Dark Ages, the Renaissance, the Reformation, industrialization and struggle for social justice . . . the familiar story, with variants especially in the later details, stresses and anticipation; all this is extremely familiar and still forms the background image of history for most of us. . . . The picture of course dovetailed with biological evolutionism, and the victory of Darwinism seemed to clinch the matter. Two quite independent disciplines, history and biology, provided, it seemed, different parts of the same continuous curve.[24]

The voyage of the *Beagle* symbolized, as it were, the journeys that brought Europeans into contact with diverse and exotic cultures, subsumed and categorized within an embracing scheme in which the West naturally stood at the top. There is no sign that evolutionary schemes today are free from this sort of ethnocentrism. Where can one find such a scheme in Western social science which holds that traditional India is at the head of the scale? Or ancient China? Or, for that matter, modern India or China?[25]

However, there is no need to pose such questions — which are obviously not logically waterproof in terms of their damaging implications for evolutionary theories — to show that history is not a 'world-growth story'. The history of *Homo sapiens* is more accurately portrayed as follows. No one can be sure when *Homo sapiens* first appeared, but what is certain is that for the vast bulk of the period during which human beings have existed they have lived in small hunting-and-gathering societies. Over most of this period there is little discernible progression in respect of either social or technological change: a 'stable state' would be a more accurate description. For reasons that remain highly controversial, at a certain point class-divided 'civilizations' come into being, first of all in Mesopotamia, then elsewhere. But the relatively short period of history since then is not one marked by the continuing ascent of civilization; it conforms more to Toynbee's picture of the rise and fall of civilizations and their conflictual relations with tribal chiefdoms. This pattern is ended by the rise to global pre-eminence of the West, a phenomenon which gives to 'history' quite a different stamp from anything that has gone before, truncated into a tiny period of some two or three centuries. Rather than seeing the modern world as a further accentuation of conditions that existed in class-divided societies, it is much more illuminating to see it as placing a caesura upon the traditional world, which it seems irretrievably to corrode and destroy. The modern world is born out of discontinuity with what went before rather than continuity with it. It is the nature of this discontinuity — the specificity of the world ushered in by the advent of industrial capitalism, originally located and founded in the West — which it is the business of sociology to explain as best it can.

Let me conclude by briefly listing four dangers which evolutionary thought courts — dangers which are best avoided by breaking with it in a radical way. They are those of what I shall call (1) unilineal compression, (2) homological compression, (3) normative illusion and (4) temporal distortion.

The first danger, unilineal compression, means the tendency of evolutionary thinkers to compress general into specific evolution. Thus feudalism precedes capitalism in Europe and is the social nexus from which capitalism develops. It is therefore, in one sense at least, the necessary forerunner of capitalism. Is feudalism, then, a general 'stage' in the evolution of capitalism?[26] Surely not, although there are versions of Marxism, and other schools of social though also, that would have it thus.

By homological compression, the second danger, I refer to the tendency of some writers to imagine that there is a homology between the stages of social evolution and the development of the individual personality. It is worth discussing this in at least moderate detail because although it does not directly depend upon the postulates of evolutionism discussed thus far, it is none the less quite often associated with evolutionary thought. Baldly stated, it is supposed that small, oral cultures are distinguished by forms of cognition, affectivity or conduct found only at the relatively early stages of the development of the individual in more evolved societies. The level of complexity of societal organization, for instance, may be supposed to be mirrored by that of personality development. A correlate of this view is that increased complexity of society implies a heightened degree of repression of affect. Freud's *Civilization and its Discontents* is the *locus classicus* of such a standpoint. Freud uses the term 'civilization' to refer to 'the whole sum of the achievements and the regulations which distinguish our lives from those of our animal ancestors and which serve two purposes — namely to protect men against nature, and to adjust their mutual relations'.[27] In strongly emphasizing progressive control over the material world, Freud's discussion of 'civilization' — a notion about which much more could be said — shares some strong affinities with historical materialism. Perhaps it is not as surprising as may appear at first sight, then, that some Marxists have picked up other aspects of Freud's conception of social development.

Marcuse's attempt to harness Freud's interpretation of 'civilization' to a critique of the capitalist mode of production accepts the fundamentals of Freud's view. The transmutation of 'animal man' into the 'human being' represents a movement from primitive barbarism to civilization:

From	To
immediate satisfaction	delayed satisfaction
pleasure	restraint of pleasure
joy (play)	toil (work)
receptiveness	productiveness
absence of repression	security[28]

Marcuse differs from Freud only in supposing that the 'struggle with nature' that is the basis of human material existence can be alleviated by the productive forces generated by, but not capable of humane expression within, the economic order of capitalism.

A comparable utilization of Freud, although stripped of the vision of a radical reconstitution of society, is to be found in the writings of Elias. Elias builds his theory very directly around the theorem that increasing complexity of social life necessarily entails increased psychological repression:

> From the earliest period of the history of the Occident to the present, social functions have become more and more differentiated under the pressure of competition. The more differentiated they become, the larger grows the number of functions and thus of

people on whom the individual depends in all his actions. . . . As
more and more people must attune their conduct to that of others,
the web of actions must be organized more and more strictly and
accurately. . . . The individual is compelled to regulate his conduct
in an increasingly differentiated, more even and stable manner. . . .
The web of actions grows so complex and so extensive, the effort
to behave 'correctly' within it becomes so great, that beside the
individual's conscious self-control an absolute, blindly functioning
apparatus of self-control is firmly established.[29]

Elias does stress certain specific characteristics of the modern
West, but these are largely submerged in a generalized evolutionism. In the 'less complex societies' there is lower individual self-
control, greater spontaneous expression of emotion, etc. People
in such societies are rather like children, spontaneous and
volatile.

If this view is wrong, as I believe it to be, there is a variety of
implications that can be drawn as regards both the nature of
modern capitalism and the liberating potential that it might
contain.[30] But why is it wrong, and what type of perspective
should replace it? In some part we have to look to the findings of
modern anthropology, which surely dispel the idea that 'primitive
societies' are primitive in anything other than their material
technology. The study of language perhaps provides something
of a baseline here. There simply is no discernible correlation
between linguistic complexity and the level of material 'advance-
ment' of different societies. This fact in itself would indicate that
there is unlikely to be any general differences of psychic
organization between oral cultures on the one hand and
'civilizations' on the other. We have to be careful even with the
supposition that civilizations are more complex than oral cultures.
Civilizations — but, above all, that specific form of global order
ushered in by the ascendancy of the West over the past two
centuries — involve greater time-space distanciation than do oral
cultures. They bracket more extensive segments of time
(probably) and space (certainly). However, some features of social
activity found in oral cultures, such as those associated with
kinship institutions, are exceptionally complex. Of course, it
might be pointed out that Freud's view, and that of others who
have adopted a similar position, is centred upon the repression of
affect, or relative lack of it, in oral cultures. But the evidence

simply does not support the proposition that such cultures are universally associated with spontaneity of emotional expression. Some oral cultures (as the ego psychologists, among others, have sought to demonstrate) have very strong moral prohibitions that cover a range of daily conduct, and the repressions inculcated in child training may be very severe.[31]

By the tendency of evolutionary theory to normative illusion, the third danger, I mean the inclination to identify superior power, economic, political or military, with moral superiority on an evolutionary scale. Such an inclination is no doubt closely related to the ethnocentric connotations of evolutionism, but it is not exactly the same thing. The concept of adaptation is again a hazardous one in this connection. It has an ethically neutral sound, as if superior 'adaptive capacity' were *ipso facto* superiority in respect of normatively superior social traits. When applied to human societies, however, the term is more often than not a synonym for sheer might. If the adage that might does not confer right is an old one, it is frequently forgotten by evolutionary theorists as a consequence of their very evolutionism.[32]

Finally, by temporal distortion, the fourth danger, I mean the proclivity of evolutionary thinkers to presume that 'history' can be written only as social change, that the elapsing of time is the same thing as change, the confusion of 'history' with 'historicity'.

Is historical materialism a form of evolutionism? With certain reservations, we may say that it is, if the term is understood in a certain way. Suppose 'historical materialism' is understood in a very general sense. The term thus appropriated can refer to the idea, stated in the quotation 'human beings make history', that human social life is formed and reformed in *praxis* — in the practical activities carried out in the enactment of everyday life. This is exactly the kind of view I have tried to argue for in setting out the basic tenets of structuration theory. But 'historical materialism' is more commonly used, especially among those who designate themselves Marxists, in a much more definite sense and one which certainly has a great deal of textual support in Marx. This is 'historical materialism' based on the scheme of societal development which Marx and Engels sketch out in the first few pages of *The German Ideology* and in the *Communist Manifesto* and which Marx states succinctly and brilliantly in the 'Preface' to *A Contribution to the Critique of Political Economy*.

The views established in these sources conform to all the main criteria by which I have identified evolutionism and also carry some of its noxious secondary implications. It is true that Marx sometimes wrote as though he were doing no more than producing a history of Western Europe. But he was surely not just writing an interpretative account of one corner of the world. His scheme of development, involving tribal society, the ancient world, feudalism, capitalism, plus the Asiatic mode of production, is an evolutionary framework in which adaptation, in the guise of the expansion of the forces of production, plays the leading role. Why is the Asiatic form of society 'stagnant' compared with the West? Because it does not allow for the development of the forces of production beyond a certain point. It would, of course, be a mistake to bracket Marx too closely with other versions of nineteenth-century evolutionism, his admiration for Darwin notwithstanding. His preoccupation with the increasing mastery of nature which human beings achieve expresses a version of the notion of adaptation not essentially different from many other uses of the idea. But in Marx there is an inverted Hegelian dialectic, tortured into a particular developmental shape, that has no direct analogue in more orthodox evolutionary theories.

Marx's evolutionism is a 'world-growth story' and displays the shortcomings of unilineal compression and temporal distortion. But one must object to it primarily in terms of the role it accords to adaptive mechanisms. Childe's version of historical materialism may be in some respects a peculiarly crude one, but it does have the virtue of bringing into the open assumptions that are often more surreptitiously made. The fact that human beings must survive in the material environments in which they live tells us nothing about whether what they do in order to survive plays a dominant role in social transformation.

I do not think it possible to repair the shortcomings of either evolutionary theory in general or historical materialism in particular.[33] That is why I speak of deconstructing them. We cannot replace them, in other words, with a theory of a similar form. In explaining social change no single and sovereign mechanism can be specified; there are no keys that will unlock the mysteries of human social development, reducing them to a unitary formula, or that will account for the major transitions between societal types in such a way either.

M

Analysing Social Change

The foregoing considerations do not mean that we cannot generalize about social change and do not imply that we should relinquish all general concepts in terms of which change might be analysed. Five concepts are particularly relevant in this respect. I have mentioned three — structural principles, time-space edges and intersocietal systems — in the previous chapter. To these I want to add the notions of *episodic characterization* (or, more briefly, episodes) and *world time*.[34]

Structural principles	Analysis of modes of institutional articulation
Episodic characterizations	Delineation of modes of institutional change of comparable form
Intersocietal systems	Specification of relations between societal totalities
Time-Space edges	Indication of connections between societies of differing structural type
World time	Examination of conjunctures in the light of reflexively monitored 'history'

All social life is episodic, and I intend the notion of episode, like most of the concepts of structuration theory, to apply to the whole range of social activity. To characterize an aspect of social life as an episode is to regard it as a number of acts or events having a specifiable beginning and end, thus involving a particular sequence. In speaking of large-scale episodes I mean identifiable sequences of change affecting the main institutions within a societal totality, or involving transitions between types of societal totality. Let us take as an example the emergence of agrarian states. To treat the formation of a state as an episode means analytically cutting into 'history', that is, identifying certain elements as marking the opening of a sequence of change and tracing through that sequence as a process of institutional transmutation. State formation has to be studied in the context of the involvement of a pre-existing society in broader intersocietal relations (without, of course, neglecting endogenous forms of change), examined in the context of the structural principles implicated in the relevant societal totalities. Thus the accumulation of surplus production on the part of spatially proximate village communities in areas of high potential fertility may be one type of pattern leading to the emergence of a state combining those communities under a single order of administration. But it is only one among others. In many cases the co-ordination of military power used coercively to establish a rudimentary state apparatus is the most important factor. Agrarian states always exist along time-space edges in uneasy relations of symbiosis and conflict with, and partial domination over, surrounding tribal societies, as well, of course, with other states which may struggle for hegemony over a given area. To insist that social change be studied in 'world time' is to emphasize the influence of varying forms of inter-societal system upon episodic transitions. If all social life is contingent, all social change is conjunctural. That is to say, it depends upon conjunctions of circumstances and events that may differ in nature according to variations of context, where context (as always) involves the reflexive monitoring by the agents involved of the conditions in which they 'make history'.

We can categorize modes of social change in terms of the dimensions represented below, these being combined in the assessment of the nature of specific forms of episode. In analysing the origins of an episode, or series of episodes studied in a comparative fashion, various sorts of consideration are ordinarily relevant. In the modern world the expansion in the time-space distanciation of social systems, the intertwining of different modes of regionalization involved in processes of uneven development, the prominence of contradictions as structural features of societies,[35] the prevalence of historicity as a mobilizing force of social organization and transmutation — all these factors and more supply a backdrop to assessing the particular origins of an episode.

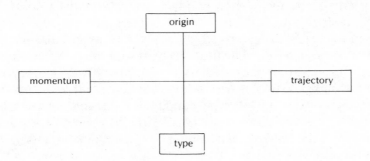

In referring to the type of social change involved in an episode I mean to indicate both how intensive and how extensive it is — that is to say, how profoundly a series of changes disrupts or reshapes an existing alignment of institutions and how wide-ranging such changes are. One idea that is relevant here, which I have outlined in some detail in other sources,[36] is that there may be 'critical thresholds' of change characteristic of transitions between overall societal types. A set of relatively rapid changes may generate a long-term momentum of development, that development being possible only if certain key institutional transformations are accomplished initially. 'Momentum' refers to the rapidity with which change occurs in relation to specific forms of episodic characterization, while 'trajectory' concerns the direction of change, as mentioned earlier.

Let us look briefly at the problem of the emergence of agrarian states in order to illustrate the concepts just introduced. How far can the development of such states be regarded as a single type of episode? Even such an apparently innocuous question turns out to be much harder to answer than is suggested by the relative simplicity of most theories which have been put forward about such states — for example, that they have their origins in warfare, in irrigation schemes, in the rapid accumulation of surplus production and so on. To make an episodic characterization, as I have mentioned, means making a number of conceptual decisions: about what social form is the 'starting point' of a presumed sequence of change, about what the typical trajectory of development is and about where the 'end point' is said to be.

First of all, we might register that the term 'state' is an ambiguous one. It can refer either to the overall form of a 'state-based society' or to governmental institutions of a definite type within such a society. To simplify the issue, I shall take 'state' for this purpose to mean the second of these alternatives. The initial characterization problem, then, becomes one of deciding the main contrasts being looked for in juxtaposing circumstances in which certain political institutions exist to those in which they do not. This question does seem to admit of an answer, although not an uncontroversial one. Following Nadel, we may suppose that a state exists when the following conditions are found: (a) centralized organs of government, associated with (b) claims to legitimate territorial control and (c) a distinct dominant elite or class, having definite modes of training, recruitment and status attributes.[37] Such a formulation, or one very much like it, has been adopted by many prominent contributors to the field, notably in the case of classic discussion of Fortes and Evans-Pritchard.[38] What is the obverse, the type of social situation from which states develop? The answer might be thought to be self-evident — societies which do not possess state institutions as defined above. But matters are not, in fact, so obvious, or they are so only if we unthinkingly apply an endogenous model. For it is probably not usually the case that state institutions develop within an already constituted 'society' that remains more or less unchanged. On the contrary, the development of states very often fuses previously unarticulated social entities and may at the same time break up others that have existed hitherto.

We have to bear this point in mind when distinguishing states from chiefdoms. It may be that the latter are usually the antecedents of the former (and remain when states are destroyed or collapse), but the one rarely derives simply from the 'expansion' or 'internal differentiation' of the other. The distinction between states and chiefdoms is by no means as easy to make as is seemingly often presumed in the anthropological literature. The normal basis of the distinction has to do with centralization. In contrast to states, chiefdoms have a range of equivalent office holders, under the chief; these offices entail more or less the same power and status. There is no doubt that this distinction does help to order the relevant empirical materials. None the less, the dividing line can be variously placed. Consider, for example, the case of Tahiti.[39] Here there were three endogenous descent groups, stratified in some degree by status and political responsibility. Chiefs, presided over by a paramount chief, were drawn from the upper of these groups within different parts of the island. But are these groups worth calling 'states'? Claessen says yes,[40] but the author who has devoted most energy to studying ancient Tahitian society, Oliver, says no.[41]

The difference of opinion is not so much empirical as conceptual. It is important because it is symptomatic of the difficulties involved in specifying classes of social objects. My view is that Claessen makes the criteria for the existence of states too lax. Of course, it is apparent enough that criteria of classification and the predication of definite mechanisms of institutional articulation are not independent issues. One cannot start out with a theoretically neutral taxonomy and then later inject a theoretical interpretation into it. Thus on the basis of a survey of twenty-one 'early states' Claessen claims that there is no specific association between such states and urbanism. But, in fact, nearly all of the examples cited to reach this conclusion belong to his category of 'inchoate states', which would seem to me to be more accurately designated as chiefdoms.[42]

How should we specify the trajectory of change to be looked at? As posed in the existing literature, this question is often answered not only within an endogenous framework but also with regard to implicitly evolutionary premises. That is to say, it is posed in a unidirectional way, as to do only with the development of states, the existence of the state being taken as the end-point of the process. But why should episodes involving agrarian states be thought of exclusively, even primarily, in this fashion? The development of a state in one particular region very often coincides with, and perhaps brings about, the dissolution or attenuation of other neighbouring states. The dissolution of states is no less common an occurrence than their initial formation, and there is little rationale for concentrating on the one process to the exclusion of the other — especially in so far as they are recurrently linked together. I would therefore be inclined to characterize the issue as follows. In understanding processes of institutional change affecting agrarian states, we are seeking to analyse the conditions giving rise to the intersecting relations between chiefdoms and state forms.

Expressed in this way, it should be clear why such a position is at odds with the usual concentration on the 'origins' of the state. It is also unsurprising that the large literature on the 'origins' of the state has not come up with support for the sorts of all-enveloping generalization that have often been ventured. These fall into various types, according to the causal forces given priority.[43] Probably the most influential are those which emphasize demographic factors, war and the growth of the forces of production. Childe's writings have had a substantial impact upon theories which are in the third of these categories; in archaeology his work has probably been a more important source of Marxist influence than the writings of Marx and Engels themselves. Theories of this type tend to be strongly evolutionary and to presume that the 'origins' of the state are associated with either sheer technological change or the accumulation of surplus production. Where such views do not amount to false functionalist 'explanations', they are simply inconsistent with empirical data. There are some cases which come close to fitting the bill — that is to say, where surplus accumulation precedes the development of a state and where an emergent ruling class 'pushes' towards state formation. But these are exceptional.[44] Phases of state formation are often connected with declining productivity and wealth rather than the reverse, although sometimes goods may be plundered from surrounding areas.

The 'warfare theory' has attracted many adherents because if there is one aspect of agrarian (and industrialized) states which is more or less chronic, it is participation in war. Spencer's version of evolutionism, of course, attributed great significance to warfare prior to the development of the industrial age. War is definitely very commonly involved in the formation and the disintegration of states — which, as I have stressed, is often one and the same process. But it is one thing to say that states frequently engage in warlike activities; it is another to say that such activities play a dominant or determinant role in the origins of those states and yet another to say that they play this role in the formation (or decline) of all agrarian states. The first statement is unobjectionable. The second is at best only partially valid. The third is simply erroneous. Demographic theories scarcely fare better. They usually suggest that population increase, the result of increasing birth rates in populations whose available living space is relatively confined, creates pressure leading to centralization of authority and differentiation of power.[45] Certainly, state-based societies are larger, often very much larger, than tribal orders. Demographic theories are often associated with the idea that the 'neolithic revolution' stimulates population increase, leading to state formation. But this does not work on either a general or a more specific level. The beginning of the neolithic is distant from the development of any known state-based societies. In more specific terms, it does not turn out that those states which were formed in physically confined areas always follow a build-up of population pressure. There are some instances that seem to accord fairly well with the theory, but many do not. Thus, examining state formation in the Valley of Mexico and in Mesopotamia, Dumont reaches the conclusion that population growth cannot explain the development of state forms, although the former is associated with the latter.[46] Other research indicates that population may decline in the period prior to state formation.[47]

Some accounts of state formation emphasize relations between societies other than that of war. Thus Polanyi has studied the impact of long-distance trade on the development of states.[48] To my knowledge, no one has offered this as a generalized theory of state formation; if anyone did, it would fare even worse than those mentioned above. This sort of viewpoint does at least call attention to aspects of the importance of intersocietal systems in processes of state formation and decay. However, the mention neither of war nor of trade confronts the analytical issue of the nature of intersocietal systems. As I have stressed in the previous chapter, it will not do to think of such systems only as a series of relations linking clearly delimited societal wholes. To study such systems means at the same time to discard the assumption that the question of what a 'society' is admits of a ready and easy answer. Consider again the sorts of example discussed by Eberhard. In a single geographical arena numerous societies may exist in relatively close physical proximity but without much direct contact between them, although all are nominally or actually subject to political rule from a centre.[49] By contrast, in such an arena there may exist ingerlaced groupings quite differently located in time-space — this is one of the phenomena I have in mind in speaking of 'time-space edges'. Thus, as in traditional China, in Moghul India the bulk of the Indian farmers had virtually no contact with the Moghuls. Their languages, customs and religion were different. The big merchants were only peripherally part of 'Moghul society', but most of their contacts and affiliations with groups were distributed over large distances, stretching across the subcontinent and the whole of the Near East. Much the same was true of the priests, who belonged to associations spanning the subcontinent and sometimes beyond.

> We should not be astonished to find certain folk tales in the whole Near East, in some parts of South Asia and, finally, on the Fu-kien coast of China, while we do not find them in the Philippines or on Hainan Island. Miao tribes in Kui-chou for centuries preserved their own customs, beliefs and tales in spite of Chinese settlements only a few miles away in which other customs, beliefs and tales

were propagated. Miao and Chinese in such places did not interact, as a rule, except in the fields of economic exploitation or military aggression. But the Miao in Kui-chou might have had the same customs as Miao in Viet-nam because — as we can often prove — some contacts were maintained even over long distances and long periods.[50]

The points made so far suggest that theories of the 'origins' of the state tend to suffer from shortcomings deriving from the characterization of episodes in an endogenous and/or evolutionary form and a failure to examine societal organization and change in the context of intersocietal systems. But to these have to be added a neglect of the impact of 'world time'. Putting these together, we can come to see that the type of theory often looked to as explaining 'state origins' turns out to be a chimera. In speaking of the influence of 'world time', I do not mean the arranging of events or happenings in a calendar of world history. I mean two things referred to by Eberhard in his use of the phrase (although these are not clearly distinguished by him). Each concerns factors limiting generalizations that might be made about types of episode. One refers to conjunctures, the other to the influence of human knowledgeability on social change. By 'conjunctures' I mean the interaction of influences which, in a particular time and place, have relevance to a given episode — in this case, state formation or decline. The conjuncture of circumstances in which one process of development occurs may be quite different from that of another, even if their 'outcomes' — e.g. the consolidation of a similar type of state apparatus — are similar. In order to understand how this may come about, it is essential to consider human reflexivity — and this is exactly what many theories of state formation do not do. Conjunctural conditions could be treated as comparable with the 'boundary conditions' of laws were it not the case that they can enter into the thinking, and therefore the conduct, of human actors who are aware of them.

Adopting bits of each of the theories previously mentioned above, Claessen and Skalnik list the following elements as relevant to explaining state formation, although these are not always found, they say, and their relative importance may vary from instance to instance:

(1) population growth or pressure;

(2)   war, conquest or their threat;
(3)   technological progress or the production of a surplus;
(4)   ideology and legitimation;
(5)   the influence of already existing states.[51]

While these are offered as if they were 'factors' of equivalent logical status, (5) is, in fact, different from the others. Taking (5) seriously means coping with all the issues I have mentioned previously in regard to intersocietal systems, time-space edges and 'world time'. It is simply absurd to compress these into a single additional 'factor' to be added to the other ones mentioned.

We can begin to unpack some of the problems involved by considering the distinction introduced by Fried, and widely adopted since then, between 'pristine' and 'secondary' states.[52] Pristine or primal states are those which develop in areas where no state forms have previously existed; secondary states are those developing in areas where others have existed before them or are to be found nearby. The differences between these supply at least one main axis in 'world time' and bring intersocietal relations directly into play. I take it that my previous discussion has indicated that the empirical identification of primal states is exceedingly difficult. It is not possible to define primal states as those which have become formed in geographically isolated environments. For the influence of forms of political organization which are simply 'known about' are enough to make a state a secondary state. Thus Egypt of the Old Kingdom is sometimes regarded as a primal state on the basis that it apparently developed in a geographically protected *milieu* (although the archaeological evidence on this is, in fact, very meagre). But all that this means is that no previous state form is known to have existed there. The impact of pre-existing Mesopotamian states certainly cannot be discounted.[53]

The implication I wish to draw is that the categories of primal and secondary states are highly imbalanced. Instances of primal states are hard to come by, and in the nature of the case we are never going to be able to be sure that cases which look to be plausible candidates for belonging in the category are any more than that. For it may be, of course, that traces of prior state influences have simply disappeared. It certainly follows that, while there is no bar to speculating about the modes of development of primal states, it may be quite misleading to treat what is known about them as a basis for theorizing about processes of state formation in general. It is likely to be very much more fruitful to regard 'secondary states' as prototypical — that is to say, states which develop in a world, or in regions of the world, where there are already either states or political formations having a considerable degree of centralization.

In a world of already existing states there is no difficulty in explaining the availability of the idea of the state, or of models of state formation, that could be followed by aspiring leaders and their followerships. We are all familiar with the fact that the leaders of Japan in recent times quite deliberately — although after a good deal of external pressure from the West — decided to adopt a certain model of industrial development derived from prior European and American experience. While this example is no doubt unusual in so far as the changes initiated were quite sudden and very far-reaching, it is hardly only in recent times that human beings in one context have been concerned to emulate, or borrow from, those in another in order to offset their power or influence. The steps involved in state formation, in other words, have probably hardly ever been unknown to those who have played leading parts in such a process. It is enough to surmise that state builders have almost always been aware of major aspects of the nature and basis of power of centralized political formations in order to explain a good deal about how states have come into being and declined. We do not have to imagine that it was ever common for individuals or groupings to have overall organizational plans in mind for social change and then to set about implementing them. That is very largely a phenomenon of the modern era.

What, then, might a theory of state formation look like, recast in these terms? First of all, we have to remember the point that the operation of generalized 'social forces' presumes specifiable motivation on the part of those influenced by them. To speak of, for example, 'population expansion' as a contributing cause of state formation implies certain motivational patterns prompting definite sorts of response to that expansion (and involved in bringing it about). Second, the influence of 'world time' means that there are likely to be considerable differences in respect of the major influences upon state formation; an overall account which will fit in some cases will not do so in others. This does not mean that generalizations about state formation as a type of episode are without value. However, they will probably apply to a more limited range of historical contexts and periods than the originators of most of the more prominent theories have had in mind.

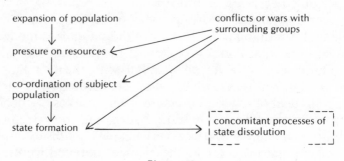

Figure 12

Carneiro's theory might be taken as an example. A formal representation of it can be given as in figure 12. Carneiro emphasizes the importance of warfare in the origin of states. But warfare is more or less chronic in societies of all kinds, he says, and is thus not a sufficient explanation of state formation. War tends to lead to the formation of states, he claims, when those involved are penned into physically circumscribed areas of agricultural land, such as the Nile, Tigris—Euphrates and Indus valleys, the Valley of Mexico or the mountain and coastal valleys of Peru. In such circumstances warfare may come to set up a pressure upon scarce resources where migration out of the area is unlikely to occur. Established ways of life come under strain, inducing some groups to seek military ascendancy over others and fostering attempts to centralize control over production. Population growth tends to be a highly important contributory factor both in stimulating conflicts over resources and in promoting centralization of administrative authority.[54] An entire valley eventually becomes unified under a single chiefdom, which, with further concentration of administrative resources, becomes distinguishable as a state. The state may then push its own boundaries outwards to conquer and absorb surrounding peoples. It is here (although Carneiro does not say so) that the theory presumes the primacy of certain types of motive — and, we can add, the likely influence of strategies, models or diffuse influences from pre-existing political forms. It has to be inferred that in the face of pressure on resources and established modes of conduct, those involved do not alter such modes of conduct so as to renew social co-operation. Unequal division of resources does not follow mechanically from population pressure. Also, tendencies towards the strengthening of centralized control will not happen willy-nilly in such a situation. They are likely to involve some sort of reflexive understanding of 'social needs' by actors engaged in policies that strengthen such control, although no one might intend the outcomes which actually come about.

As is common in much of the relevant anthropological and archaeological literature, Carneiro's discussion is offered as a theory of the 'origin of the state'. The phrase normally tends to refer to primal states, although this is not made wholly clear in what the author has to say. I think it is more valuable, for reasons already mentioned, to move away from the distinction between primary and secondary states. The very same pattern as Carneiro treats as involved in the 'origin' of the state may also be a process of political dissolution or fragmentation. Carneiro's theory is an interesting and elegant one, but it does not follow that in order to be defended it has to apply to all known cases of state formation, even if it were possible easily to distinguish primal from secondary states. Carneiro admits that cases can be readily found which the theory does not seem to fit. He then tries to modify it in such a way as to give it universal application, believing that if it does not have such a universal character there must be something wrong with the theory. States do not always develop in physically confined geographical areas. To cover such cases, Carneiro introduces a concept of what he calls 'resource concentration'. Where natural resources are particularly concentrated within any given area, people tend to become drawn to that area, leading to a crowding of population within it. Once there is a fairly dense population within the area in question, the pattern of state development will tend to occur. However, thus extended the theory no longer looks as plausible, and it is surely best to conclude that it only covers certain types of cases of state formation, not all. Of course, it is very important to seek to discover just where the limits of its validity lie. But the fact that it serves to illuminate only a given range of instances does not necessarily imply that it is logically flawed.

Change and Power

Anyone who reflects upon the phrase 'human beings make history', particularly within the broader scope of Marx's writings, is inevitably led to consider questions of conflict and power. For, in Marx's view, the making of history is done not just in relation to the natural world but also through the struggles which some human beings wage against others in circumstances of domination. A deconstruction of historical materialism means discarding some of the main parameters in terms of which Marx organized his work. But in the case of power and its relation to conflict — somewhat paradoxically — it is an effort of reconstruction that is needed. Let me look at why that should be.

A relatively superficial, although by no means unimportant, objection to Marx's various observations on conflict and domination might be that they greatly exaggerate the significance of class struggle and class relations in history. Whatever 'history' is, it is certainly not primarily 'the history of class struggles', and domination is not founded in some generalized sense upon class domination, even in the 'last instance'. A more fundamental problem, however, is the concept of power presumed, although rarely given direct expression, in Marx's writings. For Marx associates power (and the state, as its embodiment) with schism, with a division of interest between classes. Power is thus linked to conflict and is represented as characteristic only of class societies. While Marx was able to develop a formidable analysis and indictment of domination in class-divided and capitalist societies, socialism appears as a society in which domination is transcended. In this respect Marxism and socialism more generally, as Durkheim discerned,[55] share a good deal in common with their nineteenth-century opponent, utilitarian liberalism. Each participates in a 'flight from power', and each ties power inherently to conflict. Since in Marx power is grounded in class conflict, it poses no specific threat in the anticipated society of the future: class division will be overcome as part and parcel of the initiation of that society. For liberals, however, who deny the possibility of achieving such a revolutionary reorganization of society, the threat of power is omnipresent. Power signals the existence of conflict and the potentiality of oppression; thus the state should be organized in such a way as to minimize its scope, taming it through parcelling it out in a democratic fashion.[56]

A reconstructed theory of power would begin from the premise that such views are untenable. Power is not necessarily linked with conflict in the sense of either division of interest or active struggle, and power is not inherently oppressive. The barrage of critical attacks which Parson's analysis of power provoked[57] should not allow us to ignore the basic correctives which he helped to introduce into the literature. Power is the capacity to achieve outcomes; whether or not these are connected to purely sectional interests is not germane to its definition. Power is not, as such, an obstacle to freedom or emancipation but is their very medium — although it would be foolish, of course, to ignore its constraining properties. The existence of power presumes structures of domination whereby power that 'flows smoothly' in processes of social reproduction (and is, as it were, 'unseen') operates. The development of force or its threat is thus not the type case of the use of power. Blood and fury, the heat of battle, direct confrontation of rival camps — these are not necessarily the historical conjunctures in which the most far-reaching effects of power are either felt or established.

These things having been said, however, it is necessary to separate structuration theory from both of the variant pathways trodden by Parsons and by Foucault. In associating power with so-called 'collective goals', Parsons sacrifices part of the insight that the concept of power has no intrinsic relation to that of interest. If power has no logical connection with the realization of sectional interests, neither does it have any with the realization of collective interests or 'goals'. More substantively, Parsons's concentration upon normative consensus as the foundation of the integration of societies leads him seriously to underestimate the significance of contestation of norms; and of the manifold circumstances in which force and violence, and the fear of them, are directly involved in the sanctioning of action.[58] Foucault's rehabilitation of the concept of power, on the other hand, is achieved only at the cost of succumbing to a Nietzschean strain in which power is seemingly prior to truth. In Foucault, as in Parsons, although for different reasons, power is not related to a satisfactory account of agency and knowledgeability as involved in the 'making of history'.

In order to develop these various observations further, I want to discuss several aspects of power within the conceptual framework of the theory of structuration. A primary concern must be the issue of how power is generated. We have to take very seriously indeed Parsons's contention that power is not a static quantity but expandable in relation to divergent forms of system property, although I shall not adopt the ideas he worked out in pursuing the implications of this view.

The notion of time-space distanciation, I propose, connects in a very direct way with the theory of power. In exploring this connection we can elaborate some of the main outlines of domination as an expandable property of social systems. Power, I have described in the opening chapter, is generated in and through the reproduction of structures of domination. The resources which constitute structures of domination are of two sorts — allocative and authoritative. Any co-ordination of social systems across time and space necessarily involves a definite combination of these two types of resources, which can be classified as below:

Allocative Resources	Authoritative Resources
1 Material features of the environment (raw materials, material power sources)	1 Organization of social time-space (temporal-spatial constitution of paths and regions)
2 Means of material production/reproduction (instruments of production, technology)	2 Production/reproduction of the body (organization and relation of human beings in mutual association)
3 Produced goods (artifacts created by the interaction of 1 and 2)	3 Organization of life chances (constitution of chances of self-development and self-expression)

These are not fixed resources; they form the media of the expandable character of power in different types of society. Evolutionary theories have always tended to give priority to those in the left-hand column, the various sorts of material resources employed in 'adaptation' to the environment. But, as my preceding discussion has indicated, authoritative resources are every bit as 'infrastructural' as allocative resources are. I do not at all want to deny the influence of the surrounding natural habitat upon patterns of social life, the impact that major sorts of technological invention may have or the relevance of the material power resources that may be available and harnessed to human use. But it has long been conventional to emphasize these, and I think it very important to demonstrate the parallel significance of authoritative resources. For, like Marxism, we are still prisoners of the Victorian era in so far as we look first of all to the transformation of the material world as the generic motive force of human history.

It is clear that the garnering of allocative resources is closely involved with time-space distanciation, the continuity of societies across time and space and thus the generation of power. Hunters and gatherers have little means of storing food and other material requisites and utilize the given storehouse of nature in providing for their needs the year around. They are in a very immediate fashion dependent upon the bounty of nature — a fact which, however, does not necessarily imply impoverishment. Moreover, ritual, ceremonial and religious activities ordinarily loom much larger than do the relatively limited material requirements of daily life. In agrarian communities at least some kind of productive technology is employed, and the storehouse which the natural world provides is augmented in various ways that facilitate the 'stretching' of social relations across time-space. That is to say, different seasonal crops are grown, products are stored where this is technically possible, fields are allowed to lie fallow to protect the productive capacity of the society in the long term and so on. In class-divided societies there may be a further development of agrarian *per capita* productivity, although this is certainly by no means always the case as compared with that of smaller peasant communities. Irrigation schemes and other technical innovations usually do not so much increase average productivity as regularize and co-ordinate production. In larger agrarian states storage of food and other perishable goods becomes of the first importance. In modern capitalism purchase and sale of manufactured foods is as fundamental to social existence as the exchange of the whole gamut of other commodities: it is not an exaggeration to say that the expansion of capitalism to form a new world economy would not have been possible without the development of a range of techniques for the preservation and storage of perishable goods, particularly food.[59] But then capitalism also generates, and is dependent upon, rates of technical innovation, coupled with a massive utilization of natural resources, which are on an altogether different plane from anything which went before.

Described in such a manner, human history would sound (and has very often been made to sound) like a sequence of enlargements of the 'forces of production'. The augmenting of material resources *is* fundamental to the expansion of power, but allocative resources cannot be developed without the transmutation of authoritative resources, and the latter are undoubtedly at least as important in providing 'levers' of social change as the former. The organization of social time-space refers to the forms of regionalization within (and across) societies in terms of which the time-space paths of daily life are constituted. Hunting-and-gathering communities, and the relatively few instances of larger nomadic cultures, are the only societies whose overall time-space organization implies regular movement of the whole group through time-space. 'Only' is misplaced here. For hunting-and-gathering societies have been the most typical form of human social organization upon this earth until very recent times. Spatial fixity — the pinning down of locales to definite 'built environments', especially in the form of cities — marks a new departure in human history.

The second category of authoritative resources, the production/ reproduction of the body, should not be assimilated to category 2 in the classification of allocative resources. Of course, the means of material reproduction are necessary to the reproduction of the human organism; for most of human history material limits of various sorts have kept down the overall growth of population. But the *co-ordination* of numbers of people together in a society and their reproduction over time is an authoritative resource of a fundamental sort. Power does not, of course, depend solely upon the size of a population brought together within an administrative order. But size of system organization does make a very significant contribution to the generation of power. The various constraining and enabling characteristics of the body that I discussed in chapter 3 are relevant here — indeed, they are the basis upon which administrative resources in this sense are to be analysed. However, we have to add to these the category of life chances, a phenomenon again by no means sheerly dependent upon the material productivity of a society. The nature and scale of power generated by authoritative resources depends not only on the arrangement of bodies, regionalized on time-space paths, but also on the life chances open to agents. 'Life chances' means, in the first instance, the chances of sheer survival for human beings in different forms and regions of society. But it also connotes the whole range of aptitudes and capabilities which Weber had in mind when he introduced the term. Take just one example: mass literacy. A literate population can be mobilized, and can mobilize itself, across time-space in ways quite distinct from those pertaining within largely oral cultures.

I have already referred to the importance of storage of allocative resources as a medium of the expansion of domination, a theme familiar in the literature of evolutionary theory. Much less familiar, but of essential importance to the engendering of power, is the storage of authoritative resources. 'Storage' is a medium of 'binding' time-space involving, on the level of action, the knowledgeable management of a projected future and recall of an elapsed past. In oral cultures human memory is virtually the sole repository of information storage. However, as we have seen, memory (or recall) is to be understood not only in relation to the psychological qualities of individual agents but also as inhering in the recursiveness of institutional reproduction. Storage here already presumes modes of time-space control, as well as a phenomenal experience of 'lived time', and the 'container' that stores authoritative resources is the community itself.

The storage of authoritative and allocative resources may be understood as involving the retention and control of information or knowledge whereby social relations are perpetuated across time-space. Storage presumes *media* of information representation, modes of information *retrieval* or recall and, as with all power resources, modes of its dissemination. Notches on wood, written lists, books, files, films, tapes — all these are media of information storage of widely varying capacity and detail. All depend for their retrieval upon the recall capacities of the human memory but also upon skills of interpretation that may be possessed by only a minority within any given population. The dissemination of stored information is, of course, influenced by the technology available for its production. The existence of mechanized printing, for instance, conditions what forms of information are available and who can make use of it. Moreover, the character of the information medium — as McLuhan, that now forgotten prophet, consistently stressed — directly influences the nature of the social relations which it helps to organize.[60]

It is the containers which store allocative and authoritative resources that generate the major types of structural principle in the constitution of societies indicated in the previous chapter. Information storage, I wish to claim, is a fundamental phenomenon permitting time-space distanciation and a thread that ties together the various sorts of allocative and authoritative resources in reproduced structures of domination. The city, which only ever develops in conjunction with the elaboration of new forms of information storage, above all writing, is the container or 'crucible of power' upon which the formation of class-divided societies depends. Although I have quoted it before elsewhere,[61] I cannot resist mentioning again here Mumford's observation, which summarizes this point in an exemplary way:

> the first beginning of urban life, the first time the city proper becomes visible, was marked by a sudden increase in power in every department and by a magnification of the role of power itself in the affairs of men. A variety of institutions had hitherto existed separately, bringing their numbers together in a common meeting place, at seasonable intervals: the hunters' camp, the sacred monument or shrine, the palaeolithic ritual cave, the neolithic agricultural village — all of these coalesced in a bigger meeting place, the city. . . . The original form of this container lasted for some six thousand years; only a few centuries ago did it begin to break up.[62]

It began to break up, one should say, under the impact of modern capitalism, which developed in societal contexts that helped to form, and were shaped by, a new type of power container: the nation-state. The disappearance of city walls is a process convergent with the consolidation of a highly elaborated type of administrative order operating within tightly defined territorial boundaries of its own.

Critical Notes: Parsons on Evolution

While over the past few decades there have been forceful advocates of an evolutionary standpoint, such as Leslie White, it would probably be true to say that their work has not made a substantial impact upon theoretical thinking in the social sciences. It is therefore of some interest that one of the major contributors to such thinking, Talcott Parsons, should have sought to breathe fresh life into evolutionary theory, albeit only in the later development of his work. Since Parsons's account of evolutionism has indeed mobilized considerable support, I shall consider it in some detail here.

Social evolution, Parsons argues, is an extension of biological evolution, even if dependent upon substantially different mechanisms. There is no reason to assume that there is a sudden break between biological and social evolution. The 'watershed between subhuman and human', as Parsons calls it, marks a phase in a very long-term process of development. Both forms of evolution can be understood in terms of universals — 'evolutionary universals'. An evolutionary universal, in Parsons's terminology, is any type of development 'sufficiently important to further evolution' that it is likely to crop up on more than one occasion in different conditions.[1]* Vision is offered as an example of an evolutionary universal in the sphere of the organic world. The capability of vision allows for a wider range of co-ordinating responses to the surrounding environment and thus has great adaptive value. Vision has not emerged only in one part of the animal kingdom but has come about independently in phyla-molluscs, insects and vertebrates. The visual organs of these groups are not of a single anatomical form and cannot be regarded as belonging to a single evolutionary process, but vision does seem to be a prerequisite for all higher levels of biological evolution.

The biological potential of human beings for social evolution depends upon the evolutionary universals of the hands and the

*References may be found on pp. 279–80.

brain. Having independently movable fingers and an opposing thumb allows for an extraordinary variety of manipulations of objects in conjunction with arms having mobile joints. The human brain is so much more developed than those of other species that it makes possible the mastery of modes of activity and of cognition unknown among the lower animals, above all the capacity for the creation and use of language. These traits give human beings adaptive advantages over the other species. The concept of adaptation, Parsons claims, is essential to both biological and social evolution. Adaptation, he says, should not be understood to mean just the passive adjusting of a given species or type of social system to environmental conditions but should include more active survival factors. The adaptation of a 'living system' can involve 'an active concern with mastery, or the ability to change the environment to meet the needs of the system, as well as an ability to survive in the face of its unalterable features'.[2] This often means the capacity to cope with a range of environmental challenges, and especially with circumstances that provoke uncertainty. An evolutionary universal, in sum, is any organic or social trait which augments the long-run adaptive capabilities of a living system to such a degree that it becomes a prerequisite for higher levels of development. There is only one major difference between biological and social evolutionary universals: the first are not open to diffusion, while the second are. Thus the conditions under which an adaptive advantage originates may be different from those which facilitate its later adaption by other social groupings.

Human beings live in societies and create cultures. The symbolic aspects of culture, as Parsons describes them, are vital to adaptation. The 'symbol' replaces the gene as the chief organizing component of social evolution. Although based upon a set of general organic capabilities, the symbolic qualities of social systems have to be learned anew by each generation. 'Cultural orientations' do not implement themselves as genetic programmes do. Communication is the basis of culture and language the basis of communication. Language is thus an elementary evolutionary universal; there is no known human society which does not possess a language. According to Parsons, symbol systems have a directive role both in social organization generally and in social change. This is because they are at the top of a cybernetic hierarchy in human societies. In Parsons's 'action scheme' they rank above the social system, personality and the organism. The physical environment conditions, or sets limits to, the modes of conduct formed within societies, but it is the cultural system which most directly regulates them.[3]

In its earliest forms culture is more or less synonymous with religion. Religion, Parsons argues, is one of four evolutionary universals found in 'even the simplest action system'. The others are communication through language plus kinship and technology: 'their presence constitutes the very minimum that may be said to mark a society as truly human.'[4] These relate to the overall properties of action and thus to the general framework of biological evolution. Evolution away from the most elemental types of action system can be analysed as a process of progressive differentiation, which refers to functional specialization. Differentiation can lead — although not inevitably — to increased adaptive capacity in respect of each specific function that is separated out, a process of 'adaptive upgrading'. The lines along which differentiation proceeds can be worked out in these terms. Given the cybernetic nature of social systems, these lines must be *functional*. The increasing complexity of systems, in so far as it is not due only to segmentation, involves the development of subsystems specialized about more specific functions in the operation of the system as a whole and of integrative mechanisms which interrelate the functionally differentiated subsystems.[5] These subsystems — pattern maintenance, integration, polity and economy — are the basis of Parsons's analysis.

In the simplest types of society, primitive society, the four subsystems show only a very low level of differentiation. Primitive societies are characterized by a specific system of 'constitutive symbolism', which accords the group a definite cultural identity, separate from others. Such symbolism is always directly connected with kinship relations — for example, in the form of a myth of ancestral gods who founded the community. The myth both unites the group and provides an interpretative framework for coping with the exigencies of, and threats from, the natural world. One of the distinguishing features of primitive societies is that constitutive symbolism is comprehensively involved in the various spheres of life. It enters into religious, moral and technological activities, permeating them and rendering them part of a cohesive social unity. Parsons takes as an example (as Durkheim did) the aboriginal societies of Australia. The social organization of these Australian societies consists almost wholly of kinship relations and the modes in which they articulate with totemic practices, exchange relations and transactions with the environment. Economic aspects of the latter are of the 'simplest sort', depending upon hunting and the gathering of berries, roots and various sorts of edible insects. The tribal groups range over fairly broad tracts of territory, and although their constitutive symbolism has definite territorial reference, there are no clearly defined territorial boundaries between different groups. While kinship relations are of essential importance, there is no vertical differentiation between kin units; no set of clans has markedly greater power, wealth or religious prominence than any other. The Australian societies are functionally differentiated by gender and by age, but otherwise they consist of equivalent segmental groupings linked by kinship ties.

The most primitive societies, such as the Australian groups, can be distinguished from the 'advanced primitive type'. The transition is marked by the breakdown of equivalence between kinship groups. This may happen when one group manages to secure resources which allow it to control the formation of marriage ties; these resources may then be used to accumulate material wealth and other bases of power. A tendency to the vertical differentiation of society replaces the more egalitarian character of the simpler societies. Economic change is associated with such a process: settled residence, agricultural or pastoral production replace the more errant procedures of hunting and gathering. There is still not a differentiated 'economy', but enhanced material productivity creates economic pressures towards the consolidation of property rights and stability of territorial control. However it may come about, stratification is the first and most basic evolutionary universal in the transition from more to less primitive societies. Stratification tends first of all to emerge through the elevation of one lineage to a privileged rank; the senior individual in that lineage then usually takes the title of monarch. Advanced primitive societies are considerably more heterogeneous than their forerunners, involving ethnic, religious and other oppositions, as well as class divisions. The African kingdoms, such as the Zulu, are the prime examples of societies of this type. Parsons accepts that in the Zulu kingdom, and in others resembling it, military power was of major significance in shaping and consolidating the social order. But he emphasizes that probably of greater importance was the formation of a developed religious culture, legitimizing the position of the king and fostering social solidarity.

Advanced primitive societies, however, still belong to the first phase of evolution which Parsons distinguishes. The second is that of 'intermediate' societies, which contain two subtypes, the 'archaic' and the 'advanced intermediate'. Both are associated with the existence of writing. Archaic societies are characterized only by what Parsons calls 'craft literacy', that is, writing which is used mainly for administrative accounting and for the codification of magical and religious precepts. Literacy is the prerogative of small priestly groups and not part of the general education of the dominant class or classes. Ancient Egypt offers an example of an archaic society. A society of this type has a 'cosmological' religious order, which both generalizes and systematizes constitutive symbolism more than in primitive communities. It has a political and administrative apparatus, separated out in some degree from religious duties. Archaic societies have adaptive qualities superior to those of primitive ones because they concentrate functional responsibility in the domains of the religious and the political. These factors are further developed in the advanced intermediate type of society, which consists of 'historic empires' such as Rome or China. All of these have been deeply involved with the 'world religions' of which Max Weber wrote. They are characterized by the massive scale of their cultural innovations as a result of 'philosophic breakthroughs' which distinguish between the sacred and the material world; kings are no longer gods.

Specialized cultural legitimation is one evolutionary universal that is brought into sharp definition by the advent of historic empires. Its focus is political, it being the means of the consolidation of governmental authority. 'Meeting the legitimation need' implies the emergence of specialized political leaders in addition to the ruler.

> Over an exceedingly wide front and relatively independently of particular cultural variations, political leaders must in the long run have not only sufficient power, but also legitimation for it. . . . The combination of differentiated cultural patterns of legitimation with socially differentiated agencies is the essential aspect of the evolutionary universal of legitimation.[6]

A second evolutionary universal is the emergence of bureaucratic organization. Accepting Weber's thesis concerning the indispensability of bureaucracy for the effective large-scale mobilization of power, Parsons argues that advanced intermediate societies show a wide expansion of the administrative co-ordination of government, armed forces and other differentiated institutional sectors. A third universal introduced by historic empires is the use of money in relation to market exchange. Market exchange, according to Parsons, is a system of power that avoids some of the 'dilemmas' of political power. Political power depends ultimately upon punitive sanctions imposed by an administrative body; money shares some of the qualities of political power but is a more generalized resource which is spread among 'consumers' as well as 'producers', a resource that emancipates people both from loyalty to specific political groups and from ascriptive kinship ties. But these three evolutionary universals all presuppose a fourth: 'a highly generalized universalistic normative order',[7] exemplified in a system of law. However, this brings us to the threshold of modernity because some historic empires have developed bureaucratic organization and markets to a fairly high degree without a comparable extension of forms of generalized law.

The development of the modern West, the highest evolutionary form in Parsons's scheme, is related to two 'seed-bed' societies that had a specific long-range influence, Israel and Greece. (A symptomatic comment here is: 'Buddhism is by far the most conspicuous cultural complex mentioned so far that had its most profound influence *outside* the society in which it originated. But because it did not lead towards modernity and because it had little basic significance for Western society, we have not discussed it extensively.')[8] How did some of the cultural features of these two societies become so widely diffused from their points of origin? And what made possible the cultural innovations which they produced? As regards the second of these questions, Parsons argues that in fact only small societies with a reasonable degree of political independence could have given rise to such cultural novelty. It could not have come about in large empires with their extended territory and variety of competing interests. The first problem is solved precisely by the subsequent loss of independence on the part of both societies: their cultural innovations became taken up by important strata within larger social entities. Judaic and Greek culture was adopted largely by 'scholar classes' rather than by dominant political groups; subsequently these cultural influences became the 'principal societal anchorages' of established traditions in the West. The modern type of society has emerged in this 'single evolutionary area', the West.[9]

The emergence of Western society, Parsons asserts, represents a further breakthrough in adaptive capacity as compared with intermediate societies. The features of the West permitting greater differentiation than could be achieved hitherto include the further development of markets, the universalization of law and democratic association involving citizenship rights for the mass of the population. Taken together, these have furthered the consolidation of the 'territorial unity' of societies having their own clear boundaries. The development of universalized law can be traced through the articulation of Continental Roman law and English common law. The second is most important in terms of facilitating freedom of contract and the protection of private property. It is, Parsons says, 'the most important single hallmark of modern society'; the English legal order was 'a fundamental prerequisite of the first occurrence of the Industrial Revolution'.[10] It is also the condition of the development of mass democracy. Democracy is in turn the condition of the effective exercise of power in a highly differentiated society. Those societies which do not become democratic, including 'communist totalitarian organizations', will not have the adaptive advantages of those that do. Which society is farthest along the evolutionary route today? Why, the United States! A comforting, if not especially original, conclusion for an American sociologist to reach after a grand survey of human evolution as a whole.[11]

This sounds like the sort of thing that gets sociology a bad name — at least in the remainder of the world. It might be tempting to ignore it on the basis of the qualification that Parsons adds towards the conclusion of his work on evolution: that the reader should not be too concerned about the detail of his discussion because what matters is 'the *idea* of the evolutionary universal and its grounding in the conception of generalized adaptive capacity'.[12] In general I shall indeed observe this recommendation, but, as I shall indicate, Parsons's approbation of the USA is entirely in line with his version of evolutionary thought.

Parsons's theory meets all of the criteria I have mentioned as distinctive of evolutionism. Evolution, he makes clear, is more than just 'history', and his account claims social and biological evolution to be both conceptually and substantially connected. The familiar notion of adaptation once more makes its appearance. Parsons specifies the progression in which he is most interested (the differentiation of institutions) and has an overall interpretation of the mechanics of change that depends upon the 'cybernetic' influence of values and symbols. It also displays several of the secondary weaknesses of evolutionary thought and by no means watches the red light carefully enough to avoid the mishaps to which evolutionary theories are so often subject.

Parsons attaches considerable importance to the idea that social evolution is an extension of biological evolution. Now, there is obviously a sense in which this thesis is unobjectionable. After all, it seems to be the case that physical characteristics of the body (a large and neurologically complex brain, upright posture and so on) were the precondition for the developments of human society. The early development of human social association and culture was probably a survival trait allowing for the evolutionary success of *Homo sapiens*. But what follows from this if we discount the aesthetic appeal of a theory that explains biological and social development with a single set of concepts? The answer is: nothing. Biological evolution has to do with changes in heredity, in the genetic traits of succeeding generations; these are explained economically and effectively by a small number of relatively simple mechanisms. Social evolution concerns the relations both between human societies and the material environment and between such societies. The characterization of 'evolution' cannot aptly be accorded to these phenomena, nor can a given sequence of changes be explained in 'evolutionary' fashion, unless the operation of similar mechanisms be demonstrated. Parsons's theory is typical of evolutionary accounts in arguing as if such a demonstration were given by the (undeniable) fact that biological evolution has been interconnected with the early development of human culture. What should be shown with evidence is taken as if it were a source of evidence.

The concept of adaptation which Parsons introduces is as vague and all-embracing as any in the literature, although it is not thereby untypical. Adaptation, he makes clear, has something to do with 'survival' and something to do with interaction with the material world but is by no means limited to these. It is more broadly connected with the reduction of uncertainty — an idea Parsons borrows from systems theory, as he does that of the cybernetic influence of symbols and values. But since 'uncertainty' is nowhere defined, the thesis either is conceptually so diffuse as to be virtually useless or, if pushed more towards a definite empirical content, seems to be at best implausible. Suppose we take two senses Parsons may have in mind: the reduction of uncertainties about the vagaries of nature and the reduction of uncertainties in respect of future events. Neither seems even to advance unequivocally with the types of society Parsons portrays along his evolutionary scale, let alone contribute to their differential 'survival'. Increased control over the material environment, yielded by technological development or the manipulation of authoritative resources, is by no means the same as reduced uncertainty of outcomes. A technologically more 'effective' farmer, for example, might be more vulnerable to variations in the weather than a hunter and gatherer. As regards the reduction of future unpredictabilities, who could suppose that the world in which we now live, with its massive yet fluctuating rates of technological and economic change, political uncertainties and the presence of nuclear weaponry, is less uncertain than that of palaeolithic humanity?

Moreover, the guiding mechanism of evolution that Parsons ties to the increasing adaptive capacity of his evolutionary universals — the cybernetic control yielded by constitutional symbolism — is surely quite unconvincing. Parsons evidently establishes this approach in conscious opposition to historical materialism, and other theories which he takes to resemble it in holding that technology, or economic organization more generally, are the leading forces influencing social change. But it is no more plausible than are the theories he opposes. Once more an argument by analogy seems to be confused with the production of evidence. In mechanical control systems cybernetic controls of low energy can govern movements involving much greater energy expenditure. Parsons then compares this with the control of the gene over protein synthesis and other aspects of cell metabolism, as if the latter example somehow added weight to his argument about the controlling influence of 'constitutive symbolism' over social change. The supposed conceptual parallel does double duty. It is appealed to as a source of the thesis of the controlling position of symbols and values, but then Parsons also writes as though it also in some way helped validate that thesis.

Suppose it were the case that the scheme of adaptive capacity plus the 'cybernetic' influence of constitutive symbolism did provide a general explanatory framework for social evolution roughly analogous to that by means of which biologists explain natural evolution. The problem of what 'survival' means in the case of human societies, an issue that must be coupled in some degree with that of what a 'society' is, would still demand much more attention than Parsons gives them. In biological evolution survival and extinction are exclusive and clear alternatives, being linked to the conditions that determine differential reproduction. A population which cannot effectively compete for the environmental inputs it needs cannot transmit its genes and hence dies out. But there is no real analogue to these circumstances in the social world. If adaptive capacity is defined so widely as to include mobilization for war, the social units clearly often fail to 'adapt' in so far as they are subjugated or destroyed by others. But whole types of society do not usually die out in this way. Moreover, if colonized or subordinated to other groups, rather than being wiped out, pre-existing forms of social organization often continue to exist in recognizably similar guise within an altered social context. The question of whether they have managed to 'survive' or not then turns a good deal upon what we decide is a 'society' or the appropriate unit of analysis for evolutionary study. Parsons begs the question in large part by building an answer to it into his actual classification of societies. It is a mark of evolutionary inferiority that 'primitive societies' lack clearly defined boundaries.[13] An alternative view of the matter, however, would be that the definition of what is to count as a distinct 'society' is more difficult to formulate than Parsons presumes it to be — until, at least, one approaches the era of modern nation-states.

Parsons's theory exemplifies nearly all the damaging tendencies to which I have suggested evolutionary accounts are typically subject. It presents, seemingly without qualms, a 'world-growth story'; it slips into unilineal compression; and it almost makes a deliberate virtue of what I have called the normative illusion.

Symptomatic of Parsons's particular 'world-growth story' is the discussion provided of 'primitive societies'. Parsons rather casually mentions that the Aboriginal societies of Australia are 'among the most primitive societies known'[14] without much further elaboration. He thinks of them at the lowest end of the scale, he makes it clear, in terms of their lack of differentiation, low development of the economy and pre-eminence of kinship. But what of the complexity of the kinship system, the richness of Australian cultural productions of ritual and art? These go virtually unmentioned because Parsons makes the typical evolutionary elision between 'primitiveness' on certain dimensions, such as technology, and 'primitiveness' of societies as a whole. What of the tremendous diversity of small oral cultures that have existed across time and space, rightly emphasized by the 'cultural relativists'?[15] If Parsons were concerned only with formulating a conception of general evolution (that is, if he were not an evolutionist at all, in my understanding of the term), lack of reference to such diversity, and to the fact that these societies have dominated most of human history, could perhaps be justified. But he is certainly interested in specific evolution too, trying to indicate the main direction of change whereby 'primitive societies' become transformed into 'advanced primitive societies' and these into systems of the 'intermediate' type.

Unilineal compression is evident in Parsons's account of the impact of the 'seed-bed' societies, where there is a marked shift in the forms of his discussion. Whereas in relation to foregoing evolutionary types Parsons ranges over vast expanses of history, in analysing the rise of the West his discussion inevitably becomes narrower in its emphasis. It is surely unconvincing to suppose that the cultural inheritances from Israel and Greece necessarily have greater adaptive value than other borrowings which might have been made from elsewhere. The fact that they did become embodied within European culture indicates nothing about their evolutionary value, as Parsons has earlier specified it. Parsons here reads 'evolutionary necessity' (the claim that one type of societal organization shows traits that have to appear before a 'higher' type can come into being) into 'historical necessity' (the circumstance that since the designated elements did become part of European society, things 'must' have happened in that way).

Finally, normative illusion. Parsons's view that half a million years of human history culminate in the social and political system of the United States would be more than faintly ridiculous if it did not conform quite neatly to his particular 'world-growth story'. It is given whatever specious appeal it might have by its connection with the theme of increasing adaptive capacity associated with evolution. Although Parsons might claim that his interpretation is strictly analytical and carries no evaluative overtones, such is palpably not the case. If, for example, 'democracy' is defined in a specific way, as more or less equivalent to 'liberal democracy as exemplified by the political order of the United States', and if 'democracy' is made into an evolutionary universal for societies on the highest level of evolution, then what other conclusion can there be other than that which Parsons draws? But it is as empty as most of the tenets of evolutionism tend to be.

References

Change, Evolution and Power

1   Sometimes 'determination' becomes another name for an objectivism that seeks to explicate conduct primarily via structural constraint. Wright, for example, seeks to identify 'a series of distinct relationships of determination' based upon a 'differentiated scheme of structural causality compatible with Marxist theory'. He distinguishes several modes of determination, but I shall mention only two to convey the flavour of what he has to say: 'structural limitation' and 'selection'. The former refers to ways in which the structural properties of societies set limits to what is possible within those societies. Thus, Wright asserts, the 'economic structure' of feudalism limits the form of the state that appears in feudal systems. While a representative democracy with universal suffrage was 'structurally impossible' within feudalism, a fairly wide variety of state forms are compatible with feudal orders. 'Selection' refers to 'those social mechanisms that concretely determine ranges of outcomes, or in the extreme case [?] specific outcomes, within a structurally limited range of possibilities'. Wright connects 'selection' with the determination of 'specific historical conjunctures'. In feudalism, economy and state relate in such ways as to shape the forms of class division which occur, these forms of class conflict becoming expressed as concrete struggles between definite groups.

The notion of 'determination' here is ambiguously formulated. When Wright speaks of the determination of 'specific outcomes' or 'historical conjunctures' he seemingly has in mind a very generalized sense of the term. Understood in this way, Wright's view would involve a full-blown species of structural determinism, a version of a 'structural sociology' in which human conduct is to be explained as the outcome of social causes. But other remarks that Wright makes suggest that he does not wish to adopt such a standpoint. Structural features of social systems, as his first category indicates, set limits within which an indeterminate range of outcomes can come about. 'Determination' here means 'constraint' and does not discriminate between the several senses which, I have suggested, that term characteristically embraces. To repeat, 'structure' cannot be identified with 'constraint', and the constraining aspects of structural properties cannot be regarded as a generic form of 'structural causality'. Since these points have been already dealt with, there is no need to labour them further. See Erik Olin Wright, *Class, Crisis and the State* (London: New Left Books, 1978), pp. 15—18.

2 Cf. *CPST*, pp. 230—3.
3 *NRSM*, chapter 2.
4 Nisbet has pointed out, however, that social and biological evoltionism also developed separately and that 'it is one of the more serious misconceptions of much modern writing in the history of social thought that nineteenth-century social evolutionism was simply an adaptation of the ideas of biological evolutionism, chiefly those of Charles Darwin, to the study of social institutions.' Robert A. Nisbet, *Social Change and History* (London: Oxford, 1969), chapter 5.
5 Talcott Parsons, 'Evolutionary universals in society', in A. R. Desai, *Essays on Modernisation of Underdeveloped Societies* (Bombay: Thacker, 1971); idem, *Societies, Evolutionary and Comparative Perspectives* (Englewood Cliffs: Prentice-Hall, 1966).
6 Cf. 'Durkheim's political sociology', in *SSPT*.
7 Karl Marx, 'Preface' to *A Contribution to the Critique of Political Economy,* in Karl Marx and Friedrich Engels, *Selected Writings* (London: Lawrence and Wishart, 1968).
8 Auguste Comte, *Physique sociale* (Paris: Hermann, 1975), p. 16.
9 *Societies, Evolutionary and Comparative Perspectives*, p. 2.
10 Julian H. Steward, *Theory of Culture Change* (Urbana: University of Illinois Press, 1955), p. 248.
11 Julian Huxley, 'Evolution, cultural and biological', in William C. Thomas, *Current Anthropology* (Chicago: University of Chicago Press, 1956), p. 3.

N

12   Leslie A. White, *The Evolution of Culture* (New York: McGraw-Hill 1959), pp. 29—30.

13   Marshall D. Sahlins and Elman R. Service, *Evolution and Culture* (Ann Arbor: University of Michigan Press, 1960), pp. 12—13. For other definitions see, *inter alia*, the following: V. Gordon Childe, *The Progress of Archaeology* (London: Watts, 1944); Theodosius Dobzhansky, *Mankind Evolving* (New Haven: Yale University Press, 1962); Sol Tax, *The Evolution of Man* (Chicago: University of Chicago Press, 1960); Robert A. Manners, *Process and Pattern in Culture* (Chicago: Aldine, 1964); Betty J. Meggers, *Evolution and Anthropology: a Centennial Appraisal* (Washington: Anthropological Society, 1959); L. Stebbins, *The Basis of Progressive Evolution* (Chapel Hill: University of North Carolina Press, 1969); Leslie A. White, 'Diffusion vs. evolution: an anti-evolutionist fallacy', *American Anthropologist*, vol. 44, 1945; Alexander Alland, *Evolution and Human Behaviour* (Garden City: Natural History Press, 1967); Eliot D. Chapple, *Culture and Biological Man* (New York: Holt, Rinehart & Winston, 1970); George W. Stocking, *Race, Culture and Evolution* (New York: Free Press, 1968).

14   Leslie A. White, 'Evolutionary stages, progress, and the evaluation of cultures', *Southwestern Journal of Anthropology*, vol. 3, 1947; idem, *The Evolution of Culture,* chapter 2.

15   For relevant discussions, see John W. Bennett, *The Ecological Transition* (New York: Pergamon Press, 1976); Alexander Alland, *Adaptation in Cultural Evolution* (New York: Columbia University Press, 1970); M.-H. Appley, *Adaptation-Level Theory: A Symposium:* (New York: Academic Press, 1971); J. Cohen, *Man in Adaptation* (Chicago: Aldine, 1968); Arthur S. Boughey, *Man and the Environment* (New York: Macmillan, 1971); René Dubos, *Man Adapting* (New Haven: Yale University Press, 1965); Ronald Munson, *Man and Nature* (New York: Felta, 1971); George A. Theodorson, *Studies in Human Ecology* (New York: Row, Peterson, 1961); Andrew P. Vayda, *Environment and Cultural Behaviour* (New York: Natural History Press, 1969); Niles Eldredge and Ian Tattersall, *The Myths of Human Evolution* (New York: Columbia University Press, 1981).

16   There are biologists who would dispute this, however. Thus Ehrlich *et al.*: 'Because of the extremely loose application of the term adaptation in the biological literature, it might be wise to drop it completely.' Paul R. Ehrlich *et al., The Process of Evolution* (New York: McGraw-Hill, 1974), p. 337.

17   Roy A. Rappaport, 'Ritual, sanctity and cybernetics', *American Anthropologist*, vol. 73, 1971, p. 60. For critical remarks, see Anne

Whyte, 'Systems as perceived', in J. Friedman and M. J. Rowlands, *The Evolution of Social Systems* (Pittsburgh: University of Pittsburgh Press, 1978).

18 Thomas G. Harding, 'Adaptation and stability', in Sahlins and Service, *Evolution and Culture*, pp. 45 and 48. Cf. Niklas Luhmann, 'Funktion und Kausalität', in *Soziologische Aufklärung,* Köln—Opladen, 1970, vol. 1.

20 V. Gordon Childe, 'Prehistory and Marxism', *Antiquity,* vol. 53, 1979, pp. 93—4. (This article was originally written in the 1940s but not published in Childe's lifetime.)

21 *CCHM,* chapter 3. I do not see how the following statement of Lenski's can be defended: 'Like a species, a human society is an "isolated" population whose members share a pool of information and are therefore bound to a common evolutionary path.' Gerhard Lenski, *Human Societies* (New York: McGraw-Hill, 1970), p. 60. For critical comments, see Pamela J. Utz, 'Evolutionism revisited', *Comparative Studies in Society and History,* vol. 15, 1973.

22 Herbert Spencer, *The Principles of Sociology* (New York: Appleton, 1899), vol. 2, p. 110.

23 Cf. Colin Renfrew, 'Space, time and polity', in Friedman and Rowlands, *The Evolution of Social Systems.*

24 Ernest Gellner, *Thought and Change* (London: Weidenfeld & Nicolson, 1964), pp. 12—13.

25 V. S. Naipaul, *India, a Wounded Civilization* (Harmondsworth: Penguin, 1976).

26 Sahlins, 'Evolution: specific and general', in Sahlins and Service, *Evolution and Culture,* pp. 30—1.

27 Freud, *Civilisation and its Discontents* (London: Hogarth, 1969), p. 26.

28 Herbert Marcuse, *Eros and Civilization* (New York: Vintage, 1955), p. 12.

29 Norbert Elias, *The Civilising Process,* vol. I, *The History of Manners* (Oxford: Blackwell, 1978), vol. 2, pp. 232—3.

30 I pursue some of these themes in *Between Capitalism and Socialism,* vol. 2 of *CCHM.*

31 See some of the examples discussed in A. Kardiner, *The Individual and His Society* (New York: Columbia University Press, 1939).

32 Perhaps it is worth re-emphasizing that this is a peril of evolutionism, not its logical implication. Habermas is one author who has discussed this and many other points about evolutionism in an illuminating and, as always, acute way. See Jürgen Habermas, *Communication and the Evolution of Society* (Boston: Beacon, 1979), especially

chapters 3 and 4; and 'Geschichte und Evolution', in *Zur Rekonstruktion des historischen Materialismus* (Frankfurt: Suhrkamp, 1976).

33   As does Cohen's recent, philosophically sophisticated interpretation of historical materialism: G. A. Cohen, *Karl Marx's Theory of History, a Defence* (Oxford: Clarendon Press, 1978).

34   The second of these concepts I take from Eberhard. See Wolfram Eberhard, *Conquerors and Rulers* (Leiden: Brill, 1965).

35   *CCHM*, chapter 10.

36   *CSAS; CPST,* pp. 228ff.

37   S. F. Nadel, *A Black Byzantium* (London: Oxford University Press, 1942).

38   M. Fortes and E. E. Evans-Pritchard, *African Political Systems* (London: Oxford University Press, 1940).

39   Douglas L. Oliver, *Ancient Tahitian Society* (Honolulu: University of Hawaii Press, 1974).

40   Henri J. M. Claessen, 'The early state in Tahiti', in Henri J. M. Claessen and Peter Skalnik, *The Early State* (The Hague: Mouton, 1978).

41   Oliver, *Ancient Tahitian Society.*

42   Henri J. M. Claessen; 'The early state: a structural approach', in Claessen and Skalnik, *The Early State.*

43   See Ronald Cohen, 'State origins: a reappraisal', in Claessen and Skalnik, *The Early State*; Robert L. Carneiro, 'A theory of the origin of the state', *Science*, no. 169, 1970; Morton H. Fried, *The Evolution of Political Society* (New York: Random House, 1967); W. Koppers, 'L'Origine de l'état', *6th International Congress of Anthropological and Ethnological Sciences,* Paris, 1963, vol. 2; Lawrence Krader, *Formation of the State* (Englewood Cliffs: Prentice-Hall, 1968); G. Lenski, *Power and Privilege* (New York: McGraw-Hill, 1966); Robert Lowie, *The Origin of the State* (New York: Harcourt, Brace, 1927); Elman R. Service, *Origins of the State and Civilization* (New York: Norton, 1975).

44   Cf. Service, *Origins of the State and Civilization.*

45   Carneiro, 'A theory of the origin of the state'.

46   Louis Dumont, 'Population growth and cultural change', *Southwestern Journal of Anthropology,* vol. 21, 1965; Service, *Origins of the State and Civilization.*

47   Henry T. Wright and Gregory Johnson, 'Population, exchange and early state formation in southwestern Iran', *American Anthropologist,* vol. 77, 1975.

48   Karl Polanyi, *Trade and Markets in Early Empires* (Glencoe: Free Press, 1957).

49 Eberhard, *Conquerors and Rulers,* pp. 9ff.
50 Ibid., p. 10.
51 Henri J. M. Claessen and Peter Skalnik, 'Limits, beginning and end of the early state', in Claessen and Skalnik, *The Early State,* p. 625.
52 Fried, *The Evolution of Political Society.*
53 Compare the judgements of Wilson and Kelley: John A. Wilson, *The Culture of Ancient Egypt* (Chicago: University of Chicago Press, 1951); Allyn L. Kelley, 'The evidence for Mesopotamian influence in pre-dynastic Egypt', *Newsletter of the Society for the Study of Egyptian Antiquities,* vol. 4, no. 3, 1974.
54 Carneiro, 'A theory of the origin of the state'.
55 Emile Durkheim, *Socialism* (New York: Collier-Macmillan, 1962).
56 Cf. Bertrand Badie and Pierre Birnbaum, *Sociologie de l'état* (Paris: Grasset, 1979), pp. 189ff.
57 Including my own commentary in '"Power" in the writings of Talcott Parsons', in *SSPT.*
58 Cf. also Niklas Luhmann, *Trust and Power* (Chichester: Wiley, 1979), p. 127, who asserts that 'the close association of the powerful with the dangerous is really only adequate for archaic societies and archaic ways of thinking. . . .' This seems extraordinarily sanguine in a nuclear age.
59 Cf. Boris Frankel, *Beyond the State* (London: Macmillan, 1983). This is one of the few books to emphasize the significance of mass food production and preservation for the development of capitalism.
60 Marshall McLuhan, *The Gutenberg Galaxy* (London: Routledge, 1962).
61 *CCHM,* p. 96.
62 Lewis Mumford, 'University city', in Carl H. Kraeling and Robert M. Adams, *City Invisible* (Chicago: University of Chicago Press, 1960), p. 7.

Critical Notes: Parsons on Evolution

1 Talcott Parsons, 'Evolutionary universals in society', *American Sociological Review,* vol. 29, 1964, p. 339.
2 Ibid., p. 340.
3 *Societies, Evolutionary and Comparative Perspectives* (Englewood Cliffs: Prentice-Hall, 1966), pp. 9—10.
4 'Evolutionary universals in society', p. 342.
5 *Societies, Evolutionary and Comparative Perspectives,* p. 24. See also 'The problem of structural change', in Victor Lidz and Talcott

Parsons, *Readings on Premodern Societies* (Englewood Cliffs: Prentice-Hall, 1972), pp. 52ff.

6   'Evolutionary universals in society', p. 346.
7   Ibid., p. 351.
8   *Societies, Evolutionary and Comparative Perspectives,* p. 95.
9   Talcott Parsons, *The System of Modern Societies* (Englewood Cliffs: Prentice-Hall, 1971), p. 1.
10 'Evolutionary universals in society', p. 353.
11 *The System of Modern Societies,* chapter 6.
12 'Evolutionary universals in society', p. 357.
13 The empty character of this view is apparent in the following quotation: 'it is . . . clear that no society could attain what we will call the "advanced primitive" level of societal evolution without developing relatively clear-cut boundedness. Thus, a lack of boundedness seems to be an important mark of a society's primitiveness.' *Societies, Evolutionary and Comparative Perspectives,* pp. 37—8.
14 Ibid., p. 36.
15 I do not mean to imply that the only choice available in respect of the normative connotations of social theory lies between cultural relativism on the one side and evolutionism on the other.

6
Structuration Theory, Empirical Research and Social Critique

A Reiteration of Basic Concepts

It might be useful at this point to recapitulate some of the basic ideas contained in the preceding chapters. I shall summarize these as a number of points; taken together, they represent the aspects of structuration theory which impinge most generally upon problems of empirical research in the social sciences.

(1)   All human beings are knowledgeable agents. That is to say, all social actors know a great deal about the conditions and consequences of what they do in their day-to-day lives. Such knowledge is not wholly propositional in character, nor is it incidental to their activities. Knowledgeability embedded in practical consciousness exhibits an extraordinary complexity — a complexity that often remains completely unexplored in orthodox sociological approaches, especially those associated with objectivism. Actors are also ordinarily able discursively to describe what they do and their reasons for doing it. However, for the most part these faculties are geared to the flow of day-to-day conduct. The rationalization of conduct becomes the discursive offering of reasons only if individuals are asked by others why they acted as they did. Such questions are normally posed, of course, only if the activity concerned is in some way puzzling — if it appears either to flout convention or to depart from the habitual modes of conduct of a particular person.

(2)   The knowledgeability of human actors is always bounded on the one hand by the unconscious and on the other by unacknowledged conditions/unintended consequences of action. Some of the most important tasks of social science are to be found in the investigation of these boundaries, the signficance of unintended consequences for system repro- duction and the ideological connotations which such boundaries have.

(3)   The study of day-to-day life is integral to analysis of the reproduction of institutionalized practices. Day-to-day life is bound up with the repetitive character of reversible time — with paths traced through time-space and associated with the constraining and enabling features of the body. However, day-to-day life should not be treated as the 'foundation' upon which the more ramified connections of social life are built. Rather, these more far-flung connections should be understood in terms of an interpretation of social and system integration.

(4)   Routine, psychologically linked to the minimizing of unconscious sources of anxiety, is the predominant form of day-to-day social activity. Most daily practices are not directly motivated. Routinized practices are the prime expression of the duality of structure in respect of the continuity of social life. In the enactment of routines agents sustain a sense of ontological security.

(5)   The study of context, or of the contextualities of interaction, is inherent in the investigation of social reproduction. 'Context' involves the following: (a) the time-space boundaries (usually having symbolic or physical markers) around interaction strips; (b) the co-presence of actors, making possible the visibility of a diversity of facial expressions, bodily gestures, linguistic and other media of communication; (c) awareness and use of these phenomena reflexively to influence or control the flow of interaction.

(6)   Social identities, and the position-practice relations associated with them, are 'markers' in the virtual time-space of structure. They are associated with normative rights, obligations and sanctions which, within specific collectivities, form roles. The use of standardized markers, especially to do with the bodily attributes of age and gender, is fundamental in all

societies, notwithstanding large cross-cultural variations which can be noted.

(7) No unitary meaning can be given to 'constraint' in social analysis. Constraints associated with the structural properties of social systems are only one type among several others characteristic of human social life.

(8) Among the structural properties of social systems, structural principles are particularly important, since they specify overall types of society. It is one of the main emphases of structuration theory that the degree of closure of societal totalities — and of social systems in general — is widely variable. There are degrees of 'systemness' in societal totalities, as in other less or more inclusive forms of social system. It is essential to avoid the assumption that what a 'society' is can be easily defined, a notion which comes from an era dominated by nation-states with clear-cut boundaries that usually conform in a very close way to the administrative purview of centralized governments. Even in nation-states, of course, there are a variety of social forms which cross-cut societal boundaries.

(9) The study of power cannot be regarded as a second-order consideration in the social sciences. Power cannot be tacked on, as it were, after the more basic concepts of social science have been formulated. There is no more elemental concept than that of power. However, this does not mean that the concept of power is more essential than any other, as is supposed in those versions of social science which have come under a Nietzschean influence. Power is one of several primary concepts of social science, all clustered around the relations of action and structure. Power is the means of getting things done and, as such, directly implied in human action. It is a mistake to treat power as inherently divisive, but there is no doubt that some of the most bitter conflicts in social life are accurately seen as 'power struggles'. Such struggles can be regarded as to do with efforts to subdivide resources which yield modalities of control in social systems. By 'control' I mean the capability that some actors, groups or types of actors have of influencing the circumstances of action of others. In power struggles the dialectic of control always operates, although what use agents in subordinate

positions can make of the resources open to them differs very substantially between different social contexts.

(10) There is no mechanism of social organization or social reproduction identified by social analysts which lay actors cannot also get to know about and actively incorporate into what they do. In very many instances the 'findings' of sociologists are such only to those not in the contexts of activity of the actors studied. Since actors do what they do for reasons, they are naturally likely to be disconcerted if told by sociological observers that what they do derives from factors that somehow act externally to them. Lay objections to such 'findings' may thus have a very sound basis. Reification is by no means purely characteristic of lay thought.

These points suggest a number of guidelines for the overall orientation of social research.

First, all social research has a necessarily cultural, ethnographic or 'anthropological' aspect to it. This is an expression of what I call the double hermeneutic which characterizes social science. The sociologist has as a field of study phenomena which are already constituted as meaningful. The condition of 'entry' to this field is getting to know what actors already know, and have to know, to 'go on' in the daily activities of social life.[1]* The concepts that sociological observers invent are 'second-order' concepts in so far as they presume certain conceptual capabilities on the part of the actors to whose conduct they refer. But it is in the nature of social science that these can become 'first-order' concepts by being appropriated within social life itself. What is 'hermeneutic' about the double hermeneutic? The appropriateness of the term derives from the double process of translation or interpretation which is involved. Sociological descriptions have the task of mediating the frames of meaning within which actors orient their conduct. But such descriptions are interpretative categories which also demand an effort of translation in and out of the frames of meaning involved in sociological theories. Various considerations concerning social analysis are connected with this:

(1) Literary style is not irrelevant to the accuracy of social

*References may be found on pp. 368—72.

descriptions. This is more or less important according to how far a particular piece of social research is ethnographic — that is, is written with the aim of describing a given cultural *milieu* to others who are unfamiliar with it.

(2) The social scientist is a communicator, introducing frames of meaning associated with certain contexts of social life to those in others. Thus the social sciences draw upon the same sources of description (mutual knowledge) as novelists or others who write fictional accounts of social life. Goffman is able quite easily to intersperse fictional illustrations with descriptions taken from social science research because he seeks very often to 'display' the tacit forms of mutual knowledge whereby practical activities are ordered, rather than trying to chart the actual distribution of those activities.

(3) 'Thick description' will be called for in some types of research (especially that of a more ethnographic kind) but not in others. It is usually unnecessary where the activities studied have generalized characteristics familiar to those to whom the 'findings' are made available, and where the main concern of the research is with institutional analysis, in which actors are treated in large aggregates or as 'typical' in certain respects defined as such for the purposes of the study.

Second, it is important in social research to be sensitive to the complex skills which actors have in co-ordinating the contexts of their day-to-day behaviour. In institutional analysis these skills may be more or less bracketed out, but it is essential to remember that such bracketing is wholly methodological. Those who take institutional analysis to comprise the field of sociology *in toto* mistake a methodological procedure for an ontological reality. Social life may very often be predictable in its course, as such authors are prone to emphasize. But its predictability is in many of its aspects 'made to happen' by social actors; it does not happen in spite of the reasons they have for their conduct. If the study of unintended consequences and unacknowledged conditions of action is a major part of social research, we should none the less stress that such consequences and conditions are always to be interpreted within the flow of intentional conduct. We have to include here the relation between reflexively monitored and unintended aspects of the reproduction of social systems, and the 'longitudinal' aspect of unintended consequences of contingent acts in historically significant circumstances of one kind or another.

Third, the social analyst must also be sensitive to the time-space constitution of social life. In part this is a plea for a disciplinary coming together. Social scientists have normally been content to let historians be specialists in time and geographers specialists in space, while they maintain their own distinctive disciplinary identity, which, if it is not an exclusive concern with structural constraint, is bound up with a conceptual focus upon 'society'. Historians and geographers, for their part, have been willing enough to connive at this disciplinary dissection of social science. The practitioners of a discipline, apparently, do not feel secure unless they can point to a sharp conceptual delimitation between their concerns and those of others. Thus 'history' may be seen as about sequences of events set out chronologically in time or perhaps, even more ambiguously, about 'the past'. Geography, many of its representatives like to claim, finds its distinctive character in the study of spatial forms. But if, as I have emphasized, time-space relations cannot be 'pulled out' of social analysis without undermining the whole enterprise, such disciplinary divisions actively inhibit the tackling of questions of social theory significant for the social sciences as a whole. Analysing the time-space co-ordination of social activities means studying the contextual features of locales through which actors move in their daily paths and the regionalization of locales stretching away across time-space. As I have accentuated frequently, such analysis is inherent in the explanation of time-space distanciation and hence in the examination of the heterogeneous and complex nature assumed by larger societal totalities and by intersocietal systems in general.

In order to comment upon the empirical implications of the foregoing remarks, I shall consider several separate pieces of research. To preserve a degree of continuity with examples I have used before, I shall use as illustrative cases material to do with education and with the state. Since the modern state everywhere encompasses attempts to monitor institutional reproduction through influencing the nature of educational systems, these two 'areas' of research are, in fact, closely bound up with one another. The first example is a well-known study of conformity and rebellion in a working-class school in the Midlands of England. It is primarily ethnographic in character and contrasts in this respect, and in the country of its origin, with the second, a questionnaire study of educational mobility in Italy. The third and fourth examples draw upon empirical material directly concerned with the activities and involvements of modern states. One describes not so much a particular research project as the work of an author who has tried to combine empirical material with a theoretical explanation of the contradictory character of 'capitalist states'. The other refers to a specific piece of research — an attempt to analyse the origins of the divide between 'the City' and 'industry' that has been a notable feature of British society for some two centuries or more.

I shall use each piece of research to illustrate certain partly distinct conceptual issues. Looking to begin with at what I take to be in many respects an exemplary research report, I shall detail several of the main empirical emphases which connect with the major tenets of structuration theory. I shall subsequently concentrate upon three specific problems. How should we empirically analyse structural constraint? How might we give empirical flesh to the notion of structural contradiction? And what type of research is appropriate to the study of the *longue durée* of institutional change?

Two important qualifications must be made before moving on to the main content of the discussion. In specifying some of the connections between structuration theory and empirical research, I shall not be concerned with an assessment of the virtues and the drawbacks of different types of research method or technique. That is to say, I shall not seek to analyse whether ethnographic research is or is not superior to, say, the use of questionnaires. I shall, however, offer some comments upon the relation between so-called 'qualitative' research and 'quantitative' research. Moreover, I shall want to pursue the discussion in a direction not ordinarily held to be closely related to problems of empirical work — by indicating how social research is tied to social critique. In the concluding sections of this chapter I shall try to show why structuration theory is intrinsically incomplete if not linked to a conception of social science as critical theory.

These latter aspects of the discussion might seem, on the face of things, to move on quite a different plane from discussion of empirical research. But the connection is, in fact, a very close one indeed. For it will not do only to consider in what ways empirical study can be illuminated via the concepts developed in preceding parts of this book. All research is carried on in relation to explicit or implied explanatory objectives and has potential practical consequences both for those whose activities are investigated and for others. Elucidation of the character of these objectives and consequences is not easy, and demands coming to terms with some of the problems posed when a model based directly upon appeal to the logical form of natural science is abandoned. In examining these problems, I shall endeavour to limit as far as possible any forays into epistemology. My aim is to analyse what follows from the basic claim underlying all social research — that the researcher communicates new knowledge previously unavailable (in some sense or other) to the members of a social community or society.

The Analysis of Strategic Conduct

According to structuration theory, two types of methodological bracketing are possible in sociological research. In institutional analysis structural properties are treated as chronically reproduced features of social systems. In the analysis of strategic conduct the focus is placed upon modes in which actors draw upon structural properties in the constitution of social relations. Since this is a difference of emphasis, there is no clear-cut line that can be drawn between these, and each, crucially, has to be in principle rounded out by a concentration upon the duality of structure. The analysis of strategic conduct means giving primacy to discursive and practical consciousness, and to strategies of control within defined contextual boundaries. Institutionalized properties of the settings of interaction are assumed methodologically to be 'given'. We have to take care with this, of course, for to treat structural properties as methodologically 'given' is not to hold that they are not produced and reproduced through human agency. It is to concentrate analysis upon the contextually situated activities of definite groups of actors. I shall suggest the

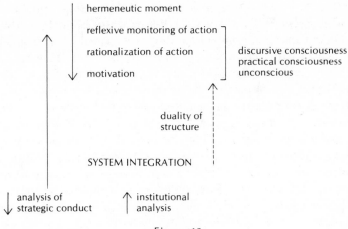

hermeneutic moment

reflexive monitoring of action

rationalization of action   discursive consciousness
practical consciousness
motivation   unconscious

duality of
structure

SYSTEM INTEGRATION

analysis of
strategic conduct   institutional
analysis

Figure 13

following tenets as important in the analysis of strategic conduct: the need to avoid impoverished descriptions of agents' knowledge-ability; a sophisticated account of motivation; and an interpretation of the dialectic of control.

Consider the research described by Paul Willis in his book *Learning to Labour.*[2] Willis was concerned to study a group of working-class children in a school located in a poor area of Birmingham. Although the group studied was quite small, Willis's research is both compelling in its detail and suggestive in drawing implications that range far beyond the context in which the study was actually carried out. As I shall try to show, it conforms closely to the main empirical implications of structuration theory. What gives the research these qualities? In some considerable part, at least, the answer is that Willis treats the boys concerned as actors who know a great deal, discursively and tacitly, about the school environment of which they form a part; and that he shows just how the rebellious attitudes which the boys take towards the authority system of the school have certain definite unintended consequences that affect their fate. When leaving school the boys take up unskilled, unrewarding jobs, thus facilitating the reproduction of some general features of capitalist-industrial labour. Constraint, in other words, is shown to operate through the active involvement of the agents concerned, not as some force of which they are passive recipients.

Let us look first of all at discursive and practical consciousness as reflected in Willis's study. Willis makes it clear that 'the lads' can say a great deal about their views on authority relations in the school and why they react to them as they do. However, such discursive capabilities do not just take the form of propositional statements; 'discourse' has to be interpreted to include modes of expression which are often treated as uninteresting in sociological research — such as humour, sarcasm and irony. When one of 'the lads' says of the teachers, 'They're bigger than us, they stand for a bigger establishment than we do. . .',[3] he expresses a propositional belief of the sort familiar from responses to interview questions posed by researchers. But Willis shows that humour, banter, aggressive sarcasm — elements of the discursive stock in trade of 'the lads' — are fundamental features of their knowledgeable 'penetration' of the school system. The joking culture of 'the lads' both displays a very complex understanding of the basis of teacher's authority, and at the same time directly questions that authority by subverting the language in which it is normally expressed. As Willis points out, 'pisstakes', 'kiddings' and 'windups' are difficult to record on tape and especially to represent in the print of research reports. But these, and other discursive forms that rarely find their way into such reports, may show as much about modes of coping with oppressive social environments as more direct comments or responses. In the author's words:

> The space won from the school and its rules by the informal group is used for the shaping and development of particular cultural skills principally devoted to 'having a laff'. The 'laff' is a multi-faceted implement of extraordinary importance in the counter-school culture . . . the ability to produce it is one of the defining characteristics of being one of 'the lads' — 'We can make them laff, they can't make us laff.' But it is also used in many other contexts: to defeat boredom and fear, to overcome hardship and problems — as a way out of almost anything. In many respects the 'laff' is the privileged instrument of the informal, as the command is of the formal . . . the 'laff' is part of an irreverent marauding misbehaviour. Like an army of occupation of the unseen, informal dimension, 'the lads' pour over the countryside in a search for incidents to amuse, subvert and incite.[4]

On the level of both discursive and practical consciousness it might seem as though the conformist children — those who more or less accept the authority of the teachers and their educational goals, rather than rebelling against them — would be most knowledgeable about the social system of the school. However, Willia makes a good case to the effect that on both levels of consciousness 'the lads' are more knowledgeable than the conformists. Because they actively contest the authority relations of the school, they are adept at picking out where the bases of the teachers' claims to authority lie, and where their weakest points are as the wielders of discipline and as individual personalities. Opposition is expressed as a continuous nagging at what teachers expect and demand, usually stopping short of outright confrontation. Thus in the classroom the children are expected to sit still, to be quiet and to get on with their work. But 'the lads' are all movement, save when the teacher's stare might freeze one of them transitorily; they gossip surreptitiously or pass open remarks that are on the verge of direct insubordination but can be explained away if challenged; they are always doing something else other than the work required of them but are ready with some sort of spurious justification when it is required. They have invented 'experiments with trust' without, it seems, having read Garfinkel: "'Let's send him to Coventry when he comes", "Let's laugh at everything he says", "Let's pretend we can't understand and say, 'How do you mean?' all the time.'"[5]

How should one assess the motivational content of the oppositional activities of 'the lads'? This depends in some degree upon material which Willis did not set out directly to explore. But it is clear that regarding 'the lads' as skilled and knowledgeable agents suggests a different account of their motivation from that implied in the 'official' view of them, as 'louts' or 'wreckers' unable to appreciate the importance of the educational opportunities the school offers — the counterpart to the sociologese of 'imperfect socialization'. The motives which prompt their activities and underlie the reasons they have for what they do cannot be well-explicated as a result of a deficient understanding of the school system or its relations with other aspects of the social *milieux* that are the backdrop to their lives. Rather, it is because they know a great deal about the school and the other contexts in which they move that they act as they do. Such knowledge may be carried primarily in their practical activities or in discourse which is highly contextualized, although in Willis's account 'the lads' emerge as much more articulate than others in the school would probably acknowledge. However, the bounds of what they know about the circumstances in which they live out their lives are fairly confined. Certainly, they realize that their chances of getting anything other than inferior and unedifying jobs are poor, and this realization influences their rebellious attitudes towards the school. But they have at most an imprecise awareness of aspects of the wider society that influence the contexts of their own activity. It might be plausible to infer a general underlying motivational pattern — perhaps partly unconscious — of an attempt to establish modes of conduct which inject some kind of meaning and colour into a drab set of life prospects that are, however diffusely, accurately seen as such. We cannot satisfactorily understand the motivation of 'the lads' unless we see that they do grasp, although in a partial and contextually confined way, the nature of their position in society.[6]

Willis describes in a very insightful manner the dialectic of control within the school setting. Both 'the lads' and their teachers are specialists in the theory and practice of authority, but their respective views as to its necessity and formal objectives are deeply opposed. Teachers recognize that they need the support of the conformist children to make the sanctions available to them stick, and that power cannot be exercised effectively if punitive sanctions have to be applied frequently. The deputy head reveals himself as a dextrous Parsonian theorist of power when he comments that the running of a school depends mainly upon the existence of a certain moral consensus, which cannot be forcibly implanted in children. Punitive sanctions should be used only as a last resort because they are a sign of the failure of effective control rather than the basis of it: 'You can't go throwing suspensions around all the time. Like the football referees today, I mean they're failing because they're reduced to the ultimate so quickly, somehow. . . . the yellow card comes out first of all, and once they've done that, they've either got to send the player off or ignore everything else he does in the game.'[7] Teachers know this, and 'the lads' know that they know it. Hence 'the lads' are able to exploit it to their own advantage. In subverting the mechanics of disciplinary power in the classroom, they assert their autonomy of action. Moreover, the fact that the school is somewhere in which they spend only part of the day and part of the year is vital to the 'counter-culture' which they have initiated. For it is out of school, away from the gaze of the teachers, that pursuits can be freely engaged in which would be anathema in the school setting.

Unintended Consequences: Against Functionalism

Willis's research is not only a superb ethnographic study of an informal group within a school; it is also an attempt to indicate how the activities of 'the lads', within a restricted context, contribute to the reproduction of larger institutional forms. Willis's study is unusual, compared with a great deal of social research, because he stresses that 'social forces' operate through agents' reasons and because his examination of social reproduction makes no appeal to all to functionalist concepts. His interpretation of the connection between the school 'counter-culture' and wider institutional patterns, expressed concisely, runs as follows. The oppositional modes of behaviour of 'the lads' while at school leads them to want to leave school to go out to work. They want the financial independence which work will provide; at the same time, however, they have no particular expectations about any other types of reward that work might offer. The aggressive, joking culture which they have developed within the school *milieu* actually quite strongly resembles that of the shop-floor culture of the work situations into which they tend to move. Hence they find the adjustment to work relatively easy, and they are able to tolerate the demands of doing dull, repetitive labour in circumstances which they recognize to be uncongenial. The unintended and ironical consequence of their 'partial penetration' of the limited life chances open to them is actively to perpetuate the conditions which help to limit those very life chances. For having left school with no qualifications and entered a world of low-level manual labour, in work which has no career prospects and with which they are intrinsically disaffected, they are effectively stuck there for the rest of their working lives. 'The working-class lad is likely to feel that it is already too late when the treacherous nature of his previous confidence is discovered. The cultural celebration has lasted, it might seem, just long enough to deliver him through the closed factory doors'[8] — or, more often nowadays, to a life of chronic unemployment or semi-employment.

Now, all of this could have been stated in a functionalist mode and 'explained' in functional terms. Thus it could be argued that industrial capitalism 'needs' large numbers of people either to work in unrewarding manual labour or to be part of an industrial reserve army of the unemployed. Their existence is then 'explained' as a response to these needs, somehow brought about by capitalism — perhaps as a result of some unspecified 'social forces' which such needs call into play. The two types of account can be contrasted, as below:

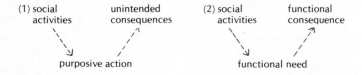

In (1), the sort of view developed by Willis, a given set of social activities (the oppositional behaviour of 'the lads') is interpreted as purposeful action. In other words, those activities are shown to be carried on in an intentional way, for certain reasons, within conditions of bounded knowledgeability. Specification of those bounds allows the analyst to show how unintended consequences of the activities in question derive from what the agents did intentionally. The interpretation involves an attribution of rationality and of motivation to the agents concerned. The actors have reasons for what they do, and what they do has certain specifiable consequences which they do not intend. In (2) little attempt is made to detail the intentionality of the agents' conduct. It is probably assumed that the conduct is intentional in some way, that it has, in Merton's terminology, manifest functions. But usually in functionalist interpretations this is not regarded as especially interesting because attention is concentrated upon attributing rationality to a social system, not to individuals. The identification of a functional need of the system is presumed to have explanatory value, calling into play consequences which in some way meet that need. Merton's functional interpretation of the Hopi rain ceremonial (see pp. 12—13) fits this scheme exactly. The intentional features of Hopi participation in the ceremonial are given short shrift — the 'purpose' of the rain ceremonial is to bring rain, and this it does not do. On the face of things, participation in the ceremonial is an irrational activity. However, we can identify a functional need to which the ceremonial corresponds, generating a positively functional consequence. Small societies need a unitary value system to hold them together; participation in the rain ceremonial reinforces such a value system by regularly bringing the community together in circumstances in which adherence to group values can be publicly affirmed.

I have previously indicated why (2) will not do and why it is not an explanation at all of whatever activities are in question. Cohen has recently suggested an ingenious way in which it might be rescued, however.[9] This is by postulating what he calls 'consequence laws'. Interpretation (2) is not an explanation because it does not supply a mechanism linking the positing of a functional need and the consequences that are presumed to ensue for the wider social system in which the activities to be explained are involved. In establishing 'consequence laws' we set up generalizations to the effect that whenever a given social item is functional for another, the first social item is found to exist. Subsumption of a particular instance of social activity under a consequence law can be regarded as an 'unelaborated' functionalist explanation. But 'unelaborated' functionalist explanations are not explanations at all and, moreover, have the dangerous side-property of implying that a higher degree of cohesion exists than may in fact be the case in the social systems to which they refer. To say that (2) is 'unelaborated' is to admit ignorance of the causal connections which link the social item or activities concerned with their functional consequences. What would these connections be if discovered? They would be precisely of the sort given in (1) — a specification of intentional action (or types of intentional action) having unintended outcomes (or types of outcomes). In other words, (2) is viable only when transmuted into (1). But in (1) it is not necessary to use the term 'function' at all. The term 'function' implies some sorts of teleological quality that social systems are presumed to have: social items or activities are held to exist because they meet functional needs. But if the fact that they have functional outcomes does not explain why they exist — only an interpretation of intentional activity and unintended consequences does that — the activities may become more readily severed from those outcomes than 'consequence laws' would imply. The conduct of 'the lads' leads to consequences functional for the reproduction of capitalist wage labour as a result of their 'partial penetration' of their life circumstances. But this very 'partial penetration', as Willis argues, may be potentially radicalizing for the individuals involved, in which case it could lead to disruptive rather than cohesive consequences for the wider social system.

The work of functionalist authors has been very important in social research precisely because it has directed attention to the disparities between what actors intend to do and the consequences which ensue from what they do. But we can identify, and attempt to resolve, the issues involved more unambiguously by dispensing with functionalist terminology altogether. There are three types of circumstance in which functionalist language is commonly used. All are important in social analysis but can easily be expressed in non-functionalist terms.

Suppose we render Willis's findings in a functionalist mode, as follows: 'Education, in a capitalist society, has the function of allocating individuals to positions in the occupational division of labour.' First, such a statement is acceptable if understood as an implicit counterfactual.[10] Many functionalist assertions, or purported 'explanations', can be read in this way. In fact, they set up a relation which calls for explanation, rather than explaining it. We can express the statement in a different manner, without using 'function', as follows: 'In order for the occupational division of labour to be maintained, the educational system has to ensure that individuals are allocated differentially to occupational positions.' The force of 'has to' here is counterfactual; it involves identifying conditions that must be met if certain consequences are to follow. It sets up a research problem, and understood as asking a question rather than as answering one, it is entirely legitimate. But the use of the term 'function' can be misleading because it suggests that the 'has to' refers to some sort of need that is a property of the social system, somehow generating forces producing an appropriate (functional) response. We might suppose that we have resolved a research problem when all that has been done is actually to establish a problem that demands research. Second, the statement may be read as referring to a feedback process which depends wholly upon unintended consequences. As I have already indicated, to say 'Education . . .

has the function of allocating individuals. . . .' fudges over the differences between intended and unintended aspects of social reproduction. It is therefore not clear in such statements how far the processes in question are the result of 'causal loops', and how far they are incorporated in processes of what I have earlier called reflexive self-regulation. Social needs exist as causal factors implicated in social reproduction only when they are recognized as such by those involved at some point and acted upon by them. The educational system in which 'the lads' are involved was supposedly established in order to further equality of opportunity. Its substantive results, in respect of perpetuating immobility, run counter to this, but they are not so planned by the Ministry of Education or some other directive body of the state. If they were — if education were deliberately organized by powerful decision-makers in order to perpetuate the class system — the process concerned would be substantially different. Of course, this is a complex matter. All modern education systems involve attempts at reflexive regulation, which often lead to consequences that rebound upon those who initiate educational policies. But to leave these complexities unstudied is to fail to grasp the actual conditions of reproduction. The result can be some form of objectivism — whatever happens does so as the result of social forces as inevitable as laws of nature. Alternatively, however, there could be a tendency to accept some kind of conspiracy theory. Whatever happens does so because someone or other designed that it should. If the former, the characteristic view of functionalism, is associated with not according enough importance to intentional action, the second derives from failing to see that the consequences of activities chronically escape their initiators.

The Duality of Structure

I take it that it is clear from my discussion earlier in this book that the concept of the duality of structure, fundamental to structuration theory, is implicated in the ramified senses that the terms 'conditions' and 'consequences' of action have. All social interaction is expressed at some point in and through the contextualities of bodily presence. In moving from the analysis of strategic conduct to a recognition of the duality of structure, we have to begin to 'thread outwards' in time and space. That is to say, we have to try to see how the practices followed in a given range of contexts are embedded in wider reaches of time and space — in brief, we have to attempt to discover their relation to institutionalized practices. To pursue the illustration drawn from Willis's work, how far do 'the lads', in developing an oppositional culture within the school, draw upon rules and resources more broadly involved than in the immediate contexts of their action?

We can specify analytically what is involved in making the conceptual move from the analysis of strategic conduct to examination of the duality of structure as below (institutional analysis would begin at the other end, as the upward arrow indicates):

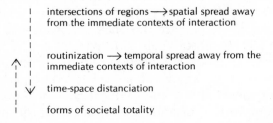

Transferring analysis from the situated activities of strategically placed actors means studying, first, the connections between the regionalization of their contexts of action and wider forms of regionalization; second, the embeddedness of their activities in time — how far they reproduce practices, or aspects of practices, that are long-established; third, the modes of time-space distanciation which link the activities and relationships in question to features of overall societies or to inter-societal systems.

Willis actually provides a very perceptive discussion of some of these phenomena, even if his terminology is different. The formal hierarchy of the school, of course, incorporates modes of conduct and normative expectations that are broadly spread across different sectors of the society, although strongly influenced by class divisions. The school as a locale is physically separate from the workplace and is temporally separated from the experience of work in the life spans of children. While school and workplace share overall patterns of disciplinary power, they are not merely aspects of a single institutional form. As Willis points out, the discipline of the school has a strongly moralized tone to it, which is lacking in the workplace. School discipline embodies an 'abstract educational paradigm, maintaining and reproducing what it makes possible'.[11] The moral character of this axis of authority, or the normative claims on which it is focused, influences the nature of the rebellious subculture. In their manifest disregard for the minutiae of school routines 'the lads' do more than deviate behaviourally from what is expected of them; they show their rejection of the moral prerogatives upon which the teachers' authority supposedly rests. The resources available to the staff in seeking to assert their authority, however, at the same time involve more than these claims to legitimation. The staff are 'resource centres' for the distribution of knowledge, recognized as a scarce commodity by the conformist children, if not by 'the lads', and they have the more direct control over the timing and spacing of activities that make up the organization of classrooms and of the school timetable as a whole. Of course, in all this the teaching staff are drawing indirectly upon entrenched sources of institutional support in the wider society.[12]

For their part, the attitudes and conduct of 'the lads' are certainly not wholly invented *de novo* by them; they draw upon a fund of experience built into their lives outside the school and built up historically within working-class communities in general. Children who disaffiliate themselves from the norms and expected behaviour of the school environment are able to make use of this fund of experience. In transforming elements of it and bringing them to bear upon the school *milieu*, they help to reproduce those very characteristics in the wider context, although they use it innovatively, not in a mechanical fashion. The neighbourhood and the street provide symbolic forms of youth culture that are also in a more direct way the source of themes articulated in the counter-school culture. Willis mentions too the importance of stories related by adults about life on the shop floor, especially those concerned with attitudes towards authority. Parents help to transmit working-class culture to their children, but obviously they do not all behave in an identical fashion or share the same views. Moreover, there is a considerable degree of independent fashioning of outlook between parents and children. Some parents express attitudes quite similar to those of 'the lads', while others disapprove strongly and forcibly of their behaviour. Yet others, who are wary of the values of the school or are hostile to them, have children who conform closely to expected standards of school conduct. The interchange between the activities of 'the lads' and influences from the broader society, in other words, is one which is 'worked upon' by all involved.

As a reflexively monitored social phenomenon, the national school system makes use of sociological research and psychology. Both have filtered down into the practical organization of this particular school (no doubt the teachers there are now thoroughly familiar with Willis's own study). There has been a move towards a somewhat more 'progressive' outlook in respect of the organization of the curriculum and of classroom teaching arrangements. One of the main contexts in which 'the lads' come into direct contact with academic research drawn from the wider society is in relation to vocational guidance, which there is now a statutory requirement for all schools to provide. Careers guidance is influenced mostly by psychological theory and psychological testing and is taken seriously inside the school. As Willis shows, despite a certain egalitarian aura, careers guidance strongly reflects middle-class values and aspirations. Centred upon 'work', the views promulgated tend to contrast rather vigorously with the attitudes and ideas about work which — in their own particular appropriation — 'the lads' have picked up from parents and others in the neighbourhood and community. They make fun of, or are indifferent towards, the material provided in careers lessons. But this response is not simply a negative one. They consider that they have insights into the true character of work denied to the conformist children — and perhaps they have. The conformists have to do things the 'hard way', through acquiring qualifications, because they have not the wit to do better. Survival in the world of work demands guts, determination and an eye to the main chance.

It is not hard to see how these views, picked up and elaborated from established working-class environments of labour, help to plunge 'the lads' into those very environments when they leave school. The sources of discontinuity with the 'official' norms of the school in some part offer continuity, unofficially, with the contexts of work. It is the counter-school culture which provides the main guide that 'the lads' follow in going out to work. Often in the views of both the boys and their parents there is a direct connection between authority relations in the school and at work, providing cognitive and emotive links between the two that are quite different from those 'officially' sanctioned in either. We can see in this a temporally long-established and spatially widespread basis of experience, renewed in varying ways by each generation for whom the disparate and physically separate social worlds of school and work are bridged. The views of 'the lads' towards the school orient them towards the future, but they see the future as 'flat' — more of the same — rather than as having any of the progressive qualities associated with the essentially middle-class notion of a career. They are not interested in choosing particular jobs, and they drift into what they do rather than deliberately confronting a range of alternatives and then opting for one among them. 'The lads', as Willis makes clear, commit themselves to a life of generalized labour. They do not have any such notion of 'generalized labour' in mind. Motivated by a desire for the best wages that can be got immediately and by the presumption that work is essentially disagreeable, they make such a commitment in their conduct.

Looked at in a wider time-space framework, then, there is a process of the regeneration of working-class culture which both helps give rise to, and is effected through, the situated activities of groups like 'the lads'. As Willis comments:

> The informal and formal processes of the school are obviously vital in preparing labour power in a certain way, but the home, family, neighbourhood, media and non-productive working-class experience in general are equally vital for its continuous reproduction and daily application to the labour process. In a converse way it is important to assess the degree to which the shop floor, both in its objective dimensions and in the oppositional culture it throws up, reacts back upon the non-productive sites of the reproduction of labour power and influences them in a certain way so that, as we have seen with the counter-school culture, there may be an unseen and often unintended circle of meaning and direction which acts ultimately to preserve and maintain a particular configuration — perhaps again at a tangent to the intentions of official policy.[13]

In raising the question of labour power a connection is provided with the transformation/mediation relations I discussed illustratively in chapter 5. I shall not cover this ground again but shall simply indicate how the structural relations involved may be worked through analytically in terms of the situated activities of the counter-school culture. Other structural sets, besides that discussed previously, implicated in the reproduction of industrial capitalism as an overall societal totality, can be represented as follows:[14]

```
private property  :  money  :  capital  :  labour contract  :  industrial authority
```

```
private property  :  money  :  educational advantage  :  occupational position
```

The transformations on the left-hand side of the first set are the same as analysed before. However, the convertibility of the structural properties towards the right-hand side depend upon ways in which the labour contract is 'translated' into industrial authority. As Marx showed in great detail, the form of the capitalist labour contract is quite different from the ties of fealty which existed between lord and serf in the feudal order. The capitalist labour contract is an economic relation between employer and employee, the meeting of two 'formally free' agents in the labour market. One main aspect of the new form of labour contract is that the employer hires not 'the worker' but the worker's labour power. The equivalence of labour power is essential — as is that provided by the unitary exchange medium of money — to the structural transformations involved in the existence of industrial capitalism as a generic type of production system. Abstract labour is quantifiable in equivalent units of time, making the qualitatively different tasks that individuals carry out in the various branches of industry interchangeable to the employer. The labour contract is transformed into industrial authority via the economic power which employers, as a class, are able to exert over workers once the vast majority of the latter are rendered propertyless.

According to Marx, for these relations to exist 'the owner of money must meet in the market with the free labourer, free in the double sense, that as a free man he can dispose of his labour power as his own commodity, and that on the other hand he had no other commodity for sale, is short of everything necessary for

the realisation of his labour power.'[15] Now the 'must' here could
be read or implying a functional 'explanation' of the phenomena
in question, as if the statement explains why those phenomena
come about. There certainly are strong functionalist leanings in
Marx's formulation of some of the key arguments in his account
of capitalist development. But let us agree to interpret the 'must'
in the way which I have suggested is unobjectionable, as posing a
question to be answered. Such questions can be asked not just in
relation to the early origins of capitalism but also in regard of its
continued reproduction as an overall institutional order — there
are no mechanical forces which guarantee that reproduction
from day to day or from generation to generation.

What Willis's research helps to indicate, in the situated contexts
of action of 'the lads', is how the structural relations identified
above are sustained in, and reproduced by, that action. Because
of their very 'partial penetration' of the school system, their
indifference to the character of work, yet willingness to enter the
world of labour, 'the lads' constitute themselves as 'abstract labour
power'. The assumption that all work is the same confirms the
conditions of the exchangeability of labour power structurally
involved in the capitalist labour contract. There is pathos here,
because if Willis's account is valid, the oppositional culture of
'the lads' effectively leads them to integrate their activities more
closely, in some respects, with the institutions of the order they
oppose than do the conformists. However, in the very complexity
of this relationship we can see the importance of not attempting
merely to 'read off' action from structure or vice versa — of
resisting, in other words, the dualism of objectivism and of
subjectivism. The situated activities of 'the lads', complicated as
they are in respect of the meshing of intended and unintended
consequences, are only one tiny corner of a massively complex
overall process of institutional reproduction. The same conclusion
has to be reached if we consider the right-hand side of the other
structural set, the institutional features making for the convertibility of educational advantage into differentiated occupational
positions. There are some relatively direct ways in which
possession of money can be converted into educational advantage,
that in turn can be translated into privileged occupational
position. Thus private education can be purchased, yielding higher
possibilities of achieving occupational rewards than are open to

those moving through the state educational sector. But the translation of one into the other for the most part involves much more complex reproduction circuits.

The identification of structural sets is a very useful device for conceptualizing some of the main features of a given institutional order. But, as I have emphasized previously, structures refer to a virtual order of relations, out of time and space. Structures exist only in their instantiation in the knowledgeable activities of situated human subjects, which reproduce them as structural properties of social systems embedded in spans of time-space. Examination of the duality of structure, therefore, always involves studying what I have earlier called dimensions or axes of structuration.

The Problem of Structural Constraint

Let me now move on to the question of structural constraint. Here I shall take leave of the boys of Hammertown school. I do not want to imply that ethnographic research such as that carried out by Willis is refractory to consideration of this problem. On the contrary, much of what Willis has to say can be understood precisely as a subtle and theoretically sophisticated, as well as empirically rich, inquiry into the nature of structural constraint. But neither have I any wish to claim that ethnographic studies have any sort of primacy over other types of social investigation, and for purposes of institutional analysis we are often (though not inevitably) interested in larger aggregates than can comfortably be dealt with in ethnographic terms. Let me shift countries as well as research studies, and use as a basis for discussion research carried out into educational opportunity in Piemonte, in north-west Italy.[16] The research reports the results of a questionnaire and an interview survey carried out among high school pupils, involving in all some 3,000 individuals. Those interviewed in the larger of the two pieces of research were all young people who had started to look for work not more than a year prior to being contacted.

The research was thus concerned with themes quite similar to those of Willis's study, especially with attitudes towards school and work. It also exemplifies aspects of the reflexive monitoring of system reproduction on the part of the state so characteristic of contemporary societies. The individuals interviewed were registered in lists set up by an Act of Parliament which had the objective of aiding school-leavers in finding employment. The Act offered benefits to employers taking on young people and allowed for various forms of training on the job and so on. The research project was itself part of the attempt of the authorities reflexively to influence conditions of social reproduction. It was sponsored by the local government partly in response to a rather surprising outcome of previous policy concerned with school-leavers. The government had offered 600 quite well-paid jobs to out-of-work high school and college graduates for a period of a year. However, a third of those to whom the jobs were offered refused them. Such a reaction confounded those who had initiated the policy, who had apparently believed that the unemployed would take any reasonably well-paid employment which was offered. To investigate the matter, they financed the study.

The author of the research report, Gambetta, analyses his material in such a way as to bring it to bear very firmly upon questions of structural constraint. In taking up various educational options, he asks, are individuals 'pushed' or do they 'jump'? In what sense, if any, are there forces akin to those portrayed by 'structural sociologists' which impel individuals into specific courses of action? Gambetta first of all sets up the research results in a manner resembling a myriad of other studies in which this type of standpoint has been adopted. Thus, for example, class background can be shown to influence the nature of educational choice. An 'upper-class' child has four times the chance of reaching higher education than one from a 'working-class' background. What do such differences tell us? They do not, as they stand, indicate the mechanisms whereby the observed correlations are produced; and whatever influences are responsible are far from unequivocal in their effects, for many upper-class children do not enter higher education, while a certain proportion of working-class children do. None the less, such observations do indicate that there is more influencing educational choice than factors which could effectively be represented as an aggregate of separately taken decisions. Reviewing similar findings for a range of studies carried out mostly in North America, Leibowitz demonstrates that the 'explained' variance in completed years of schooling in terms of socio-economic background ranges between 10 and 47 per cent.[17]

Clearly, these connections are only diffusely expressed when given in the form of such gross correlations. Gambetta therefore seeks to look more closely at sources of inter-class variance, controlling statistically for a number of possibly influential factors. Controlling for economic differences as indexed by per child family income, and for 'cultural resources' as measured by parents' education, the results show that father's occupation — probably the single most common empirical index of class background used in research — still has considerable effect upon educational destination. The results also indicate a sequential process of effects occurring. Working-class children are more likely than others to be weeded out at a relatively early stage in terms of leaving school at the earliest available opportunity. But those who do stay on are more likely to go to university than higher-class children who stay on; the latter, in other words, are more likely to leave once the more advanced phases of the educational process are reached. This suggests that higher-class families perhaps tend more or less automatically to keep their children in education beyond the ordinary school-leaving age. In other words, there are influences 'pushing' upwards, not just downwards, against working-class children. Working-class parents do not tend to keep their children in education unless there is some particular reason to do so — an exceptionally gifted child, one particularly motivated to remain in school, and so on.

Were the working-class children pushed, or did they jump? Were they 'pulled from the front' through having what Willis calls a 'partial penetration' of the life chances confronting them? By further statistical analysis of his material, Gambetta is able to show that working-class children are considerably more responsive to lack of educational success, prior to the initial decision of whether to stay on at school or leave, than are higher-class children. This suggests that working-class families and children have a realistic understanding of the difficulties they face in 'getting on' in the school system. We can at least venture an interpretation of why working-class children, having stayed on at school, tend to be less likely to leave than the others. For these children, and for their parents, staying on involves more of a commitment (to values that are culturally 'alien') than in the case of those in the higher classes. The material costs are also greater, since for the parents the marginal cost of keeping a child in school is more substantial than for higher-class families. Once the commitment has been made, there is a greater cultural and material 'investment' to be protected than in the case of the higher-class children.

Knowledge of labour markets, as well as attitudes towards work in general, can be presumed to influence such decisions. Here Gambetta discusses a conception of behaviour in labour markets which has attracted considerable attention in Italy: the 'parking theory'. According to this view, the length of education tends to be inversely related to chances of social mobility at early school-leaving ages. In order to avoid being unemployed, pupils stay on longer at school. The implied motivational account in the parking theory is that, *ceteris paribus*, work is preferred to school. Those who have proposed the theory[18] have given an account of actors' motives and reasons which is both largely implicit and 'thin'. None the less, the parking theory is interesting because it yields certain counter-intuitive possibilities — for example, it indicates that length of education, in certain circumstances, may be inversely related to the level of economic development of a neighbourhood or a region. Thus Barbagli found that, in Italy as a whole, average *per capita* income is positively correlated with rate of school attendance in the age group 11−15. On the other hand, the rate of staying on, after the age at which it is legally possible to leave school, is correlated negatively with *per capita* income and with other measures of provincial economic development. He concludes that, as a result of the greater difficulties in finding employment, those in poorer provinces tend to stay on at school.[19]

Since, however, the parking theory is 'thin' in motivational terms, it does not allow us to consider various possible interpretations of such results. For example, would the pattern of staying on at school be the same if there were no possible economic benefits to be derived from longer school attendance? Here the parking theory would suggest conclusions different from those of 'human capital' theories, which regard educational decisions in cost-benefit terms. In order to assess these variant possibilities Gambetta correlated decision to stay on in education to university level with economic differences in the Piemonte region. The results indicate that this is not just a matter of

P

negative choice, as the parking theory suggests; staying on is in some part a positive decision, 'pulled' by the attractions of the opportunities that further education offers. But 'human capital' theories are themselves oversimplified in terms of the motivational assumptions they involve, as the research shows. Moreover, such theories are unable to grasp unintended outcomes of a plurality of separately considered courses of action. There may be perverse consequences which result unintentionally from decisions to stay on in order to maximize occupational rewards. Each individual might act in the expectation of higher benefits, but if too many act in this way, the expected benefits evaporate.[20]

The question Gambetta originally posed — were they pushed or did they jump? — leads him to go beyond the usual confines of structural sociology. He is able to analyse his empirical material in such a way as to move from an institutional perspective towards the study of purposive conduct. His research subjects are more than just 'sociological dopes'. Rather than directly discussing Gambetta's analysis of his results, however, I shall follow lines of thought developed in a previous chapter. Let me repeat what I have said about constraints on action previously. First, constraints do not 'push' anyone to do anything if he or she has not already been 'pulled'. In other words, an account of purposive conduct is implied even when the constraints limiting courses of action are very severe. Second, constraints are of various kinds. It is important in this case to distinguish between constraint deriving from differential sanctions and structural constraint. Third, to study the influence of structural constraint in any particular context of action implies specifying relevant aspects of the limits of agents' knowledgeability.

Let us take these issues in reverse order. So far as the third point is concerned, it is apparent that a good deal of what Gambetta has to say is in fact to do with identifying the bounds of agents' knowledgeability. For instance, he devotes some considerable attention to specifying what parents and children are likely to know about labour markets in their local area. This is manifestly important. The same is true of knowledgeability in respect of the schol *milieu*. A study of a statistical type cannot produce material of the richness of detail offered in Willis's work. But inferences can be made — and backed up by the research material, as Gambetta shows — about the sorts of knowledge parents and children are likely to have of the 'cash value' of education.

In regard of the second point, it should be pointed out that there are various sorts of sanction which affect the position of the children; these can quite easily be distinguished from sources of structural constraint. School attendance and the minimum school-leaving age are fixed by law. Parents and children sometimes disregard this legal obligation, especially in southern areas of Italy, but for most it sets the framework within which the sorts of decisions analysed by Gambetta are taken. Children are also subject to informal sanctions on the part of parents and of other figures in the school. Since parents have to support those of their progeny who stay on at school, they have a strong economic sanction with which to influence whether or not their children go on into further education; of course, a range of other more subtle sanctioning mechanisms are also likely to be involved. Studies like Willis's make it apparent enough that a variety of such mechanisms exist in the school environment also.

Let me move finally to the first issue. Identifying structural constraint in a specific context or type of context of action demands consideration of actors' reasons in relation to the motivation that is at origin of preferences. When constraints so narrow the range of (feasible) alternatives that only one option or type of option is open to an actor, the presumption is that the actor will not find it worth while to do anything other than comply. The preference involved is the negative one of wishing to avoid the consequences of non-compliance. If the agent 'could not have acted otherwise' in the situation, it is because only one option existed, given that agent's wants. This *must* not be confused, as I have consistently emphasized, with the 'could not have done otherwise' that marks the conceptual boundary of action; it is exactly this confusion that structural sociologists tend to make. Where only one (feasible) option exists, awareness of such limitation, in conjunction with wants, supplies the reason for the agent's conduct. It is because the constraint — understood as such by the actor — is the reason for that conduct that the ellipsis of structural sociology is readily made.[21] Constraints also, of course, enter into the reasoning of actors when a wider range of options is involved. Again we have to be careful here. Formal models of preference or decision-making may, in any particular set of circumstances, offer an analytically powerful way of interpreting connections between structural properties, but they do not substitute for more detailed investigations of agents' reasoning which ethnographic research provides. Consider once more the conduct of 'the lads'. An 'economic' model undoubtedly makes some sense of their reasoning. Seeing that formal education has little to offer them in respect of work prospects, they effectively decide to cut their losses by getting out to work as soon as they possibly can. However, such a representation of their behaviour conveys nothing of the subtleties or the complexity which Willis's study reveals.

Gambetta's study is concerned with the influence of structural constraint within the immediate situation of action which confronts the school-leavers. Such a restricted focus is no doubt justified, given the inevitably confined nature of any individual piece of research. But obviously the influence of structural constraints over the course of action in question could potentially be examined in much more depth. Thus one could investigate how the actors' motives and processes of reasoning have been influenced or shaped by factors in their upbringing and prior experiences and how those factors have in turn been influenced by general institutional features of the wider society. However, such 'social forces' could in principle themselves be studied in exactly the same way as the phenomena directly involved in Gambetta's research. Structural constraints, in other words, always operate via agents' motives and reasons, establishing (often in diffuse and convoluted ways) conditions and consequences affecting options open to others, and what they want from whatever options they have.

Contradiction and the Empirical Study of Conflict

Pursuing the connected topics of education and the state provides a material thread of continuity in proceeding to consider a further range of questions relevant to empirical work. I have suggested in an earlier chapter that the concept of contradiction can be usefully connected to notions of structural properties and structural constraint. My discussion in that chapter was both relatively short and highly abstract. I claimed that the notion of contradiction can be given a clear sense in social theory, and that it is worth distinguishing from conflict, where the latter term denotes some form of active antagonism between actors and collectivities. Let me now attempt to defend this claim in an empirical context, concerning myself only with what I earlier called 'structural contradiction'. The most important and interesting of recent attempts to give the concept of contradiction a definite empirical content are to be found in the work of authors influenced by game theory, who adopt a viewpoint explicitly linked to methodological individualism.[22] One of these authors, Boudon, has written extensively upon education and state policy. The work of another, Elster, is one of the main sources Gambetta drew upon in the study just analysed.

Boudon and Elster associate contradiction with the unintended consequences of action, a subclass of the 'perverse effects' that may result from the intentional acts of a plurality of individuals. Elster distinguishes two varieties of contradiction thus understood: that involving 'counterfinality', and that involving 'suboptimality'.[23] The first of these is associated with what Elster calls the fallacy of composition — the mistaken view that what is possible for one person in a given set of circumstances is necessarily possible simultaneously for everyone else in those circumstances. For example, it does not follow from the fact that anyone can deposit all his or her money in a bank, and gain interest on it, that everyone can do so.

Elster's point is that many instances of the fallacy of composition can be redescribed as involving contradictory social relations. Contradictory consequences ensue when every individual in an aggregate of individuals acts in a way which, while producing the intended effect if done in isolation, creates a perverse effect if done by everyone. If all the audience in a lecture hall get to their feet to obtain a better view of the speaker, no one will in fact do so. If each farmer in a given area attempts to acquire more land by cutting down trees, resulting in soil erosion because of deforestation, everyone will end up with less land than in the first place. These are outcomes not only that no one intends but also that run counter to what everyone in the situation wants; none the less, they derive from conduct that is intended to satisfy wants, and could do so for individuals, were it not for the fact that the conduct in question becomes generalized. Consider Marx's discussion of the tendency of the rate of profit to fall in capitalist economies.[24] In circumstances in which the economy is growing at such a pace as to absorb available sources of labour, wages will tend to increase as employers experience a scarcity of suitable labour power. To offset this, employers introduce technical innovations which save on labour costs. While individual industrialists may derive greater profitability from such a response, the overall amount of surplus value, and therefore of profit, in the economy declines, since the ratio of constant to variable capital has risen. Once all those in a given sector of the economy have introduced the same technological innovation, they may all be worse off than they were before.

The second type of contradictory relation, suboptimality, is defined in terms of game theory. It is where all participants in a game-theoretical situation opt for a solution strategy, aware that the other participants will do so as well and that all could have obtained as much, and one more, if another strategy had been adopted. Unlike the case of counterfinality, those involved are aware of the outcomes to which their behaviour can lead in various conjunctions with the action of others. Supposing farmers producing a particular crop will be able to secure higher profits if they form a cartel. If a cartel is formed, it will be even more profitable for the individual farmer to flout the cartel agreement, in order to gain from it without being bound by it. As all the farmers are aware that such is the case, no cartel is established.[25] Boudon has applied a somewhat comparable interpretation to research into education and social mobility. In the 1960s higher education expanded in virtually all the industrialized countries. As educational levels rose, more and more people took up occupations for which, according to the formal demands of the work involved, they were markedly over-qualified. Partly as a response to the frustrations thus incurred, in many countries there was set up what has come to be called 'short-cycle' higher education — short courses offering more flexible, short-term options. However, few chose to enter such courses. Why should this be? Boudon suggests that the failure of short-cycle education can be understood in terms analogous to those of the prisoner's dilemma — a suboptimal result of rational decisions taken by the student population in cognizance of their probable outcome. Research shows that persons choosing short-cycle courses of study do indeed have chances of getting well-paid jobs not inferior to those who have followed longer, more traditional courses. Most students also seem to be aware of this fact. So one would intuitively assume — as did the governments which instituted them — that a high proportion of students would choose the short-cycle courses. Obvious though it might appear, Boudon points out, this assumption would be incorrect. The choices students make depend, as does the prisoner's dilemma, upon the fact that each individual is choosing in the knowledge that others are making choices from the same alternatives. Students actually do maximize their chances by choosing long-term education, even knowing that others are likely to think the same way and even though some individuals would profit more from selecting the short-term option.[26]

The formulations of Elster and Boudon are attractive because they enable a clear meaning to be given to contradiction (although Boudon does not himself use the term) and because they indicate how the notion might be accorded an empirical content. The consequences of intended acts are contradictory when those consequences are perverse in such a way that the very activity of pursuing an objective diminishes the possibility of reaching it. The difficulties with such a conception of contradiction, however, are fairly obvious. It is closely associated with the use of models drawn from game theory. Now, there is no doubt that game-theoretical models can be very useful in empirical research, in respect of suggesting both problems to be investigated and how research results might be interpreted. Boudon's work in the sociology of education is a case in point. But the scope of the application of game theory in the social sciences nevertheless seems limited. Although game-theoretical models may be elegant and satisfying when stated abstractly or mathematically, their relation to actual conduct is often quite tenuous.

The empirical applications of game-theoretical models are easiest to defend when certain particular circumstances are found: when definite 'decisions' are to be made; where the alternative consequences involved are quite easily specified; and where the decisions in question are taken separately by an aggregate of individuals not in direct communication with one another. Such circumstances are not infrequently discovered in modern societies, but there are very many contexts of social life which are not of such a kind. If the linkage with game theory is one source of limitation upon this type of approach to the concept of contradiction, another is the affiliation with methodological individualism, explicitly adopted by Elster in particular. The connection may be logically a contingent one, but it is not hard to see why the two tend to go together. Contradiction is located by Elster in the disjunction between individual acts, undertaken separately, and their composite consequences. It is largely limited to what I have called the analysis of strategic conduct. In this standpoint there is no way of understanding contradiction as implicated in the structural conditions of system reproduction.

It is such an understanding which I advocate as having a broader significance for social theory than that suggested by Elster and Boudon and as offering more scope for empirical work. I want not to question the importance of their ideas but rather to complement them. Contradictory outcomes of the sort they discuss may be supposed often to be linked systematically to what I have termed structural contradiction. I wish to understand the concept of contradiction less abstractly than they do, in addition to separating it from the premises of methodological individualism. That is to say, I want to connect the notion in a substantive way to the overall types of societal totality distinguished earlier, such that although there may be many examples of secondary contradiction, these are derivative of the dominant contradictory modes in which societies are structured. However, as I have defined them, primary and secondary structural contradictions still preserve the same core of meaning which Elster gives to the term; the conditions of system reproduction depend upon structural properties which act to negate the very principles upon which they are based.

As an example of some pertinent reflections upon the primary contradiction of capitalist states, let me refer to some of Offe's writings on the subject.[27] They are logically and substantively compatible — at least, in some of their main aspects — with the ideas I have advanced in this book, and they have generated a good deal of illuminating empirical work. The institutional form of the capitalist state is described in terms of the following traits (among others).

(1) 'Political power is prohibited from organizing production according to its own political criteria.' In other words, large

sectors of economic organization are co-ordinated not by government but by activities engaged in within 'private' spheres of economic enterprise. The institutional foundation of these spheres is to be found in private property and in the secular 'ownership' of labour power.

(2) 'Political power depends indirectly — through the mechanisms of taxation and dependence on the capital market — on the volume of private accumulation.' That is to say, the state is funded by taxation derived from processes of economic development which state agencies do not directly control.

(3) 'Since the state depends on a process of accumulation which is beyond its power to organize, every occupant of state power is basically interested in promoting those conditions most conducive to accumulation'.[28]

The third point is an important addition to the first two, since it serves to avoid the implication of an untutored functionalism. It is made clear that the phenomena identified in the first two points are known to those in state agencies, which act in the light of that knowledge.

Why is the capitalist state, thus characterized, a contradictory social form? Because the very conditions that make possible the state's existence call into play, and depend upon, mechanisms that run counter to state power. 'Private appropriation', to use the traditional terminology, demands 'socialized production' at the same time as it negates it. Another way to express this — developed in an analytically powerful way by Offe — is to say that, while the state depends upon the commodity form, it also depends simultaneously upon negating the commodity form. The most direct expression of commodification is the buying and selling of values; when values are no longer treated as exchangeable in terms of money, they lose their commodified character. The contradictory nature of the capitalist state is expressed in the push and pull between commodification, de-commodification and re-commodification. Take as examples the provision of health care and public transport. The setting up of socialized medicine means de-commodifying important aspects of health care and establishing them on basis other than that of whether or not individuals who need treatment can pay for it. However, those who have least need of socialized medicine — the more affluent sections of the population, which tend to opt for private medicine even though publicly provided medical services are available — have to contribute disproportionately to paying for it via graduated taxation. They are likely therefore to apply pressure to putting some of the services of public medicine back upon a commercial basis. Much the same applies to public transport. Those in the higher tax brackets, who contribute most to the financing of public transport, are likely to do much of their travelling in private cars. They will probably therefore be resistant to policies which treat public transport as a general good for the community rather than as a commercially viable set of services. Since those in lower income groups are likely to have opposing views, government policy may vacillate between the denationalization and renationalization of such services as successive parties, representing different class interests, come to power.[29]

Offe's analysis raises in a trenchant fashion the problem of the relation between contradiction and conflict, but before taking this up directly I want to pursue the theme of secondary contradiction. Primary contradictions may be linked in a variety of more or less direct ways with secondary ones. Some may be very general in character, but others may be much more contextualized. Consider the following examples, chosen at random from the sociological literature. They are instances of perverse outcomes, but I think it can reasonably be said that they express contradictions.

(1)   A study of the elderly and the provision of supplementary benefits. In the United States supplementary insurance benefits were introduced to improve the lot of old people on low incomes. But these had the effect of raising the level of their income such that they received a few dollars over the requirements of eligibility for state medical aid. Consequently, medical coverage was denied to them, so that many were worse off than before.

(2)   A study of the police. In New York City, in order to reduce the cost of overtime worked by officers on the existing staff, additional patrolmen were placed on the streets. However, the main source of police overtime is the processing of arrests. The increased number of police on the streets led to more arrests being made, thus exacerbating the situation the new policy was supposed to remedy.

(3)   An analysis of urban rioting in Detroit. A large-scale effort was made in the late 1960s to try to prevent a recurrence of riots in the ghettos of Detroit by providing increased welfare benefits and employment opportunities for those in inner-city areas. However, large numbers of poor people were attracted to the city from outside to take advantage of the programmes offered. Many of these were unable to find employment in the city and thus swelled the ranks of the unemployed further. Others took jobs which might otherwise have fallen to the city's own chronically unemployed. The conditions diagnosed as conducive to the outbreak of rioting were thus augmented rather than reduced.[30]

Such examples serve to drive home the likely connection between structural contradiction, contradiction in the sense of Elster and Boudon, and the occurrence of social conflict. Briefly put, I want to advance the following proposal: contradiction is likely to be linked directly to conflict where perverse consequences ensue or are considered by those involved to be likely to ensue. I do not suggest that contradictions always generate perverse consequences or that all perverse consequences are contradictory. But contradiction is a sort of structural perversity and is likely constantly to throw off perverse consequences in the modes in which it is exposed in the conduct of situated actors. Perverse outcomes are likely to generate resentment, and therefore at least potential mobilization for struggle, precisely because of their 'rebound effects'. That is to say, things are worse than they were before in circumstances in which all or the majority of those involved could expect them to be better. The study of perverse consequences of a contradictory kind is thus fruitful ground for the examination of the origins of conflicts. But we can see that it is very limiting to identify contradiction with such consequences *per se*; for on the one hand structural contradiction need not lead to perverse consequences at all, and on the other perverse consequences are not the only circumstances associated with contradiction that can stimulate conflict.

Perverse consequences, it may be said, are contingent outcomes that may be brought about in circumstances of structural contradiction. More generic stimulating conditions of conflict are to be found in the association between contradiction and collective interests. Capitalism is a class society, and the contradiction between 'private appropriation' and 'socialized production' is locked into class divisions which in turn express opposing interests. The articulation between contradictions and interests may, of course, vary. But it is reasonable to assert that the greater the convergence of contradictions, primary and secondary, the more there will be an overriding alignment of interest divisions, and the more likely that open conflict will develop along the 'fault line' of those contradictions. We may suggest that there are three sets of circumstances particularly relevant to examining the relation between contradiction and conflict: the *opacity* of action, the *dispersal of contradictions* and the prevalence of *direct repression*.[31] By the 'opacity' of action, I mean, in Willis's terms, the degree of penetration which actors have of the contradictory qualities of the social systems in which they are involved. Insight into the nature of contradictions may initiate action directed towards resolving or overcoming them. But it would be a specious argument that links such insight only to social change. Contradiction is a source of dynamism, but an understanding of this on the part of lay actors can promote attempts to stabilize a given state of affairs as much as to transform it. The importance of this point is substantively very considerable in respect of Marx's prognostications about the supposed transition from capitalism to socialism. Marx held that as the members of the working class come increasingly to grasp the contradictory nature of capitalist production, they will mobilize to change it. He does not seem to have attached much weight to the possibility that dominant groups in the society might acquire an understanding of the system sophisticated enough in some part to stabilize it. The expanding role of the state can be seen just in these terms. The state is not just caught in the push and pull of primary contradiction; state agencies may seek to monitor the conditions of system reproduction in such a way as to minimize the conflicts that might otherwise tend to break out.

The degree of fusion or dispersal of contradictions is likely to vary according to two main sets of conditions. One is that of 'uneven development', the other that of regionalization. Little needs to be said about the concept of uneven development here, or about its empirical applications. It is usually associated with Marxist thought, and particularly with the writings of Trotsky and Lenin, but its elucidation and application have by no means been confined to Marxism. The notion does, however, have a broader application than has ordinarily been recognized. It has usually been thought of only in relation to large-scale processes of change; there is no reason why it cannot be useful in more restricted time-space contexts as well. The idea of regionalization is certainly relevant here. A particular regional 'spread', in conjunction with differential rates of change, may serve to produce a build-up of contradictions and probably also of perverse consequences. This is exactly the sort of situation, for example, which Lenin diagnosed as pertaining in Russia after the turn of the twentieth century. Other forms of regionalization, however, may produce a diffusion or segmentation of contradictions. Where this is the case, conflict which occurs is likely to be both fragmented and cross-cutting, so that the outcomes of some struggles will cancel out those of others. By direct repression I mean the use of force or the threat of its use to inhibit the emergence of active struggle. The use of force may normally be taken precisely as one of the expressions of the occurrence of conflict, but the threat of its use, or certain tactical shows of force, may also equally well serve to prevent sources of dissension from emerging as overt struggle. Anyone who is prone to argue that control of the means of violence cannot be used to dampen conflicts of a profound and deep-lying kind should ponder cases such as that of South Africa.[32]

Institutional Stability and Change

I shall look finally at a piece of research which, unlike the others discussed, has been in some part directly influenced by structuration theory. The work in question is Ingham's recent investigation of the role of the City in Britain over the past two hundred years or so.[33] The empirical problem that Ingham sets out to study is how the City, the financial centre based in London, has maintained its pre-eminence over Britain's industrial capital for such a lengthy period. His more general concern is with the nature of the modern state.

The organizations that collectively make up the City, according to Ingham, are concerned mainly with activities that can be described as 'commercial'. These activities involve, among other things, the financing of trade, the insurance of commodities and transport, and foreign exchange transactions. They have to do not only with the relations between Britain and other states but also with the ramifications of capitalistic enterprise on a global scale. Most significant in this respect is the part the City has played in the management of domestic currency as 'world money', a means of exchange valid internationally. Ingham criticizes theories which treat the City as being concerned with 'finance capital'. The activities of the City are certainly financial in the sense that they are bound up with the circulation of capital, but the City is concerned primarily with brokerage in all forms, with profit-making from providing intermediary services between those directly engaged in the productive use of capital.

Ingham shows that in order to understand adequately the survival of the power of the City since the late eighteenth century, it is necessary to reject the endogenous style of theorizing which has dominated the previous literature and to grasp how leading organizations within the City have reacted to contingent political events. Both Marx and later Marxists, such as Hilferding, sought to explain (or to explain away) the role of the City in terms mainly of endogenous conceptions of capitalist development. Marx recognized, and commented upon, the distinctive qualities of the City in British economic life in the nineteenth century, and he analysed the origins of these in terms of some of the traits of the British economy as it moved from the dominance of commercial to that of industrial capital. But the development of industrial capitalism, according to Marx's view, would soon oust commercial and banking capital from such a central position. As industrial production advanced, productive capital would come to predominate economically and politically over the more traditionally established 'bankocracy'. Marx's discussion of the matter provides little clue, therefore, as to how it has come about that the economic and political power of the City has been sustained in the long term. Hilferding's standpoint, worked out at a later date, is equally flawed. According to Hilferding, the formation of 'finance capital' — the merging of banking and large-scale industry — has occurred at a more leisurely pace in Britain than elsewhere. But the same process will eventually occur there as has taken place in other societies. Britain's manufacturing supremacy in the nineteenth century allowed the country temporarily to lag behind; however, international competition would ensure that the same pattern would eventually emerge.[34]

Such a pattern has not come into being. Why not? Ingham's thesis is that modern British society has been marked by being not only the first industrial economy but also a centre for world commercial transactions. The most important traits of the City, Ingham argues, have to be understood in relation to the nature of nation-states. States have their own currencies but cannot easily control the flow of these outside their own territories; moreover, the values and stability of different currencies vary widely. The City early on — partly, but by no means wholly, because of Britain's industrial strength in the nineteenth century — became a centre for an accepted form of 'world money' and an international clearing house for the settlement of transactions. The virtual monopoly which the City was able to achieve over certain types of commercial transaction, plus the introduction of the gold—sterling standard, depended upon a range of political conditions. These have to be distinguished from the sources of Britain's industrial supremacy. The importance of the City, and of sterling, has lasted well beyond the point at which Britain was the world's leading industrial power. By the end of the First World War the United States had become the world's strongest economy, but, contrary to the expectations of many in the 1920s and 1930s, New York did not supplant London as the world's main clearing house.

According to Ingham's account, these phenomena are to be understood in the following terms. In the early nineteenth century a series of fiscal reforms was introduced in Britain. The intention of the reformers was mainly to try to cope with the long-standing debts that the state had accumulated, exacerbated by the Napoleonic Wars. The result, however, was to further a concentration of monied interests, separate from the industrial entrepreneurs, in the City institutions. The burgeoning wealth of the City made possible the survival of certain sectors of the aristocracy when faced by the diminishing importance of the agrarian economy which was its power base. As part of a 'gentlemanly exchange', City merchants and bankers in turn acquired the trappings of aristocracy. It was not only a definite type of class power which was enhanced by the particular processes affecting the development of the City in the nineteenth century; these same processes led to the perpetuation, and indeed strengthening, of 'pre-industrial' commercial capitalism. The City was physically separate from the industrial North — a dramatic example of regionalization! — remaining both economically and politically distinct from the centres of industrial capitalism. It became strongly centralized under the control of the Bank of England, and the banking system became oriented first and foremost to maintaining the stable role of sterling as a 'trusted' form of world money.[35] A further important aspect of this process was the state's fiscal policy in ensuring sterling's formal validity, which the City's narrowly economic activity alone could not guarantee.

What is important about Ingham's appraisal of British economic and political development, in this context at any rate, is less the question of whether or not it is valid than the general theoretical standpoint it expresses. In criticizing endogenous models Ingham's analysis avoids what might be regarded as the developmental determinism that is built into many theories about modern societies. By this I mean a type of thinking about social change which implies that in a society of a given type there is only 'one way forward', which every particular society must at some point follow if it is of that type. Thus 'industrial capitalism', it might be supposed, has certain generic patterns of development that are repeated in all societies which can be so characterized. If some societies do not display these patterns, it must be because they are lagging behind; for some reason their development has been retarded. This type of thinking very often also involves a particular version of functionalism. If certain processes of development are 'necessary' to a society, or type of society, it is because they are functionally required by the institutional order of that society. The implied functional needs 'explain' why a certain path of development 'must' be followed. It should be emphasized again that the 'must' here is justified only if understood in a counter-factual context. Thus it might be argued that what 'must' or 'had to' happen in Britain at the turn of the twentieth century was a scrapping of the 'obsolete' commercial role of the City in the face of the 'needs' of industrial capital. Such an argument is at least potentially illuminating if understood counter-factually. In other words, we can ask the question: what were the consequences for industrial capital of the fact that the position of power of the City was maintained? But if the 'must' is taken to have explanatory force, the result is a positive barrier to understanding why things took the course they did, as Ingham's work demonstrates in pellucid fashion.

The research successfully skirts a further tendency associated with endogenous models. This is the presumption that the society which is most advanced in respect of whatever social traits are being studied can be treated as an exemplar for research purposes.[36] Thus in the nineteenth century Britain was regarded, by Marx among many others, as showing other societies an image of their own future; as the most industrially advanced country Britain presaged developments that others were bound to follow. Quite understandably, there are few who would regard Britain in such a way in the closing decades of the twentieth century. . . . But has the style of thinking that this view represents disappeared along with Britain's retreat into economic obscurity? By no means. Nowadays it is the United States, as the most 'economically advanced' society, that fulfils a comparable role in social theory and in research — even if rarely as unequivocally as in Parsons's version of evolutionism. Now, I do not deny that it may be useful, for some purposes, to rank societies according to their level of development in respect of criteria of one sort or another. It is also legitimate and necessary to attempt to specify what is generic to the institutional order of different societies. But 'comparative research' must be what the term says. That is to say, we have to recognize that 'typical' processes of development can be assessed only by direct comparison between different societies, not by assuming that any one society can be treated as a model of an endogenous development process.

The original rise to prominence of the City, Ingham makes clear, was largely an unintended outcome of fiscal measures instituted for other reasons. What therefore for Marx, and for most subsequent Marxists, belonged only to the early phases of capitalist development, commercial brokerage and usury, became a lasting feature of British capitalism. Precisely because the dominant position of the City was gradually linked to its role as a broker for transactions across national boundaries, the same phenomenon was unlikely to be repeated elsewhere. But if the dominant position which the City established in the early part of the nineteenth century was substantially unintended, subsequent policies defending and expanding its power were usually of a quite different sort. After the turn of the twentieth century the

British economy faced intensified competition from other industrialized and industrializing countries. In these circumstances the economic hegemony of the City became seriously threatened, internally and externally. In large part, as Ingham's analysis discloses, policies promoted by groups either in banking or in the Treasury, or in both, were actively and successfully directed at defending the privileged role of City organizations.

Ingham's research displays a particular and compelling sensitivity to problems of 'world time'. The City came to take on its modern form in relation to a definite conjuncture of events in the early part of the nineteenth century. Its persistence as a centre of commercial activities was dependent upon Britain's position as the leading industrial power and upon the involvement of the country in a worldwide expansion of capitalistic relations. Those who pushed through the fiscal reforms of the early nineteenth century believed that the merchants, who had managed to take over a great deal of erstwhile Dutch and French trade, would be able to consolidate Britain's economic strength on the basis of combining a Free Trade policy with adherence to the Gold Standard. The President of the Board of Trade, Huskissen, for instance, invoked comparisons with Venice in previous centuries. The effectiveness of such influences was possible, however, only because of the particular class alliance which Ingham describes. Moreover, the conditions of the initial consolidation of the power of the City, he makes clear, were substantially different from those allowing for the sustaining of that power in subsequent periods. During the nineteenth century the role of the City in the world economy has a direct economic base in the success of Britain as an industrial producer. In the twentieth century this ceased to be the case; the 'industrial' and 'commercial' sectors of the British economy became oriented to different sets of involvements. It was the City's position as a world monetary broker, by then established internationally, which enabled it to sustain its power. But by this time, because of the changing nexus of circumstances nationally and internationally, the prosperity of the City probably actually presupposed the relative decline of British industry.

Ingham's work demonstrates that the conditions which influenced the rise of the City, and which have subsequently sustained its privileges, are in some substantial degree political.

The City is probably best not regarded as a 'part' of the state, but both internally and externally its economic power has depended in a profound way upon political factors. The hegemony of the City within the British economy has been fostered by the close links that have existed between the 'bankocracy' and the higher levels of government. But the role of the City has also been vitally shaped by its focal position in brokerage activities on an international scale. It is evident that no conception which treats the state either as a unitary phenomenon or as some sort of collective actor could cope with the materials that Ingham analyses. Certain key policy dimensions — for example, those concerned with the Gold Standard in the 1930s — have strongly affected the fate of the City. They can be adequately understood only in terms of shifting allegiances and coalitions between strategically placed groupings of individuals, sometimes having outcomes that none of them intended.

On a more general plane, lessons can be drawn from the analysis of the modern state that are similar to those I have indicated follow from the study of traditional states. The study of 'state formation', as I have sought to demonstrate, is likely to be very seriously misconceived if understood either in a quasi-evolutionary way or in terms of endogenous notions. An adequate 'theory' of the traditional or the modern state simply cannot look like most of the theories which currently predominate in the literature. For one thing, the level of generality which such theories can be presumed to have is likely to be much lower than their proponents imagine. Of course, for a general category like 'agrarian state' or 'capitalist state' to exist at all there must be certain common institutional features which they share, and from this it can be inferred that they also are likely to share some common dynamic tendencies. But to demonstrate what these are is not at all the same as explaining sequences of development or change which take place. The sorts of knowledge which certain individuals or groups, especially the more powerful, may have of such dynamic tendencies can become part of those very tendencies and can act to shape them in specific ways. Factors which are of determinate importance in one time and place, or at one particular conjuncture, may become relatively insignificant elsewhere by virtue of the very influence which they had first of all. The conditions which originally gave rise to the City's dominance over industry were not the same as those which allowed that position later to be sustained.

Some of the problems raised by the nature of theories and generalizations will be taken up in the sections which follow. But in concluding this part of the discussion, it may be as well to raise a question which might be provoked in the reader's mind by the empirical studies I have used to illustrate some of the contentions of structuration theory. Ingham's work might have been partly influenced by these contentions, but the other studies analysed were written quite independently. Why bother with cumbersome notions like 'structuration' and the rest if first-rate social research can be done without them? There are various comments which should be made in response to this. The ideas built into structuration theory allow, in the ways I have tried to demonstrate, for various quite basic criticisms and emendations to be made to the research work analysed. If this is so of what I take to be superior pieces of research, such criticisms would have to be made much more forcibly of research of poorer quality. Moreover, all of the research analysed was informed by serious and prolonged theoretical reflection about the issues investigated. It is perhaps particularly important to stress this in respect of Willis's work. One might easily portray it as nothing less, but nothing more, than an outstandingly perceptive piece of ethnography. In fact, Willis's book contains a substantial theoretical analysis of problems of social reproduction, and there can be no doubt that this was a major stimulus to the research conducted as well as to the mode of its interpretation. Since Willis's theoretical discussion follows lines similar, at least in some ways, to the views I have developed, it is not surprising that his research work should provide an especially illuminating source for examining the implications of those views.

However, there is a point to be made more important than either of these. There is, of course, no obligation for anyone doing detailed empirical research, in a given localized setting, to take on board an array of abstract notions that would merely clutter up what could otherwise be described with economy and in ordinary language. The concepts of structuration theory, as with any competing theoretical perspective, should for many research purposes be regarded as sensitizing devices, nothing more. That is to say, they may be useful for thinking about research problems and the interpretation of research results. But to suppose that being theoretically informed — which it is the business of everyone working in the social sciences to be in some degree — means always operating with a welter of abstract concepts is as mischievous a doctrine as one which suggests that we can get along very well without ever using such concepts at all.

Drawing Together the Threads: Structuration Theory and Forms of Research

In the preceding sections I have discussed a variety of forms of social research, which it is not possible to draw together under a single heading. That is to say, research work is undertaken to attempt to clarify many different issues, according to the nature of the problems the investigator sets out to illuminate. In indicating some of the implications of structuration theory for empirical research, I do not mean to suggest that there is only one format of research which everyone henceforth should adopt. That is part of the point of concentrating upon studies which have mostly been undertaken outside any immediate influence of the concepts I have elaborated. I said earlier that I did not propose to analyse the relevance that structuration theory may or may not have for evaluating specific types of research methods — participant observation survey research, and so on. It is, however, both possible and worth while to look more generically at the tasks of social research informed by structuration theory and at the consequences of the foregoing discussion of research work for the traditional debate between 'qualitative' and 'quantitative' methods in social research.

∧	Hermeneutic Elucidation of Frames of Meaning	(1)
	Investigation of Context and Form of Practical Consciousness	(2)
	(The Unconscious)	
	Identification of Bounds of Knowledgeability	(3)
∨	Specification of Institutional Orders	(4)

The methodological 'insertion' of the research investigator into whatever material is the object of study can be made at any of the four levels indicated above. All social research presumes a hermeneutic moment, but the presumption may remain latent where research draws upon mutual knowledge that is unexplicated because researcher and research inhabit a common cultural *milieu*. The more vociferous advocates of quantitative research repress the essential significance of (1) in two ways. They either take (1) to be purely descriptive rather than explanatory, or else they fail to see that it enters into the formulation of their research work at all. But research concerned with (1) may be both explanatory and generalizing. It has to do with answering why-questions that stem from the mutual unintelligibility of divergent frames of meaning. Naturally, such questions arise across the varying contexts of single societies as well as between societies. Research which is geared primarily to hermeneutic problems may be of generalized importance in so far as it serves to elucidate the nature of agents' knowledgeability and thereby their reasons for action, across a wide range of action-contexts. Pieces of ethnographic research like that of Willis — or like, say, the traditional small-scale community research of fieldwork anthropology — are not in themselves generalizing studies. But they can easily become such if carried out in some numbers, so that judgements of their typicality can justifiably be made.

Hermeneutic aspects of social research are not necessarily illuminating to those who are the subjects of that research, since their main outcome is the elucidation of settings of action considered as 'alien *milieux*'. Such is not the case with the investigation of practical consciousness. Studying practical consciousness means investigating what agents already know, but by definition it is normally illuminating to them if this is expressed discursively, in the metalanguage of social science. Only for ethnomethodology is the analysis of practical consciousness a circumscribed 'field' of study. For all other types of research the interpretation of practical consciousness is a necessary element, implicitly understood or explicitly stated, of broader features of social conduct.

As I have consistently stressed, identifying the bounds of agents' knowledgeability in the shifting contexts of time and space is fundamental to social science. The investigation of (3), however, presumes some considerable knowledge of levels (1), (2) and (4). Without them we are back with an untutored form of structural sociology. The study of the unintended consequences and unacknowledged conditions of action, as I have emphasized when discussing Willis's research, can and should be carried on without using functionalist terminology. What is 'unintended' and 'unacknowledged', in any context or range of contexts of action, is usually by no means a simple matter to discover. No study of the structural properties of social systems can be successfully carried on, or its results interpreted, without reference to the knowledgeability of the relevant agents — although many proponents of structural sociology imagine that this is exactly what defines the province of 'sociological method'.

Level (4), the specifying of institutional orders, involves analysing the conditions of social and system integration via identification of the main institutional components of social systems. Those institutional forms are most important which, in terms of designated structural principles, can be specified as overall 'societies'. Once more, however, I have been at some pains to stress that it is only with many reservations that the main unit of analysis in social science can be said to be a 'society'. Institutional orders frequently cross-cut whatever decisions can be recognized between overall societies.

It is in the relation between (1) and (2) on the one hand and between (3) and (4) on the other that a division between 'qualitative' and 'quantitative' methods is often located. A fondness for quantitative methods has, of course, long been a trait of those attracted to objectivism and structural sociology. According to this type of standpoint, analysing conditions of social life that stretch well beyond any immediate contexts of interaction is the prime objective of social science, and grasping the 'hardened' nature of the institutional components of social life can best be accomplished through classification, measurement and statistical methods. Obviously the idea that the overriding concern of the social sciences is with uncovering law-like generalizations about social conduct is closely related to this proclivity. There is a strong, and often deliberate, echoing of the 'macro'/'micro' division here. Those who favour quantitative methods as the main basis of what makes social science 'science' are prone to emphasize the primacy of so-called macrosociological analysis. Those who advocate qualitative methods as the foundation of empirical research in the social sciences, on the other hand, emphasize (1) and (2) in order to point up the necessarily situated and meaningful character of social inter-action. They tend often to be directly hostile to the use of quantitative methods in social science, on the grounds that quantification and the use of statistical method impose a fixity on social life that it does not in fact have. It is not difficult to see in the conflict between these positions a methodological residue of the dualism of structure and action, and showing such a dualism to be spurious will allow us to tease out further some of the empirical implications of the duality of structure.

To see how this is so, let us return again to that concept, in an empirical setting different from those discussed so far. The following is a transcript of a strip of interaction in a courtroom. Those involved are a judge, a public defender (PD) and a district attorney (DA), and their exchange concerns a prisoner who has pleaded guilty to a second-degree burglary charge. The question being discussed is what sentence the culprit should be given.

> PD: Your honour, we request immediate sentencing and waive the probation report.
> JUDGE: What's his record?
> PD: He has a prior drunk and a GTA [grand theft, auto]. Nothing serious. This is just a shoplifting case. He did enter the K-Mart with intent to steal. But really all we have here is a petty theft.
> JUDGE: What do the people have?
> DA: Nothing either way.
> JUDGE: Any objections to immediate sentencing?
> DA: No.
> JUDGE: How long has he been in?
> PD: Eighty-three days.
> JUDGE: I make this a misdemeanour by PC article 17 and sentence you to ninety days in County Jail, with credit for time served.[37]

Such a situated strip of interaction, like any other, can readily be prised open to indicate how what seems a trivial interchange is profoundly implicated in the reproduction of social institutions. Each turn in the talk exchanged between participants is grasped as meaningful by them (and by the reader) only by the tacit invocation of institutional features of the system of criminal justice. These are drawn upon by each speaker, who (rightly) assumes them to be mutual knowledge held also by the others.

Note that the content of such mutual knowledge presumes vastly more than just awareness of the tactics of 'proper procedure' in such cases, although that is also involved. Each participant knows a vast amount about what a 'legal system' is, about normative procedures of law, about what prisoners, advocates, judges do, etc. In order to 'bring off' the interaction, the participants make use of their knowledge of the institutional order in which they are involved in such a way as to render their interchange 'meaningful'. However, by invoking the institutional order in this way — and *there is no other way* for participants in interaction to render what they do intelligible and coherent to one another — they thereby contribute to reproducing it. Moreover, it is essential to see that in reproducing it they also reproduce its 'facticity' as a source of structural constraint (upon themselves and upon others). They treat the system of justice as a 'real' order of relationships within which their own interaction is situated and which it expresses. And it is a 'real' (i.e., structurally stable) order of relationships precisely because they, and others like them in connected and similar contexts, accept it as such — not necessarily in their discursive consciousness but in the practical consciousness incorporated in what they do.

It is important not to confuse this observation with the famous dictum of W. I. Thomas that if actors 'define situations as real, then they are real in their consequences'. Thomas's proposition suggests that there are circumstances which are not in fact 'real' (i.e., are fictitious or imaginary), but nevertheless have actual consequences because people believe in them. Merton took this as a starting-point for his formulation of the self-fulfilling prophecy, in which a state of affairs comes to exist by the very fact of its announcement. Now, I do not doubt at all the importance both of the self-fulfilling prophecy and of a range of phenomena linked to it. But it is not the prototype of the 'facticity' of structural properties contained in the duality of structure. The point is a more subtle and more profound one, linking the very possibility of the mutual intelligibility and coherence of situated interaction to 'facticity' on a broadly based institutional level.

Notice also how intimately and fundamentally the 'facticity' of the institutional order is linked to power, which it both expresses and facilitates in the details of the interaction. For the 'acceptance-as-real' that is built into the mutually intelligible continuity of the interaction is the very foundation of the legal system as an expression of modes of domination. 'Acceptance-as-real' embodied in concrete modes of procedure plainly does not mean the same thing as discursively according legitimation to the system, although of course it by no means precludes it either. As a system of power relations, 'acceptance-as-real' has much more far-reaching implications than does the actual differential power that the participating agents are able to bring to the interaction to make their particular views count. However, it is noticeable that the sequence of talk does not follow the more 'democratic' rules that conversations between peers ordinarily display, and does directly reflect differential power. Thus the judge has the right to interrupt what the others say, to pose particular types of questions and to control the sequence of talk, which the others do not have, at least to the same degree. The fact that the conversation does not have a conventional turn-taking form is made intelligible by the mutual acknowledgement that the judge has a certain institutionalized social identity, allocating him definite prerogatives and sanctions.

Let me formulate this at a more general level to make its connotations clear. All social interaction is situated within time-space boundaries of co-presence (whether or not this be extended via media such as letters, telephone calls, etc.). Its situated character, as I have discussed in detail in chapters 1 and 2, is directly involved with the indexical nature of the 'bringing off' of mutually intelligible communication. But the situatedness of interaction is not a barrier to that institutional 'fixity' demonstrated by institutional orders across time and space. It is its very condition, just as the existence of those institutional orders is the condition of the most transient forms of social encounter or conversation. The reflexive monitoring of social conduct is intrinsic to the 'facticity' which the structural properties of social systems display, not something either marginal or additional to it. Wilson has expressed this in the following way. As an account of the significance of the concept of the duality of structure, I could not better it:

> the social world is constituted by situated actions produced in particular concrete situations, that are available to the participants for their own recognition, description, and use as warranted

grounds for further inference and action on those same occasions as well as subsequent ones. Situated actions are produced through context-free, context-sensitive mechanisms of social interaction, and social structure is used by members of society to render their actions in particular situations intelligible and coherent. In this process, social structure is an essential resource for and product of situated action, and social structure is reproduced as an objective reality that partially constrains action. It is through this reflexive relation between social structure and situated action that the transparency of displays [the mutual intelligibility of conduct] is accomplished by exploiting the context-dependence of meaning.[38]

Once the point of this is fully understood, the idea that there is either a clear-cut division or a necessary opposition between qualitative and quantitative methods disappears. Quantitative techniques are usually likely to be demanded when a large number of 'cases' of a phenomenon are to be investigated, in respect of a restricted variety of designated characteristics. But both the collection and interpretation of quantitative material depends upon procedures methodologically identical to the gathering of data of a more intensive, 'qualitative' sort. This is why Gambetta's study can be used to focus upon some of the same problems as those investigated by Willis. Gambetta's data concern a large number of individuals, Willis's material only a handful. Gambetta's work involves the use of a battery of sophisticated research methods, while Willis's study consists wholly of ethnographic reporting. But Gambetta's research, no less than that of Willis, presupposes a grasp of situated action and meanings without which the formal categories of the theoretical metalanguage employed by the researcher would have neither sense nor application. All so-called 'quantitative' data, when scrutinized, turn out to be composites of 'qualitative' — i.e., contextually located and indexical — interpretations produced by situated researchers, coders, government officials and others. The hermeneutic problems posed by ethnographic research also exist in the case of quantitative studies, although these may be in some large part 'buried' by the extent to which the data involved have been 'worked upon'. Attempts to produce scaling measures, eliminate selection bias, produce consistent sampling techniques, etc., operate within these confines. They do not in any way logically compromise the use of quantitative methods, although no doubt they lead us to appraise the nature of quantitative data rather differently from some of the advocates of structural sociology.

(1) and (2) are thus as essential for undrstanding (3) and (4) as vice versa, and qualitative and quantitative methods should be seen as complementary rather than antagonistic aspects of social research. Each is necessary to the other if the substantive nature of the duality of structure is to be 'charted' in terms of the forms of institutional articulation whereby contexts of interaction are co-ordinated within more embracing social systems. The one point which does need to be forcibly stressed is that social researchers should be alert to the modes in which quantitative data are produced. For, unlike the movement of mercury within a thermometer, social data are never only an 'index' of an independently given phenomenon but always at the same time exemplify what it is they are 'about' — that is, processes of social life.

Mutual Knowledge versus Common Sense

Empirical research self-evidently has no rationale if it does not somehow generate new knowledge which was not available before. Since all social actors exist in situated contexts within larger spans of time-space, what is novel to some such actors is not to others — including, among those others, social scientists. It is, of course, in these 'information gaps' that ethnographic research has its specific importance. In a broad sense of the term this sort of research is explanatory, since it serves to clarify puzzles presented when those from one cultural setting encounter individuals from another which is in some respects quite different. The query 'Why do they act (think) as they do?' is an invitation to enter the culturally alien *milieu* and to make sense of it. To those already within that *milieu*, as Winch and many others have pointed out, such an enterprise may be inherently unenlightening. However, much social research, in terms of both the empirical material it generates and the theoretical interpretations which may be linked to it, has critical connotations for beliefs which agents hold. To investigate what such connotations might be we have to consider the question of exactly in what sense the social sciences reveal new knowledge and how such knowledge might connect with the critique of false belief. These matters are complex, and I shall not attempt to deal here with more than certain aspects of them.

The critical endeavours of the social sciences, like those of natural science, are bound up with the logical and empirical adequacy of reported observations and theories associated with them. As Schutz and many others have quite rightly emphasized, the critical character of social science in this respect normally departs quite sharply from the beliefs and theories-in-use incorporated within the conduct of day-to-day social life. All social actors, it can properly be said, are social theorists, who alter their theories in the light of their experiences and are receptive to incoming information which they may acquire in doing so. Social theory is by no means the special and insulated province of academic thinkers. However, lay actors are generally concerned above all with the practical utility of the 'knowledge' that they apply in their daily activities, and there may be basic features of the institutional organization of society (including, but not limited to, ideology) which confine or distort what they take to be knowledge.

It is surely plain that the 'revelatory model' of natural science cannot be directly transferred to the social sciences. Common-sense beliefs about the natural world are corrigible in the light of the findings of the natural sciences. There are no particular logical difficulties in understanding what is going on in such circumstances, even though there may be social barriers to the reception of scientific ideas.[39] That is to say, lay beliefs are open to correction, in so far as this is necessary, by the input of novel scientific theories and observations. The natural sciences can in principle demonstrate that some of the things that the lay member of society believes about the object world are false, while others are valid. It is more complicated, for better or for worse, in the social sciences. The 'findings' of the social sciences, as I have emphasized, are not necessarily news to those whom those findings are about.

The issues involved here have become very murky indeed as a result of the push and pull between objectivist and interpretative formulations of social science. The former have tended to apply the revelatory model in an uninhibited way to the social sciences.

That is to say, they have regarded common-sense beliefs involved in social life to be unproblematically corrigible in terms of the enlightenment which the social sciences can deliver. Those influenced by hermeneutics and ordinary-language philosophy, however, have established powerful objections to this naive standpoint. Common-sense beliefs, as incorporated in day-to-day language use and action, cannot be treated as mere impediments to a valid or veridical characterization of social life. For we cannot describe social activity at all without knowing what its constituent actors know, tacitly as well as discursively. Empiricism and objectivism simply suppress the whole issue of the generation of social descriptions via the mutual knowledge which sociological observers and lay members of society hold in common.[40] The trouble is, having reached this conclusion, those advocating interpretative forms of social science find it difficult or impossible to maintain that critical edge which the opposite type of tradition has rightly insisted upon in juxtaposing social science and common sense. The tasks of social science then seem precisely limited to ethnography — to the hermeneutic endeavour of the 'fusion of horizons'.[41] Such a paralysis of the critical will is as logically unsatisfactory as the untutored use of the revelatory model.

A way out of this impasse can be found by distinguishing mutual knowledge from 'common sense'.[42] The first refers to the necessary respect which the social analyst must have for the authenticity of belief or the hermeneutic *entrée* into the description of social life. 'Necessary' in this statement has logical force to it. The reason why it characteristically makes more sense to speak about 'knowledge' rather than 'belief' when speaking of how actors find their way around in the contexts of social life is that the generation of descriptions demands the bracketing of scepticism.[43] Beliefs, tacit and discursive, have to be treated as 'knowledge' when the observer is operating on the methodological plane of characterizing action. Mutual knowledge, regarded as the necessary mode of gaining access to the 'subject matter' of social science, is not corrigible in the light of its findings; on the contrary, it is the condition of being able to come up with 'findings' at all.

It is because mutual knowledge is largely tacit — carried on the level of practical consciousness — that it is not obvious that respect for the authenticity of belief is a necessary part of all ethnographic work in the social sciences. The attacks led by those influenced by phenomenology and ethnomethodology upon more orthodox conceptions of social science have undoubtedly been of major importance in elucidating the nature of mutual knowledge. But in speaking of 'common sense' or equivalent terms in a diffuse way they have not separated out analytically the methodological issue from that of critique. In distinguishing mutual knowledge from common sense I mean to reserve the latter concept to refer to the propositional beliefs implicated in the conduct of day-to-day activities. The distinction is largely an analytical one; that is to say, common sense is mutual knowledge treated not as knowledge but as fallible belief. However, not all mutual knowledge can be expressed as propositional beliefs — beliefs that some states of affairs or others are the case. Moreover, not all such beliefs are capable of being formulated discursively by those who hold them.

Distinguishing between mutual knowledge and common sense does not imply that these are always easily separable phases of study in actual social research. For one thing, the descriptive language used by sociological observers is always more or less different from that used by lay actors. The introduction of social scientific terminology may (but does not necessarily) call in question discursively formulated beliefs (or, where connected in an ensemble, 'theories-in-use') which actors hold. Where contested descriptions are already employed by the agents studied, any description given by observers, even using actors' categories, is directly critical of other available terminologies that could have been used. What is a 'liberation movement' from one perspective might be a 'terrorist organization' from another. The choice of one term rather than the other, of course, implies a definite stance on the part of the observer. It is less immediately apparent that the choice of a more 'neutral' term does as well; its use, however, also indicates a critical distance which the observer takes from the concepts applied by the actors directly involved.

In any research situation there may be beliefs accepted by participants which so grate upon those held by the observer that the observer expresses critical distance from them, even in what is otherwise a purely ethnographic study. An anthropologist may feel no qualms about asserting, 'The X grow their crops by planting seeds every autumn', since it is mutually held as knowledge between him or her and the members of culture X that the planting of seeds at an appropriate time of the year eventuates in a particular crop. But that anthropologist is likely to say, 'The X believe their ceremonial dance will bring rain' indicating a gap between what he or she and those in culture X believe to be the case about the conditions under which rainfall occurs.[44]

The examples mentioned in the above paragraph indicate that even purely ethnographic social research — that is, research which follows the confined goal of descriptive reportage — tends to have a critical moment. While this does not compromise the logical distinction between mutual knowledge and common sense, it does mean specifying more directly what is involved in that moment of critique, which in other types of research is usually more directly developed.

I have to emphasize at this point the modest dimensions of the discussion which follows. Analysing logically what is involved in the garnering of mutual knowledge, as well as what is involved in the critique of common-sense belief, raises questions of epistemology which it would be out of the question to discuss exhaustively here. The ideas I shall develop in what follows are intended to supply no more than an outline format, which presumes a definite epistemological view without supporting it in detail. There are two senses, I want to claim, in which social science is relevant to the critique of lay beliefs construed as common sense (which includes, but does not give any special priority to, the critique of ideology). The critical activities in which social scientists engage as the core of what they do have direct implications for the beliefs which agents hold, in so far as those beliefs can be shown to be invalid or inadequately grounded. But such implications are especially important where the beliefs in question are incorporated into the reasons actors have for what they do. Only some of the beliefs which actors hold or profess form part of the reasons they have for their conduct. When these are subjected to critique in the light of claims or findings of social science, the social observer is seeking to demonstrate that those reasons are not good reasons.

The identification of agents' reasons is normally intimately bound up with the hermeneutic problems posed by the generating of mutual knowledge. Given that this is so, we should distinguish what I shall call 'credibility criteria' from the 'validity criteria' relevant to the critique of reasons as good reasons. Credibility criteria refer to criteria, hermeneutic in character, used to indicate how the grasping of actors' reasons illuminates what exactly they are doing in the light of those reasons. Validity criteria concern criteria of factual evidence and theoretical understanding employed by the social sciences in the assessment of reasons as good reasons. Consider the famous case of the red macaws, much discussed in the anthropological literature. The Bororo of Central Brazil say, 'We are red macaws.' Debated by Von den Steinen, Durkheim and Mauss, among others, the statement has seemed to many to be either nonsensical or hermeneutically impenetrable. The issue was, however, recently taken up by an anthropologist who had the chance to reinvestigate the matter at source, among the Bororo.[45] He found that the statement is made only by men; that Bororo women tend to own red macaws as pets; that in various ways in Bororo society men are peculiarly dependent upon women; and that contact with the spirits is made by men and red macaws independently of women. It seems plausible to infer that 'We are red macaws' is a statement in which men ironically comment upon their indebtedness to women and at the same time assert their own spiritual superiority to them. Investigation of why the statement is made helps to clarify the nature of the statement. The investigation of credibility criteria, in respect of discursively formulated beliefs at any rate, usually depends upon making clear the following items: who expresses them, in what circumstances, in what discursive style (literal description, metaphor, irony, etc.) and with what motives.

Assessment of validity criteria is governed solely by the conjunction of 'internal' and 'external critique' generated by social science. That is to say, validity criteria are the criteria of internal critique which I hold to be substantially constitutive of what social science is. The main role of the social sciences in respect of the critique of common sense is the assessment of reasons as good reasons in terms of knowledge either simply unavailable to lay agents or construed by them in a fashion different from that formulated in the metalanguages of social theory. I see no basis for doubting that the standards of internal critique in the social sciences carry over directly to external critique in this respect. This statement is a strong one, and it is particularly at this

Q

juncture that a specific epistemological standpoint is presupposed. It presumes, and I presume, that it is possible to demonstrate that some belief claims are false, while others are true, although what 'demonstrate' means here would need to be examined as closely as would 'false' and 'true'. It presumes, and I presume, that internal critique — the critical examinations to which social scientists submit their ideas and claimed findings — is inherent in what social science is as a collective endeavour. I intend to risk the disfavour of the philosophically sophisticated by asserting, without further ado, that I hold these things to be the case. In a different context, however, it would clearly be necessary to defend such contentions at some considerable length.

It can be shown, I think, that there is a non-contingent relation between demonstrating a social belief to be false, and practical implications for the transformation of action linked to that belief.[46] Criticizing a belief means (logically) criticizing whatever activity or practice is carried on in terms of that belief, and has compelling force (motivationally) in so far as it is a reason for action. Where the belief in question informs a segment or aspect of conduct in relation to the natural world, showing it to be false will (*ceteris paribus*) cause the agent to change his or her behaviour in whatever respects are relevant. If this does not happen, the presumption is that other considerations are overriding in the agent's mind, that the implications of the falsity of the belief are misunderstood or that the actor does not in fact accept that its falsity has been convincingly shown. Now social beliefs, unlike those to do with nature, are constitutive elements of what it is they are about. From this it follows that criticism of false belief (*ceteris paribus*) is a *practical intervention* in society, a political phenomenon in a broad sense of that term.

How does this discussion of belief relate to the claim that all competent actors not only know what they are doing (under some description or another) but must do so for social life to have the character which it does? The question can best be answered by reference to a concrete example. Consider voting in a 'one person, one vote' situation. Such a practice clearly involves all potential voters knowing what a 'vote' is, that they are only permitted to vote once, that they can only vote in their own name, etc. It is only if participants know these things, and act appropriately, that we could talk of a 'one person, one vote' system existing at all.

How far such a phenomenon could validly be said to exist if only a certain proportion of people were fully aware of the relevant concepts is a hermeneutic problem. To say that actors 'must' know what they are doing for voting to exist is to specify what counts as a valid description of the activity. However, there is no doubt that *some* persons involved might not know what voting is, or might not know all the procedures involved in voting, and that their activity could influence the outcome of the vote. Generalizing, we could say that any individuals can make mistakes about what is involved in any aspects of any social convention. But no one can be mistaken most of the time about what he or she does, or that person will be regarded as incompetent by other actors; and there is no aspect of any convention that most agents can be wrong about most of the time. Of course, we have to recognize other possibilities. Agents positioned in some sectors of a society might be quite ignorant of what goes on in others; actors might believe that the outcomes of their activities are different from what they in fact are; and the redescription of a context of action in the concepts of social science might represent what is going on in ways different from those with which the agent is familiar.

We can assume, to repeat, that new knowledge developed in the social sciences will ordinarily have immediate transformational implications for the existing social world. But what is covered by *ceteris paribus?* Under what conditions will this not be so?

(1) Most obvious, where the circumstances described or analysed are to do with past events and relate to social conditions which no longer pertain. In case it should be thought that this again allows for a clear-cut distinction between history and social science, it should be pointed out that even purely ethnographic studies of dead cultures may very well be treated as illuminating current circumstances, often by the very contrasts they reveal. We undoubtedly cannot say in principle that knowledge about situations that no longer exist is irrelevant to other contexts in which that knowledge might be drawn upon in a transformative way. The influence of 'Caesarism' in nineteenth-century politics in France, satirized by Marx, is a good example.

(2) Where the conduct in question depends upon motives and reasons which are not altered by new information that

becomes available. The relationships involved here may be very much more complicated than may appear at first sight. What seem to be two sets of independent phenomena (for example, the statement of a generalization and activities referred to by that generalization) may in fact be intimately connected. Most of the more familiar 'laws' or generalizations of neo-classical economics, it might be thought, are statements knowledge of which will not alter the circumstances to which they relate. That is to say, they depend upon patterns of motivation and reasoning on the part of lay agents which are unlikely to alter no matter how far those generalizations become familiar. But the development of economics has played a role in creating the very conditions in which the generalizations in question hold, promoting a calculating attitude towards the deployment of capital and so on — a phenomenon I shall discuss further below.

(3)　Where the new knowledge or information is used to sustain existing circumstances. This may, of course, happen even where the theories or findings concerned could, if utilized in certain ways, modify what they describe. The selective appropriation of social scientific material by the powerful, for example, can turn that material to ends quite other than those that might be served if it were more widely disseminated.

(4)　Where those who seek to apply the new knowledge are not in a situation to be able to do so effectively. This is evidently often a matter of access to the resources needed to alter an existing set of circumstances. But it must also be pointed out that the possibility of discursively articulating interests is usually assymetrically distributed in a society. Those in the lower echelons of society are likely to have various limitations upon their capabilities of discursively formulating interests, particularly their longer-term interests. They are less likely than those in superordinate positions to be able to transcend the situated character — in time and in space — of their activities. This may be so because of inferior educational opportunities, because of the more confined character of their typical *milieux* of action (in Gouldner's terms, they are more likely to be 'locals' than cosmopolitans) or because those in superordinate positions simply have a greater range of accessible information available to them.

Those in the lower echelons are also unlikely to have access to a coherent and conceptually sophisticated discourse in terms of which to connect their interests to the conditions of their realization.

(5) Where what is claimed as knowledge turns out to be in some part false. It is surely evident enough that there is no necessary convergence between the validity of ideas or observations produced in the social sciences and their appropriation by lay actors. Various possibilities derive from this, including that whereby views which were originally false can become true as a result of their propagation (the self-fulfilling prophecy). It by no means inevitably follows that the adoption of invalid findings will be unconsequential in respect of the conduct they purport to describe.

(6) Where the new knowledge is trivial or uninteresting to the actors to whom it has reference. This case is rather more significant than might appear because of the differences that may exist between the preoccupation of lay actors and those of social observers. As Schutz puts it, the relevances of social scientists are not necessarily the same as those of the actors whose behaviour they seek to explicate.

(7) Where the *form* of knowledge or information generated inhibits its actualization or conceals certain ways in which it might be actualized. By far the most important case in question is that of reification. But the possible implications which this raises are again complex. Reified discourse produced in the social sciences may have different effects where the discourse of lay actors is also reified than where it is not.

Generalizations in Social Science

Social life is in many respects not an intentional product of its constituent actors, in spite of the fact that day-to-day conduct is chronically carried on in a purposive fashion. It is in the study of the unintended consequences of action, as I have often emphasized, that some of the most distinctive tasks of the social sciences are to be found. It is also here that the prime concern of social scientists inclined towards objectivism and structural sociology is located. Those who speak of the explanatory objectives of the social sciences as bound up with the discovery of laws do not do so when outcomes are more or less completely intended. Thus, for example, the drivers of cars regularly stop when traffic lights are red and start off again when they go green. But no one suggests that stopping at traffic lights can be represented as a law of human social conduct. The laws involved are of a juridical kind. Drivers know what the red lights are for, how they themselves are supposed to react according to the codes of traffic behaviour, and when they stop on the red or start on the green they know what they are doing and do it intentionally. The fact that such examples are not talked of as laws, even though the behaviour involved is very regular, indicates that the problem of laws in social science is very much bound up with unintended consequences, unacknowledged conditions and constraint.

By 'laws' structural sociologists ordinarily mean universal laws of the kind thought to exist in the natural sciences. Now, there are many debates about whether or not such laws do in fact exist in natural science and, if so, what their logical status is. But let us suppose that they do exist and follow the standard interpretation of their logical form. Universal laws state that whenever one set of conditions, specified in a definite way, is found, a second set of conditions will be found also where the first set causes the second. Not all causal statements, of course, are laws, and not all causal relations can be subsumed under (known) laws. Nor are all statements of a universal form laws. Hempel gives the example 'All bodies consisting of pure gold have a mass of less than 100,000 kilograms.' There is no known case where this statement does not hold, but unless some causal mechanism were discovered to explain why this should be so, it would probably not be regarded as an example of a law.[47] Do universal laws exist in the social sciences? If not, why have so many of those affiliated with structural sociology typically placed all of their eggs in that particular explanatory basket? The plain answer to the first question is that they do not. In natural science, or at least in some of the major areas of natural science, there are many examples of laws that appear to conform to the universal law type. In social science — and I would include economics, as well as sociology within this judgement — there is not a single candidate which could be offered uncontentiously as an instance of such a law in the realm of human social conduct. As I have argued elsewhere,[48] modjat Scherish the social sciences are not latecomers as compared with natural science. The idea that with further research such laws will eventually be uncovered is at best markedly implausible.

If they do not exist, and will never exist, in social science, why have so many supposed that the social sciences should pursue such a chimera? No doubt in considerable part because of the sway that empiricist philosophies of natural science have held over the social sciences. But this is surely not all there is to it. Also involved is the supposition that the only worthwhile knowledge about social actors or institutions which the social sciences should be interested in obtaining is that which those actors do not themselves possess. With this comes the inclination to reduce knowledge imputed to actors to a minimum, thus broadening the scope for the operation of causal mechanisms which have their effects independently of the reasons that individuals have for what they do. Now, if this kind of view is not viable, on grounds I have discussed in some detail in this book, we have to look again at the nature of laws in social science. That there are no known universal laws in social science is not just happenstance. If it is correct to say, as I have argued, that the causal mechanisms in social scientific generalizations depend upon actors' reasons, in the context of a 'mesh' of intended and unintended consequences of action, we can readily see why such generalizations do not have a universal form. For the content of agents' knowledgeability, the question of how 'situated' it is and the validity of the propositional content of that knowledge — all these will influence the circumstances in which those generalizations hold.

Men lavcr haun ikba selv en generalisering?

Once more at the risk of upsetting the more philosophically minded reader, I propose simply to declare that reasons are causes, accepting that this no doubt implies a non-Humean account of causality. More properly put, in the terminology I have introduced: the rationalization of action is causally implicated, in a chronic manner, in the continuation of day-to-day actions.[49] The rationalization of action, in other words, is a major element of the range of causal powers than an individual, *qua* agent, displays. This is so because doing something for reasons means applying an understanding of 'what is called for' in a given set of circumstances in such a way as to shape whatever is done in those circumstances. To have reasons for doing something is not the same as to do something for reasons, and it is the difference between these that spells out the causal impact of the rationalization of action. Reasons are causes of activities which the individual 'makes happen' as an inherent feature of being an agent. But since the reflexive monitoring of action is bounded, as I have frequently insisted, there are causal factors which influence action without operating through its rationalization. It follows from what has been said previously that these are of two types: unconscious influences and influences which affect the circumstances of action within which individuals carry on their conduct.

The second of these is by far the more important for purposes of social analysis, but since 'circumstances of action' is a very general term, it needs spelling out somewhat. All action occurs in contexts that, for any given single actor, include many elements which that actor neither helped to bring into being nor has any significant control over. Such enabling and constraining features of contexts of action include both material and social phenomena. In so far as social phenomena are concerned, it has to be emphasized that what for one individual is a controllable aspect of the social *milieu* may be for others something which 'happens' rather than something which is 'made to happen'. Many of the most delicately subtle, as well as the intellectually most challenging, features of social analysis derive from this.

Now, it can be accepted that all abstract generalizations in the social sciences are, explicitly or implicitly, causal statements. But, as I have been concerned to stress throughout this book, it matters a great deal what type of causal relations are involved. That is to say, situations where those concerned 'make happen' a regularized outcome differ substantially from those in which such an outcome 'happens' in a way which no participant has intended. Since agents' knowledge about the conditions influencing the generalization is causally relevant to that generalization, these conditions can be altered by changes in such knowledge. The self-fulfilling prophecy is one, but only one, example of this phenomenon.

Caution is in order here. There are always boundary conditions to the operations of laws in natural science. But these do not affect the invariant causal relation that is at the core of the explanatory tasks for which reference to the law can be made. In the case of generalizations in social science, the causal mechanisms are inherently unstable, the degree of instability depending upon how far those beings to whom the generalization refers are likely to display standard patterns of reasoning in such a way as to produce standard sorts of unintended consequence. Consider the sort of generalization suggested by Gambetta's study: 'the higher up children of working-class origins are in an educational system, the lower the chance they will drop out, as compared to children from other class backgrounds.' Here the unintended consequences pointed to form a statistical pattern, the result of an aggregate of decisions of individuals separated in time and space. I take it that no one would suggest this to express a universal law, but it is none the less a potentially illuminating generalization. The causal relation it presumes depends upon the kinds of decision-making specified by Gambetta. But, as that author points out, if the parents or children (from any of the classes) got to know about the generalization, they could build it into their assessment of the very situation it describes and therefore in principle undermine it.

We can say, as many others have, that generalizations in the social sciences are 'historical' in character as long as we bear in mind the many senses which that term can assume. In this particular connotation it means only that the circumstances in which generalizations hold are temporally and spatially circumscribed, depending as they do upon definite mixes of intended and unintended consequences of action. Given that such is the case, is it worth calling generalizations in the social sciences 'laws'? This depends entirely upon how strictly one wishes to interpret the term 'law'. In my opinion, since in natural science 'law' tends to be associated with the operation of invariant relations, even in the case of laws that are not universal in form, it is preferable not to use the term in social science. In any case, it is important to avoid the implication of the advocates of structural sociology that 'laws' are found only when unintended consequences are involved in a significant way in respect of a given series of phenomena. Generalizations about human social conduct, in other words, may directly reflect maxims of action which are knowingly applied by agents. As I have stressed in this chapter, just how far this is the case in any specified set of circumstances it has to be one of the main tasks of social research to investigate.

The Practical Connotations of Social Science

The social sciences, unlike natural science, are inevitably involved in a 'subject—subject relation' with what they are about. The theories and findings of the natural sciences are separate from the universe of objects and events which they concern. This ensures that the relation between scientific knowledge and the object world remains a 'technological' one, in which accumulated knowledge is 'applied' to an independently constituted set of phenomena. But in the social sciences the situation is different. As Charles Taylor puts it: 'While natural science theory also transforms practice, the practice it transforms is not what the theory is about. . . . We think of it as an "application" of the theory.' In the social sciences, 'the practice is the object of the theory. Theory in this domain transforms its own object.'[50] The implications of this are very considerable and bear upon how we should assess the achievements of the social sciences as well as their practical impact upon the social world.

If we were to accept the view of those who suppose that the social sciences should be simulcra of the natural sciences, there is no doubt that the former must be accounted a failure. Social science has not come up with the sorts of precise law found in the more sophisticated areas of natural science and, for reasons to which I have already alluded, will not do so. On the face of things, it would look as though the demise of the aspiration to create a 'natural science of society' marks the end of the idea that the social sciences could ever affect 'their world', the social world, to the degree that the natural sciences have influenced 'theirs'. For generations those who have proposed naturalistic sociologies have done so on the basis of the notion that social science needs to 'catch up' with natural science both intellectually and practically. In other words, it is held that the natural sciences have demonstrably outstripped the social sciences in terms of their intellectual achievements and, therefore, their practical consequences. The problem is for the social sciences to recover the ground that has been lost in order to apply their findings to control events in the social world in a parallel fashion. Comte's programme was founded upon this type of standpoint, and it is

one which has thereafter been consistently reiterated in one guise
or another.

The following is a typical formulation of it, from an author whc
otherwise is far from being a follower of Comte:

> As social scientists we share with all fairly educated people in the
> world a general disturbing understanding that in our field of study
> progress is very much slower than in the natural sciences. It is their
> discoveries and inventions which are compelling radical changes in
> society, while ours, up till now, have been very much less
> consequential. There is spreading a creeping anxiety about the
> dangerous hiatus inherent in this contrast. While man's power over
> nature is increasing fast and, indeed, acceleratingly fast, man's
> control over society, which means in the first place over his own
> attitudes and institutions, is lagging far behind. In part, at least, this
> is due to a slower pace in the advance of our knowledge about man
> and his society, the knowledge that should be translated into
> action for social reform.[51]

At first sight nothing looks more obvious than that the
transformative impact of the natural sciences has been incom-
parably greater than that of the social sciences. Natural science
has its paradigms, its agreed-upon findings, knowledge of high
generality expressed with mathematical precision. In the natural
sciences the 'founders' are forgotten or regarded as the originators
of ideas that have only antiquarian interest. The fusion of science
and technology has generated forms of material transformation
on the most extraordinary scale. Social science, on the other
hand, is apparently chronically riven with disagreements, unable
to forget its 'founders', whose writings are regarded as having an
importance of a lasting kind. Governments today might on
occasion look to the social sciences as a source of information for
policy decisions; but this seems of trivial and marginal consequence when compared with the global impact of natural
science. The greater social prestige which natural science enjoys
as compared with the social sciences seems well in line with their
differential accomplishments and material influence.

But is this conventional view of social science as the poor
relation correct? One can at least say it becomes much less easy
to sustain if we take into account the significance of the double
hermeneutic. The social sciences, to repeat, are not insulated

(For meget tid på at evaluere
sig selv ...

from 'their world' in the way in which the natural sciences are insulated from 'theirs'. This certainly compromises the achievement of a discrete corpus of knowledge of the type sought by those who take natural science as a model. However, at the same time it means that the social sciences enter into the very constitution of 'their world' in a manner which is foreclosed to natural science.

Consider the following:

> A man who is made a prince by favour of the people must work to retain their friendship; and this is easy for him because the people ask only not to be oppressed. But a man who has become prince against the will of the people and by the favour of the nobles should, before anything else, try to win the people over; this too is easy if he takes them under his protection. When men receive favours from someone they expected to do them ill, they are under a great obligation to their benefactor; just so the people can in an instant become more amicably disposed towards the prince than if he had seized power by their favour.[52]

Machiavelli's theorem is not just an observation about power and popular support in politics. It was intended to be, and has been accepted as, a contribution to the actual mechanics of government. It can be said, without exaggeration, that the practice of government has never been quite the same since Machiavelli's writings became well known. Their influence is not at all easy to trace. 'Machiavellian' has become a pejorative term partly for reasons which have nothing much to do with the actual content of what Machiavelli wrote — for example, because of the reputed behaviour of rulers who put their own construction upon what he had to say. Principles which can be applied by princes can also be applied by those who are subject to their reign and by others opposed to them. The practical consequences of tracts such as Machiavelli's are likely to be tortuous and ramified. They are very far from the situation in which the findings of the social sciences are collated and assessed in one sphere (the 'internal critique' of professional specialists) and simply 'applied' in another (the world of practical action). But they are more typical of the fate of social scientific knowledge than is the latter picture.

Now, the question of whether it is justified to call Machiavelli a 'social scientist' might be disputed on the grounds that his writings precede the era in which reflection upon the nature of social institutions became systematized. Suppose, however, we look to the later period of the closing decades of the eighteenth century and the opening part of the nineteenth century. This was the time at which, it might be argued, detailed empirical research into social issues was initiated. Some have regarded the period as the first phase in which the social sciences were given an evidential base which could begin to resemble that of natural science. However, what is striking is that the techniques of research developed, and the 'data' generated, immediately became a significant part of the society which they were used to analyse. The burgeoning of official statistics is both symptom and material result of this process. Their gathering was made possible by the use of systematic methods of social surveying. The development of such methods is inseparable from the new modes of administrative control which the collection of official statistics permitted. Once established, official statistics in turn allowed for new types of social analysis — research into, for example, demographic patterns, crime, divorce, suicide, etc. However the literature on these topics in turn was re-incorporated in the practice of those concerned with the production of the relevant statistics. Literature on suicide, for example, is widely read by coroners, court officials and others, including those who contemplate or carry out suicidal acts.[53]

Of course, the development of theoretical matelanguages and the specialization demanded by the intensive study of specific areas of social life ensure that the social sciences do not become wholly merged with their 'subject matter'. But once it is grasped how complex, continuous and intimate is the association between 'professional' and lay social analysts, it becomes easy to see why the profound impact of social science upon the constitution of modern societies is hidden from view. 'Discoveries' of social science, if they are at all interesting, cannot remain discoveries for long; the more illuminating they are, in fact, the more likely they are to be incorporated into action and thereby to become familiar principles of social life.

The theories and findings of the natural sciences stand in a 'technological' relation to their 'subject matter'. That is to say, the information they generate has practical significance as a 'means' applied to altering an independently given and autonomous world of objects and events. But the social sciences do not stand only in a 'technological' relation to their 'subject matter', and their incorporation into lay action is only marginally a 'technological' one. Many possible permutations of knowledge and power stem from this. To demonstrate such to be the case we might go back to the example of Machiavelli's observations about the nature of politics. The following are possible involvements and ramifications of Machiavelli's writings:

(1)   Machiavelli may in substantial part have given only a particular form of expression to what many rulers, and no doubt others too, knew already — they might very well even have known some of these things discursively, although it is unlikely that they would have been able to express them as pithily as Machiavelli did.

(2)   That Machiavelli wrote the texts he did introduced a new factor, once they became available, which did not exist previously when the same things were known, if they were known.

(3)   'Machiavellian' became a term of abuse among those who heard of the ideas that Machiavelli espoused without necessarily having any first-hand knowledge of the texts. Machiavelli was widely thought in England to be a purveyor of depravities before the first English translation of *The Prince* was published in 1640.

(4)   The sort of discourse which Machiavelli made use of in his writings was one element or aspect of fundamental changes in the legal and constitutional orders of modern states. To think about 'politics' in a particular and substantively novel way was essential to what 'politics' became.[54]

(5)   A ruler who was thought to be a follower of Machiavelli, and to try to govern according to Machiavellian precepts, might find them harder to apply than one who was not known to be such. A ruler's subjects, for example, who knew of the precept that a populace tends to be particularly receptive to favours given by one who is expected to be oppressive might be suspicious of just those favours.

(6)   Machiavelli was well aware of most of the preceding points and warned of some of their implications explicitly in *The Prince*. Several of these points therefore become even more

complex in so far as awareness of them itself becomes part of political activity.

But why should Machiavelli's formulations remain significant today, and be seriously discussed as relevant to existing societies, if they have been in varying ways absorbed into those societies? Why cannot those working in the social sciences forget their 'founders', as natural scientists do? The answer might have to do precisely with the constitutive character of the ideas which a thinker like Machiavelli both formulates and represents. Machiavelli provides us with the means of considered reflection upon concepts and practices which have become part of the nature of sovereignty, political power, etc., in modern societies. In studying his writings we get a sense of what it is that is distinctive of the modern state because Machiavelli wrote at a relatively early period in its development. No doubt also Machiavelli uncovers, or gives a specific discursive form to, principles of government which have very generalized application to states of all kinds. However, the main reason why Machiavelli's writings do not 'date' is that they are a series of (stylistically brilliant) reflections about phenomena which they have helped to constitute. They are formulations of modes of thought and action which are relevant to modern societies not only in their origins but also in their more permanent organizational form. An archaic natural scientific theory is of no particular interest once better ones have come along. Theories which become part of their 'subject matter' (while perhaps in other ways resisting such incorporation) necessarily retain a relevance which antiquarian natural science theories do not have.

Furthering the critical character of social science means fostering a developed conceptual awareness of the practical connotations of its own discourse. The fact that the social sciences are deeply implicated in what it is they are about suggests a basic role for the history of ideas. Thus, for example, Skinner's studies of the emergence of modern forms of discourse on the post-medieval state demonstrate how these have become constitutive of what the state is.[55] In showing that the nature of the modern state presumes a citizenry which itself knows what the modern state is and how it works, Skinner helps us to see how specific and distinctive that state form is and how intertwined with discursive changes which became part of lay social practices.

The social sciences cannot provide (relevant) knowledge that can be 'held back', ready to stimulate appropriate social interventions where necessary. In natural science the evidential criteria involved in deciding among theories and hypotheses are (in principle, and usually also in practice, with exceptions such as Lysenkoism) in the hands of its specialist practitioners. They can get on with the job of sifting evidence and formulating theories without interruption from the world to which the evidence and the theories refer. But in the social sciences this situation does not pertain — or, more accurately put, it pertains least in respect of theories and findings which have most to offer in terms of their revelatory value. This is a large part of the reason why the social sciences might appear to provide much less information of value to policy-makers than do the natural sciences. The social sciences necessarily draw upon a great deal that is already known to the members of the societies they investigate, and supply theories, concepts and findings which become thrust back into the world they describe. The 'gaps' which can be made to appear between the specialist conceptual apparatus and findings of the social sciences and the knowledgeable practices incorporated into social life are very much less clear than in natural science. Viewed from a 'technological' standpoint, the practical contributions of the social sciences seem, and are, restricted. However, seen in terms of being filtered into the world they analyse, the practical ramifications of the social sciences have been, and are, very profound indeed.

Critical Notes: Social Science, History and Geography

Historians, I have said, cannot properly be regarded as specialists along a dimension of time, any more than geographers can be regarded as specialists along a dimension of space; such disciplinary divisions, as ordinarily conceived, are concrete expressions of the repression of time and space in social theory. They have a counterpart in the idea that social science is concerned with laws of a universal, or at least a highly general, nature. Here we have the neat traditional breakdown between social science and history, the one supposedly preoccupied with generalization that is indifferent to time and place, the other analysing the unfolding of events situated in time-space. I do not think it necessary, in the light of the main ideas I have sought to develop in this book, to labour the point as to why this traditional idea is hollow.

If historians are not specialists in time, what of the view that they are specialists in the study of the past? This view is not only perhaps intuitively attractive but has been defended by many eminent historians as well as philosophers. Oakeshott explicates the term 'historical past' as follows.[1]* The world which an individual perceives, he says, is 'unmistakably present'. I stand on a kerb in a street and observe what goes on around me. As I stand there, time passes, but I attend to a 'continuous present', in which 'the passage of time is marked by no noticeable change or even suggestion of movement.'[2] I see a man with a wooden leg hobbling by. He is part of the 'continuous present', unless I perceive him not as a man with a wooden leg but as a man who has lost his leg. Such an awareness of the past, Oakeshott argues, is brought about not by neglect of the present but by a particular interpretation of the present that attends to what is evoked by the word 'lost'. The present in historical understanding is composed

*References may be found on pp. 371–2.

of whatever are recognized as survivals or relics of a 'conserved past':

> an historian's only entry into the past is by means of these survivals. And the first concern of an historical inquiry is to assemble them from where they lie scattered in the present, to recover what might have been lost, to impose some kind of order upon this confusion, to repair the damage they may have suffered, to abate their fragmentariness, to discern their relationships, to recognise a survival in terms of its provenance, and thus to determine its authentic character as a bygone practical or philosophical or artistic, etc., performance.[3]

Through fragments of the past which have survived, the historian attempts to recover those aspects of the past which have not done so.

This interpretation of the nature of history could be understood in two somewhat different ways, conceiving history to be concerned either with the recovery of a lost past or with specific techniques of textual hermeneutics somehow peculiar to the historian. According to the first interpretation, history would have a definite 'subject matter' of its own; according to the second, the distinguishing feature of history would be primarily methodological. But neither of these has much plausibility when examined a little more closely. By 'present', as his example of the individual on the street corner makes clear, Oakeshott means something close to what I have called 'presence'. But the limits of presence are spatial as well as temporal. The interpretative retrieval of a lost past cannot easily be severed — and neither should it be — from the interpretative elucidation of cultural differences scattered 'laterally' across the face of the globe. For all such analysis involves the co-ordination of the temporal and spatial in subtle and intricate ways. The reader who does not concede this point will not have much sympathy with structuration theory as I have developed it in the preceding pages. If Oakeshott's view is regarded as a methodological one, on the other hand, it implies that the distinctiveness of history lies in the arts of the historian, as a specialist in the interpretation of texts or relics which survive from past eras. This idea certainly has a great deal of support among historians, and not without reason, for it is evident enough that the expert perusal and elucidation of texts or material relics is a primary preoccupation of historical research. Many social scientists might also see a division of labour between history and social science along these lines; those actors in whom the social scientist is interested, being alive, can be communicated with directly, while those in whom the historian is interested, being dead, cannot be. The difference is plainly an important one, not only because the living can answer questions whereas the dead cannot but also because the living can also answer back. That is to say, they can actively question, or alter their activity in terms of, whatever 'findings' are disseminated about them. However, it does not follow that a worthwhile division could be made between history and social science along these lines. For most social science is done in and through texts and other 'secondary' materials, as history is. The efforts a social scientist might expend in direct communication with the agents who are the subjects of his or her research investigations are likely to be tiny compared with those which must be spent working through textual materials. Moreover, how far there are interpretative problems to be resolved in making sense of texts — using them as exemplifications as well as descriptions of a given context of activity — depends not upon 'distance' in time but upon how much has to be made of how little, and upon the degree of cultural difference involved.

If there are two disciplines, then, whose intersection concerns the limits of presence, they are surely those of archaeology and hermeneutics: archaeology, because this is the subject *par excellence* which is concerned with relics or remains, the bric-à-brac washed up on the shore of modern times and left there as the social currents within which it was created have drained away; hermeneutics, because all survivals of a 'conserved past' have to be interpreted, regardless of whether they are pots or texts, and because this task of recovering the past is conceptually and methodologically indistinguishable from mediating the frames of meaning found in coexisting cultures.

If social science is not, and cannot be, the history of the present, and if it is not, and cannot be, concerned simply with generalizations out of time and place, what distinguishes social science from history? I think we have to reply, as Durkheim did (albeit having followed a different line of reasoning to arrive at this result): nothing — nothing, that is, which is conceptually coherent or intellectually defensible. If there are divisions between social science and history, they are substantive divisions of labour; there is no logical or methodological schism. Historians who specialize in particular types of textual materials, languages or 'periods' are not freed from involvement with the concepts of, and the dilemmas inherent in, social theory. But, equally, social scientists whose concerns are the most abstract and general theories about social life, are not freed from the hermeneutic demands of the interpretation of texts and other cultural objects. Historical research is social research and vice versa.

To say this is surely no longer the heresy it may once have been. Let us first of all consider what has been happening from the side of history. Abrams summarizes things very well when he says of the work of historians:

> the really significant development of the past twenty years has been the publication of a solid body of theoretically self-conscious historical work which has progressively made nonsense of earlier conceptions of history as somehow, in principle, not engaged in the theoretical world of the social sciences. Social change is made by people doing new things. As the acknowledged masterpieces of the discipline of history become increasingly theoretically explicit, and as the unity of theoretical method between history and sociology becomes thereby steadily more obvious, the continued insistence of a rump of professional historians that theory is not part of their trade becomes steadily less firmly the effective basis of the 'institution' of history and steadily more plainly an ineffectual nostalgia.[4]

The key phrase here is 'unity of theoretical method'. The problems of social theory, of agency, structure and forms of explanation, are problems shared in general by all the social sciences, whatever the division of labour that in other respects may exist between them.

Stone has written perceptively of the influence of the social sciences upon history over the two decades mentioned by Abrams.[5] Stone distinguishes several ways in which those involved in the 'new history' have been influenced by the social sciences. Historians, he agrees with Abrams, have been made more aware of their inescapable involvement with social theory. That is to say, they have come to accept that they cannot leave entirely implicit the theoretical presuppositions that guide their work; in making them explicit, they are putting on the table cards which previously they might have preferred to keep concealed in their hands. Other contributions from the social sciences have been more methodological. Quantifying methods have been applied with some success to a range of different historical issues — a phenomenon of importance if only because the use of such methods is a quite novel departure in history.

In respect of these contributions, however, there has been a contrary pressure from those concerned to advance the claims of so-called 'narrative history'. The debate between the advocates of the 'new history' on the one side and proponents of 'narrative history' on the other in some main respects can aptly be seen as the historians' version of the self-same dualism of action and structure that has dogged the development of social science in general. Those who favour narrative history object to the manner in which the 'new history' tends to offer accounts of human conduct which imply that such conduct is the outcome of social causes outside the influence of the actors involved. They are right to do so. For the usefulness of importing into history styles of theorizing that are flawed at source is likely to be strictly limited. But to propose 'narrative history' as an alternative to 'analytical history', as if we have to opt for one wholly at the expense of the other, is surely mistaken.

Narrative history is supposedly the telling of stories, in conscious acknowledgement of the common root which 'history' has with 'story' and of the fact that *histoire* means both. The stories told have to conform to the demands of factual evidence, but what holds them together and commands the assent of the reader is the coherence of the plot, the mode in which the purposive character of the activity of those described is conveyed and the contexts of activity described. Thus Elton remarks, in the course of describing what narrative history is: 'In order that action may be understood, its setting, circumstances and springs must be made plain',[6] a statement which is unobjectionable. As discussed by Elton and others, narrative and what I have earlier referred to as ethnography are more or less the same thing. But just as it does not follow that the use of ethnographic techniques has to be inevitably associated with subjectivism, so it does not follow that narrative history has any logical connection with a theoretical position which would reject structural concepts. The advocates of narrative history are quite justified in objecting to the indiscriminate importation of the concepts of structural sociology into the work of historians. But they are not right to suppose that such concepts can be ignored altogether. What makes a narrative a persuasive 'story' is not just the coherence of the plot but, as Elton says, understanding the 'setting, circumstances, and springs' of action. However, the settings and circumstances within which action occurs do not come out of thin air; they themselves have to be explained within the very same logical framework as that in which whatever action described and 'understood' has also to be explained. It is exactly this phenomenon with which I take structuration theory to be concerned.

Let us briefly look at the matter from the aspect of recent developments in social science, concentrating particularly upon sociology. Sociology one might say, has its origins in modern history, conceived of as the analysis of the origins and impact of industrial capitalism in the West. But where such problems were taken up by the post-Second World War generation of sociological writers, they often succumbed to the forms of evolutionism I have earlier been concerned to criticize. Evolutionism, it should be clear, can easily be an enemy of history rather than the ally it might superficially seem to be. For it encourages a high-handed disrespect for matters of historical detail by cramming human history into pre-packed schemes.

Where evolutionism has not made much headway there has been a very strong tendency to identify 'sociology', and its separation from 'history', in just these terms which I have earlier condemned as vacuous. Lipset's description of such a view is characteristic:

> the task of the sociologist is to formulate general hypotheses, hopefully set within a larger theoretical framework, and to test them. . . . History must be concerned with the analysis of the particular set of events or processes. Where the sociologist looks for concepts which subsume a variety of particular descriptive categories, the historian must remain close to the actual happenings and avoid statements which, through linking behaviour at one time or place to that elsewhere, lead to a distortion in the description of what occurred in the set of circumstances being analysed.[7]

But what this division describes is one between generalizing concerns and more specific ones, not between sociology and history.[8]

The term 'sociology' was invented by Comte and, until quite recent times, for the most part preserved a strong connection with the style of thinking of which he was so prominent a representative. Many who have disavowed both evolutionism and functionalism have none the less associated sociology with some of the main tenets of objectivism. The 'general hypotheses' of which Lipset speaks are commonly thought of in the manner I have discussed above, as laws which express causal relations that operate somehow independently of the volition of the agents to whose conduct they refer. It is not just the contrast between the 'nomothetic' and the 'idiographic' that sociologists tend to have in mind here. If, as structural sociology suggests, the distinctiveness of sociology is to be found precisely in its overriding concern with structural constraint, the implication can be drawn that historians work in closer touch with the contextualized activities of purposive agents. If it is in this manner that 'sociological' concepts are understood when imported into history, it is easy to see why the advocates of narrative history are suspicious of them and how they can defend what they do *as* 'history', compared with 'sociology'. Both sides lend support to a disciplinary dichotomy that makes no logical or methodological sense.

What has changed, and is changing, sociology is no doubt in very large degree the decline of the hegemony which objectivism and functionalism once enjoyed. The repression of time in social theory, as perpetrated by sociologists at any rate, was definitely also a repression of history — time, history, social change all tend to be assimilated within functionalism.[9] But there has also come about a disillusionment with the two types of tradition which dominated the analysis of the industrially advanced societies until some two decades ago — the 'theory of industrial society' on the one hand and Marxism on the other.[10] In the period after the Second World War both of these tended to have a strong evolutionary tinge to them, as well as displaying several of the secondary traits I have indicated are associated with evolutionism. In particular, each tended to be heavily Europocentric. The challenge which 'dependency' and 'world system' theory posed to these developmental schemes has played some considerable part in attacking Europocentric assumptions. But there is also clear evidence of the impact of the 'new history', which has indicated that many of the suppositions which sociologists made about pre-capitalist Europe were probably basically mistaken.[11]

However, sociologists have a great deal more to learn from the work of historians than most would currently admit. One might propose as a key example the work of Braudel, lauded among the 'new historians' but still largely unknown to those who conceive themselves to be working in 'sociology'. Braudel's writing displays the early influence which sociology, particularly as filtered through the *Année Sociologique* group, had upon the development of history in France. No doubt in some ways it reflects the shortcomings of the sociological views of that group. But it also goes far beyond the limitations of those views in other respects, and not only in its substantive content but also in its theoretical sophistication holds out great interest for sociology. The 'dialogue between structure and conjuncture'[12] which Braudel wants to capture is parallel to that which I seek to represent in a more detailed way in structuration theory. Braudel is the historian of the *longue durée*, but he is also explicitly concerned to connect the contingent and the short-term with institutions that endure over long periods of time.

Who could seem further apart, at first sight, than Braudel and Goffman? Wholly incompatible figures, one might think, and even to mention them in the same breath seems faintly ludicrous. Braudel studies history over several centuries, while Goffman resolutely avoids any analysis of the development of the institutional contexts with which social activity occurs. Yet both anchor their studies in the events of daily life. What connects them is a pre-eminent concern with time, not as chronological duration but as inherent in the complexities of social reproduction. As I have tried to indicate, we can learn a lot from Goffman about how the most deeply sedimented institutions are reproduced; Goffman is not aptly regarded as the theorist of the trivial or the ephemeral. *Per contra*, Braudel should not be seen as proposing the study of vast sweeps of history in which individual actors appear as the playthings of irresistible social currents, a 'deterministic, fatalistic history'.[13] History is the structuration of events in time and space through the continual interplay of agency and structure. the interconnection of the mundane nature of day-to-day life with institutional forms stretching over immense spans of time and space.

In pointing to important convergences between the work of historians and sociologists today I do not wish to suggest only that history should become more sociological and sociology more historical. There is more at stake than that. A recovery of time and space for social theory means theorizing agency, structure and contextuality as the focus for research problems in both.

Contextuality means space as well as time, and here we can turn to the relation between geography and sociology. Geography has long been a less intellectually fashionable subject than history, and there are far fewer discussions in the literature of the relation between geography and sociology than there are of history and sociology. Many sociologists have worried about how far 'sociology' is, or should be, 'historical' — in different ways, according to how each term is understood — but to my knowledge very few have felt the same disquiet in respect of geography. This is probably due not just to the differential intellectual repute of history and geography but also to the greater transparency which the concept of space seems to have as compared with that of time. Distance in space is apparently easy to comprehend and to cope with conceptually; distance in time is not. It might seem to follow from such reasoning both that space can be left to the geographers and that the study of spatial forms is relatively uninteresting. But this conclusion would be a superficial one. The phrase might seem bizarre, but human beings do 'make their own geography' as much as the 'make their own history'. That is to say, spatial configurations of social life are just as much a matter of basic importance to social theory as are the dimensions of temporality, and, as I have often accentuated, for many purposes it is appropriate to think in terms of time-space rather than treating time and space separately.

The roots of human geography in the late nineteenth century have a certain amount in common with those of sociology; as in the case of history, human geography was influenced in a significant manner by Durkheim and those affiliated to the *Année Sociologique*. This is true of both Ratzel and Vidal de la Blanche, perhaps the two most influential figures in the early formation of geography. Ratzel's watchword was 'Die Menscheit ist ein Stück der Erde',[14] but he also emphasized the importance of social organization as an independently established phenomenon. Durkheim rightly saw in Ratzel's work a 'potential ally' for the conception of sociology that he wished to develop.[15] Vidal's concept of *genre de vie* directly expresses the influence of Durkheim; as taken over by Lucien Febvre, Vidal's ideas have had a major impact upon the work of French historians, including Braudel.[16] Braudel's concentration upon the Mediterranean area as a whole, rather than upon boundaries defined by nation-states or political designations of 'Europe', strongly reflects the emphases of Vidal. The influence of Ratzel and Vidal within sociology subsequently, however, has been weak. In the decades following the Second World War sociology and geography mostly went in their own separate directions.

Since then, however, things have changed. The detectable convergence of research has perhaps not been as great as that between history and sociology, but human geography has certainly largely recovered the close affiliation with sociology which it used to enjoy in previous generations.[17] The 'new geography' of the 1960s, like the 'new history', was strongly influenced by the importation of quantitative methods from elsewhere in the social sciences. The idea that geography is primarily about the study of regionalization tended to be displaced by a more abstract emphasis upon spatial form. Echoing the flux of ideas elsewhere in the social sciences, the 'new geography' has already substantially succumbed to critiques of empiricism which have had such a strong impact throughout modern social and political thought. The result, however, is that the work of geographers today has as much to contribute to sociology as sociologists can offer in return. For human geography has come to contain many of the same concepts, and to be involved with the same methodological debates, as sociology.

In the preceding chapters I have tried to make clear what I regard as some of the chief respects in which geographical concepts can be incorporated into structuration theory. I do not, of course, mean to suggest that the work of Hägerstrand and his followers exhausts what geography has to offer sociology. But it is particularly relevant to structuration theory for reasons I have attempted to specify. It offers insights of a theoretical nature, when subjected to a proper critical assessment, but also research techniques that can be directly applied in empirical work. Time-geography offers three advantages over established social research techniques, with which, of course, it can in any case be combined. One is that it sensitizes research work to the contextualities of interaction, especially in so far as these connect with the physical aspects of the *milieux* in which actors move. Most social research, as practised by sociologists, has been averse to examining connections between physical and social aspects of *milieux*, with the honourable exceptions of the Chicago school and so-called 'ecological' theorists.[18] Another is that it directs our attention to the significance of routinization in the day-to-day activities that are at the core of social institutions. The third is that, in developing the idea of day-to-day life as a series of intersecting time-space paths, time-geography offers a mode of charting and of analysing patterns of social reproduction.[19]

The attempt to supplant the notion of regionalization in geography by more abstract models of spatial form I regard largely as a mistaken endeavour. I do not think it useful to seek to make the analysis of regionalization the specific and peculiar concern of geography. As I have tried to emphasize, regionalization is a notion that should be seen as having a major role in social theory. Regionalization is best understood not as a wholly spatial concept but as one expressing the clustering of contexts in time-space. As such it is a phenomenon of quite decisive significance to sociology, on both a theoretical and an empirical level. No single concept helps more to redress the misleading divisions between 'micro-' and 'macro-sociological' research; no concept helps more to counter the assumption that a 'society' is always a clear-cut unity with precisely defined boundaries to it. As adopted within sociology, the problems with the notion of regionalization are, first, that it has figured primarily within urban sociology; second, that it has been used primarily with reference to neighbourhoods; and, third, that urban sociology has traditionally been understood as one 'field' of sociology among others.

Each of these usages should be called in question. As I have tried to formulate it, regionalization is certainly not equivalent to 'regional science' but none the less has a very broad usage. 'Urban sociology' is one of the main concerns that has been shared by geographers and sociologists and where interchange between the two disciplines has been most profuse. There are interesting parallels between the work of Vidal, based mainly on rural environments, and that of the Chicago school, based upon urban ones. Park knew of the writings of French human geography, although he seems to have worked out his main concepts independently of 'it. It is unfortunate that Park's influence has been strongest in respect of urban ecology, marked by a formalist conception of space and emphasizing an objectivist standpoint. In his later work Park adhered to the view that if we are able to 'reduce all social relations to relations of space', we can envisage that 'it would be possible to apply to human relations the fundamental logic of the physical sciences.'[20] But in his earlier writings he emphasized much more the neighbourhood as a contextualizing phenomenon, ordered by and expressing distinctive social traits as *genres de vie*. It is this sort of emphasis which needs to be retained, while being regarded as associated with regionalization in general rather than with urban neighbourhoods in particular.

Urban sociology is not merely one branch of sociology among others. It is of the first importance to stress this, and in acknowledging it recent developments in urban theory have helped further to crumble some of the divisions between geography and sociology. As I have indicated previously, a consideration of the nature of cities is of major importance in analysing issues that are usually presented as purely logical in character, including especially the micro/macro problem. The term 'city' is misleading here. If cities have virtually everywhere played a key role in the organization of large-scale societies, the city in class-divided societies is not the city of the modern era. In so far as modern urbanism is expressive of a new type of organization of time-space, it is discontinuous with traditional cities, and its origins are coterminous with those of the capitalist-industrial type of society. There is no need to agree with all the themes of Castells's work to accept that he has been important in shifting the emphasis in urban theory away from 'urban sociology' towards a stress on the generic significance of urbanism for social theory.[21] The analysis of urbanism, as the basis of the 'created environment', would certainly occupy a main position in any empirical programme of study which structuration theory might help generate about industrialized societies today.

What can sociologists learn from the work of geographers? Not only the importance of regionalization and techniques of studying it, but also the significance of what geographers traditionally call place (but I prefer to call locale) in the reproduction of social practices. Pred's writings may be quoted as an instructive example, combining as they do the empirical study of urbanism with a perspective influenced by both time-geography and structuration theory.[22] As Pred quite rightly points out, the concept of the 'situated' character of social interaction can be adequately fleshed out empirically only if we grasp how the 'reproduction of particular cultural, economic and political institutions in time and space are continuously bound up with the temporally and spatially specific actions, knowledge build-up, and biographies of particular individuals'.[23] The co-ordination of the daily paths of individuals within a given range of locales, plus what some researchers have called a 'sense of place', are concretized aspects of the duality of structure. The dialectic of 'daily path' and 'life path' is the way in which the continuity of the biography of the individual is expressed in, and also expresses, the continuity of institutional reproduction. A sense of place seems of major importance in the sustaining of ontological security precisely because it provides a psychological tie between the biography of the individual and the locales that are the settings of the time-space paths through which that individual moves. Feelings of identification with larger locales — regions, nations, etc. — seem distinguishable from those bred and reinforced by the localized contexts of day-to-day life. The latter are probably much more important in respect of the reproduction of large-scale institutional continuities than are the former.[24] Pred suggests that research should explore the double sense which the phrase 'taking place' can assume. Social activity takes place in definite locales, but this is not to be understood just as the passive localization of such activity within particular situations. Human activities 'take place' by appropriating and transforming nature, nowhere more evidently so than in the created environment of modern urbanism.

What, by way of return, can geographers learn from sociologists? Perhaps little indeed, since over the last few years geographers have become well aware of the debates and issues current in sociology. One contribution which can be made, however, is to help to break down the supposition that there can be a distinctive 'science of space'. In human geography spatial forms are always social forms. Consider the assertion, representative of a certain type of geographical literature, that geography is concerned to establish 'the spatial connections between sets of facts by finding spatial laws' and to elucidate 'the connections between the laws themselves, by constructing spatial theories, which are the patterns or systems in the domain of spatial problems'.[25] Such formulations, of course, express a conception of laws which I have earlier discarded as inapt; they represent an attempt to form a 'social physics in a spatial context'.[26] More important, however, they suppose that space has its own intrinsic nature, a proposal that is logically questionable and empirically unfruitful. Space is not an empty dimension along which social groupings become structured, but has to be considered in terms of its involvement in the constitution of systems of interaction. The same point made in relation to history applies to (human) geography: there are no logical or methodological differences between human geography and sociology!

References

Structuration Theory, Empirical Research and Social Critique

1   Cf. *NRSM*, chapter 3.
2   Paul Willis, *Learning to Labour* (Farnborough: Saxon House, 1977).
3   Ibid., p. 11.
4   Ibid., pp. 29–30.
5   Ibid., p. 33.
6   Cf. especially ibid., chapter 5.
7   Quoted ibid., p. 64.
8   Ibid., p. 107.
9   G. A. Cohen, *Karl Marx's Theory of History, a Defence* (Oxford: Clarendon Press, 1978).
10 Here I draw upon my discussion in 'Commentary on the debate', a debate about functionalism, in *Theory and Society*, vol. II, 1982.
11 Willis, *Learning to Labour*, p. 66.
12 Ibid., pp. 68ff.
13 Ibid., p. 107.
14 See *CPST*, pp. 104–6.
15 Karl Marx, *Capital*, vol. 1 (London: Lawrence and Wishart, 1970), p. 169.
16 Reported in Diego Gambetta, 'Were They Pushed or did They Jump?', Ph.D. dissertation, Cambridge University, 1982.

17 A. Leibowitz, 'Family background and economic success: a review of the evidence', in P. Taubman, *Kinometrics: Determinants of Socioeconomic Success Between and Within Families* (Amsterdam: North Holland, 1977).

18 M. Barbagli, *Disoccupazione intellettuale e sisterna scolastico in Italia* (Bologna: Il Mulino, 1974).

19 Ibid.; quoted in Gambetta, 'Were They Pushed or did They Jump?', pp. 225—6.

20 Ibid., pp. 243—4.

21 *NRSM*, chapter 3.

22 Jon Elster, *Logic and Society, Contradictions and Possible Worlds* (Chichester: Wiley, 1978); idem, *Ulysses and the Sirens* (Cambridge: Cambridge University Press, 1979); Boudon, *The Unintended Consequences of Social Action* (London: Macmillan, 1982).

23 Elster, *Logic and Society*, chapter 5.

24 Ibid., pp. 113—18.

25 This is the phenomenon made well known by Olsen; see Mancur Olson, *The Logic of Collective Action* (Cambridge, Mass.: Harvard University Press, 1963).

26 Boudon, *The Unintended Consequences of Social Action*, chapter 4; critical comments are made by Elster in *Logic and Society*, pp. 126—7.

27 See especially the now classic article by Offe and Ronge: Claus Offe and Volker Ronge, 'Theses on the theory of the state', *New German Critique*, vol. 6, 1975.

28 Ibid., p. 250.

29 Offe's own research has been concerned particularly with education and labour markets. His argument is that educational and training policies are strongly influenced by the perceived need to enhance the saleability of labour power. 'Laissez faire', and 'welfare state-protective' policies are compared with ones concerned with 'administrative re-commodification': see Claus Offe, *Struktur-probleme des kapitalistischen Staates* (Frankfurt: Suhrkamp, 1972); idem, *Berufsbildungsreform* (Frankfurt: Suhrkamp, 1975).

30 Each of these three cases comes from Sam D. Sieber, *Fatal Remedies* (New York: Plenum Press, 1981), pp. 60—1, 67—8, 85.

31 *CPST*, p. 144.

32 A point made by Skocpol; see Theda Skocpol, *States and Social Revolutions* (Cambridge: Cambridge University Press, 1979), p. xii.

33 G. K. Ingham, *Capitalism Divided? The City and Industry in Britain* (London: Macmillan, 1984).

34 Rudolf Hilferding, *Finance Capital* (London: Routledge, 1981).

35   Ingham, *Capitalism Divided?*
36   I have criticized this tendency in several sources; see *Capitalism and Modern Social Theory* (Cambridge: Cambridge University Press, 1971), chapter 15; *CSAS,* Introduction; *CPST,* chapter 6.
37   The example comes from Thomas P. Wilson, to whose work on this matter I am greatly indebted. See 'Qualitative "versus" quantitative methods in social research', Department of Sociology, University of California at Santa Barbara, 1983 (mimeo). Published in German in the *Kölner Zeitschrift für Soziologie und Sozialpsychologie,* vol. 34, 1982. See also Douglas W. Maynard and Thomas P. Wilson: 'On the reification of social structure', in Scott G. McNall and Gary N. Howe, *Current Perspectives in Social Theory,* vol. 1 (Greenwich, Conn.: JAI Press, 1980).
38   Wilson, 'Qualitative "versus" quantitative methods in social research', p. 20.
39   Cf. *CPST,* pp. 248–53.
40   Peter Winch, *The Idea of a Social Science* (London: Routledge, 1963).
41   Hans-Georg Gadamer, *Truth and Method* (London: Sheed & Ward, 1975).
42   *CPST,* pp. 250–3.
43   *NRSM,* pp. 150–3.
44   Ibid.
45   J. C. Crocker, 'My brother the parrot', in J. D. Sapis and J. C. Crocker, *The Social Use of Metaphor* (Philadelphia: University of Pennsylvania Press, 1977); also discussed in Dan Sperber, 'Apparently irrational beliefs', in Martin Hollis and Steven Lukes, *Rationality and Relativism* (Oxford: Blackwell, 1982).
46   Roy Bhaskar, *The Possibility of Naturalism* (Brighton: Harvester, 1979), pp. 80ff.
47   Carl G. Hempel, *Philosophy of Natural Science* (Englewood Cliffs: Prentice-Hall, 1966), p. 55.
48   'Classical social theory and the origins of modern sociology', in *PCST.*
49   See *NRSM,* chapter 1, and *passim.*
50   Charles Taylor; 'Political theory and practice', in Christopher Lloyd, *Social Theory and Political Practice* (Oxford: Clarendon Press, 1983), p. 74. Cf. Also Alasdair MacIntyre, 'The indispensability of political theory', in David Miller and Larry Siedentop, *The Nature of Political Theory* (Oxford: Clarendon Press, 1983).
51   Gunnar Myrdal, 'The social sciences and their impact on society', in Teodor Shanin, *The Rules of the Game* (London: Tavistock, 1972), p. 348.

52 Niccolò Machiavelli, *The Prince* (Harmondsworth: Penguin, 1961), p. 69.
53 See J. Maxwell Atkinson, *Discovering Suicide* (London: Macmillan, 1978).
54 See Quentin Skinner, *The Foundations of Modern Political Thought,* 2 vols. (Cambridge: Cambridge University Press, 1978); idem, *Machiavelli* (Oxford: Oxford University Press, 1981).
55 Skinner, *The Foundations of Modern Political Thought.*

Critical Notes: Social Science, History and Geography

1   Michael Oakeshott, *On History* (Oxford: Basil Blackwell, 1983).
2   Ibid., p. 7.
3   Ibid., p. 32.
4   Cf. Philip Abrams, *Historical Sociology* (London: Open Books, 1982), p. 300.
5   Lawrence Stone, *The Past and the Present* (London: Routledge, 1981), pp. 16ff. and *passim.*
6   G. R. Elton, *The Practice of History* (London: Fontana, 1967), p. 173.
7   S. M. Lipset, 'History and sociology: some methodological considerations', in S. M. Lipset and Richard Hofstadter, *Sociology and History* (New York: Basic Books, 1968), pp. 22—3.
8   Cf. Arthur L. Stinchcombe, *Theoretical Methods in Social History* (New York: Academic Press, 1978).
9   Cf. 'Functionalism: après la lutte', in *SSPT.*
10 See 'Classical social theory and the origins of modern sociology', in *PCST.*
11 Charles Tilly, *As Sociology Meets History* (New York: Academic Press, 1981), pp. 37ff.
12 F. Braudel, *The Mediterranean and the Mediterranean World in the Age of Philip II* (London: Fontana, 1973), vol. 2, p. 757.
13 Stone, *The Past and the Present,* p. 19.
14 Friedrich Ratzel, *Anthropogeographie* (Stuttgart, 1899), vol. 1, p. 23.
15 Emile Durkheim, review of *Anthropogéographie,* vol. 1, *L'Année Sociologique,* vol. 3, 1898—9, p. 551. However, in this and in other reviews Durkheim was also very critical of Ratzel.
16 Lucien Febvre, *A Geographical Introduction to History* (London: Routledge, 1950).
17 Cf., *inter alia,* Derek Gregory, *Ideology, Science and Human Geography* (London: Hutchinson, 1978).

R

18   See, for example, Amos H. Hawley, *Human Ecology* (New York: Ronald Press, 1950).

19   Some important applications in this respect are offered in T. Carlstein, *Time, Resources, Society and Ecology* (Lund: Department of Geography, 1980).

20   R. Park, 'Human ecology', *American Sociological Review*, vol. 42, 1936, p. 2. It is true that Park sometimes softened this position somewhat.

21   Manuel Castells, 'Is there an urban sociology?' in C. G. Pickvance, *Urban Sociology: Critical Essays* (London: Tavistock, 1976), and other publications. Cf. also the voluminous writings of Henri Lefebvre.

22   See especially Allan Pred, 'Power, everyday practice and the discipline of human geography', in *Space and Time in Geography* (Lund: Gleerup, 1981); Nigel Thrift and Allan Pred, 'Time-geography: a new beginning', *Progress in Human Geography*, vol. 5, 1981; and Allan Pred, 'Structuration and place: on the becoming of sense of place and structure of feeling', in *Journal for the Theory of Social Behaviour,* vol. 13, 1983.

23   Pred, 'Structuration and place', p. 46.

24   Anne Buttimer and David Seamon, *The Human Experience of Space and Place* (New York: St Martin's Press, 1980); Yi-Fu Tuan, 'Rootedness versus sense of place', *Landscape*, vol. 24, 1980.

25   D. Amedeo and R. G. Colledge, *An Introduction to Scientific Reasoning in Geography* (New York: Wiley, 1975), p. 35.

26   Derek Gregory, *Ideology, Science and Human Geography* (London: Hutchinson, 1978). p. 73.

Glossary of Terminology of Structuration Theory

This list includes either neologisms or terms employed differently from established usage. It is intended only to summarize formulations offered in the text, not to elucidate them further.

Allocative resources	Material resources involved in the generation of power, including the natural environment and physical artifacts; allocative resources derive from human dominion over nature
Analysis of strategic conduct	Social analysis which places in suspension institutions as socially reproduced, concentrating upon how actors reflexively monitor what they do; how actors draw upon rules and resources in the constitution of interaction
Authoritative resources	Non-material resources involved in the generation of power, deriving from the capability of harnessing the activities of human beings; authoritative resources result from the dominion of some actors over others
Class-divided society	Agrarian states in which there is class division of discernible kinds but where such class division is not the main basis of the principle of organization of the society
Contextuality	The situated character of interaction in time-space, involving the setting of interaction, actors co-present and communication between them
Contradiction	Opposition of structural principles, such that each depends upon the other and yet negates the other; perverse consequences associated with such circumstances

Credibility criteria

The criteria used by agents to provide reasons for what they do, grasped in such a way as to help to describe validly what it is that they do

Dialectic of control

The two-way character of the distributive aspect of power (power as control); how the less powerful manage resources in such a way as to exert control over the more powerful in established power relationships

Discursive consciousness

What actors are able to say, or to give verbal expression to, about social conditions, including especially the conditions of their own action; awareness which has a discursive form

Double hermeneutic

The intersection of two frames of meaning as a logically necessary part of social science, the meaningful social world as constituted by lay actors and the metalanguages invented by social scientists; there is a constant 'slippage' from one to the other involved in the practice of the social sciences

Duality of structure

Structure as the medium and outcome of the conduct it recursively organizes; the structural properties of social systems do not exist outside of action but are chronically implicated in its production and reproduction

Episodic Characterization

The designation, for comparative purposes, of forms of institutional change; episodes are sequences of change having a specifiable opening, trend of events and outcomes, which can be compared in some degree in abstraction from definite contexts

External critique

Critique of lay agents' beliefs and practices, derived from the theories and findings of the social science

Historicity

The identification of history as progressive change, coupled with the cognitive utilization of such identification in order to further that change. Historicity involves a particular view of what 'history' is, which means using knowledge of history in order to change it

Homeostatic loops	Causal factors which have a feedback effect in system reproduction, where that feedback is largely the outcome of unintended consequences
Institutional analysis	Social analysis which places in suspension the skills and awareness of actors, treating institutions as chronically reproduced rules and resources
Intersocietal systems	Social systems which cut across whatever dividing lines exist between societies or societal totalities, including agglomerations of societies
Internal critique	The critical apparatus of social science, whereby theories and findings are subjected to evaluation in the light of logical argument and the provision of evidence
Knowledgeability	Everything which actors know (believe) about the circumstances of their action and that of others, drawn upon in the production and reproduction of that action, including tacit as well as discursively available knowledge
Locale	A physical region involved as part of the setting of interaction, having definite boundaries which help to concentrate inter-action in one way or another
Mutual knowledge	Knowledge of 'how to go on' in forms of life, shared by lay actors and sociological observers; the necessary condition of gaining access to valid descriptions of social activity
Ontological security	Confidence or trust that the natural and social worlds are as they appear to be, including the basic existential parameters of self and social identity
Practical consciousness	What actors know (believe) about social conditions, including especially the conditions of their own action, but cannot express discursively; no bar of repression, however, protects practical consciousness as is the case with the unconscious

Rationalization of action	The capability competent actors have of 'keeping in touch' with the grounds of what they do, as they do it, such that if asked by others, they can supply reasons for their activities
Reflexive Monitoring of action	The purposive, or intentional, character of human behaviour, considered within the flow of activity of the agent; action is not a string of discrete acts, involving an aggregate of intentions, but a continuous process
Reflexive Self-regulation	Causal loops which have a feedback effect in system reproduction, where that feedback is substantially influenced by knowledge which agents have of the mechanisms of system reproduction and employ to control it
Regionalization	The temporal, spatial or time-space differentiation of regions either within or between locales; regionalization is an important notion in counter-balancing the assumption that societies are always homogeneous, unified systems
Reproduction circuit	An institutionalized series of reproduction relations, governed either by homeostatic causal loops or by reflexive self-regulation
Routinization	The habitual, taken-for-granted character of the vast bulk of the activities of day-to-day social life; the prevalence of familiar styles and forms of conduct, both supporting and supported by a sense of ontological security
Social integration	Reciprocity of practices between actors in circumstances of co-presence, understood as continuities in and disjunctions of encounters
Stratification model	An interpretation of the human agent, stressing three 'layers' of cognition/motivation: discursive consciousness, practical consciousness and the unconscious
Structuration	The structuring of social relations across time and space, in virtue of the duality of structure
Structural principles	Principles of organization of societal totalities; factors involved in the overall institutional alignment of a society or type of society

Structural properties	Structured features of social systems, especially institutionalized features, stretching across time and space
Structure	Rules and resources, recursively implicated in the reproduction of social systems. Structure exists only as memory traces, the organic basis of human knowledgeability, and as instantiated in action
Structures	Rule-resource sets, implicated in the institutional articulation of social systems. To study structures, including structural principles, is to study major aspects of the transformation/ mediation relations which influence social and system integration
System	The pattering of social relations across time-space, understood as reproduced practices. Social systems should be regarded as widely variable in terms of the degree of 'systemness' they display and rarely have the sort of internal unity which may be found in physical and biological systems
System integration	Reciprocity between actors or collectivities across extended time-space, outside conditions of co-presence
Time-space distanciation	The stretching of social systems across time-space, on the basis of mechanisms of social and system integration
Time-space edges	Connections, whether conflictual or symbiotic between societies of differing structural types
Validity criteria	The criteria appealed to by social scientists to justify their theories and findings and assess those of others
World time	Conjunctures of history that influence the nature of episodes; the effects of the understanding of historical precedents upon episodic characterizations

Bibliography

Abrams, Philip, *Historical Sociology* (London: Open Books, 1982)

Alland, Alexander, *Evolution and Human Behaviour* (Garden City: Natural History Press, 1967)

Alland, Alexander, *Adaptation in Cultural Evolution* (New York: Columbia University Press, 1970)

Amedeo, D., and R. G. Golledge, *An Introduction to Scientific Reasoning in Geography* (New York: Wiley, 1975)

Anderson, Perry, *Arguments Within English Marxism* (London: Verso, 1980)

Anscombe, G. E. M., 'The first person', in Samuel Guttenplan, *Mind and Language* (Oxford: Blackwell, 1972)

Appley, M.-H., *Adaptation-Level Theory: A Symposium* (New York: Academic Press, 1971)

Archer, Margaret S., 'Morphogenesis versus structuration: on combining structure and action', *British Journal of Sociology*, vol. 33, 1982

Ariès, P., *Centuries of Childhood* (Harmondsworth: Penguin, 1973)

Artaud, Antonin, *Le théâtre et la science* (Paris: Seuil, 1947)

Atkinson, Maxwell J., *Discovering Suicide* (London: Macmillan, 1978)

Bachrach, Peter, and Morton S. Baratz, 'The two faces of power', *American Political Science Review,* vol. 56, 1962

Bachrach, Peter, and Morton S. Baratz, *Power and Poverty* (New York: Oxford University Press, 1970)

Badie, Bertrand, and Pierre Birnbaum, *Sociologie de l'état* (Paris: Grasset, 1979)

Banks, J. A., *The Sociology of Social Movements* (London: Macmillan, 1972)

Barbagli, M., *Disoccupazione intellettuale e sisterna scolastico in Italia* (Bologna: Il Mulino, 1974)

Becker, Ernest, *The Birth and Death of Meaning* (New York: Free Press, 1962)

Bennett, John W., *The Ecological Transition* (New York: Pergamon Press, 1976)

Benyon, Huw, *Working for Ford* (London: Allen Lane, 1973)

Bergström, Lars, *The Alternatives and Consequences of Actions* (Stockholm: Almqvist, 1966)

Bettelheim, Bruno, *The Informed Heart* (Glencoe: Free Press, 1960)

Bhaskar, Roy, *The Possibility of Naturalism* (Brighton: Harvester, 1979)

Biddle, Bruce J., *Role Theory* (New York: Academic Press, 1979)

Blacking, John, *The Anthropology of the Body* (London: Academic Press, 1977)

Blau, Peter M., 'Structural effects', *American Sociological Review,* vol. 25, 1960

Blau, Peter M., 'A formal theory of differentiation in organizations', *American Sociology Review*, vol. 35, 1970

Blau, Peter M., *Approaches to the Study of Social Structure* (London: Collier-Macmillan, 1975)

Blau, Peter M., 'A macrosociological theory of social structure', *American Journal of Sociology*, vol. 83, 1977

Blau, Peter M., *Inequality and Heterogeneity* (New York: Free Press, 1977)

Blau, Peter M., 'Comments on the prospects for a nomothetic theory of social structure', *Journal for the Theory of Social Structure,* vol. 13, 1983

Blumer, Herbert, 'Collective behaviour', in Alfred M. Lee, *Principles of Sociology* (New York: Barnes & Noble, 1951)

Boomer, Donald S., and D. M. Laver, 'Slips of the tongue', *British Journal of Disorders of Communication,* vol. 3, 1968

Boudon, Raymond, *The Uses of Structuralism* (London: Heinemann, 1971)

Boudon, Raymond, *The Unintended Consequences of Social Action* (London: Macmillan, 1982)

Boughey, Arthur S., *Man and the Environment* (New York: Macmillan, 1971)

Bourdieu, Pierre, *Outline of a Theory of Practice* (Cambridge: Cambridge University Press, 1977)

Braudel, F., *The Mediterranean and the Mediterranean World in the Age of Philip II,* 2 vols., (London: Fontana, 1973)

Brazelton, T. B., *et al.,* 'The origins of reciprocity', in M. Lewis and L. Rosenblum, *The Infant's Effects on the Caregiver* (New York: Wiley, 1974)

Brown, Penelope, and Stephen Levinson, 'Universals in language use: politeness phenomena', in Esther N. Goody, *Questions and Politeness* (Cambridge: Cambridge University Press, 1978)

Bruner, J. S., *Beyond the Information Given* (New York: Norton, 1973)

Buttimer, Anne and David Seamon, *The Human Experience of Space and Place* (New York: St Martin's Press, 1980)

Caillois, Roger, *Man, Play and Games* (London: Thames & Hudson, 1962)

Carlstein, T., et al., *Timing Space and Spacing Time*, vol. I of *Making Sense of Time* (London: Arnold, 1978)

Carlstein, T., *Time, Resources, Society and Ecology* (Lund: Department of Geography, 1980)

Carlstein, T., 'The sociology of structuration in time and space: a time-geographic assessment of Giddens's theory', *Swedish Geographical Yearbook* (Lund: Lund University Press, 1981)

Carneiro, Robert L., 'A theory of the origin of the state', *Science,* no. 169, 1970

Castells, Manuel, 'Is there an urban sociology?', in C. G. Pickvance, *Urban Sociology: Critical Essays* (London: Tavistock, 1976)

Chapple, Eliot D., *Culture and Biological Man* (New York: Holt, Rinehart & Winston, 1970)

Cherry, E. C., 'Some experiments on the recognition of speech with one and two ears', *Journal of the Acoustical Society of America,* vol. 25, 1953

Childe, V. Gordon, *The Progress of Archaeology* (London: Watts, 1944)

Childe, V. Gordon, 'Prehistory and Marxism', *Antiquity,* vol. 53, 1979

Claessen, Henri J. M., and Peter Skalnik, *The Early State* (The Hague: Mouton, 1978)

Clark, P. A., 'A review of the theories of time and structure for organisational sociology', *University of Aston Management Centre Working Papers,* no. 248, 1982

Cohen, J., *Man in Adaptation* (Chicago: Aldine, 1968)

Cohen, G. A., *Karl Marx's Theory of History: A Defence* (Oxford: Clarendon Press, 1978)

Cohen, Ronald, 'State origins: a reappraisal', in Claessen and Skalnik, *The Early State*

Cohn, Norman, 'Mediaeval millenarianism: its bearing upon the comparative study of millenarian movements', in Silvia L. Trapp, *Millenial Dreams in Action* (The Hague: Mouton, 1962)

Collins, Randall, 'Micro-translation as a theory-building strategy', in K. Knorr-Cetina and A. V. Cicourel, *Advances in Social Theory and Methodology* (London: Routledge, 1981)

Collins, Randall, 'On the micro-foundations of macro-sociology', *American Journal of Sociology,* vol. 86, 1981

Colson, F. H., *The Week* (Cambridge: Cambridge University Press, 1926)

Comte, Auguste, *Physique Sociale* (Paris: Herman, 1975)

Crocker, J. C., 'My brother the parrot', in J. D. Sapis and J. C. Crocker, *The Social Use of Metaphor* (Philadelphia: University of Pennsylvania Press, 1977)

382   Bibliography

Davidson, Donald, 'Agency', in *Essays on Actions and Events* (Oxford: Clarendon Press, 1980)
De Sola Pool, Ithiel, *The Social Impact of the Telephone* (Cambridge, Mass.: MIT Press, 1981)
Deutsch, J. A., and D. Deutsch, 'Attention: some theoretical considerations', *Psychological Review*, vol. 70, 1963
Ditton, Jason, *The View from Goffman* (London: Macmillan, 1980)
Dobzhansky, Theodosius, *Mankind Evolving* (New Haven: Yale University Press, 1962)
Dubos, René, *Man Adapting* (New Haven: Yale University Press, 1965)
Dumont, Louis, 'Population growth and cultural change', *Southwestern Journal of Anthropology*, vol. 21, 1965
Durkheim, Emile, review of *Anthropo-Geographie*, vol. 1, *L'Année Sociologique* vol. 3, 1898—9
Durkheim, Emile, *Socialism* (New York: Collier-Macmillan, 1962)
Durkheim, Emile, *The Rules of Sociological Method* (London: Macmillan, 1982)
Eberhard, Wolfram, *Conquerors and Rulers* (Leiden: Brill, 1965)
Ehrlich, Paul R., *et al.*, *The Process of Evolution* (New York: McGraw-Hill, 1974)
Eldredge, Niles, and Ian Tuttersall, *The Myths of Human Evolution* (New York: Columbia University Press, 1981)
Elias, Norbet, *The Civilising Process* (Oxford: Blackwell, 1978)
Elias, N., and J. Scotson, *The Established and the Outsiders* (Leicester: University of Leicester Press, 1965)
Elster, Jon, *Logic and Society, Contradictions and Possible Worlds* (Chichester: Wiley, 1978)
Elster, Jon, *Ulysses and the Sirens* (Cambridge: Cambridge University Press, 1982)
Elton, G. R., *The Practice of History* (London: Fontana, 1967)
Ericksen, Gordon E., *The Territorial Experience* (Austin: University of Texas Press, 1980)
Erikson, Erik H., *Childhood and Society* (New York: Norton, 1963)
Erikson, Erik H., *Identity and the Life Cycle* (New York: International Universities Press, 1967)
Erikson, Erik H., *Identity, Youth and Crisis* (London: Faber & Faber, 1968)
Febvre Lucien, *A Geographical Introduction to History* (London: Routledge, 1950)
Feinberg, Joel, 'Action and responsibility', in Max Black, *Philosophy in America* (Ithaca: Cornell University Press, 1965)
Feld, Maury D., *The Structure of Violence* (Beverly Hills: Sage, 1977)
Forer, P., in Carlstein *et al.*, *Timing Space and Spacing Time*
Fortes, M., and E. E. Evans-Pritchard, *African Political Systems* (London: Oxford University Press, 1940)

Foucault, Michel, *Folie et déraison* (Paris: Plon, 1961)
Foucault, Michel *et al.*, *Moi, Pierre Rivière . . .* (Paris, Plon: 1973)
Foucault, Michel, *Discipline and Punish* (Harmondsworth: Penguin, 1979)
Frankel, Boris, *Beyond the State* (London: Macmillan, 1983)
Freud, Sigmund, 'The Psychical mechanism of forgetfulness' (1980)
Freud, Sigmund, *An Outline of Psychoanalysis* (London: Hogarth, 1969)
Freud, Sigmund, *Civilisation and its Discontents* (London: Hogarth, 1969)
Freud, Sigmund, *Introductory Lectures on Psychoanalysis* (Harmondsworth: Penguin, 1974)
Freud, Sigmund, *The Psychopathology of Everyday Life* (Harmondsworth: Penguin, 1975)
Fried, Morton H., *The Evolution of Political Society* (New York: Random House, 1967)
Friedman, Andrew L., *Industry and Labour* (London: Macmillan, 1977)
Fromkin, Victoria A., 'The non-anomalous nature of anomalous utterances', *Language*, vol. 47, 1971
Gadamer, Hans-Georg, *Truth and Method* (London: Sheed & Ward, 1975)
Gailey, H. A., *A History of Africa, 1800 to the Present*, 2 vols. (New York: Houghton-Mifflin, 1970−2)
Gambetta, Diego, 'Were they pushed or did they jump?', Ph.D., University of Cambridge, 1982
Garfinkel, Harold, 'A conception of, and experiments with, "trust" as a condition of stable concerted actions', in O. J. Harvey, *Motivation and Social Interaction* (New York: Ronald Press, 1963)
Gellner, Ernest, *Thought and Change* (London: Weidenfeld & Nicolson, 1964)
Gibson, J. S., *The Ecological Approach to Visual Perception* (Boston: Houghton-Mifflin, 1979)
Giddens, A., *Capitalism and Modern Social Theory* (Cambridge: Cambridge University Press, 1971)
Giddens, A., *New Rules of Sociological Method* (London: Hutchinson/ New York: Basic Books, 1976)
Giddens, A., *Studies in Social and Political Theory* (London: Hutchinson/New York: Basic Books, 1977)
Giddens, A., *Central Problems in Social Theory* (London: Macmillan/ Berkeley: University of California Press, 1979)
Giddens, A., *The Class Structure of the Advanced Societies*, rev. edn (London: Hutchinson/New York: Harper & Row, 1981)
Giddens, A., *A Contemporary Critique of Historical Materialism*, vol. 1 (London: Macmillan/Berkeley: University of California Press, 1981)
Giddens, A., *Profiles and Critiques in Social Theory* (London: Macmillan/Berkeley: University of California Press, 1982)

384 Bibliography

Ginzburg, Carlo, *The Cheese and the Worms* (London: Routledge, 1980)
Goffman, Erving, *Asylums* (Harmondsworth: Penguin, 1961)
Goffman, Erving, *Behaviour in Public Places* (New York: Free Press, 1963)
Goffman, Erving, *Interaction Ritual* (London: Allen Lane, 1972)
Goffman, Erving, *Frame Analysis* (New York: Harper, 1974)
Goffman, Erving, *Forms of Talk* (Oxford: Blackwell, 1981)
Goffman, Erving, *The Presentation of Self in Everyday Life* (New York: Doubleday, 1959)
Gorz, André, *Farewell to the Working Class* (London: Pluto, 1982)
Gouldner, Alvin W., *The Coming Crisis of Western Sociology* (London: Heinemann, 1971)
Gregory, Derek, 'Solid geometry: notes on the recovery of spatial structure', in Carlstein *et al., Timing Space and Spacing Time*
Gregory, Derek, *Ideology, Science and Human Geography* (London: Hutchinson, 1978)
Gregory, Derek, *Regional Transformation and Industrial Revolution* London: Macmillan, 1982)
Grousset, René, *The Empire of the Steppes* (New Brunswick: Rutgers University Press, 1970)
Habermas, Jürgen, *Zur Logik der Sozialwissenschaften* (Tübingen: Siebeck & Mohr, 1967)
Habermas, Jürgen, 'On systematically distorted communication', *Inquiry*, vol. 13, 1970
Habermas, Jürgen, *Communication and the Evolution of Society* (Boston: Beacon, 1979)
Habermas, Jürgen, *Theorie des kommunikativen Handelns*, 2 vols. (Frankfurt: Suhrkamp, 1981)
Hägerstrand, T., 'What about people in regional science?', *Papers of the Regional Science Association*, vol. 24, 1970
Hägerstrand, T., 'Space, time and human conditions', in A. Karlqvist, *Dynamic Allocation of Urban Space* (Farnborough: Saxon House, 1975)
Hägerstrand, T., *Innovation as a Spatial Process* (Chicago: University of Chicago Press, 1976)
Hägerstrand, T., 'Survival and arena: on the life-history of individuals in relation to their geographical environment', in Carlstein *et al., Human Geography and Time Geography*, vol. 2 of *Making Sense of Time*
Hall, Edward T., *The Silent Language* (New York: Doubleday, 1959)
Hall, Edward T., *The Hidden Dimension* (London: Bodley Head, 1966)
Harding, Thomas G., 'Adaptation and stability', in Sahlins and Service, *Evolution and Culture*

Harré, R., and P. F. Secord, *The Explanation of Social Behaviour* (Oxford: Blackwell, 1972)

Hawley, Amos H., *Human Ecology* (New York: Ronald Press, 1950)

Hayek, F. A., *Individualism and Economic Order* (Chicago: University of Chicago Press, 1949)

Hempel, Carl G., *Philosophy of Natural Science* (Englewood Cliffs: Prentice-Hall, 1966)

Hilferding, Rudolf, *Finance Capital* (London: Routledge, 1981)

Hodgson, Marshall G. S., 'The interrelations of societies in history', *Comparative Studies in Society and History*, vol. 5, 1962—3

Huizinga, Jan, *Homo Ludens* (London: Routledge, 1952)

Huxley, Julian, 'Evolution, cultural and biological,' in William C. Thomas, *Current Anthropology* (Chicago: University of Chicago Press, 1956)

Ingham, G. K., *Capitalism Divided? The City and Industry in Britain* (London: Macmillan, 1984)

Janelle, D. G., 'Spatial reorganisation: a model and concept', *Annals of the Association of American Geographers*, vol. 58, 1969

Kardiner, A., *The Individual and His Society* (New York: Columbia University Press, 1939)

Kautsky, John H., *The Politics of Aristocratic Empires* (Chapel Hill: University of North Carolina Press, 1982)

Kelley, Allyn L., 'The evidence for Mesopotamian influence in pre-dynastic Egypt' *Newsletter of the Society for the Study of Egyptian Antiquities*, vol. 4, no. 3, 1974

Koppers, W., 'L'Origine de l'état', *6th International Congress of Anthropological and Ethnological Studies*, Paris, 1963, vol. 2

Krader, Lawrence, *Formation of the State* (Englewood Cliffs: Prentice-Hall, 1968)

Labov, William, 'Rules for ritual insults', in David Sudnow, *Studies in Social Interaction* (New York: Free Press, 1972)

Laing, R. D., *Self and Others* (Harmondsworth: Penguin, 1971)

Layder, Derek, *Structure, Interaction and Social Theory* (London: Routledge, 1981)

Leibowitz, A., 'Family background and economic success: a review of the evidence', in P. Taubman, *Kinometrics: Determinants of Socioeconomic Success Between and Within Families* (Amsterdam: North Holland, 1977)

Lenski, G., *Power and Privilege* (New York: McGraw-Hill, 1966)

Lenski, G., *Human Societies* (New York: McGraw-Hill, 1970)

Lévi-Strauss, Claude, *Totemism* (London: Merlin, 1964)

Lévi-Strauss, Claude, *The Savage Mind* (London: Weidenfeld & Nicolson, 1966)

386 *Bibliography*

Lévi-Strauss, Claude, *Structural Anthropology* (London: Allen Lane, 1968)
Lipset, S. M., 'History and sociology: some methodological considerations', in S. M. Lipset and Richard Hofstadter, *Sociology and History* (New York: Basic Books, 1968)
Lockwood, David, 'Social integration and system integration', in George Z. Zollschan and W. Hirsch, *Exploration in Social Change* London: Routledge, 1964)
Lowie, Robert, *The Origin of the State* (New York: Harcourt, Brace, 1927)
Luhmann, Niklas, 'Funktion und Kausalität', in *Soziologische Aufklärung* (Köln—Opladen, 1970)
Luhmann, Niklas, *Trust and Power* (Chichester: Wiley, 1979)
Lukes, Steven, *Power: A Radical View* (London: Macmillan, 1974)
Lukes, Steven, 'Methodological individualism reconsidered', in *Essays in Social Theory* (London: Macmillan, 1977)
Machiavelli, Niccolò, *The Prince* (Harmondsworth: Penguin, 1961)
MacIntyre, Alasdair, 'The indispensability of political theory', in David Miller and Larry Siedentop, *The Nature of Political Theory* (Oxford: Clarendon Press, 1983)
MacIntyre, Alasdair, *After Virtue* (London: Duckworth, 1981)
Mackie, J. L., 'The transcendal "I"', in Zak Van Straaten, *Philosophical Subjects* (Oxford: Clarendon Press, 1980)
McLuhan, Marshall, *The Gutenburg Galaxy* (London: Routledge, 1962)
Manners, Robert A., *Process and Pattern in Culture* (Chicago: Aldine, 1964)
Marcuse, Herbert, *Eros and Civilization* (New York: Vintage, 1955)
Marsh, Peter, *et al.*, *The Rules of Disorder* (London: Routledge, 1978)
Marx, Karl, 'Preface' to *A Contribution to the Critique of Political Economy* in Karl Marx and Friedrich Engels, *Selected Writings* (London: Lawrence & Wishart, 1968)
Marx, Karl, *Capital* (London: Lawrence & Wishart, 1970)
Marx, Karl, *Grundrisse* (Harmondsworth: Penguin, 1976)
Mayhew, Bruce H., 'Structuralism versus individualism', Parts 1 and 2, *Social Forces,* vol. 59, 1980
Mayhew, Bruce H., 'Causality, historical particularism and other errors in sociological discourse', *Journal for the Theory of Social Behaviour,* vol. 13, 1983
Maynard, Douglas W., and Wilson, Thomas P., 'On the reification of social structure', in Scott G. McNall and Gary N. Howe, *Current Perspectives in Social Theory* (Greenwich, Conn.: JAI Press 1980), vol. 1
Meggers, Betty J., *Evolution and Anthropology: A Centennial Appraisal* (Washington: Anthropological Society, 1959)

Melbin, M., 'The colonisation of time', in Carlstein *et al., Timing Space and Spacing Time*

Merleau-Ponty, M., *Phenomenology of Perception* (London: Routledge, 1974)

Meringer, R., and C. Mayer, *Versprechen und Verlesen* (Vienna, 1895)

Merton, R. K., 'The unanticipated consequences of purposive social action', *American Sociological Review*, vol. 1, 1936

Merton, R. K., 'Manifest and latent functions', in *Social Theory and Social Structure* (Glencoe: Free Press, 1963)

Mommsen, Wolfgang, 'Max Weber's political sociology and his philosophy of world history', *International Social Science Journal*, vol. 17, 1965

Mumford, Lewis, 'University city', in Carl H. Kraeling and Robert M. Adams, *City Invisible* (Chicago: University of Chicago Press, 1960)

Munson, Ronald, *Man and Nature* (New York: Felta, 1971)

Myrdal, Gunnar, 'The social sciences and their impact on society', in Teodor Shanin, *The Rules of the Game* (London: Tavistock, 1972)

Nadel, S. F., *A Black Byzantium* (London: Oxford University Press, 1942)

Naipaul, V. S., *India: A Wounded Civilisation* (Harmondsworth: Penguin, 1976)

Neisser, Ulric, *Cognition and Reality* (San Francisco: Freeman, 1976)

Neisser, Ulric, *Memory Observed* (San Francisco: Freeman, 1982)

Nisbet, Robert A., *Social Change and History* (London: Oxford University Press, 1969)

Oakeshott, M., *On History* (Oxford: Blackwell, 1983)

Offe, Claus, *Strukturprobleme des kapitalistischen Staates* (Frankfurt: Suhrkamp, 1975)

Offe, Claus, *Berufsbildungsreform* (Frankfurt: Suhrkamp, 1975)

Offe, Claus, and Ronge Volker, 'Theses on the theory of the state', *New German Critique*, vol. 6, 1975

Oliver, Douglas L., *Ancient Tahitian Society* (Honolulu: University of Hawaii Press, 1974)

Olson, Mancur, *The Logic of Collective Action* (Cambridge, Mass.: Harvard University Press, 1965)

Palm, R., and A. Pred, 'The status of American women: a time-geographic view', in D. A. Lanegran and R. Palm, *An Invitation to Geography* (New York: McGraw-Hill, 1978)

Park, R., 'Human ecology', *American Sociological Review*, vol. 42, 1936

Parkes, Don, and Nigel Thrift, *Times, Spaces and Places* (Chichester: Wiley, 1980)

Parsons, Talcott, 'Evolutionary universals in society', *American Sociological Review*, vol. 29, 1964

Parsons, Talcott, *Societies: Evolutionary and Comparative Perspectives*

(Englewood Cliffs: Prentice-Hall, 1966)

Parsons, Talcott, 'Evolutionary universals in society', *American Sociological Review*, vol. 29, 1964

Parsons, Talcott, *The System of Modern Societies* (Englewood Cliffs: Prentice-Hall, 1971)

Piers, G., and Singer, M. B., *Shame and Guilt* (Springfield: Addison, 1963)

Pitkin, Hanna F., *Wittgenstein and Justice* (Berkeley: University of California Press, 1972)

Pocock, J. G. A., 'The origins of the study of the past,' *Comparative Studies in Society and History,* vol. 4, 1961—2

Polanyi, Karl, *et al., Trade and Market in the Early Empires* (New York: Free Press, 1957)

Pollard, Andrew, 'Teacher interests and changing situations of survival threat in primary school classrooms', in Peter Woods, *Teacher Strategies* (London: Croom Helm, 1980)

Pred, Alan, 'The choreography of existence: comments on Hägerstrand's time-geography', *Economic Geography*, vol. 53, 1977

Pred, Alan, 'The impact of technological and institutional innovations of life content: some time-geographic observations', *Geographical Analysis*, vol. 10, 1978

Pred. Alan, 'Power, everyday practice and discipline of human geography', in *Space and Time in Geography* (Lund: Gleerup, 1981)

Pred, Alan, 'Structuration and place: on the becoming of sense of place and structure of feeling', *Journal for the Theory of Social Behaviour*, vol. 13, 1983

Psathas, George, *Everyday Language: Studies in Ethnomethodology* (New York: Irvington, 1979)

Rappaport, Roy A., 'Ritual, sanctity and cybernetics', *American Anthropologist*, vol. 73, 1971

Ratzel, Friedrich, *Anthropo-Geographie*, 2 vols., (Stuttgart, 1899—91)

Renfrew, Colin, 'Space, time and polity', in J. Friedman and M. J. Rowlands, *The Evolution of Social Systems* (London: Duckworth, 1977)

Ricoeur, Paul, 'Existence and hermeneutics', in *The Conflict of Interpretations* (Evanston: Northwestern University Press, 1974)

Rose, Gillian, *The Melancholy Science* (London: Macmillan, 1978)

Rykwert, Joseph, *The Idea of a Town* (London: Faber & Faber, 1976)

Sacks, Harvey, and Emmanuel A. Schegloff, 'A simplest systematics for the organisation of turn-talking in conversation', *Language,* vol. 50, 1974

Sahlins, Marshall D., and Elman R. Service, *Evolution and Culture* (Ann Arbor: University of Michigan Press, 1960)

Sargant, William, *Battle for the Mind* (London, Pan, 1959)

Sartre, Jean-Paul, *Critique of Dialectical Reason* (London: New Left Books, 1976)

Schafer, Kermit, *Prize Bloopers* (Greenwich, Conn.: Fawcett, 1965)

Schelling, Thomas, 'Dynamic models of segregation', *Journal of Mathematical Sociology*, vol. 4, 1971

Schelling, Thomas, 'On the ecology of micromotives', *Public Interest*, vol. 25, 1971

Schintlholzer, Birgit, *Die Auflosung des Geschichtbegriffs in Strukturalismus*, doctoral dissertation, Hamburg, 1973

Searle, John R., *Speech Acts* (Cambridge: Cambridge University Press, 1969)

Service, Elman R., *Origins of the State and Civilization* (New York: Norton, 1975)

Shils, Edward, *Tradition* (London: Faber & Faber, 1981)

Shotter, John, '"Duality of structure" and "intentionality" in an ecological psychology', *Journal for the Theory of Social Behaviour*, vol. 13, 1983

Skinner, Quentin, *The Foundations of Modern Political Thought*, 2 vols. (Cambridge: Cambridge University Press, 1978)

Skinner, Quentin, *Machiavelli* (Oxford: Oxford University Press, 1981)

✓ Skocpol, Theda, *States and Social Revolutions* (Cambridge: Cambridge University Press, 1979)

Sieber, Sam D., *Fatal Remedies* (New York: Plenum Press, 1981)

Spencer, Herbert, *The Principles of Sociology* (New York: Appleton, 1899)

Spengler, Oswald, *The Decline of the West* (London: Allen & Unwin, 1961)

Sperber, Dan, 'Apparently irrational beliefs', in Martin Hollis and Steven Lukes, *Rationality and Relativism* (Oxford: Blackwell, 1982)

Stebbins, L., *The Basis of Progressive Evolution* (Chapel Hill: University of North Carolina Press, 1969)

✓ Steward, Julian H., *Theory of Culture Change* (Urbana: University of Illinois Press, 1955)

Stinchcombe, Arthur L., *Theoretical Methods in Social History* (New York: Academic Press, 1978)

Stocking, George W., *Race, Culture and Evolution* (New York: Free Press, 1968)

Stone, Lawrence, *The Past and the Present* (London: Routledge, 1981)

Strawson, P. F., *The Bounds of Sense* (London, Methuen, 1966)

Sullivan, Harry Stack, *The Interpersonal Theory of Psychiatry* (London: Tavistock, 1955)

Tax, Sol, *The Evolution of Man* (Chicago: University of Chicago Press, 1960)

Taylor, Charles, 'Political theory and practice', in Christopher Lloyd, *Social Theory and Political Practice* (Oxford: Clarendon Press, 1983)

Tenbrük, F. H., 'Zur deutschen Rezeption der Rollenalyse', *Kölner Zeitschrift for Soziologie*, vol. 3, 1962

Thalberg, Irving, 'Freud's anatomies of self', in Richard Wollheim, *Freud, A Collection of Critical Essays* (New York: Doubleday, 1974); revised in Richard Wollheim and James Hopkins, *Philosophical Essays on Freud* (Cambridge: Cambridge University Press, 1982)

Theodorson, George A., *Studies in Human Ecology* (New York: Row, Peterson, 1981)

Thompson, E. P., *The Making of the English Working Class* (Harmondsworth: Penguin, 1968)

Thompson, E. P., *The Poverty of Theory* (London: Merlin, 1978)

Thompson, J. B., *Critical Hermeneutics* (Cambridge: Cambridge University Press, 1981)

Thrift, Nigel, 'On the determination of social action in space and time', *Society and Space*, vol. 1, 1982

Thrift, Nigel, 'Flies and germs: a geography of knowledge', in Derek Gregory and John Urry, *Social Relations and Spatial Structures* (London: Macmillan, 1984)

Thrift, Nigel, and Allan Pred, 'Time-geography: a new beginning', *Progress in Human Geography*, vol. 5, 1981

Tilly, Charles, *As Sociology Meets History* (New York: Academic Press: 1981)

Toulmin, Stephen, 'The genealogy of "consciousness"' in Paul F. Secord, *Explaining Human Behaviour* (Beverly Hills: Sage, 1982)

Touraine, Alain, *The Self Production of Society* (Chicago: University of Chicago Press, 1977)

Treisman, A. M., 'Strategies and models of selective attention', *Psychological Review*, vol. 76, 1969

Turner, Stephen P., 'Blau's theory of differentiation: is it explanatory?', *Sociological Quarterly*, vol. 18, 1977

Tuun, Yi-Fu, 'Rootedness versus sense of place', *Landscape*, vol. 24, 1980

Utz, Pamela J., 'Evolutionism revisited', *Comparative Studies in Society and History*, vol. 15, 1973

van Doorn, Jacques, *The Soldier and Social Change* (Beverly Hills: Sage, 1975)

Vayda, Andrew P., *Environment and Cultural Behaviour* (New York: Natural History Press, 1969)

Vico, G., *The New Science* (Ithaca: Cornell University Press, 1968)

Vygotsky, L. S., *Mind in Society* (Cambridge, Mass.: Harvard University Press, 1978)

Waley, Arthur, *Three Ways of Thought in Ancient China* (London: Allen & Unwin, 1939)

Wallace, Walter L., 'Structure and action in the theories of Coleman and Parsons', in Blau, *Approaches to the Study of Social Structure*

Wallerstein, Immanuel, *The Modern World-System* (New York: Academic Press, 1974)

Watkins, J. W. N., 'Historical explanation in the social sciences', in P. Gardiner, *Theories of History* (Glencoe, Free Press, 1959)

Weber, Max, *Economy and Society*, 2 vols. (Berkeley: University of California Press, 1978)

Weber, Max, *The Methodology of the Social Sciences* (Glencoe: Free Press, 1949)

Wertheimer, M., 'Psychomotor coordination of auditory and visual space at birth', *Science*, vol. 134, 1962

White, Leslie A., 'Diffusion vs evolution: an anti-evolutionist fallacy', *American Anthropologist*, vol. 44, 1945

White, Leslie A., 'Evolutionary stages, progress, and the evaluation of cultures', *Southwestern Journal of Anthropology*, vol. 3, 1947

White, Leslie A., *The Evolution of Culture* (New York: McGraw-Hill, 1959)

Whyte, Anne, 'Systems as perceived', in J. Friedman and M. J. Rowlands, *The Evolution of Social Systems* (Pittsburgh: University of Pittsburgh Press, 1978)

Wieder, Lawrence D., 'Telling the code', in Roy Turner, *Ethnomethodology* (Harmondsworth: Penguin, 1974)

Willis, Paul, *Learning to Labour* (Farnborough: Saxon House, 1977)

Wilson, John A., *The Culture of Ancient Egypt* (Chicago: University of Chicago Press, 1951)

Wilson, Thomas P., 'Qualitative "versus" quantitative methods in social research', Department of Sociology, University of California at Santa Barbara, 1983 (mimeo); published in German in the *Kölner Zeitschrift fur Soziologie und Sozialpsychologie*, vol. 34, 1982

Winch, Peter, *The Idea of a Social Science* (London: Routledge, 1963)

Wittgenstein, Ludwig, *Philosophical Investigations* (Oxford: Blackwell, 1972)

Wolf, Dennie, 'Understanding others: a longitudinal case study of the concept of independent agency', in George E. Forman, *Action and Thought* (New York: Academic Press, 1982)

Wright, Erik Olin, *Class, Crisis and the State* (London: New Left Books, 1978)

Wright, Henry T., and Gregory Johnson, 'Population, exchange and early state formation in southwestern Iran', *American Anthropologist*, vol. 77, 1975

Zerubavel, Evitar, *Patterns of Time in Hospital Life* (Chicago: University of Chicago Press, 1979)

Zerubavel, Evitar, *Hidden Rhythms* (Chicago: University of Chicago Press, 1981)

Ziff, Paul, *Semantic Analysis* (Ithaca: Cornell University Press, 1960)

Index